DISMANTLING THE
COLD WAR ECONOMY

DISMANTLING THE COLD WAR ECONOMY

∎

Ann Markusen

and

Joel Yudken

BasicBooks
A Division of HarperCollins*Publishers*

Library of Congress Cataloging-in-Publication Data

Markusen, Ann R.
    Dismantling the cold war economy / Ann Markusen and
Joel Yudken.
        p.   cm.
    Includes bibliographical references and index.
    ISBN 0-465-00662-0
    1. Economic conversion—United States.   2. Military-
industrial complex—United States.   3. Defense
industries—United States.
I. Yudken, Joel.   II. Title.
HC110.D4M383   1992
338.4'76233'0973—dc20   91-44427
                                                              CIP

For David Markusen-Weiss
and
Rosa Cecilia Briceño

Contents

∎

List of Tables   xi

List of Figures   xiii

Preface   xv

Acknowledgments   xix

1   An Economy at War   1
    The World's High-Tech Cop   3
    Creating Defense-Dependency   4
    Stuck in the War Economy Trough   6
    Redirecting Science and Technology   8
    Breaching the War Economy Trough   10

2   The Rise of Postmodern Warfare   12
    Warfare Goes Extraterrestrial   15
    Machines at War   18
    The Boom in Military Electronics   20
    Cold War and Continual Innovation   23
    Demand- or Supply-Driven?   25
    Making Weapons Flexibly, Secretly, Expensively   27
    Separate and Better than Equal   31

3   The Aerospace Industry Comes of Age   33
    The ACE Complex   34

CONTENTS

Tight from the Start		39
From Hot War to Cold War		42
Why Not Auto?		44
Aerospace Sidekicks: Electronics, Communications, and Computers		47
A Closet Industrial Policy		51
The Fruits of Cultivating Aerospace		55
The Neglected Industrial Base		58
Trouble on the Horizon		66
4	A Wall of Separation	69
	Lockheed: A Military-Industrial Prototype	69
	Who's Who in Selling to the Pentagon	74
	Breeding Defense-Dependency	80
	Strange Bedfellows	83
	Why a Wall of Separation?	90
	How Well Does the ACE Complex Perform?	94
	The Resilience of the Wall	99
5	Innovation Goes to War	101
	Science-Based Weapons	102
	Creating the Modern Research System	105
	From Cradle to Grave	108
	Universities as the Cradle	110
	The Faustian Bargain	114
	In the Corporate Nursery	116
	The Spin-off Slump	119
	Dual-Use: The Pentagon's New Tack?	121
	The Politics of Dual-Use	124
	The Limits of Dual-Use Policy	127
6	Weapons of Paper and Pen	132
	Defense Job Growth	133
	Soldier, Sailor, Candlestick-Maker?	135
	The Military "Scientific City"	138
	The Mental Assembly Line	146
	The Eggheads	147
	The Can-Dos	151
	Military-Industrial Managers	155
	Blue-Collar Defense Workers	157

CONTENTS

Rosie the Riveter and Her Minority Coworkers   163
Redeployed Defense Workers—What Are Their
    Options?   165

7   Cold War Communities   170
    The Cold War Gunbelt   173
    How the Gunbelt Came to Be   181
    Location Theory When Government Is the Market   182
    Camp Followers   185
    The Geography of Strategic Fears   188
    Arms Geography and the Make-or-Buy Decision   190
    Cold-Shouldered by the Cold War   192
    Pork-Barreling: The Pentagon versus the Politicians   194
    Geographical Constituency Building   196
    Gunbelt Boosterism   197
    The Benefits of the Gunbelt   199
    Gunbelt Drawbacks   200
    Gunbelt Politics   203
    A Post–Cold War Gunbelt?   204

8   Scaling the Wall of Separation   208
    Big Business and the Present Build-down   210
    Smaller Firms: Headed Underwater   216
    Converting the Company May Not Convert Jobs   219
    Labor: Reconsidering the Benefits of Cold War   220
    Converting Workers   225
    Converting the Local Economy   226
    Converting Facilities   228
      Quincy Shipyards   229
      McDonnell-Douglas Aircraft   231
      Blaw-Knox Foundry   233
      Unisys Defense Computer Systems   235
    Lessons from Conversion Efforts   237
    At the Cold War Crossroads   240

9   Dismantling the Cold War Economy   241
    Toward a Nurturing Economy   242
    Competitiveness Is Not the Answer   244
    A National Economic Development Strategy   247
    Building the New Economic Order   249
    Reinvesting the Peace Dividend   252

CONTENTS

Negotiating the Strategy   255
Getting There   256

Notes   261

Index   299

List of Tables

∎

3.1 Growth in Military Sales and Dependency, 1980–85   37

3.2 Gross National Product Share of Selected
Manufacturing Industries, 1979–86   58

3.3 Trade Balance in Selected Manufacturing Industries,
1987   59

3.4 Federal versus Industry R&D Funding for Selected
Industries, 1989   65

4.1 DOD Top Military Contractors, 1988   75

4.2 NASA Top Contractors, 1988   77

4.3 Military and Space Dependency of Major Defense
Contractors, 1985–88   78

5.1 DOD Support for University Research   112

5.2 RDT&E Awards to Top Twenty Defense Contractors,
1987   117

6.1 Concentrations of Scientists and Engineers in
Manufacturing, 1980   139

6.2 Selected White-, Pink-, and Gray-Collar Military-Related
Occupations, 1986   141

6.3 Selected Blue-Collar Military-Related Occupations, 1986   142

6.4 BLS and SSE Estimates of Occupational Defense-
Dependency, 1986   144

7.1 Index of Regional DOD Prime Contracts, 1952–89   175

7.2 DOD Prime Contracts by County, 1984   179

List of Figures

∎

4.1 Military-Space Receipts of Top Contractors, 1964–88   83
7.1 Military Prime Contracts per Capita as a Percentage of
     the U.S. Average, by State, 1984   176
7.2 Military Manufacturing Job Shares as a Percentage of
     the U.S. Average, by State, 1983   181

Sources for Figure 4.1: U.S. Department of Defense, Washington Headquarter Services, Directorate of Information Operations and Reports, *100 Companies Receiving the Largest Dollar Volume of Prime Contract Awards* (Washington, D.C.: U.S. Government Printing Office, 1964–88); National Aeronautics and Space Administration, Office of Procurement, *NASA Annual Procurement Report* (Washington, D.C.: U.S. Government Printing Office, 1964–88); *Economic Indicators*. Prepared for the Joint Economic Committee by the Council of Economic Advisers (Washington, D.C.: U.S. Government Printing Office, selected issues); and Aerospace Industries Association of America, *Aerospace Facts and Figures 1989–1990* (Washington, D.C.: AIA, 1989).

Source for Figure 7.1: Ann Markusen, Peter Hall, Sabina Deitrick, and Scott Campbell, *The Rise of the Gunbelt* (New York: Oxford University Press, 1991), figure 2.8, p. 22.

Source for Figure 7.2: Ann Markusen, Peter Hall, Sabina Deitrick, and Scott Campbell, *The Rise of the Gunbelt* (New York: Oxford University Press, 1991), figure A.1, p. 181.

Preface

■

For the United States, the second half of the twentieth century has been a military-industrial era. Ideas and technologies bred by a prolonged cold war with the Soviet Union played a major role in shaping the culture of the United States. Nowhere was this more apparent, and more costly, than in the industrial economy.

We both have personal histories of exposure to the way military priorities have deformed American economic development: one as the daughter of a Honeywell aerospace engineer who worked on defense satellite control all his life, and the other as an electrical engineer who worked at Lockheed on defense satellite systems and then as co-director and director for programs of California's Center for Economic Conversion (formerly the Mid-Peninsula Conversion Project). We were each irresistibly drawn toward researching the military economy long before we knew of each other's work, and between us, we have put nearly two decades into drawing this profile.

Our central argument is straightforward. Because of the peculiarities of cold war outfitting, new atmospheric technologies, such as bombers and satellites, called forth a whole new set of industries that thrived on the continual innovation in weaponry demanded by the Pentagon. We call them Aerospace, Communications, and Electronics industries (ACE). These industries, and the new big firms that led them—Rockwell, Lockheed, McDonnell-Douglas, General Dynamics, Hughes, Northrop—were marked off from the rest of American commercial business by a "wall of separation." Behind the wall, they developed a business culture that favored glitz and gimmickry over cost minimization and concentrated marketing efforts on lobbying and negotiating with the Pentagon.

Over the decades, whenever defense cuts became fashionable or imperative, the companies found it increasingly difficult to scale the wall. Meanwhile, their business practices had created an unusual and dependent work force, heavily populated with scientists and engineers whose missions were narrowly specialized and often shrouded in secrecy. Because the plants producing weaponry were located in new, outlying locations far from the traditional manufacturing belt, and because government had subsidized the migration of the work force and the building of new infrastructure to accommodate them, whole communities, even cities, became increasingly defense-dependent.

Meanwhile, year after year, the continued siphoning off of billions of dollars from the public treasury constituted a quiet industrial policy, but one aimed narrowly at the newly emergent ACE industries. Not only did they receive enormous research and development subsidies but they also were rewarded with outright government purchase of major portions of their output. Not surprisingly, they are the industries that have added jobs in the past decade and are the nation's net trade winners. Back in the heartland, saddled with aging plants and a shutout of government support, traditionally strong American industries like steel, autos, machining, and consumer electronics languished, making them attractive targets for government-supported industries in Europe and Japan.

By the late 1980s, when the most recent buildup could no longer be sustained, the contours of a stubborn and downward-spiraling cycle began to show through. As Congress began a series of inevitable cuts, defense contractors scrambled to close plants and cut their losses while vigorously pressing Congress to reverse its course and candidly admitting their unfitness and unwillingness to shift to commercial ventures. Workers in some plants tried relatively unsuccessfully to get their companies to consider conversion, seeing that few jobs existed in the moribund commercial marketplace. Sometimes they succumbed to company-organized political offensives to revive aging weapons programs. Communities bred on defense projects sent desperate appeals to their congressional representatives to stop or slow the cuts, because alternative economic development ideas seemed like pipe dreams.

The cycle is clear, and it is potentially ruinous. Defense dependence makes large and key economic sectors unfit for commercially competitive markets. This situation can be cured only by cutting defense budgets and redirecting national resources into broad industrial reinvigoration. But politicians are afraid to take the big steps to do so, because millions of constituents and well-heeled business backers are so desperate to defend their livelihoods. The result: the comparative advantage of the United States is increasingly confined to weapons systems and their high-tech spinoffs.

The specter of the United States as the world's cop, paid by other countries to mobilize airpower and personnel for foreign military arenas like the Gulf in 1990–91, is not attractive. Nor is that of a nation compelled to sell arms to close the trade gap. Furthermore, neither of these courses can compensate for the slow deterioration in the underlying state of the economy. Breaking the cycle has never been more critical and perhaps never more difficult.

For the coming decade, and the coming century, the United States must make a bold new set of national commitments to address fundamental economic, social, and environmental problems. To accomplish this, the federal government should take a leadership role, working collaboratively with diverse interests in the private sector and in regions, states, and communities, to mobilize the necessary economic, financial, technological, and human resources. Dismantling the cold war economy and converting it to one based on economic stability, a healthy populace, and a clean environment will take a lot of courage, entrepreneurship, and creativity. But it can be done.

Acknowledgments

■

This account of the current state of America's military-industrial complex could not have been written without the time and insights shared with us by dozens of military contractors, military personnel, trade unionists, public officials, and public interest group members. They are too numerous to mention, but their comments, often in their own inimitable language, are peppered throughout the book.

We are grateful to the National Science Foundation, and to the Geography and Regional Science Program directors Ronald Abler and Thomas Baerwald in particular, for funding portions of the research in chapters 6 and 7, and to the Ploughshares Foundation, and Sally Lilienthal, for underwriting the survey of conversion efforts in chapter 8. On those projects, we also owe much to our colleagues Pete Hall, Scott Campbell, Sabina Deitrick, and Catherine Hill. Our interpretations of the research findings remain our own.

A number of people read portions of the manuscript and gave us excellent feedback. Among them, we would like to thank particularly Marc Baldwin, Bob Beauregard, Jurgen Brauer, Michael Closson, Tom Geoghegan, David Gold, Catherine Hill, Candace Howes, Bob Lake, Roberta Lynch, Fred Rose, Max Sawicky, and Phil Shapira. Others, including Greg Bischak, Michael Black, Michael Borrus, Gary Chapman, Bennett Harrison, David Henry, Josh Lerner, John Lovering, Richard Oliver, and Barbara Simons, have been important sources of ideas, information, data, and inspiration, as well as encouragement, along the way.

Chapter 7 draws on more extensive discussions previously published in *The Rise of the Gunbelt* and in "Government as Market: Industrial Location in the U.S. Defense Industry," in Henry Herzog, Jr., and Alan Schlottmann, *Industrial Location and Public Policy*. We are grateful to Oxford University Press and University of Tennessee Press, respectively, for permission to include them. Portions of chapter 8 were drawn from "Converting the Military Industrial Economy: The Experience of Six Facilities," in the *Journal of Planning Education and Research*, which also gave us permission to reprint.

To Rutgers and Northwestern universities, we owe thanks for support during the period of writing. Rutgers's generosity in establishing the Project on Regional and Industrial Economics was a big shot in the arm. Helzi Noponen, as de facto office designer and manager during the first year and a half of PRIE, deserves praise as the book's fairy godmother. At PRIE, we enjoyed the spirited and quality research assistance of Wei Ping Wu, Yang Shao, Vickie Gwiasda, Scott Ballinger, and Deirdre FitzGerald. Nothing would have gotten out the door, and many mistakes would doubtless have been made, without the careful, consistent, and good-humored oversight of Kim Smith.

In Martin Kessler, we enjoyed an editor who not only pierced the veil over long-winded passages and waffling language but encouraged us over marvelous cuisine during the confusing weeks of the Gulf War, when we wondered whether military spending might not continue to be high fashion.

Our friends and families deserve thanks many times over for their tolerance of occasional absences and babbling at the dinner table or, worse, those lapses over the poised fork when a chapter's main theme suddenly burst through a clogged-up brain. They know who they are.

1

An Economy at War

■

THE economy of the United States has been at war for more than five decades. U.S. factories equipped the military in the successful "good war" of the 1940s. Then the infant aerospace industry filled the nation's nuclear arsenals with effective deterrents for the cold war. As the cold war waned, military contractors cranked out high-tech weapons for new "hot" wars in areas like Vietnam and the Persian Gulf. Ever since the Depression, preparing for warfare has been a permanent and potent American preoccupation. Consuming considerable human, financial, and public-sector resources, a military-oriented economy is, and has been, the industrial policy of the United States.

Like Janus, the Roman god of gateways, this economic commitment displays two faces. One is the vigorous face of American military hegemony, based upon considerable technological superiority in arms and their deployment. After its successful deployment of the Liberator bomber and the A-bomb in the Second World War, the ICBM (intercontinental ballistic missile) and the communication satellite during the cold war, and the Patriot missile and computer-managed battlefield in the Gulf War of 1991, the United States has demonstrated decisively that devoting R&D moneys, top scientific and engineering talent, and large procurement contracts to military missions does pay off in military prowess.

The second face is that of a domestic economy scarred by prolonged commitments of physical, technological, and human resources. This face has aged less well over the decades. Permanent commitments to war preparedness have created whole new industries and firms shaped and nourished by Pentagon budgets. Aerospace, electronics, communications, and computing have all benefited from

1

continual infusions of government R&D funding and from large government orders in key developmental stages. Some segments of these industries have progressed away from their military masters to serve commercial markets in aircraft, computers, and other high-tech paraphernalia. They form the core of whatever competitive advantage the U.S. economy retains in international markets.

But the power of these sectors, and their military progenitors, to sustain American economic leadership and provide a satisfactory standard of living is increasingly in doubt. Other nations' leading firms have stolen the thunder, capturing Pentagon-financed innovations and embedding them in commercial products faster than American producers can. Even the semiconductor industry, an American creation, has fallen to foreign competition and now suffers a negative trade balance.

Furthermore, as military missions become more and more esoteric, cross-fertilization between the military and commercial sectors of the economy becomes less and less likely. In the 1980s the pioneer's baton passed from military to commercial research labs in many industries; in computing and semiconductors, for instance, commercial technologies are now generations ahead of military ones. While American firms labor to produce a Stealth bomber, a laser gun, or a software system to demanding military specifications, their counterparts abroad are free to lavish their best brains and resources on commercial developments with far greater payoffs to the economy. What cold war expertise cross-fertilizes best is conventional weaponry, the kind employed with precision in the Gulf War.

Even if American military-industrial high-tech firms were to remain dominant in commercial as well as government markets, the jobs and economic activity generated would not compensate for the losses that this single-minded policy has inflicted on the rest of the industrial economy. The preemption of resources for military-industrial missions, particularly precious and scarce scientific and technical labor, has ill served purely commercial industries such as machine tools, industrial equipment, steel, autos, and consumer electronics. In these industries, stiff competition from abroad, often from countries with targeted industrial policies, has eroded American market share and humiliated domestic producers with large gains in net imports.

Furthermore, the machine and computer technologies developed to automate warfare have unintentionally automated commercial production as well, ejecting millions of blue-collar workers from manufacturing jobs at an artificially rapid pace. This group's slide into the lower middle class, in contrast to the smaller but marked increase in stature and pay of the military-oriented science and engineering professions, has contributed to the nation's worsening income distribution.

Military-led industrial policy in the United States, unlike Japanese and German industrial policy, operates as a *command* segment of the economy; the outright purchase of matériel, equipment, and research is its major mechanism. Over the entire postwar period, the Pentagon spent nearly $10.5 trillion (in 1990 dollars), accounting for a substantial portion of the annual deficit and the total accumulated public debt.[1] To raise the borrowed funds to finance these expenditures, the government has jacked up interest rates, further discouraging new private investment in nonmilitary activities. Increasingly, low productivity gains, higher deficits, and high real interest rates have led to economic stagnation and placed a vise grip on the economy, squeezing profits and wages.

Janus looked forward and backward, in opposite directions; the Janus face of the permanent war economy, however, looks up and down. One visage, youthful and dazzled, is tilted toward the sky, where the spectacular performances of fighter bombers, satellites, space shuttles, and defensive missiles confirm the payoff of large, sustained military expenditures. The other visage, weary and stressed, looks down into the trough where the American economy seems to be headed.

The World's High-Tech Cop

The Gulf War of 1991 demonstrated the ability of the United States, despite record budget and trade deficits, falling real wages, and worsening income inequality, to marshal its industrial and human resources to accomplish what no other nation could. The war pitted a U.S.-led multinational military force against heavily armed Iraqi land forces, following that nation's occupation of neighboring Kuwait. In a few short weeks, aircraft guided by highly sophisticated communications systems delivered a massive blitz of conventional explosives that destroyed the relatively well armed Iraqi army and the industrial capacity that equipped it. The strategy and the success of the relentless allied bombing campaign were charted daily on colorful maps for the entire television-viewing world. Many, though not all, of the new conventional weapons—some expressly designed for "low-intensity conflict" in "special Third World situations"—worked better than the designers and their military clients had dared to hope. Unbelievably, little American blood was shed.

For many observers, the achievements of the upgraded American arsenal vindicated the enormous expenditures undertaken by the Reagan administration in its eight years of unprecedented peacetime buildup in the 1980s. While some worried about the cost of the war—estimated at around $100 billion—others pointed out that the financial contributions of other nations prevented the United States from losing money on the war at all! Yet others pointed to the lucrative new markets for arms sales that the Gulf exhibition surely opened up; many countries would now strive to obtain the Patriot missiles and fancy electronic gear that had enabled the United States to obliterate Iraqi military installations in short order.[2]

But the specter of the United States assuming the role of the world's cop, and raising the revenues to do so by charging other countries, is troublesome. It is tantamount to acknowledging that the U.S. economy's chief competitive advantage lies in the design and production of instruments of war. In such a future, the United States would sell to other countries, both developed and underdeveloped, its expertise, its war-making technologies, and the services of its young military men and women. Funds from Japan, Germany, and other beneficiaries of U.S. intervention in local conflicts around the world would be used by the U.S. government for salaries to defense industry workers, wages for troops, and dividends to defense company stockholders. The recipients could buy from abroad the computers, videocassette recorders, autos, and machine tools that the United States could no longer produce competitively.

Regrettably, the United States appears to be in danger of pursuing just such a strategy. Under the Bush administration, the nation seems headed ever more resolutely down the path of renewed support for the defense industry and continued indifference toward the plight of all other segments of the domestic economy. Meanwhile, other nations are pursuing industrial policies designed to strengthen their commercial high-technology sectors and to raise the standard of living of their citizens.

Creating Defense-Dependency

Other futures are, of course, possible. A concerted effort to dedicate a portion of the nation's economic surplus and professional skills to new societal problems like environmental protection, waste management, and alternative energy development could generate significant new technologies and rebuild American competitive advantage. But one great deterrent to redirecting the economy is the degree of "defense-dependency" bred into a number of key sectors, firms, occupations, and communities. Over the decades, the unique missions of the cold war shaped an entire segment of the American economy. Between defense firms and their civilian counterparts there grew a "wall of separation" more durable than another product of the cold war, the Berlin Wall.

The rise of the aerospace-communications-electronics (ACE) complex is both a major burden and yet perhaps the best hope for the American economy. The crucial formative years of the ACE complex were the 1950s, when the cold war got under way. In stark contrast to the way hot wars are conducted, with hundreds of battalions of troops wielding hand-held weapons or driving ground vehicles like tanks and trucks, cold wars are waged and won in the research lab. Instead of a hot war's thousands of mass-produced guns and uniforms and tanks—not all that different from the consumer goods that can be manufactured in the same facilities—cold war factories turn out small numbers of highly specialized, atmospherically delivered weapons.

These weapons must not be *used,* since the point of cold war is deterrence. Nevertheless, cold wars are won by besting your opponent's weaponry, not by stockpiling the same old thing; weapons must be constantly re-created and updated. Furthermore, to make their long-distance threats effective the modern bomber and ballistic missile require enormously sophisticated electronic guidance and communications gear. Thus, cold war weaponry requires a large share of the available scientific and engineering expertise in a continual process of basic research, design, development, and experimentation.

To produce this type of gear, the defense industry requires an industrial configuration entirely different from the capital-intensive plants that crank out steel, machine tools, and consumer goods. Its facilities must have fewer fixed machines but larger numbers of skilled laborers. Its firms need to have internal structures and priorities that are appropriate for performance-oriented, and relatively cost-insensitive, military missions. Engineers tend to occupy the highest echelons of defense management. Reliance on defense contracts fosters a business community that is better at tolerating the red tape of selling to the government than at marketing on a mass scale. Defense firms must also accommodate themselves to government ownership of plants and stiff requirements for secrecy and security. Over the decades, a whole new set of firms heavily oriented toward the Pentagon as market have entered the Fortune 500.

These firms have become permanent features of the American industrial landscape. Because the business culture favored by the Pentagon diverges so remarkably from that of the older commercial industries, defense firms and their plants have been disproportionately located far from the traditional industrial heartland. Heartland business was indifferent, even hostile, to government contracting in the 1950s, an era of booming consumer demand and seemingly infinite commercial markets for machinery. Without the discipline of cost-consciousness, and free to settle wherever they wished, military contractors were drawn toward certain key military installations and followed the air force in particular toward its preferred locations in the West. They have shaped their host communities into the "Gunbelt"—a string of large cities and smaller towns across the country that are heavily dependent upon the federal government for the continuing good health of their economies. The new residents of these communities include aerospace, nuclear, and electrical engineers.

Pentagon contracts to universities and defense contractors for R&D activity over the past fifty years have swelled the ranks of both scientists and engineers, and many are trained to work on top-secret, highly specialized projects. To complement this brain power, the ranks of highly skilled blue-collar workers have also grown in Gunbelt locations. They have been moved in large numbers around the country, from the heartland to the Gunbelt, a dramatic migration of skilled labor financed by U.S. taxpayers.

Stuck in the War Economy Trough

Over the decades, civilian economic growth in the United States has become more and more sluggish. The number of jobs generated by military spending and in the defense-initiated commercial high-tech sectors has not been enough to offset losses in other areas of the industrial economy. From 1980 to 1985, during the height of the Reagan administration buildup, defense manufacturing added 600,000 jobs to the economy, but 1.6 million jobs were lost in non-defense industry. A better industrial future for the United States clearly lies down the road taken by non–military spending Japan and Germany—toward preeminence in high-quality, mass-produced consumer goods and in leading-edge technologies devoted to socially useful ends. To support such an about-face, the nation's infrastructure and human capital would need considerable refurbishing and retraining. But substantial rigidities and adjustment problems are making the transfer of resources from the military-industrial sector to other sectors quite difficult. The nation seems to be stuck in the war economy trough.

By the 1970s, despite an overwhelming post–Vietnam War mandate to rein in the military-industrial complex, the entire edifice had become so highly specialized and dramatically differentiated from the rest of the business community that it could not easily turn to commercial alternatives. A number of well-publicized failures—for instance, the ventures by Boeing-Vertol and Rohr into mass-transit vehicles— underscored the formidable barriers to easy conversion and helped propagate a myth that the big defense contractors could not do anything else well.

Faced with the choice of either going commercial with their own R&D initiatives or searching for another angle on the federal government, most defense firms chose the latter. Working hand in glove with the Pentagon, they designed a whole new generation of cold war weaponry (Trident subs, MX missiles) and a raft of radically updated conventional arms (Bradley fighting vehicles, new fighter bombers, Patriot missiles). By the end of the 1970s, the ink was beginning to dry on contracts that would boost the federal defense budget by more than 42 percent in real dollars from 1980 to 1987. In a few short years, real military spending climbed to the level it had reached during the Vietnam War.[3]

The apparent end of the cold war in 1989 and the growing concern over the budget deficit slapped a lid on military spending in the late 1980s. By 1990, in the midst of a short-lived public euphoria about a peace dividend, a number of top military contractors were loudly worrying about their futures. Despite the shot in the arm of the Gulf War, many still attend the meetings of the half-dozen or so task forces on conversion that have sprung up around the nation. Many firms are so pessimistic about their ability to do anything other than defense work that they have adopted the strategy of simply hunkering down and laying off workers until the next buildup—inevitable in their view—begins. In the battle of the budget, they are choosing trench warfare.

Many others touched by the defense economy are also reluctant to take aggressive steps to alter its course. It is not hard to see why. The experience of plant closings and job losses in numerous other sectors of the economy in the past decade has shaken workers, communities, and politicians. Switching from defense to commercial production would not be easy even in better economic times. In the short run, a reallocation of national spending from producing B-2 bombers to upgrading the nation's infrastructure would require contracting more often with firms that employ civil engineers and construction workers. It is estimated that it would take a year to train an electrical engineer to be a civil engineer, and at least six months to train an aircraft assembler to work construction.[4] Furthermore, some infrastructure projects are in regions of the country far from the locus of military-industrial production; shifting from defense to commercial production could temporarily cause inflationary pressures in some industries and regions while creating considerable displacement and recession in others.[5]

Members of Congress find it difficult to vote for budget cuts that will affect their own districts, even if they favor military budget cuts in principle. When local economies provide no alternatives for the workers and communities faced with such cuts, the pressure on individual members of Congress increases all the more. To cope with a clear imperative to close military bases, Congress recently set up an elaborate process that invests initiating authority in an independent commission and ensures that any congressional acquiescence will take place as far as possible from the biennial election dates.

At least 6.7 million Americans work in military-related jobs, not including those whose livelihoods come from defense-related space and energy projects or from foreign arms sales. These workers support families and other workers in their local economies through their expenditures on food, clothing, housing, and so on. The cuts of 20 percent in military spending slated to take place over the first half of the 1990s would substantially displace many of them.[6] Their unions and their communities know this. Many unions have played a lead role in crafting conversion legislation that would set up programs to absorb these shocks. Some communities have initiated conversion task forces, military spending, impact assessment, and special conversion projects. Yet many are loath to embrace so-called alternative use planning if no provision is made for those left behind.

Redirecting Science and Technology

The cold war and its prophet and facilitator, the nuclear bomb, proved beyond a doubt that cadres of scientists and engineers, bankrolled by the government, could produce revolutionary new technologies. These technologies, with differing degrees of success, gave us commercially viable materials and products that have altered the face of industrial society—nuclear power, jet airplanes, supercomputers, and lasers, to name a few. Guided by the American model, other nations have concluded that setting aside a portion of their wealth for investment in new technologies will make them market leaders in new product lines. But over the decades, the payoffs from American military-sponsored research have shrunk and become more confined to strictly military products, like F-16s and Patriot missiles.

Any new nonmilitary economic development strategy for the United States must thus grapple with the question of how to support new R&D. Officials of the Pentagon's Defense Advanced Research Projects Agency (DARPA), the de facto national industrial R&D agency for the past few decades, have pioneered the notion that national security is as much a question of economic strength as of military prowess. With the support of congressional allies, the agency has undertaken an extensive program of selective R&D funding of special projects to enhance the ability of American companies to compete internationally. Some of these projects—for instance, the Sematech research consortium for leading-edge semiconductor research—have already been implemented. Under attack by laissez-faire conservatives within the Bush administration and by other Pentagon officials, the agency's mission has been recast as one of generating "dual-use" technologies to serve both military and civilian goals.

Critics of the defense domination of such efforts point to the increasing failure of military technologies to generate appropriate civilian technologies and to the worsening performance of even high-tech industries in international competition. They also point out that using a dual-use criterion limits severely the types of R&D projects that can be supported. These critics prefer the idea of establishing a civilian technology agency, perhaps housed in the Department of Commerce, whose mandate would be to pick "critical" technologies and fund their development.

In our view, both of these strategies are misconceived. U.S. defense-led industrial policy was successful for forty years because the government not only funded research and development but provided a market for the product of those efforts. A technology agency that simply tries to pick winning technologies, considering neither the nature of demand nor social policy, is sure to be as ineffective as an industrial policy that tries to pick winners and losers. Such an agency, whether military or civilian, could become a tremendous money sink, and it could re-create the same defense-dependency of university and corporate scientists and engineers that is now such a problem. To work, a technology policy must include commitments by the government and by private parties to purchase the equipment and services pioneered.

For instance, renewed national commitments to environmental cleanup, solid-waste disposal, alternative energy development, and housing the homeless should encompass not only a research agenda but an effort to develop markets for the products of that research. Unlike commitments to developing B-2 bombers or battlefield management systems, these commitments need not cost taxpayers money. They can be implemented through regulations, which cost very little. For instance, the use of electric autos could be mandated as a means of achieving air quality requirements, thereby creating a market for the necessary new technologies. Or such innovation can be encouraged through one-of-a-kind demonstration projects. For instance, the feasibility of inexpensive, energy-efficient manufactured housing as a solution to the housing crisis could be shown in a government-subsidized new-town project.

Furthermore, the issues of science and technology policy and conversion of military to civilian activity must be joined. Military spending in all its guises—research as well as procurement—has diverted resources and policy attention from other social needs and industrial sectors; only an integrated R&D, spending, and industrial policy will successfully revitalize the economy without further squandering resources and creating even more hardship in the interim. Specific plans for converting plants and work forces from one set of activities to another are integral to new economic development efforts.

Breaching the War Economy Trough

In the absence of viable alternatives, defense-related companies and workers and their communities will probably support continued heavy commitments to military spending. They will do so even at great personal cost—the average American family has spent over $50,000 on the military just since 1975.[7] Sustaining large military budgets is attractive to some policymakers, particularly during a recession, because it is an attractive and easy way to artificially stimulate the economy. Yet maintaining commitments to military spending, whether for cold or hot war purposes, will only deepen the economic malaise that grips the nation because such commitments cannot reverse the deterioration in American competitiveness and standards of living. The prognosis for the nation's smooth adjustment to a new era of heightened competitiveness and a changing world order is not good and will be worse if the recession deepens and spreads internationally. If we are to flourish as a nation, avoid growing debt, and reverse worsening social conditions, the military budget must be cut and the wall of separation between military and civilian industry dismantled. As a nation, we must take up the historic challenge of rebuilding our economy so that it can stand the rigors of the harsh new world of global competition.

Fortunately, out of the experiments of the recent past have come a number of good ideas and success stories. A few small firms have successfully converted their military production to the civilian market. Research on conversion by union leaders and peace organizations, often working in tandem, suggests that alternative civilian products exist for many defense-oriented businesses. Communities facing base closure have successfully redeveloped military bases into schools, commercial airstrips, industrial parks, and other civilian facilities. Cities as diverse as Irvine, California, and Pittsburgh have launched high-speed mass-transit system initiatives that combine private production with public-sector infrastructure renovation. After ten years of experience with plant closings, state and local governments have initiated several new efforts, some quite successful, at marketing, technical assistance, and small-business formation. Regional job authorities, such as Pittsburgh's Steel Valley Authority, help engineer management turnovers and are a resource of first resort for workers and managers whose plants are closing.

On these foundations an integrated strategy for building new economic and industrial initiatives to meet national needs is feasible. Our version encompasses public as well as private commitments to environmental, health, housing, and infrastructure programs. Key features include a responsive science and technology policy and incentives to firms, workers, and their communities to take giant steps along a new road.

Do we think the United States can accomplish this? Absolutely. A nation that can produce the F-117 Stealth fighter, and the generations of weapons before it, has demonstrated its ability to combine teamwork, technological expertise, and planning, all under the auspices of the public sector, to accomplish a complex mission. Now it is time to set the nation's sights higher and climb out of the war economy trough.

2

The Rise of
Postmodern Warfare

∎

AMONG the showcase items in the American arsenal of the 1990s is the Peacekeeper—or MX—missile. An MX does not look all that extraordinary. Weighing ninety-seven tons and stretching seventy-one feet in length, it resembles a small, slick obelisk when upended. But its plain-looking facade is deceptive. An MX can carry ten nuclear warheads up to 6,674 miles, delivering enough destructive power to match Hiroshima and Nagasaki hundreds of times over. A refinement of the intercontinental ballistic missile (ICBM), the MX sports a sophisticated inertial guidance system and is remotely controlled with the aid of global positioning satellites. Some MX missiles are deployed in silos, others are slated to move around on the rail system. The MX is, according to two of its students, the "most expensive weapon project contemplated, the most extensive in resource consumption, most cogent in strategic significance since nuclear weapons and intercontinental missiles, and most expansive in environmental and socioeconomic implications."[1]

And, one might add, among the most controversial. President Jimmy Carter decided in 1979 to deploy 200 of them, but throughout the 1980s the MX was targeted by the peace movement as a major candidate for elimination. The plan to "mobilize" the missile by continually moving it around on rails was much derided. Its vulnerabilities and its ballooning costs were highly publicized. Despite President Ronald Reagan's enthusiasm for the MX—he redubbed it the "Peacekeeper"—through 1988 procurement had been held to fifty at a cost of about $100 million apiece. The Bush administration ordered twelve MXs, at a cost of $918 million, in fiscal 1991. Although the Bush administration has cancelled the dozen per year slated for purchase in

12

1992 and 1993, it has proposed funding *research* on the rail garrison idea at a cost of $360 million in 1992–93.[2]

The MX epitomizes the strange ways of postmodern cold warfare. It is a weapon designed *not* to be used—its value lies in its ability to deter. It is the quality of this weapon, not the quantity of it, that makes it so potent. The MX is an extraterrestrial weapon—it defies gravity thanks to the benefits of an explosion in human knowledge about flight—and a completely automated weapon, delivering enormous destructive power without any direct manning. Its design, manufacture, and deployment require highly specialized skills—to fashion the computers, instruments, radars, satellites, and guidance systems that permit it to travel and target precisely. Thousands of physicists, aeronautical engineers, and electrical engineers labored to create it. The MX is only one of many extraordinarily expensive pieces of capital equipment with which national hostilities are now mediated, and as such, it is a creature of long-term government planning.

If the First and Second World Wars were the first modern wars, then the cold war—and its progeny, the kind of high-tech hot war fought in 1991 in the Persian Gulf—are distinctively postmodern. The differences between modern and postmodern warfare cannot be overstated. The world wars were hot wars, conducted with endless battalions of men armed with huge volumes of guns and ammunition and transported on thousands of land-based vehicles, ships, and fighter planes. Such "total war" was made possible by the extraordinary productivity of the modern industrial economy. Every plant in the industrial heartland pumped out matériel for the war effort. Innovation was often forsaken in the push to turn out airplanes, steel, motor vehicles, machinery, chemicals, and other equipment faster. (For instance, during the Second World War the Army Air Corps settled for an inferior fighter plane, the P-40, produced by Curtiss-Wright in Buffalo, over designs by Bell, Lockheed, and Seversky because the P-40 could be produced in quantity a full year ahead of any other.)[3] Massive volumes of armaments, as well as the esprit and readiness of troops, determined the outcome of hostilities.

In contrast, the cold war was characterized by the replacement of manpower with highly sophisticated, electronics-intensive precision machinery. Machines, not men, came to form the core of the nation's fighting ability. As the expense and elaborateness escalated for each submarine, bomber, and missile, fewer and fewer units of each were produced. These weapons were products of the fusion of science, technology, and engineering that was so central to the cold war military competition of staying one step ahead of the adversary. New generations of weaponry followed fast on the footsteps of the last; rather than responding to foreign policy priorities, strategic planning for weaponry began to occur far in advance of foreign policy formation, in the laboratories of giant corporations and major research universities and on the drawing boards of military designers.

Science-based, capital-intensive warfare has dramatically altered both the way the United States equips itself for war and the way it conducts diplomacy. It is "products" like the Stealth bomber, the Trident submarine, the MX missile, and the Patriot missile that are the major innovative works of the postmodern war economy. Particularly in the 1980s, the application of science took weapon development beyond the boundaries of cold war competition. Precision guidance systems and computer-based battlefield management plans had obvious applications to hot war situations, to what were envisioned—erroneously, in retrospect—as "low-intensity" conflicts. Technological dominance of the conventional battlefield permitted the formulation of a whole new American foreign policy initiative—George Bush's "new world order." Highly automated, albeit expensive, weapon and delivery systems could minimize the shedding of American blood while maximizing the destruction on the other side.

How did this revolution in the tools of war come about? How did the technologies demanded in an atmospheric and automated era of military conflict alter the way contractors work? Through a relentless chain of events, a dramatically new form of warfare bred a radically different type of economic activity. Three features of postmodern warfare are central to this transformation. First, the rise of atmospheric warfare placed strenuous demands on engineering and industry. A whole new military service, the air force, evolved to manage airborne warfare and the process of equipping for it. Airborne preparedness was enhanced by the automation of warfare and the development of sophisticated, remote sensing and guidance systems, both of which fostered revolutions in computing and electronics. Expanded phalanxes of engineers were trained and recruited to create and fine-tune these systems. As it took on more engineers, the military needed fewer and fewer troops.

Second, since cold war demanded constant innovation, the lifespan of new generations of weapons became shorter and shorter while the scientific complexity of each generation grew disproportionately larger. Cold war weapons were designed to be threats, to not be used, so the quantity of weapons produced became much less important than their quality and capabilities. The scientific and engineering expertise required to generate continual innovation in high-performance weapons shifted the production process inside contractors' facilities heavily toward the white-collar end at the same time as fewer and fewer blue-collar workers were required to turn out the quantities of aircraft or ordnance they had once produced. As warfare production became more capital-intensive, requiring more highly skilled workers, military policy itself was increasingly determined by scientific and supply-side considerations.

Third, postmodern weapons had to be produced in clean, flexible, and secret environments, which we now associate with the high-tech industrial world. Entirely new work environments and business cultures were demanded by the unique nature of cold war production. The practices of minimizing production costs and marketing far and wide fell by the wayside as contractors concentrated on dazzling their sole customer, the military, with visions of craft and weapons capable of unthinkable new feats. Companies had to remain flexible enough to shift workers and machinery from one activity to another with ease. For this segment of American industry there were fewer and fewer mass-production lines; instead, thousands of highly specialized market niches, all of them within the Pentagon's five walls, proliferated. Furthermore, much of the highly touted flexibility observed in other sectors of the economy was an outgrowth of the technologies nurtured and then weaned from the cold war effort. By the time the cold war was over, its legacy was deeply embedded in all segments of American industry, but especially in that subsector that had come to be known as the military-industrial complex.

Warfare Goes Extraterrestrial

In postmodern warfare, pilots in aircraft and pilotless missiles and satellites have supplanted sailors navigating hostile waters, knights in armor, and troops in camouflage marching across deserts, slogging through swamps, or struggling with jungle vegetation. The most effective military threats are now extraterrestrial, above the frictions of land and sea. The exploration of this "third dimension to warfare" has contributed to radical alterations in the industrial base that equips war-making.[4]

The ability to move military confrontation up into the atmosphere was predicated on the development of the airplane. By the First World War, what Irving Holley, Jr., has called "the aerial weapon" was well on its way to development.[5] At first the notion was that aircraft could

15

act as the "eyes" of the army, surveying and reporting on the battlefield with bird's-eye vision. In addition, they could act "as a sort of mobile artillery, applied directly in support of ground armies."[6]

But the truly revolutionary promise of the airplane lay in its potential for bombardment. Air-delivered bombs of tremendous destructive magnitude promised to democratize warfare, to move conflicts beyond the battlefield with its battalions of well-marshaled men and into enemy factories, refineries, rail lines, and civilian neighborhoods. Strategic bombing, writes Michael Sherry, threatened "to nationalize the battle of attrition on the ground, testing how long entire peoples rather than armies could exhaust each other." (Sherry also recounts H. G. Wells's famous fictionalized forecast of aerial bombardment in *War in the Air* [1908], in which he predicted that the bomber could topple civilization not just because it kills and destroys, but because it could rip apart the economic and political fabric of society.)[7] The bomber, offering superior range, easy portability, and enormous striking power, appealed broadly to diverse constituencies.[8] Its potency was questioned by many until the dropping of atomic bombs on Hiroshima and Nagasaki. A handful of pilots in four bombers leveled Hiroshima in a few short, epoch-making minutes—the final proof of the superiority of the aerial weapon.

The availability of weapons and delivery systems that defy gravity—for such was the magic of aerial warfare—wiped away obstacles that had plagued ground commanders for years. The terrestrial environment is cluttered with lumpy and obstructed terrain, lines of communication are fragile, and troublesome human populations stand in the way. Armed aircraft, in contrast, can overfly sloughs, hillocks, and brush. The air weapon's strengths, according to the military historian Martin van Creveld, are "speed, flexibility, the ability to reach out and hit any point regardless of natural and artificial obstacles, and great potential for achieving surprise." Van Creveld argues that human populations constitute by far the most complicated environment in which war can be waged; he suggests that this is why modern technological weaponry is least effective in campaigns against guerrillas.[9]

Back in the factory, air power presented novel problems to industrial designers and military planners. The construction and deployment of aircraft required technologies and strategies quite foreign to those employed for land and sea mobility. Aircraft have to be constantly mobile, pilots have to aim under such conditions, and lines of communication have to be secured over extraordinarily long distances. Aircraft are fragile, have limited endurance, and are exceedingly vulnerable to attack and weather conditions (indeed, foul weather was the dominant problem confronting bombing strategy in Europe during the Second World War); these factors require difficult trade-offs between payload, manning levels, and fuel capacity.[10] From the outset, aircraft designers and their military clients found themselves immersed in a highly experimental production process. As Holley puts it, "Design of aircraft was not only unstable, but far less static than design of any other weapon military men had ever before encountered."[11]

In the postwar period, extraterrestrial warfare has penetrated deeply into military strategy and organizational structure. It has moved beyond fighters and bombers into missiles—including those launched by submarine—communication satellites, and space-based weapons (which promoted and were promoted by the emerging aerospace industry). Its major tools are now large weapon systems, each consisting of platforms (the bomber, the missile, the submarine, the aircraft carrier) outfitted with expensive and sophisticated equipment designed to enhance guidance, surveillance, precision, speed, stealth, and durability. Each weapon system has a linchpin, with a cast of hundreds supporting it. The aircraft carrier's entourage, for instance, includes destroyers and submarines for protection, a fleet of aircraft on its decks, a diverse set of supply ships, and a complicated global communication network.[12]

Today, such extraterrestrial products account for the bulk of military procurement budgets. By the early 1980s, for instance, the Trident submarine and the new nuclear-powered aircraft carrier, together with their missiles and aircraft, absorbed about 60 percent of the navy's procurement outlays; two fighters, the F-15 and the F-16, took up more than 40 percent of the air force share. Each program is exorbitantly expensive: the Trident cost American taxpayers over $30 billion in 1980 dollars, and the nuclear carrier, together with its planes and ships, cost $60 billion. Individual platforms weigh in with mind-boggling price tags: an F-15, for instance, costs $19 million. Distinctions between strategic and nonstrategic weapons, albeit used by the Pentagon in planning, are not particularly important when assessing each product and the demands it levies on the economy. Furthermore, it is questionable whether tactical fighters and other equipment that defend platforms carrying strategic nuclear weapons are not themselves "strategic," just as fears about the use of tactical nuclear weapons in Europe raise questions about the distinction.[13]

The new military service that managed atmospheric warfare, the air force, had distinct advantages from the outset. First, it had glamor; compared with the mass missions of sailors and infantrymen, the air force could celebrate the individual pilot-as-hero. The popularity of the pilot did much for the air force's appeal. Of course, each pilot was supported by a team of about seventy other technicians. And pilots' roles were eventually de-skilled by the accretion of automatic guidance systems, instrumentation, and cybernetics aboard the aircraft, which came to resemble manned missiles.[14]

Second, the air force possessed what Matthew Evangelista calls an "ethos of change."[15] It had weaned itself from the army during a long era of lively experimentation in every kind of gravity-defying endeavor. Its leadership was remarkably design-oriented and relied heavily upon scientists and engineers in procurement planning. It had already forged close working relationships with the dozen or so companies headed for dominance in the aerospace industry, which in turn helped build political support for further weapons development. The air force remains the most advanced of the services in R&D outlook and competence.

Of course, the air force faced stiff challenges from the other major services, the army and the navy, both of which managed to garner their share of atmospheric weaponry. The rivalry among the services for an extraterrestrial role, particularly in the 1950s when resources seemed limitless, created more and better weapons in the aggregate. The net result was the proliferation of weapons, an acceleration of the pace of weapons development, and a dramatic shift of all the services toward a high-tech, automated form of postmodern warfare.

Machines at War

Until the total wars of this century, the First and Second World Wars, war had been highly labor-intensive. Weaponry was carried and thrust or aimed (once gunpowder became available) by individual human beings. Indeed, the term "arms" embodies the notion that weapons are extensions of the human limb.

It is hard to imagine a more dramatic shift in the conduct of war than from the labor-intensive trench warfare of the First World War to the dropping of the A-bomb over Hiroshima in 1945. Both resulted in unbelievable carnage, but it was achieved in entirely different modes. The same dramatic gap appeared between the deadly aerial bombardment in Iraq in early 1991 achieved by a few hundred pilots in enormously expensive machines, and the hundreds of thousands of allied troops amassed along the Iraqi border, whose courage and sacrifice were never really required.

This substitution of aircraft for manpower was welcomed, by the public as well as the army, as a life-saving innovation designed to "remove the soldier from the hazards of duty." By the Second World War, lowering the number of human casualties of warfare had become a serious preoccupation. According to former journalist and government information officer Arthur Sweetser, an early air war advocate, "Every day's delay in building planes means three or four thousand more Americans that will not come back at all, or will come back crippled and of no use at all."[16] Policymakers justified the use of the A-bomb by invoking the specter of an invasion of Japan requiring a projected force of 2.7 million men and women and resulting in great casualties.[17] Since then, the rising resistance of the American population to the use of its young people as cannon fodder, expressed in the anti–Vietnam War movement and in anxiety about the Gulf War, has quickened the pace of substitution of automated equipment for manpower in military strategy. Bases close, but budgets for weapon systems increase.

In postmodern warfare, manpower—the brawn, courage, and physical combat skills of soldiers—has given way to the firepower and mobility of machines. Even the bomber, which required few men to achieve enormous destruction, has been challenged if not displaced by the intercontinental ballistic missile. With the ICBM, the pilot's position as deliverer of nuclear warheads has been replaced by robots. Top-of-the-line bombers like the B-1 or the Stealth are now largely automated as well; they resemble manned missiles, their pilots more or less imprisoned in them. The pilot's role as navigator, interpreter of information, and bombsighter has been almost completely usurped by complex communication and guidance equipment.[18] He remains a high-profile hero, but his job is not all that different from what the video-game player does at home or in the arcade.

Consider the Maverick missile, a prime example of automated weaponry. The Maverick is designed to "see" targets and select which ones to hit, relying on complicated and miniaturized electro-optical equipment, including a tiny television camera embedded in its nose. Its response system can be programmed to "kill" tanks, bridges, or other specific shapes that come into view. The Maverick incorporates the latest in electronic components, integrated circuits, and minicomputers for signal processing, carrying many thousand times more computing power and sensory capability than did its predecessors. Norman Augustine, CEO of Martin-Marietta, the company that designed the Maverick, and the former assistant secretary of the army, has bragged, "Our missiles will be not just smart, but brilliant."[19]

Ironically, the inexorable push toward automated weapons like the Maverick has not lowered the number of people dedicated to war readiness. Instead, it has pushed them back from the front lines into roles as mechanics and repairmen, computer programmers, procurement officials, and growing phalanxes of private-sector professional workers. In the Civil War era, nine out of ten soldiers belonged to combat-ready units. Today, only one in six do, a phenomenon known in military circles as the "declining teeth to tail" ratio.[20] As Mary Kaldor, a scholar of contemporary weaponry, has remarked, "It is easier to persuade men to work than to kill or to risk getting killed."[21] The business of killing has simply become more remote, and the deployment of an effective threat has become predominantly an industrial undertaking.

As direct war-making has become more highly automated, the business of outfitting for war has paradoxically become more labor-intensive. Factories once turned out mass-produced rifles and tanks by the thousands; now the craftsman's work of producing a handful of missiles, satellites, bombers, fighters, and nuclear-powered submarines every year takes place in structures that resemble office buildings more than factories. Mechanisms that can see, sense, analyze, and make decisions that pilots and infantrymen once made are very demanding in design and construction. Lead times as long as fifteen years are required for major weapon system development. Supporting casts of thousands are needed—scientists to invent the weapons, engineers to design them, machinists to build them, more engineers to test them, programmers to direct them, and technicians to repair them.[22]

The Boom in Military Electronics

Unlike Rosie of Second World War fame, the supporting casts are not chiefly engaged in riveting aluminum sheets together. They are more likely to be engaged in the wizardry known as "electronics." The rise of automated military air power created new challenges in the fields of instrumentation, communications, and information processing. Air missions operate at incredible speeds compared with ground warfare, and the remoteness of pilots from their commanders taxed existing methods of leadership. The result was a series of revolutionary breakthroughs between the 1920s and 1940s—the wireless radio, radar, and computers, all signaled the advent of the electronics age. Each, in turn, dramatically increased the amount of information that should and could be processed.

The wireless radio proved to be the first important breakthrough. With it, commanders could communicate with their pilots, process information fed from them, and relay tactical decisions. Air combat could take place in "real time," without the long-distance, hand-written missives that had delayed and bollixed nineteenth-century warfare.[23]

Consider the problems facing the early fighter pilot. He had to plot his course, monitor the speed of his aircraft, figure in the wind direction, and attempt to find and destroy his targets. At first, the Army Air Corps simply relied on weather forecasts, which often led to tragedy. The navy, more advanced in instrumentation, experimented as early as the First World War with direction-finding wireless telegraphy and instruments to improve navigation.[24] Radar was an even more significant breakthrough. It enabled pilots to read the position, course, and speed of opposing craft. Radar was the new eye of the system, and coupled with radio teleprinter links, searchlights, and antiaircraft batteries, it changed the face of war. Designed to increase the speed of detection and decision-making and the accuracy of response, radar dramatically accelerated the trend toward replacing human operators with machines.

Several features of aerial warfare sped up the evolution of computers. First, the need to coordinate radar, searchlights, and directions to antiaircraft artillery and pilots required expanded computing ability. Radar-related research also pioneered high-frequency electronics, upon which computers later relied heavily. Second, the need to crack codes, used by all belligerents for long-distance, radio-based communications, enhanced the desire for massive computational capacity, especially during the Second World War. Third, new demands from aeronautical research, so much more complicated than landed vehicle or even ship design, fed the pressure for innovation in business machines. Finally, paperwork had snowballed, and officers found themselves increasingly unable to cope. The information explosion demanded a shortcut to the computational and storage capacity of the human brain.[25]

At first the computer's role was limited to monitoring data linked to sensors. But gradually computers assumed the roles of intelligence analyst and decision-maker, sounding the alarm and directing automated weapons to their targets. Over time, top military management made a long-term commitment to computing research, an effort so unequivocally successful that the average F-15 now contains forty-five "black boxes"—the computer systems that virtually run the aircraft.[26]

With the rise to prominence of unmanned missiles and satellites and barely manned bombers, the overall conduct of war has become increasingly cybernetic. All-electronic communications networks have supplanted direct human interaction; decision-makers attempt to manage the conflict by remote control. According to Jack Manno, "As methods of communication, espionage, navigation, information processing and display become more refined and integrated, they make it possible to transform the earth into an electronic battlefield, its wars observed on display terminals by commanders far from the field."[27]

Military cybernetics has created nightmarish tasks for officers and political leaders. Weapon systems must be integrated across all types. Instant global communications produce rigorous demands for quick human response. Satellite messages must be processed and directions sent to a far-flung network of silos, submarines, and aircraft on bases and carriers. War planning has mushroomed into a highly complex exercise; thousands of programmers create simulations of missile attacks under a multitude of assumptions about equipment, position, speed, targets, and capabilities. The proliferation of problems in the guidance and communications area has created a new specialization, colloquially known as C³I, or "C-cubed-I"—command, control, communications, and intelligence systems. C³I consists of radio and computer hookups "designed to carry out the dream of controlling military maneuvers from one central point." As of the early 1980s, the Pentagon had invested $10–15 billion in such worldwide command and control systems, and outlays have accelerated since then.[28]

Historically, new military capabilities have sooner or later generated their own vulnerabilities. Electronic warfare is no exception. As soon as radar and computing became essential to military prowess, belligerents began to figure out ways of sabotaging their opponents' instruments and lines of communication. Ingenious ways of jamming radar or fooling it continue to be found, and much energy goes into creating and breaking communication codes and computer security systems. Electronic countermeasures and counter-countermeasures absorb increasing resources, without appreciably enhancing inherent performance.[29] This arms race may be without technological limit.

The Pentagon's fascination with automated, electronic, and extraterrestrial warfare intensified throughout the postwar period, especially in the 1980s, despite considerable criticism from both within and without. Gen. Omar Bradley spoke for many seasoned military leaders when he criticized "the permanent American desire to substitute machines for men and magic weapons for conventional armaments."[30] James Fallows, in his plea for a return to esprit de corps over technology, lambasts the "pursuit of the magic weapon," which he sees as the distinguishing feature of modern American defense. "In the years since research and engineering came to dominate the Pentagon," he contends, "more and more of the resources available for defense have been invested in the search for weapons that will make victory automatic, that will give ten men the power of ten thousand."[31] Yet automated weaponry, from F-117s and fighter bombers to Patriot missiles, proved once and for all in the Gulf War of early 1991 the overwhelming superiority of sophisticated gear over men, even men in tanks.

Cold War and Continual Innovation

The task of solving the technical problems of extraterrestrial warfare would not, in itself, have been sufficient to justify building a permanent and distinctive military-industrial complex. That required a foreign policy that harnesses the national will to large and sustained expenditures on military preparedness, and preparedness of a certain kind. The cold war between the Soviet Union and the United States, introduced by the awesome A-bomb, provided just such a rationale. It set off an unprecedented process of relentless, government-underwritten innovation. Generation after short-lived generation of high-tech nuclear weapons, launched from a battery of sophisticated delivery craft, were drafted and built, but for a strange mission—that of deterrence. The point was no longer to produce and use lethal weapons in large numbers, but to produce a few of such deadly superiority that they would ensure their own disuse.

At first glance, the nonuse of weapons might appear incompatible with a permanent jump in the peacetime military budget. Why could not these unspeakably powerful weapons simply be built and stockpiled? What accounts for the escalation in expenditure? The answer is that cold war is won by besting an opponent's weaponry—its delivery system, its lethality, its detectability, its flexibility, its directability. Each breakthrough poses new problems for the opponent, who then struggles to match the virtuosity of a new weapon technology until the initiator's competitive edge is eroded.

The U.S.-Soviet cold war resembled a seesaw ratcheting ever up-ward. Each new invention was destabilizing because it gave superior-ity to one side of the superpower duopoly. Inventions are highly diffusion-prone. It did not take long for one belligerent to master the secrets of the other's technology, however new it was. Over the decades, a pattern developed: the United States initiated a new tech-nology, and the Soviet Union copied it.[32]

Ironically, many of the innovations that made American military devices obsolete emerged from the nation's own government-spon-sored workshops. No sooner does the military have a new weapon than it worries about how opponents might disarm it. The Pentagon then gives contractors more money to either find a defense against it or develop a new offensive weapon that will penetrate any new defense system, setting in motion a pendulum that swings back and forth from offensive to defensive preoccupations.[33] The Strategic De-fense Initiative (SDI), the "Star Wars" plan for a space-based strategic defense system, is a response to the enhanced power of nuclear missiles with their multiple warheads and scattered, diverse launching pads; it is just the latest swing of the pendulum.

Where once weapons innovations were haphazard and unex-pected, preparation for war has increasingly become a process of managing technology. To keep up with the accelerated pace of change, military leaders have developed "a new awareness of inven-tion," states Martin van Creveld. Their traditional resistance to innova-tion has been irrevocably eliminated. The modern military manager is preoccupied with choosing paths of technological development and managing the organizational changes necessary to make the new weapon systems work.[34] The penchant for technological solutions has spread far beyond the strategic sphere. Those branches of the services responsible for conventional and "low-intensity" warfare have begun to mimic the high-tech innovation process of nuclear weapon delivery systems.

Government-led, high-tech innovation began to be institutional-ized in the military-industrial complex in the 1950s. The need for new generations of weapons inflated the demand for scientists and engi-neers beyond what was needed to meet the purely technical chal-lenges of atmospheric warfare. A considerable amount of labor goes into pure conceptualizing and into the basic science research that contributes to useful military equipment. More goes into planning the process of experimentation and prototype building, even more into testing and evaluation. Skilled workers are also needed to carry out security arrangements and communicate with the military customer.

Today, the production of what amounts to only dozens of highly automated weapon systems entails the work of millions of white-collar specialists. As research and development became key activities of defense contracting, more and more highly skilled labor was devoted to accelerating military capabilities.

Demand- or Supply-Driven?

Was the development of continual cold war innovation a one-way process in which contractors expanded to meet foreign policy imperatives? Some scholars accept this demand-side view. Others argue that the appetite for cold war was created in large part by political pressures from within communities of scientists, contractors, and the military services. Each of these groups, for reasons of its own, wanted to regularize infusions of R&D moneys and government sales.

F.P.

There is some evidence for the latter view. Despite the fact that nightmares of Nazi atomic bombs were dispelled long before the Second World War's end, key American bomb designers and managers of the Manhattan Project argued for using the A-bomb anyway. They pointed out to civilian political leaders that Congress might wonder about the value of the enormous investment that had gone into its construction if it were not detonated. They also argued that demonstration of the bomb's devastating power would strengthen the American hand in the anticipated postwar competition with its ally, the Soviet Union. Aerospace companies, lean and hungry after their profitable wartime contracts evaporated, were quick to clamor about the Soviet threat.[35]

The supply-side push to cold war military provisioning persisted after the war. The prosperity of the 1950s afforded savvy military and commercial entrepreneurs ample opportunity to win government support for projects of enormous proportions and almost surreal ambitions. For example, Adm. Hyman Rickover was personally and fanatically committed to his dream of a nuclear submarine. He directed Electric Boat (now a subsidiary of General Dynamics) to build a prototype. Rickover orchestrated a highly publicized keel-laying ceremony for grandstanding politicians, generating congressional and public commitment before the reactor had even been built. Rickover played on Truman and Eisenhower's desire to see nuclear energy harnessed for uses other than bombing.[36]

It is beyond our present inquiry to arbitrate among the rich and disputatious theories about the origins of the cold war.[37] Its emergence was enthusiastically welcomed by the many firms for whom its novel requirements promised funding for R&D projects that strained ordinary citizens' imaginations. Putting unmanned vehicles into space, both to deliver nuclear bombs and to monitor the entire surface of the earth, became a national enterprise of great import in the 1950s. Widespread public support, heightened by McCarthy-era anticommunism and deeply rooted in the pioneering spirit of American culture, permitted the devotion of billions of dollars annually to a consortium of new and expanded national labs—such as the Lawrence Livermore National Laboratory in California and the Oak Ridge National Laboratory in Tennessee—aerospace companies' laboratories, and engineering, math, and science programs in the universities. War outfitting became a business of science.

The formal integration of science into military planning and procurement led, inevitably, to science-initiated weapons. As Matthew Evangelista puts it, "In the United States, impetus for innovation in weapons technology comes from the bottom—from the scientists in government or private laboratories and the military officials with whom they are in close contact. In this respect, a new weapon starts with a technological idea rather than as a response to a specific threat or as a means to fulfill a long standing mission."[38] Ideas spawned in corporate laboratories, often paid for with R&D overheads from existing contracts, are marketed to colonels and their bosses. For their part, military officials have learned that novel ideas and big visions enhance their budgets. Higher political authorities are often reluctant to turn down ideas like SDI and Stealth bombers at the R&D stage, and only much later, after being built into a long-term Pentagon plan, are they presented to Congress. By then, if constituency building by the contractors and military service in question has been effective, members of Congress are pressured by the prospect of increased numbers of jobs in their home districts and campaign contributions. Often, the strategic rationale is developed long after the weapon is adopted by the military.[39]

Suspicions that the military-industrial complex drives weapons development, and that weaponry drives military policy rather than vice versa, were heightened by the Gulf War. Technologies borrowed from cold war equipment and adapted for conventional warfare were opportunistically deployed in a relatively new setting. Contractor interest in producing new weapons for "low-intensity" conflict grew throughout the 1970s. Weapons like the "smart" laser-guided bomb and the Patriot missile had been developed long before the Iraqi threat materialized. The Bush administration's "new world order" seems to have been an afterthought, a foreign policy belatedly developed to match the military capabilities generated during the Reagan-era arms extravaganza.

FP
✗

Making Weapons Flexibly, Secretly, Expensively

The new science-based war hardware demands a production process starkly different from that used in plants that make autos, steel, chemicals, and housewares for commercial markets. Not only does it require a manufacturing establishment dedicated to product quality, sophistication, and small batches of quite specialized output, it also flourishes in a production environment that is highly flexible, accustomed to risk and uncertainty, and shrouded with secrecy. The result is a whole new segment of American industry that designs and produces ever more costly products, in dramatic contrast to the mission of commercial firms, for whom cost and product price reduction are major competitive goals.

In recent years, many economy watchers have waxed enthusiastic about what they see as the resurgence of flexible manufacturing systems in contemporary industry.[40] The examples they point to are often commercially oriented, but in machine tools or computers, for instance, flexible manufacturing is more a creature of the defense effort than it is of entrepreneurs like Steve Jobs of Apple Computers or An Wang of Wang Computers. Indeed, many of the industries applauded for their vaunted flexibility are highly interpenetrated with defense spending and military procurement cultures.

When complex extraterrestrial military hardware first appeared, no one imagined that it would so radically alter the nature of manufacturing. In the beginning decades of the century, some aircraft designers believed that airplanes could be efficiently mass-produced. At the onset of the First World War, entrepreneurs—including Henry Ford, who had triumphed with innovative auto mass-production techniques in consumer markets—rushed to offer their services to the American and British governments. Ford proposed that his firm build 150,000 airplanes; he claimed that they could be as easily manufactured as motor cars and estimated that they would cost about twenty-five cents a pound to produce. (The claim was extravagant. In contrast, recall that more than twenty years later, Franklin Roosevelt's proposal that the entire U.S. aircraft industry produce 50,000 airplanes was considered exceedingly ambitious.)[41]

Although rebuffed at the time, Ford went on to develop the earliest successful American cargo airplane, the Ford Trimotor, and in the Second World War, the Ford Motor Company cranked out more than 400 Liberator bombers per month at Willow Run, the world's single largest industrial structure of its day. The Ford legacy greatly improved aircraft production techniques and efficiency. For instance, Ford insisted on humidity-controlled interior construction and pushed for standardized methods of machining and higher quality standards.[42]

But already by the Second World War, the entrepreneurs at the more military-oriented aircraft firms were balking at the Ford drive toward standardization. Ford's auto strategy relied on rigid and mechanically guided production lines on which he could employ relatively unskilled labor. In contrast, Consolidated and other West Coast companies had assembled highly skilled work forces, underwritten by government contracts. They depended much more upon the ingenuity and knowledge of workers to alter parts and make essential changes. As Dutch Kindelberger, president of North American Aviation and a consistent critic of awarding airplane contracts to auto firms, put it, "You cannot expect blacksmiths to learn how to make watches overnight."[43]

In addition, Ford's insistence on an elaborately tooled mass-production facility rankled his military-oriented competitors in California. They considered Second World War crafts like the Liberator to be makeshift. Anticipating new and dramatic breakthroughs, firms like Consolidated disparaged Willow Run as a wasteful investment, soon to be obsolete.[44] In this clash of management outlooks, Consolidated and North American presaged the culture of continual, military-funded innovation, while Ford could not wean itself from the principles that had worked so well for it in the consumer market. In addition, Ford and its sister auto companies had never developed the expertise in aircraft design that was essential to survival. As the Second World War wound down, the early great aircraft firms across the industrial heartland that had relied on mass-production strategies, such as Curtiss-Wright in Buffalo and Ford and Packard in Detroit, shifted their efforts back to the booming consumer markets and abandoned the aircraft market.

The gap in business cultures, already apparent by midcentury, has continued to widen over the years. The firms that have chosen to serve the military market, instead of providing cost-conscious services and products to thousands of nameless consumers, face an unusual set of demands from their clients. Colonels with reputations to make are more concerned with the performance characteristics of weapons and the timeliness of delivery than with the cost or efficiency of their production. Military clients worry more about quality than about quantity and cost.

The military demand for special-purpose weaponry is what distinguishes postmodern warfare and its military-industrial suppliers from the rest of American manufacturing. In the First World War, four-fifths of army equipment consisted of standard commodities produced in ordinary peacetime production facilities. By the Second World War, the rate had fallen fell to less than one-half. As the cold war set in, special-purpose hardware displaced mass-produced weaponry with a vengeance: the share of military demand met by specialized equipment escalated to 90 percent by the early 1960s.[45] Aircraft with unique missions proliferated despite pressures on the services to share models. On the seas, aircraft carriers required an expanded flotilla of smaller escort vessels to provide antiaircraft or antisubmarine protection. Demands for special-purpose electronic components exploded as increasingly complex weapons were outfitted with their very own brains.

Specialized military products are also flexible products, both in performance and in production process. Whether for cold or hot wars, contractors have concentrated on improving the deliverability, maneuverability, "intelligence," undetectability, and degree of surprise embedded in military hardware. Tactical nuclear weapons are one example. They can be delivered by fighter bomber, short-range or medium-range missile, cruise missile, or medium-caliber artillery shell. Their yield can vary from less than one kiloton to roughly a dozen kilotons, the equivalent of the Hiroshima atomic explosion. They can be built to maximize blast and minimize radioactive fallout, or the reverse. They can be directed against diverse targets, from enemy soldiers to command centers, arms depots, and airfields.[46]

As military demands for flexibility in cold war weaponry escalated, so did demands for flexibility in the organizational milieu that produces it, albeit flexibility of a certain kind. The American military demanded that companies be able to shift gears suddenly and often, as military requirements unfolded. A single weapon system might go through thousands of changes in specifications after the contract was awarded. The ability to respond flexibly to the changing needs of a single military client stood in stark contrast to the design and marketing practices of commercially oriented industries.[47]

The production and development of weaponry is often protected by high walls of secrecy. A recent example is the Stealth bomber, which was unveiled officially in late 1988 after many years of development. The mantle of secrecy over cold war logistics began with the Manhattan Project; work on the A-bomb was kept secret from both Congress and the public. Military departments funded the project, concealing its purpose, and President Roosevelt added resources, shielded from congressional scrutiny, from his special contingency fund. The system of secrecy, says Ronald Powaski, "not only prevented public debate on the question of building and using atomic weapons, it also hindered discussion within the government. Since there was virtually no debate on the question, those few who were informed came to consider the construction and use of atomic weapons foregone conclusions."[48] As a weapon's clout increasingly came to depend upon its novelty and unreplicability by the other side, colonels and contractors found it easy to make the case for secrecy and to delay oversight and public debate on the merits of any particular weapon system. Secrecy, then, reinforces the momentum of science-initiated weaponry.

The upshot of this unorthodox way of doing business is that weapons cost taxpayers enormous sums of money every year. Each generation of weapons costs between two and five times as much in constant dollars as the previous one. The latest army tank, the M-1, costs seven times as much as the Sherman tank of the Second World War. Radar-guided missiles like the Sparrow and the Phoenix, used in aerial dogfights, cost, respectively, ten and one hundred times more than the more reliable pioneer, the Sidewinder. One nuclear-powered aircraft carrier now costs more than $3 billion to build and $100 million per year to operate.

Rising costs and accelerated rates of obsolescence also cause the military to buy less of any particular weapon. With nuclear submarines costing $300 million each, the navy can now buy only one-fourth as many as it could afford of the earlier diesel-electric submarines. With the conversion from the Polaris to the Trident, the number of submarines in the U.S. fleet fell from forty-one to twenty.[49] Cost inflation is a product of the oligopolistic nature of the industry, abuses in the procurement process, and the expense of highly technical and innovative weaponry.

Ironically, cost-control initiatives by civilian managers at the Pentagon—often, like Robert McNamara, fresh from the auto or other commercial industries—have resulted in bizarre practices and counterproductive outcomes. Take the fixed-force structure, which limits the actual number of ships the navy is permitted to buy. If, as Fallows notes, the navy can have only thirteen carriers, it will push for the very best and pack on them every gadget and gimmick conceivable. When generals and colonels are judged by the sheer size of the budget they command, the incentive to keep cost up is powerful. As a result, argues Fallows, "a culture of procurement has been created in the Pentagon which draws the military toward new weapons because of their great cost, not in spite of it."[50]

Separate and Better than Equal

The conduct of postmodern warfare is unprecedented in human history. It depends not upon the muscle and willpower of humans, working cooperatively in units of equals led into battle by officers, but upon a hierarchy of highly specialized technicians sitting in central control rooms, in cockpits, and at remote control locations, reading television screens and pushing buttons. War today is not so much "manned" as "equipped," decisive victory depending heavily upon technological superiority. Much of that superiority can be delivered in terrifying form from the skies, from missiles launched from silos thousands of miles away, from submarines in unknown locations, or from fighter bombers taking off from home bases or sea-based carriers. War, as in the 1991 Persian Gulf affair, now consists of short, quick actions that take days to complete, not months or years.[51]

If the MX missile represents the pinnacle of cold war deadliness, then items like the laser-guided bomb and its infrared radar guidance system are its high-tech hot war counterparts. It was these fighter bomber—launched bombs that wreaked havoc on the Iraqi supply and communication systems in early 1991, obviating a bloody ground war. A camera with a sensor chilled to $-320°F$ in the nose cone of a Stealth bomber detects faint infrared radiation from any warmer object, including tanks or human beings. The signal is converted to an image on the pilot's computer screen, which indicates where to aim the bomb. Simultaneously, an escort craft sends out a laser beam that reflects off the target. The bomb has a light-sensing nose with its own computer that tells the bomb where to go. A thermal battery, activated at its release, runs the laser detector and the computer. An internal generator in the bomb mixes chemicals to create hot gas, driving pistons that move the bomb's guidance fins in response to computer commands.[52]

The laser-guided bomb is the logical outcome of a system of science-initiated weapons. Rivalry in military capability has bred and in turn been promoted by a unique new industrial segment—the aerospace-electronics-communications (ACE) complex. It is a separate, but far better than equal, segment of American industry. Highly privileged because of its close association with and patronage by the military, both its R&D efforts and its sales are chiefly attributable to government. Because of the long lead times required for the germination of ideas, designs, and prototypes, this segment of the economy has developed a planning process like no other segment.

It is governed by what James Kurth has labeled the "follow-on" imperative: the Pentagon keeps key firms in business by carefully generating and spreading around a steady stream of lucrative contracts.[53] Firms are not allowed to go under, at least if they are sizable, because of either poor performance or lack of business. Which firms these are, how they evolved, and how they operate are the subjects to which we next turn.

3

The Aerospace
Industry Comes of Age

■

"**O**N the modern battlefield," notes Martin van Creveld, "a blizzard of electromagnetic blips is increasingly being superimposed on—and to some extent substituted for—the storm of steel in which war used to take place." This development, he concludes, has been the single most important outcome of the technological progress in war-making in the decades since the Second World War.[1] In parallel fashion, high-tech industries have boomed at the expense of traditional basic industries. The manufacturing industries with the most spectacular postwar growth records are disproportionately those whose expertise lies in wooing military R&D funds and capturing high-tech sales to the cold war–waging Pentagon. In truth, the Department of Defense (DOD) and its sister agencies, the National Aeronautics and Space Administration (NASA) and the Department of Energy (DOE), have been fabulous patrons.

Of all the enduring myths in the United States today, perhaps one of the most powerful is the belief that we have had no industrial policy. Certainly for most industries this assumption has been valid, but for the industries and firms whose business is primarily with the Pentagon the story is very different. For a good forty years, the aerospace-communications-electronics complex (ACE) has benefited from every advantage attributed to industrial policy elsewhere—government fostering of research and development, public capital for plant construction and modernization, guaranteed markets for product, bailouts for firms in troubled periods, training funds for employee development, trade protection, export promotion, and economic adjustment for displaced workers and communities. Not surprisingly, this enormous public investment has paid off handsomely in new technologies.

In contrast, industries that have not benefited from this closet industrial policy, such as steel, machine tools, tractors, autos, and consumer electronics, have stagnated and seen their markets invaded successfully by competitors from rich and poor nations alike. Once the backbone of the nation's industrial prowess, these sectors have progressively fallen on hard times. Not only have they not been nurtured by the government, but they must compete with the military-oriented industries for domestic labor, capital, and entrepreneurial talent. Faced with uncertain markets, they have had difficulty obtaining long-term, low-interest capital for their modernization projects. Given these and other structural problems, it is not surprising that these industries have lost markets to competitors in countries, such as Japan and Germany, where industrial policy is not directed toward military priorities.

Cold war industrial policy created the ACE complex, a separate and favored set of industries and firms distinct from those that had emerged from several rounds of the American industrial revolution. In this chapter, we look at that complex and contrast its fortunes with those of civilian industries. In the next chapter, we examine the corporate leaders within the complex—how they do business and how they relate to each other and their client, the Pentagon.

The ACE Complex

The aerospace industry consists of many large and small firms that, in Herman Stekler's historic definition, "develop and manufacture vehicles, subsystems and parts essential for both atmospheric and space flight, whether manned or instrumented, or necessary for effective operation in flight or space." (Stekler reviewed various definitions of the aerospace industry and opted for the more inclusive one, which encompasses defense electronics and communications.)[2] In addition to bombers, fighters, and missiles, the industry produces satellites and space vehicles, the majority of which are devoted to military missions.[3] By 1986, there were already 1,500 satellites orbiting the world, and the number has climbed rapidly since then. The majority aid the world's military forces in navigating, reconnoitering, warning, communicating, and coordinating among central nerve centers and dispersed submarines, radar stations, and missile bases.

Closely tied to the aerospace business are the communications and defense electronics industries, whose products are vital to the remote and precise control of automated warfare. Together, they compose the aerospace-communications-electronics (ACE) complex. The dominance of these military-centered industries is an abrupt break with the past; until the interwar period, arms development and even much production were still reserved for government laboratories and arsenals. Only after a weapon was proven was it given over to the private sector to produce in quantity. The cold war changed that pattern dramatically; the private sector took over research and development as well as testing and evaluation, becoming the major initiator of new weapon systems and a powerful locus of innovation. (Although statutes still directed the services to "have supplies needed by the Department of the Army made in factories or arsenals owned by the United States," by the 1960s two decades of the military's informal preference for out-sourcing had resulted in the relative and absolute decline of production in government shipyards and arsenals.)[4]

Trillions of dollars have been spent on these industries since the Second World War. As the decades rolled by, more and more spending went to the private sector rather than to the services for manpower and operations. Between 1980 and 1989, the military procurement budget grew by 54 percent and research and development by 94 percent, while operations and maintenance grew only 25 percent.[5] The lion's share of the increase went for research, hardware, and facilities to develop, produce, house, and operate new generations of fighter bombers, tanks, attack submarines, aircraft carriers, helicopters, and air-defense missiles.

Unlike other forms of government expenditure, military purchases have characteristics that amplify their stimulative effect on the industries involved and, indirectly, on the entire American economy. First, they are unusually manufacturing-intensive. One million dollars spent on buying weapons creates many more manufacturing jobs than does the same amount spent on social security or health care or even infrastructure. About 40 percent of the military dollar goes to the manufacturing sector, either as orders or as research contracts for future products, compared with manufacturing's 20 percent share of the entire economy. Of that 40 percent, aerospace and its communications and electronics partners get the biggest chunk: 79 percent in 1990, or $62 billion out of a total of $78 billion in DOD outlays, far outpacing the $11 billion spent on ships.[6]

Second, the United States has a de facto domestic content requirement for military aerospace and related industries. The Pentagon practices an explicit "buy America" policy that discourages the purchase of war matériel on the international market. Buy America practices date from 1933, when Congress imposed penalties on government agencies that preferred foreign equipment over domestic equivalents, giving domestic firms a cushion of 6–12 percent in cost differentials. Perhaps even more important, the DOD-initiated protective legislation effectively closed the U.S. market by requiring that all arms components include American specialty metals. The Pentagon has directly intervened numerous times to cancel imports or to force domestic supply. In 1988 it bailed out Avtex, the sole remaining American supplier of rayon fibers, which are critical to the production of missiles and rockets.[7] If American suppliers are scarce, the Pentagon will sometimes underwrite the building of new plants to ensure domestic provision, as it did in the chemical feedstocks industry in the 1980s. The Pentagon prefers American suppliers for strategic reasons, fearing a cutoff in times of emergency. Congress has tended to concur, because contracts mean jobs and jobs mean votes.

Both these features of defense procurement—manufacturing intensity and high domestic content—help to explain why a select set of U.S. industries in aerospace and allied sectors have thrived in the postwar period while many commercial industries, unprotected from import erosion, have not. At the same time, the ACE industries have become increasingly dependent upon military markets. David Henry's work at the Department of Commerce (DOC) reveals an elite set of industries tightly linked to the DOD market (Table 3.1).[8] Henry calculated the direct and indirect purchases attributable to Pentagon orders for all American industries, enabling us to track the rounds of indirect purchases from prime contractors through their subcontractors and third-tier suppliers. (His procedure is an improvement on estimates based on prime contracts alone.) Topping his list are the key industries in the aerospace sector, plus shipbuilding, ordnance, and tanks. These *defense-dependent* industries all had 40 percent or more of their capacity committed to the Department of Defense by 1985. Aircraft and missiles, together with engine and parts suppliers, landed a whopping $22 billion (in 1977 dollars) in DOD sales in 1985, and communications equipment industries sold $15.7 billion to the same customer. If we include defense-related NASA purchases (5–10 percent of DOD budgets), the Department of Energy's orders for nuclear warheads, and foreign military sales (aircraft sales to foreign governments were 22 percent of Pentagon sales in 1987), the size of these industries' military business would increase significantly. Some measure of the underestimation

TABLE 3.1

Growth in Military Sales and Dependency, 1980–85 (in 1977 dollars)

INDUSTRY	MILITARY OUTPUT (BILLION $) 1985	MILITARY SHARE OF OUTPUT (%) 1980	1985
Shipbuilding	5.8	61	93
Ordnance	0.8	79	86
Missiles	5.3	69	84
Tanks	1.1	68	69
Aircraft	11.7	37	66
Communications Equipment	15.7	42	50
Machine Tools	0.4	8	34
Engineering Instruments	0.7	23	28
Optical Instruments	0.9	13	24
Electronic Components	3.0	16	20
Steel	3.4	6	12
Airlines	3.0	n.a.[a]	10
Oil Refining	5.2	4	6
Computers	2.3	5	5
Industrial Chemicals	2.0	4	5
Semiconductors	1.6	9	5
Automobiles	6.3	3	3

[a]*n.a.: not available*
SOURCES: *Compiled from David Henry and Richard Oliver, "The Defense Buildup, 1977–1985: Effects on Production and Employment,"* Monthly Labor Review *(August 1987): 3–11, and unpublished data from the Bureau of Industrial Economics, and the U.S. Department of Commerce, 1987.*

here can be gauged by looking at the category "missiles," for which there has been literally no nonmilitary demand over the period, yet it registers only 84 percent defense-dependent with the DOC data. A conservative adjustment upward of these figures to account for such sales would result in defense-dependency rates of 100 percent for missiles, 79 percent for aircraft, and 60 percent for communications equipment.

Another set of industries are *defense-related*—the middle group in Table 3.1. The high-tech supplier sectors—optical and engineering instruments and electronics—as well as the more mature machine tools industry, had between 20 and 34 percent of their market dedicated to the military at the height of the 1980s buildup. With the exception of electronic components, their total receipts were small relative to those reaped by the defense-dependent industries.

A third set of industries are *beneficiaries* of military spending in rather large absolute amounts without being dependent upon it. Among them are computers and semiconductors, the two miracle industries spawned by military research and development in earlier decades, and several materials (steel, chemicals, oil) and service (airlines) industries. Together with others not listed (such as railroads, real estate, and wholesaling), these industries sold $35 billion worth of goods and services to the Pentagon in 1985.

Recent experience shows how sensitive such dependency rates are to a boom in military spending, and thus how vulnerable these industries may be to looming cuts. After the Vietnam War, many industries' military shares declined markedly. The aircraft industry went from a high of 72 percent defense-dependent in 1968 to a low of 39 percent in 1977; electronics went from 34 percent to 15 percent.[9] The opposite occurred in the 1980s, when the Reagan administration buildup left U.S. manufacturers more dependent than ever on the military budget. Coming as they did in a period of sluggish growth and over-capacity in many industries, military orders absorbed idled resources and obscured the extent of displacement in civilian manufacturing. Furthermore, weapon system acquisitions were heavily favored by the Reagan buildup, in contrast to consumable items like ammunition, food, and clothing, which were in heavy demand during the Vietnam War. From 1980 to 1985, military aircraft and missile orders in real terms jumped 60 percent, weapons and tracked vehicles by 84 percent, and research and testing by 53 percent.[10] The Gunbelt industrial complexes benefited at the expense of the traditional mass-production factories of the heartland.

The number of industries with more than 10 percent of their output devoted to DOD orders (not including NASA or foreign military sales) rose from twenty-one in 1977 to forty-five in 1985. Some registered stunning shifts in their orientation; for instance, shipbuilding, including renovation and repair, went from being 45 percent defense-dependent in 1977 to 93 percent, and aircraft zoomed from 43 percent to 66 percent in the same period. Only 26 percent of planes actually produced were military, but on average these cost $18.6 million, compared with a unit cost of only $3 million for civilian aircraft.[11]

Some of the more traditional industries also found their dependency on military sales increasing sharply not because of enormous Pentagon orders but because their commercial markets were eroding so badly. For instance, output in the machine tool industry declined

38

by 60 percent between 1980 and 1985. Because military orders increased by 65 percent, however, the defense-dependency rate for toolmakers rose from just 3 percent in 1977 to 34 percent in 1985 (see Table 3.1). Similarly, the military's hold on industrial trucks increased from a paltry 2 percent to 22 percent in the same period.[12]

Many of the largest beneficiaries of the 1980s defense buildup, in absolute terms, were new intermediate goods industries whose commercial competitiveness, after three decades of government nurturance, enabled them to expand their nonmilitary sales. Hence, in spite of a dramatic rise in military orders, the defense-dependency rate of this group did not increase by nearly as much. Military demand for computers reached a historically high $2.3 billion in 1985, but the computer industry's defense-dependency rate had risen only modestly from 3.6 percent in 1979 to 5 percent. Radio and television communications equipment, which received a whopping $15.7 billion in government sales in 1985 (up 73 percent since 1980), increased its defense-dependency rate from 42 percent to 50 percent.[13]

Among this panoply of industries, the ACE industries stand out, not only for their defense-dependency and high absolute share of Pentagon dollars, but also because they dominate the lion's share of government R&D expenditures. From its inception, the ACE complex has followed a very different path from that of the heartland industries.

Tight from the Start

The aircraft industry, the core of what has become the aerospace industry, has a unique history. To an unparalleled degree, the industry has featured cooperation among a relatively small number of firms, garnered government patronage, and engaged in extraordinary boosterism from the outset. Its infancy and adolescence took place during wartimes, permitting top-down direction to an extent not often found in American business. Furthermore, many of its leaders have been men who began their careers in the military or who worked for significant stints in military engineering offices.

The aircraft industry was born during the First World War. Before 1914, only a handful of airplanes were produced, all out of small workshops like those of the Wright brothers and Glenn Curtiss. It was very much a craft industry; airplanes were turned out one at a time. From the start, the industry enjoyed military patronage—the Army Signal Corps ordered its first plane from the Wright brothers in 1908.

The war and the way both sides of the conflict used aircraft convinced the U.S. government to rush-order 25,000 airplanes. By 1918, $350 million had been spent to make 14,000 military airplanes, employing 175,000 people. Simultaneously, a new government institution was created, the National Advisory Committee for Aeronautics, whose purpose was to further the science and technology of aeronautics and to advise the military and other government agencies on aeronautical research.[14]

At the time, the industrial landscape of America was dominated by the big trusts that had emerged in oil, steel, chemicals, and banking. The innovative sector of the day was the small but booming auto industry, which was awash in Henry Ford's fantastic commercial success in mass-producing cars on the assembly line. From birth, the aircraft industry was distinguished from these older industrial siblings. Although the young industry was threatened by intense competition and patent fights that sometimes delayed wartime production, it benefited from a government-initiated trade association, the Manufacturers Aircraft Association, which pooled patents and shared plane-making methods. The association quickly became the single, consolidated voice of the manufacturers.

This culture of cooperation came in handy after the war. Coping with the collapse of their market from 14,000 units in 1918 to 263 in 1922, the surviving companies mounted a major campaign for government assistance. It was clear to them that despite the glamor of flying, no commercial market was going to materialize to absorb industrial capacity. After the First World War, the American industry "was left flat, over-capitalized, over-stocked with raw materials, over-organized in all executive and inspection departments, and over-manned by expert personnel and skilled labor." The association, "eager to continue the method originally a war expedient of having the Government working heart and soul with the industry, now called upon the Government officials for help in promoting the popularity of flying," reported Howard Mingos, an early industry official.[15]

The association harped on defense preparedness and found sympathizers in the military services. The report of the 1919 American Aviation Mission to Europe (comprising manufacturers, military officers, and War Department personnel), drafted by the general manager of the Manufacturers Aircraft Association, concluded that, "for economic reasons, no nation can hope in time of peace to maintain air forces adequate to its defensive need except through the creation of a great reserve in personnel, material and producing industry, through the encouragement of civil aeronautics. Commercial aviation and transportation development must be made to carry the financial load." The mission asked the government to either pay private enterprises for flying the mails or operate mail lines until they were proven commercially successful. It also recommended a complete infrastructure program of airports, weather reporting, flight control, and regulation to be paid for by the taxpayers, plus a program to conserve aircraft factories by a "well-defined and continuing program of production for military and naval purposes, over a period of years—long enough for commercial aviation to get a fair start."[16]

All of these proposals did in fact come to fruition. In the 1920s, the aircraft industry was kept afloat by the Air Mail Act, of 1925, which greatly expanded government demand for aircraft services and, indirectly, for the aircraft that provided them. Thanks to this new source of public orders, "civil" aircraft production began to exceed military production. In 1925, U.S. firms produced 447 military planes and 342 civil ones; the next year the numbers rose to 532 and 654, respectively.[17] But plane-makers' dreams of a passenger business akin to those run by the railroad and shipping industries were dashed by continued public indifference and the prohibitive cost of flying, especially as the Depression set in. As Mingos put it,

> The industry, the entire field of aviation, became involved in a vicious circle. It could not sell machines; and without sales it could not finance research and improvements in its products. And until it could produce better airplanes, machines that could be operated at a profit, there was small chance of procuring the financial support necessary for commercial expansion and technical development. The Army and Navy were the only customers.[18]

Government orders constituted at least two-thirds of the manufacturers' business from the mid-1920s until just before the Second World War. For example, 90 percent of Douglas Aircraft's income in 1933 came from the government.[19]

This patronage effectively put a small handful of firms, out of many hopefuls, at the top of a highly concentrated industry. As early as 1930, ten airframe companies received 90 percent of the military's business, and just two companies made military aircraft engines, mostly on noncompetitive bids. Not surprisingly, the youthful oligopoly made spectacular profits (which were often the subject of public outcry and congressional investigations). Pratt & Whitney, a major engine-maker, made 36 percent of its profit on navy contracts from 1927 to 1933, and 23 percent on army orders. Boeing made 21 percent on its navy contracts and 25 percent on those from the army in the same period, and Douglas made 21 percent and 18 percent respectively.[20]

The government did make a modest effort in the early years to produce military aircraft "in-house." The Vinson-Trammel Act of 1934 required the navy to build at least 10 percent of its aircraft at the Naval Aircraft Factory in Philadelphia, but even that plant licensed its engines from Curtiss-Wright. In-house production was vociferously opposed by industry, and the domination of military production boards by industrialists effectively thwarted it.[21]

Even before the Second World War, then, the aircraft industry was extraordinarily well coordinated, controlled, and dependent upon a military patronage that it cultivated assiduously. As the industrialist Mingos put it: "The industry, through its trade organization, kept repeating what it had been saying for years, that American aviation could not be given a fair start without a comprehensive and detailed national policy."[22] Concerted lobbying by the aircraft industry continued through the interwar period and bore fruit. By the start of the Second World War, the companies making up the still modest-sized industry were well poised to become big corporations on the receipts from wartime taxpayers.

From Hot War to Cold War

The Second World War was a watershed for the aircraft industry, bestowing upon it the success, size, and solidity that would make it a permanent and leading feature of the U.S. economy for the next half-century. The investments made in aircraft and related manufacturing capacity (some 92 percent of which were financed by government advances and payments under contracts) put in place an enormous and modern postwar industrial infrastructure.[23]

The impact of the war itself cannot be overstated. Pres. Franklin D. Roosevelt's target of producing 50,000 planes a year, announced in 1940, precipitated an enormous investment in plant and equipment and set off dramatic migrations of men and women to work in them. From a small set of plants producing 17,000 planes in 1940, the industry swelled to make 96,000 airplanes in 1944. By that year, the aircraft industry accounted for 12.4 percent of all manufacturing employment. The individual firms that would form the backbone of the ACE complex became giants on this rich government diet. North

American, for example, expanded from a single plant employing 6,000 workers in 1940 to five plants with 92,000 workers in 1943. To build this capacity, North American pulled in $79 million in government investments on top of a modest $5 million of its own funds.[24]

The immediate postwar period thrust the existing aircraft companies, so recently bloated with government orders, into severe recession. Sales imploded from a wartime peak of $16 billion to $1 billion by 1947, and employment fell from over one million to a low of 237,700 in 1948. Although industry analysts were hopeful, commercial sales proved not to be an alternative; sales of civilian aircraft fell steadily from 35,000 in 1946 to 2,500 in 1951, and the market was saturated as early as 1948.[25] Some big wartime contractors, such as Ford and General Motors, enthusiastically closed military-oriented plants and devoted their energies to consumer markets. Aircraft firms such as Hughes, Lockheed, Boeing, and North American (later to become Rockwell in 1967) made more or less successful efforts to create new military as well as commercial products; others—Curtiss-Wright, for example—faltered.

To enhance their prospects, the companies revived their interwar demand for an American air power policy. Calling their agenda "Air Power for Peace," the industry campaigned for a public commitment to air defense systems, expansion of domestic and international air transport, and the preservation of a strong aircraft manufacturing industry.[26] Close ties with military strategists cultivated military markets and influenced government notions of defense necessities.

The rise of the cold war, and especially the emergence of unmanned missiles as the major deterrent force, provided the industry with one way out. Ballistic missile contracts had been awarded as early as 1946, when Convair (now General Dynamics) began work on the Atlas ICBM.[27] By 1951, the year the missile business came into its own, taxpayer expenditures on development and production increased 500 percent. Missiles were challenging the airplane's role in military strategy, and by 1957 military aircraft production had begun to shrink as missile and spacecraft production grew. Airframe manufacturers switched to making missiles. Thanks to the cold war, the aircraft industry quadrupled its share of the nation's manufacturing value-added between 1947 and 1954, and by 1958 it employed nearly one million workers.[28]

As the aircraft industry reshaped itself around cold war missions, it diverged increasingly from other American industries. As continual innovation took root, defense RDT&E (research, development, testing, and evaluation) expenditures more than tripled between 1953 and 1964, and industry R&D costs ballooned as a percentage of total costs, rising from levels of 2–3 percent to 20–30 percent. More work went into special-purpose test equipment, measurement devices, and guidance and control systems than into constructing frames. More and more electronics were incorporated into each generation of weapon system—as much as 50 percent of the cost of a missile was for its electrical equipment, compared with 13–20 percent aircraft costs. Aircraft companies developed communications and electronics capabilities, and their self-image was no longer that of simple airplane makers. In the late 1950s the industry decided to formalize its identity change and redubbed itself the "aerospace" industry. By 1965 half of the industry's $15.8 billion in sales were in missiles and space vehicles, production lines that were nonexistent a decade before.[29]

By 1965, the cold war economy accounted for 10 percent of U.S. personal income and 20 percent of the nation's manufacturing output. Indirectly, it provided the livelihoods for 12–14 million Americans, including roughly 70 percent of American scientists.[30] The linchpin of this economy was the ACE complex. With its deeply entrenched cabal of large contractors and a broad array of smaller contractors, the complex was a powerful force in the institutionalization of the cold war, which, in turn, served as a rationale for further expansion of the complex.

Why Not Auto?

The uniqueness of the aircraft industry is best illustrated by comparing it with the auto industry, a sector that lent it much technology and know-how and yet never capitalized on the new atmospheric market. In three separate efforts, the auto giants entered aerospace as pioneers—as makers of commercial aircraft in the 1920s, as developers of unmanned missiles in the 1950s, and as acquirers of promising aerospace firms since then. The auto industry's failure in these attempts underscores the cultural disparity between cold war–driven aerospace and the older, mass-production–oriented industrial base.

Several leading auto companies entered the industry in its early stages, well before the futures of West Coast firms such as North American and Douglas were assured. Why this effort fizzled out is perhaps best illustrated by the 1920s saga of Henry Ford's pioneering Trimotor. After a profitable stint making Liberty bomber engines in the First World War, Henry Ford threw his company into the infant aircraft industry competition with zest. He joined forces with a local Detroit entrepreneur, William Stout, whose cargo plane design had been rejected by the military. An indefatigable inventor and genius of structural design, Stout had worked both for Packard and for the airplane equipment division of the army. His strategy was to "simplicate and add more lightness." Ford raised funds from other Detroit businessmen with an appeal to local pride: Detroit led the nation in autos—why not in planes?[31]

Stout had tried to sell his revolutionary design—an all-metal, single-engined, mass-produced monoplane—to the navy. But Ford was captivated with its commercial possibilities. He envisioned mass production for a mass market. He argued that once this was achieved, military production would be easy. By 1924 the Maiden Detroit (a terrible but deliberate pun), was the best cargo plane in existence. Ford's larger three-engine version, Trimotor, pioneered the transcontinental route over the Rockies and was the major early carrier of U.S. mails. By the late 1920s, with a goal of "a plane a day," Ford was the dominant firm in the aircraft industry, selling more than 50 percent of all multiengine transports in the United States, to both airlines and the military.[32]

What happened to Ford's highly successful aircraft business? First, a dramatic slump in demand hit the industry. On the brink of a depression Henry Ford did not foresee, the company could fill, in six months of normal manufacture, the entire aircraft industry's need for the next four years. Second, as part of an economywide trend, airlines and airplane manufacturers were being swallowed up by huge holding companies, cutting out independents like Ford. His commercial market dried up, and he began losing money. In 1933, after selling 199 Trimotors, Ford shut down the program and returned his attention to his auto business. Auto sales were booming, despite the Depression, and Ford's competition from GM and others for market share was stiff.[33]

Also at the heart of the matter was Ford's—indeed, Detroit's—business culture, which was based on the new ground-based transportation system for the American public. Ever since the Model T, Ford and his competitors had been envisioning a world of assembly line–produced commercial goods. But Ford had difficulty translating this vision into the aircraft industry, in which the client, increasingly military, and the product, with its very different performance requirements, were a far cry from auto-making.

In the postwar era, Detroit got a second chance to break into the innovative end of the industry. This time the lead firm was Chrysler.

It teamed up with the army in its race against the air force to control the first intercontinental ballistic missile.[34] The army wanted to design and develop the nuclear missile within its Redstone arsenal in Huntsville, Alabama, and then have the auto industry build it. After inviting only the "Big Three" automakers to bid, the army awarded the contracts to Chrysler. But the arsenal system was no match for the dynamism of an ascendent air force and a dedicated and desperate set of aircraft firms with no other options. Charging that the arsenal system was "socialistic," a coalition of air force and aircraft industry competitors argued that the army-Chrysler deal would lack imagination and be plagued by long delays and inefficiencies.[35] By the late 1950s the army had lost control over long-range ballistic missile production. As Charles Bright put it: "Each service tends to do business with firms it has grown accustomed to. Without this odd combination of events the auto-makers might today have a large role in the aerospace industry, for they tried to enter it at the innovation stage."[36] The auto industry had struck out a second time.

In a third attempt to enter the aerospace industry, to diversify away from cars, and to cash in on the cold war, the Ford Motor Company decided to explore acquisitions. In the early 1950s Henry Ford II sent two of his lieutenants to California, where they found a group of scientists who had just left Lockheed en masse. With the Ford "whiz kids" of 1946 in mind, Ford dreamed of building an aircraft business bigger than Boeing. He then tried to buy the Martin Company, to graft it onto this base of innovative talent, but the price was too high. Bitterly disappointed, Ford grabbed the next thing that came along, a consumer appliance business named Philco, which he wanted in order to diversify into its consumer markets. But he also got Philco's small defense electronics division, which merged with the Lockheed émigrés. The result was Ford Aerospace.[37] The division has been dramatically successful, prospering during periods of cold war buildup. Today it employs over 13,000 workers who fashion missile guidance and control units, space satellites, and C[3]I systems.

Yet after thirty years, this marriage is made on paper only. For all practical purposes, Ford Aerospace operates as a stand-alone business unit. None of its activity has ever taken place in Detroit. Even the attempt to headquarter Ford Aerospace in Dearborn failed. Resisting top management's insistence that it be located with the rest of the company in Michigan (principal Ford Aerospace operations are in Newport Beach, California, with others in Colorado, Texas, and Pennsylvania), Ford's vice-president for aerospace persistently argued that "we are in the kind of business where we should live over the shop."

Day-to-day discussions in the design-oriented aerospace business require the kind of proximity to the plant that worldwide auto manufacture and marketing do not. In 1988, after several years of tension, Ford Motor Company abandoned its attempt to keep its stepchild at home and set up dual headquarters for its subsidiary in Newport Beach, California—for "timely attention to operational issues and coordination among divisions"—and in Washington, D.C., a location that "enhanced Ford Aerospace's ability to anticipate and meet the nation's defense and space requirements."[38]

What stands out about Detroit's three-time failure in the aerospace industry is how difficult it is to introduce a truly distinctive, revolutionary technology into a region where another, entirely different technology is still robust and has command over resource markets and the business culture. Detroit, the preeminently innovative auto milieu—at least through the 1960s—failed utterly as a center for innovative aircraft activity. Interservice rivalries certainly played their role in this failure, but in large measure it was caused by the incompatibility between producing autos for a mass market and making aircraft for a single cold war military client.

Even today contractors contrast their way of doing business with the auto industry's. As one Lockheed manager observed in an interview with us in 1985:

> We can develop all kinds of things, but what we can't do then is take it and build it and put it into commercial product that's cost effective. Our culture isn't like that. Maybe our culture ought to be like that . . . well, hell, General Motors culture couldn't go out and build airplanes. This is a unique business and costs are high because you're dealing with very expensive products, you're dealing with products that have to be safe, have to be reliable, have to work the first time, and they're very, very, very sophisticated. Very difficult for this industry to try to diversify into commercial products. You might say, "Well, why doesn't the aerospace industry go out and build the ultimate, the penultimate, car that would get 85 miles to the gallon?" Well, hell, we could build it, but it'd cost $85,000 dollars!

Aerospace Sidekicks: Electronics, Communications, and Computers

The ACE complex includes the industries that inform, monitor, guide, and oversee the increasingly automated platforms that are the weapons of cold war. C³I systems, built mostly from electronic components, form the backbone of the modern military's strategic capability. As the electronics and communications payload has increased, so has the significance of industries that produce it. The myriad of commercially marketable products these industries produce is almost exclusively military in origin, owing both to R&D subsidies and guaranteed government markets.

The electronics revolution dates back to the 1930s, when military research in both the United States and Europe was crucial in developing components to modulate the high-speed, high-frequency electrical pulses essential for radar. During the Second World War, Bell Labs was funded by the military to research semiconductor materials for use in radar detection, resulting in the invention of the transistor. At least 25 percent of the Bell Labs semiconductor research budget over the subsequent critical period of 1949–58 was funded by military contracts. As late as 1959 a Senate committee estimated that 85 percent of U.S. electronics research and development was paid for by the federal government.[39]

It was not just R&D grants that greased the electronics industries' wheels, but the prospect of ensured government markets. *All* of the early semiconductor production of Western Electric, Bell's manufacturing affiliate, went to military shipments. From 1956 to 1964, the Pentagon consumed over 70 percent of the industry's output, particularly in the Minuteman missile program. For integrated circuits (developed later), the military consumed 100 percent of output in 1962, though the rate fell to less than 50 percent by the end of the decade. To this day, many segments of the electronics industry remain relatively dependent upon military expenditure for research and development, and to a lesser degree, for sales.[40]

As electronics assumed a more central role in the mechanics and cost structure of aerospace, the big aerospace firms were confronted with new competition. Especially in missiles and spacecraft, the electronics firms entered the bidding fray, hoping that their expertise in the payload would challenge the traditional lead role of the platform-makers. By the early 1960s the high-tech gear on satellites cost more than the launching vehicle itself, and on missiles it accounted for 40–50 percent of the cost.[41]

The military has encouraged participation by electronics firms as prime contractors. As early as 1958 an undersecretary of the air force announced that development and production contracts would go to electronics companies for vehicles that were primarily electronic devices with airframes designed to merely house the systems. In the smaller missile category, Raytheon, Western Electric, Bendix, Hughes,

Emerson, Sperry-Rand, and Honeywell were all awarded prime contracts early in the missile era.

The leading aircraft firms fought back by developing their own capability in electronics. Some created electronics divisions from scratch (North American, Martin), while others, such as Northrop, Lockheed, and General Dynamics, built their electronics divisions by purchasing existing electronics companies. Developing an electronics capability was particularly important in securing a foothold in the missile market. The boundary between the aircraft and missile industries had become harder to delineate as early as 1962, when electronics firms were already prime contractors for fourteen of forty-one missiles under development. Herman Stekler believes it is surprising that the airframe companies got as many missile contracts as they did and speculates that the services were slow to learn that electronics capability was displacing metal-bending as the key to system performance. Some airframe firms never made it—Grumman, McDonnell, and Republic had had no missile contracts by 1960, a handicap that led to their vulnerability to shrinkage and merger in the longer run.[42]

Like electronics, the communications equipment industry is also heavily indebted to the cold war. A huge sector of the U.S. economy, employing more than 350,000 Americans, communications is more than 50 percent dependent upon military markets and has been less successful than its electronics and computer siblings in weaning itself from the Pentagon. In 1989 sizable contracts for radar warning receivers ($213 million), surveillance radar ($200 million), a navy-sponsored advanced NATO IFF (identification, friend or foe) system ($162 million), and other search and navigation equipment constituted a significant portion of the industry's demand.[43] Like electronics, the communications industry is heavily interpenetrated by firms that are also in the aerospace industry; advantages accrue to the systems bidder that has everything on its team.

Bridging both the electronics and communications equipment sectors is the computing industry, which also owes its origins and spectacular early growth to military patronage. A massive effort to improve computing was initiated during the Second World War. The early entrepreneurs, such as the scientists J. Presper Eckert and John Mauchly, were bankrolled in the more secretive corners of the military establishment, as were most of their competitors. In the late 1940s, according to Kenneth Flamm, a historian of the computer industry,

> key players in the military first tried to convince established business
> and investment bankers that a new and potentially profitable business

opportunity was presenting itself. They did not succeed, and consequently, the Defense Department committed itself to financing an enormously expensive development program for new technologies—like the electronic computer—in which the military had a special interest.[44]

The military literally had to create a new industry because established business-machine giants, such as International Business Machines (IBM) and National Cash Register (NCR), were not interested. The navy begged NCR, promising considerable subsidies, to capitalize on its wartime lead by continuing to make high-speed analytical machinery after the war. But NCR declined, in a way reminiscent of Ford; it was eager to resume its prewar office equipment business, which was high-volume, low-risk, and profitable. IBM was so preoccupied with its role as a maker of electric accounting machines that it saw no commercial market in computers.[45]

Eventually the promise of big procurement contracts and the government's elimination of most of the risk brought companies like IBM and Honeywell into the arena. Contracts to build the first large mainframe computers went to the military aerospace companies. IBM also benefited from large chunks of government R&D spending; over half of its research and development during the 1950s and early 1960s was paid for by federal contracts, and as late as 1963 the government was still paying for 35 percent.[46]

While the military dominated computer development from the war through 1955, it also helped to spawn the commercial computer and software industries, which took off in the 1960s and are now among the the most vibrant sectors in the U.S. economy. But research on advanced, leading-edge technologies, such as supercomputers, scientific computing, artificial intelligence, software engineering, high-performance networks, and advanced computer architecture, continue to be underwritten by the Pentagon. According to Flamm, the military client

> retains a powerful influence at the most radical leading edge of architectural innovation in computers. Research on novel types of parallel architectures and the financial backing for the first working models of these new concepts rely heavily on federal funding. And development of the largest and most powerful computers of the day—even those with more conventional designs—continues to rely heavily on demand by government agencies.[47]

Computer firms also continue to vie for other kinds of enormously lucrative government contracts. In 1987, for instance, IBM, AT&T, and

Digital Equipment all competed for a $4.5 billion air force deal for 20,000 office minicomputers, part of a fiscal 1988 federal information systems budget that totalled $17 billion. Illustrating the power of this government market, 14,000 IBM employees are located in Washington, D.C.; Computer Science Corporation has located one-third of its employees there as well.[48]

A Closet Industrial Policy

Many in the United States consider targeted industry policy, with its element of favoritism, to be "un-American." Traditionally, the American public and business community have been solidly opposed to any such coddling because it is believed to be inefficient and unfair. The United States is alone in the developed world in its commitment to this extreme ideology. But this belief does not correspond to reality. Since the onset of the cold war, and even back to the 1920s and 1930s, the U.S. government, in concert with the aircraft (later aerospace) industry's trade association, has practiced an industrial policy almost unparalleled in the modern world.

What are the elements of an industrial policy? First, such a policy targets particular sectors as growth leaders, or in modern parlance, as guarantors of national economic strength and "competitiveness." Second, an industrial policy provides substantial support for research and development, through either incentives or direct provision of funds. Third, an industrial policy can provide capital for plant, equipment, and operating expenses. Fourth, it encourages industrial collaboration and planning, on advisory boards and as members of project teams. Fifth, it monitors and shapes competition by ensuring that there are neither too many producers to permit stability nor too few to avoid complete monopoly. It can do so by spreading business around and by providing special emergency assistance to any firm in deep trouble whose survival is deemed critical. Sixth, an industrial policy offers a guaranteed government market for output, especially at early stages of development, to ensure enough volume for growth and cost recovery. Seventh, it may include a trade policy of promoting exports of the industries involved and protecting them from the rigors of international competition. Finally, an industrial policy may provide adjustment assistance to firms, workers, and communities whose futures are affected by the closing of facilities.[49]

Most of these features of industrial policy, although much maligned in the United States, are present in the business cultures of its chief competitors in Asia and Europe. What is not well understood is the extent to which these policies have characterized the relationship between the Pentagon and the ACE complex for forty years in the United States.

As the history reviewed above makes clear, the U.S. government has systematically "targeted" the aerospace, communications, and computer industries since their beginnings. Especially notable is the role that government has played at times when the aircraft industry might otherwise have folded—after the First World War, during the Depression, and after the Second World War. A recent survey concludes that the United States has promoted its aircraft industry as much as other nations have promoted theirs.[50]

Aerospace has also benefited from the other ingredients of industrial policy. The government has provided massive amounts of capital for the industry, funds that other industries must raise on the private market. It has done so both through the provision of fixed capital (land, buildings, equipment) and through the advance of progress payments and loan guarantees for operating capital. It has often built plants directly with taxpayer funds, and then leased them out to companies or paid for capital construction costs and equipment purchase through contracts. As of the early 1980s, the Pentagon had invested about $18 billion in plant and equipment, with a replacement value of $100 billion. Its holdings included 146 plants and 500,000 items of equipment, 60 percent of which were in the hands of contractors. It still owns a considerable portion of contractors' facilities, including most of the plant space and equipment in the munitions and strategic missiles industries and one-third of plant and equipment in the aircraft industry.[51] This has substantially lowered the real cost of capital for companies benefiting from Pentagon contracts.

The government has continually funded leading-edge R&D work, encouraging pioneering basic research, design, and experimentation that would not have taken place otherwise. Before the Second World War, the government spent less than $100 million a year on research and development. This figure rose tenfold, to $1 billion during the war. But the cold war, in its relentless demand for innovative weaponry, has been even kinder to R&D work. By 1970 the United States was spending over $16 billion a year on research and development, or 1,600 times the prewar level. Some 90 percent of these funds were spent by three agencies—Defense, NASA, and the Atomic Energy Commission (AEC)—for direct or indirect defense purposes.[52]

The ACE industries were targeted beneficiaries of this R&D largesse. In 1956, the middle of the first cold war buildup, the government financed 87 percent of aircraft and parts industry research and development. The electrical equipment industry got 56 percent of its R&D funds from the government; the shares for scientific instruments and chemicals were 25 percent and 3 percent, respectively. Not only did this amount to a free R&D ride for the ACE industries, but at certain times, such as during the 1950s, R&D projects accounted for big chunks of the *sales,* and therefore profits, of aerospace corporations. In 1956, for instance, R&D expenditures accounted for almost 20 percent of sales of aircraft and parts firms, compared with only 3 percent for all U.S. industry; by 1960 this share had risen to 30 percent.[53] The aerospace industry continues to be the top R&D performer up to the present day, thanks to this support. In 1989 it spent $19 billion on research and development, of which the government provided almost $16 billion. Computers and machinery were next, spending $18 billion, of which $8 billion was federally funded.[54]

Collaboration by the leading firms in their planning and strategy for equipping the armed services has been carefully arranged through a superstructure of government advisory committees. In his 1981 study, Gordon Adams found that DOD had 777, and NASA 483, such committee members. Of these, quite a few were drawn from industry, with Boeing providing 23, Lockheed 20, McDonnell-Douglas 11, and Northrop 10. Frequently, the committees were considering technologies in which the companies had a major stake. For instance, Boeing sat on committees dealing with strategic targeting while it was a prime contractor on the Minuteman ICBM, and Lockheed sat on space program, intelligence, and military airlift committees, all of which worked on material central to its contracts. Adams concludes:

> The major problem that results from this special early access is one of bias. Because advisory committees are concerned with a specific issue or policy area and select their own membership, they tend to reinforce a closed, interacting network of policy-makers, all of whom have expertise in the area but who share a similar interest in the preservation of the industry-Government relationship, through closed meetings and selective membership. Wider views are not represented.[55]

The Pentagon has been vigilant in shaping competition in the aerospace industry and in protecting the stronger companies. It has also continually bailed out companies in trouble. Between 1958 and 1973, some 3,652 rescue operations were undertaken by the government to help financially troubled firms. Douglas garnered some $75 million in aid in 1967 when it was in serious financial trouble with its DC-8 and DC-9. Lockheed's loan guarantee was worth more than $350 million four years later. General Dynamics and other companies have been the beneficiaries of controversial salvage operations. Not including the controversial Lockheed bailout, the bill for such bailouts amounted to a hefty $85.9 million for this period.[56] As we shall see in the next chapter, contracts have been carefully spread around to ensure the prosperity of each major firm.

Perhaps most important, the Pentagon has provided a deep and ongoing market for the sale of aerospace products through massive procurement budgets year after year. James Clayton found in 1970 that military expenditures accounted for 82 percent of total federal purchases of goods and service in the first twenty years after the Second World War and were much more likely to be directed toward the cold war industries.[57] The infant electronics and computer industries found safe harbor in the crucial decades of the 1950s with the government, which accounted for 70 percent or more of their sales. Even today military orders account for the bulk of aerospace sales. In 1989 military aircraft, missiles, and spacecraft accounted for 77 percent ($76 billion) of the aerospace industry's sales, compared with just 23 percent for civilian aircraft ($22 billion).[58]

America's closet industrial policy for aerospace extends to the international sector. The Pentagon has offered substantial amounts of military assistance that was for decades tied to exports and continues to operate a large foreign military sales program. The civilian aircraft sector has also benefited. The U.S. Export-Import Bank has vigorously competed with the Europeans to assemble preferential financial packages for the export of aircraft. Lockheed justified its demand for a loan guarantee by pointing out that, through 1971, Boeing had received $600 million in such guarantees by the Export-Import Bank, inducing foreign airlines to purchase Boeing products. The bank has focused its efforts on commercial aircraft to the exclusion of most other sectors.[59]

Adjustment assistance for communities, workers, and companies affected by military base and plant closures is also a common feature of the Pentagon industrial policy. Since 1961 the Office of Economic Adjustment (OEA) in the Pentagon has been helping communities redevelop closed bases and even a few idled plants. Although the office's strategies and accomplishments are controversial (as we shall see in chapter 8), millions of dollars have been spent on them.

The ACE complex plays an active role in the formation and practice of this industrial policy. Some twenty industry trade associations exist to keep a close watch on Washington. They carry the weight of their industries without speaking for the specific interests of any one company, notes Gordon Adams. For example, the Aerospace Industries Association, founded in 1919, has fifty-five corporate members and a budget (as of 1991) of over $6–7 million. It helps members with "noncompetitive" problems and seeks "equitable procurement policies and practices" at DOD and NASA. The American Defense Preparedness Association, also founded in 1919, has 33,000 individual and 400 corporate members. According to Adams, "The Association freely admits that it supports the so-called military industrial complex" and takes pride in the fact that forty-eight of the top sixty prime contractors are members. The Air Force Association is the strongest of the service groups; in addition to 90,000 individuals, it has 200 corporate members. All these groups actively monitor and lobby the Pentagon and Congress on behalf of their constituents.[60]

The closet industrial policy of the Pentagon is not acknowledged by presidents or chiefs of staff, who champion free enterprise and oppose the idea of industrial policy at the same time that they oversee personnel who operate one. Everything that the much admired (and derided) "Japan Inc." practices in industries from autos to supercomputers the American government also practices, primarily for the ACE complex. The United States has been in diplomatic trouble when it has protested subsidies for Airbus, the Europeans' joint commercial jetliner, but refused to acknowledge that without military contracts, Boeing and McDonnell-Douglas would never have gotten a jet off the ground.

Recent world events, however, have finally pushed the United States out of the closet. The Pentagon has become the leading sponsor of commercially important technologies such as semiconductors, supercomputers, and high-definition television (HDTV). Although there is clearly no consensus within its walls, as we shall see in chapter 5, strong voices within the Pentagon have spoken out for explicit industrial policies to reverse the reputed decay in the military-industrial base.

The Fruits of Cultivating Aerospace

The extraordinary success of the ACE complex in the larger, more competitive world economy is a direct consequence of the massive American public commitment to the cold war. It is not surprising that aircraft, computers, electronics, and communications topped the list of export growth industries of the American economy in the 1980s, outpacing agriculture and machinery.

Military and civilian orders together doubled the share of aerospace in American manufacturing sales from 1977 to 1986. The industry has enjoyed spectacular growth since the end of the Vietnam War build-down; sales in real dollars had increased in 1986 by a whopping 87 percent over 1977. Of this, military and space program sales accounted for a disproportionate share, but civilian sales were also up more than 60 percent over the decade. The aerospace industry finished 1989 with $120 billion in sales for the year. Government remained its single largest customer, responsible for $72 billion in sales. Despite real defense cuts, military aerospace sales continued to rise through 1989 because of existing commitments, as well as a big jump in direct foreign sales. Ironically, for the billions of dollars spent on military aircraft, only 1,443 units were actually produced in 1988; 825 were sold to U.S. military agencies and 618 to foreign armed forces.[61]

Aerospace plays a particularly important role in the trade balance. Aerospace exports rose to over $31 billion in 1990, contributing a net $21 billion to the U.S. trade balance. Much of the positive aerospace balance is attributable to civilian sales, which accounted for almost 80 percent of exports in 1989, a share that has grown from a low of 48 percent in 1964. Along with high-tech products in electronics and communications, these aerospace products accounted for 42 percent of all manufactured exports in 1987, but only 25 percent of imports.[62]

The extraordinary success of American civil aircraft producers in the world market is a consequence of the long-term nurturing of aerospace by the military. In 1990 the civilian segment of the industry shipped a total of 544 transports and 591 helicopters for a total price tag of $23.5 billion. Of these, about 42 percent were sold to domestic customers, mainly the airlines, and the rest were exported. The exports attest to the dominance of American airframe companies. From 1980 through 1986, U.S. manufacturers accounted for 80 percent of total value of orders for commercial transport aircraft throughout the world, compared with 15 percent for Airbus and 5 percent for British Aerospace and Fokker combined. Boeing easily outclassed its domestic competitors, shipping a total of 289 transports to McDonnell-Douglas's 129 and Lockheed's 5. A large proportion of company receipts comes from such exports; 24 percent of McDonnell-Douglas's and 41 percent of Boeing's were accounted for by such sales in 1987. These firms have a long history of profitable exporting: from 1952 to 1984, Boeing delivered 55 percent of all commercial jets sold worldwide, and McDonnell-Douglas shipped 25 percent.[63]

The designs of several of the industry's workhorse products were lifted from work done for the military. An outstanding example is Boeing's 707, which was so closely cloned from its air force KC-135 tanker that the first prototype wheeled out of the Seattle plant had no windows in the fuselage. Boeing eventually made more than eight hundred of the tankers, which enabled it to spread its development costs and lower its price for the commercial twin much faster than would otherwise have been possible. Although a greater share of commercial work is now funded internally, the Department of Defense is still a big underwriter of aircraft engine development, and NASA spends $350–400 million a year on generic aeronautical research and testing, which complements industry efforts and reduces industry's costs.[64] In one major effort, the National Aerospace Plane Technology Program, NASA, and the air force are jointly developing a new commercial-military hypersonic aircraft, to which in 1990 alone the air force contributed $202 million and NASA $38 million. Air force support is slated to decrease by $44 million in 1991, however, while NASA's is expected to grow by $30 million.[65]

Government oversight kept the commercial industry more competitive than it might otherwise have been. In 1965, Almarin Phillips predicted that of the seven firms (four domestic and three foreign) selling aircraft to American airline companies, only one would survive. He believed that during the two previous decades "the decrease in numbers [of manufacturers of commercial planes] would likely have been greater and the possibility of entry by new producers would likely have been less had there not been huge procurement of military aircraft and related R&D through much of the period."[66] His understanding of the mechanics was better than his prediction—the Pentagon helped two American firms—Boeing and McDonnell-Douglas—to survive and tried to help a third, Lockheed. Undoubtedly, this military-bred rivalry, as commercial airplane makers, helped the American industry maintain its edge in international competition.

Computing, of course, has grown by leaps and bounds as an industry and is today much more dependent upon commercial markets than military ones. The computer sector has become central to the functioning of the modern U.S. economy, accounting for approximately 10 percent of both gross national product and the nation's capital investment. But most of its main features and key technologies owe their existence to decades of military largesse.[67] The historians Ernest Braun and Stuart MacDonald concur that, in electronics, too, military money at the very least accelerated development dramatically. They point out that the strong, early American lead in semiconductors had much to do with other nations' industries being deprived of the vast American military market.[68] To this day, in both semiconductors and computing, much of the ongoing basic research is funded through the Pentagon's Sematech Program and Strategic Computing Program.

The Neglected Industrial Base

The closet industrial policy has paid off, then, in the form of a set of U.S. industries that are commercially strong and competitive in world markets. Less well understood is the degree to which their vitality was purchased at the price of stagnation in the rest of the civilian industrial base, especially in producer goods. Compare the shares of ACE industries and commercially oriented industries in GNP growth, for instance (Table 3.2). During the buildup of 1979 through 1986, while

TABLE 3.2

Gross National Product Share of Selected Manufacturing
Industries, 1979–86

INDUSTRY	1986	CHANGE IN SHARE (%) 1979–86
Total Manufacturing	21.87	0.2
Computers, Nonelectrical Machinery	4.06	54.7
Electric and Electronic Equipment	2.29	21.4
Instruments and Related Products	0.80	13.5
Aircraft, Other Nonauto Transport	1.31	12.1
Food and Related Products	1.69	−2.0
Printing and Publishing	1.14	−3.3
Chemicals and Related Products	1.60	−7.8
Lumber and Wood Products	0.58	−11.6
Apparel and Other Textile Products	0.53	−14.5
Motor Vehicles and Equipment	1.20	−20.1
Petroleum and Coal Products	0.71	−21.5
Primary Metal Industries	0.94	−39.6

SOURCE: *Bureau of Economic Analysis, U.S. Dept. of Commerce, "National Economic Product Accounts" (tables 6.1, 6.2), compiled by U.S. Congress, Office of Technology Assessment,* Paying the Bill: Manufacturing and America's Trade Deficit *(Washington, D.C.: U.S. Government Printing Office, June 1988), table 3.*

the share of GNP of manufacturing output as a whole held steady, the military-led industries increased their shares of domestic output dramatically. Nonelectrical machinery increased its share by 55 percent, all of it accounted for by the spectacular growth in computers. Electronics, instruments, and nonmotor vehicles (the last dominated by aircraft) increased their shares by 12–22 percent. In contrast, steel, autos, and apparel decreased their shares by 14–40 percent.[69] What these contrasting figures show is a profound restructuring in the source of manufactured goods—Americans are buying more from abroad because imports are better and cheaper.

The contrasts in trade balance are striking among the twelve manufacturing industries listed in Table 3.3. While aircraft posted a surplus of $12.5 billion in 1987, instruments $3 billion, and computers $1 billion, apparel had a negative trade balance of $16.9 billion, motor vehicles $53.3 billion, and iron and steel $8.5 billion. Indeed, adverse trade balances in steel, autos, textiles and apparel, and electronics

TABLE 3.3

Trade Balance in Selected Manufacturing Industries, 1987

INDUSTRY	TRADE BALANCE (BILLION $)
Total Manufacturing	− $137.7
Aircraft and Other Transportation Equipment	12.5
Chemicals	9.6
Professional, Scientific, and Control Instruments	3.0
Military Arms, Ammunition, Vehicles	2.0
Computing and Office Machinery	1.0
Industrial Machinery	− 6.7
Semiconductors and Other Electrical Equipment	− 7.0
Iron and Steel	− 8.5
Telecommunications and Sound-reproducing Equipment	− 15.6
Wearing Apparel and Accessories	− 16.9
Motor Vehicles	− 53.3

SOURCE: *U.S. Department of Commerce, Office of Trade and Investment Analysis, compiled by U.S. Congress, Office of Technology Assessment,* Paying the Bill: Manufacturing and America's Trade Deficit *(Washington, D.C.: U.S. Government Printing Office, June 1988), table 12.*

other than computers accounted for more than three-quarters of the entire American deficit. The result was considerable job loss: in steel, autos, and textiles and apparel, employment dropped by 600,000 from 1979 to 1986.[70]

Overall, even with the strength of computers and aircraft, the composition of American imports has been changing in an alarming manner. In 1967 more than 60 percent of the nation's imports consisted of petroleum, food products, and industrial supplies; automotive and capital goods accounted for only 18 percent. By 1987 imports of the latter had spurted to almost 40 percent and imports of the former had dropped below 40 percent. At the same time, durables exports, once the pride of the nation, barely increased their share of exports. The result is a troublesome and growing trade deficit as U.S. commercial firms steadily lose ground to their foreign competitors. In the auto industry, for instance, Japanese producers account for the bulk of the deterioration in the American market. In 1987, 21 percent of the cars sold in the United States were made in Japan, another 6 percent were made by Japanese companies in the United States, and another 9 percent were imported from other foreign countries. Japanese steel made considerable inroads into U.S. markets in the 1970s and 1980s. In electronics, too, Japanese firms have been challenging American prowess. By the end of the 1980s, the Japanese had cornered the market on dynamic random access memory (DRAM) devices, a crucial and large component in computers. Germany has also emerged as a powerful competitor in machine tools, specialty tools, industrial equipment, and electronics.[71]

While the United States was busy lavishing its industrial policy on the ACE complex, diverting to military commitments resources that might have been made available to civilian industries, Japan and Germany concentrated their initiatives on their commercial sectors. In the United States the best talent went into the engineering professions in heavy demand and paying premium salaries because of Pentagon funding. Aeronautical and electrical engineers, with their pick of graduate research fellowships, have been on the top of the American totem pole, while civil and industrial engineers have lost prestige, unlike in Japan, where those occupations are held in high esteem. According to critics, the closet U.S. industrial policy, by depleting resources, has contributed to several deepening macroeconomic problems in the economy: inflation, unemployment, a collapse in productivity gains, and a worsening in income distribution. In addition, it often created esoteric technologies that were many times more expensive than necessary and therefore difficult to apply to commercial endeavors.[72]

It is hard to determine exactly what the state of the American economy and its leading nonmilitary sectors might be today had our industrial policy been conducted differently. The dimensions of the resource diversion are fairly clear: between 20 to 30 percent of the engineering and scientific work force of the nation (the share was actually much higher in the first postwar decades) has been devoting itself to the development of military technology. Lloyd Dumas argues that since the United States already produces fewer engineering graduates than Japan, Japanese companies have a 56 percent lead over U.S. firms in the availability of this labor pool for commercial activity.[73]

The stock of physical capital accumulated and owned by the Department of Defense had reached $474.9 billion in 1983, even at heavily discounted prices. Over 56 percent of this stock was weaponry, and another 24 percent was equipment and supplies that were not of much use to the commercial economy. Pentagon budgets from 1947 through 1981 accounted for 46 percent of the reproducible assets of American national wealth. That represents a considerable number of forgone opportunities. New investment in the United States during the 1980s continued to be skewed toward military ends. The net investment in plant equipment by all U.S. manufacturing concerns over the three-year period 1980–82 was $8.8 billion; in 1982 alone, the Department of Defense invested $3.3 billion in new plant equipment. Furthermore, in the same period that DOD lavished funds on military infrastructure, public works investment in the United States for highways, sewers, and mass transit fell off precipitously. Total investment in public works by all levels of government fell 21 percent from 1965 to 1977, from $38.6 billion per year to $30.4 billion, and estimates of necessary repair and reconstruction amount to several trillion dollars.[74]

A quick look at the neglected American industries reveals the bad fruit that was borne of the closet industrial policy. Autos make an interesting contrast with aerospace, not only because of their intertwined genealogies but also because the two industries have long competed to be the single largest source of U.S. manufacturing employment. From 1945 to the early 1970s, the American auto industry paid the highest wages in the world for industrial work, produced the most inexpensive cars, and was a huge net exporter. In 1963 the value of North American exports exceeded imports by 50 percent, half of the exports going to Europe and half to developing countries. In 1973 the American market was on a par with Europe's, with a net positive auto trade balance of $3 billion. By 1980 the situation had deteriorated dramatically. America had lost more than one-quarter of its market, chiefly to Japan, a country whose industrial policy was to explicitly target the U.S. market while permitting only marginal growth of its own. In that year, auto imports from Japan were three times as high as U.S. exports to Japan. So successful was Japan that by the late 1980s, 40 percent of all Japanese autoworker jobs were dependent upon exports to the American market, and one-third of Japan's total worldwide surplus was its auto surplus with the United States. In the 1980s the American auto work force declined from 1.6 million to 1 million, yielding to aerospace the role of lead domestic manufacturer.[75]

Why did the American auto industry lose ground so steadily? There are many reasons, including substantial and pernicious oligopoly in the industry and an ingrown management preoccupied with disciplining labor and managing rather than with serving the market. But the diversion of top engineering talent away from the automotive field, the absence of government R&D aid, the deterrence of government-induced high interest rates, antitrust policy, and the ineffectiveness of trade policy, which permitted galloping imports, all contributed. In contrast, the Japanese government assembled a package of incentives—R&D subsidies, training, low-cost capital, managed cooperation among firms, and export promotion with domestic market protection—that powerfully assisted Japanese firms in achieving inroads into U.S. markets.

Steel is another example. For more than a century, steel was a core industry in the United States, providing infrastructure for the nation's transportation system and feeding industrialization in the machinery, auto, and equipment industries. Through the 1950s, the American steel industry was the most productive in the world, and its pay scales set standards for the rest of the United States. But by the 1980s the industry was in deep trouble. Employment had fallen by more than 60 percent between the late 1970s and 1990, when imports accounted for more than one-quarter of domestic consumption. The top firm, U.S. Steel, had literally x-ed steel out of its corporate name when it became USX in the late 1980s, after pruning its steel work force from 75,000 to 20,000.[76] While an ossified industrial structure deserves much of the blame, the highly capital-intensive steel industry also suffered from not being offered the subsidies enjoyed by its competitors in the form of low-cost capital, R&D support, and trade assistance.

Without government involvement, the steel industry was more or less left to fund its own innovation. As a result, American R&D expenditures per ton of steel were about $1.30 in 1972, when the European Community was spending $1.46 per ton and Japan $2.26 per ton. Industry research and development continued to suffer through the 1970s. Unlike both private- and public-sector European and Japanese managers, who consider research and development a means to meeting competitive problems, U.S. government leaders have been preoccupied with nurturing aerospace. While the Strategic Defense Initiative (SDI) was being sold as a $60 billion R&D program for the aerospace industry, the steel industry could not get $15 *million* for its Leapfrog Technology Program, despite support from President Reagan's science adviser, George Keyworth.[77]

Consumer electronics is a third area in which the U.S. competitive lead was destroyed by neglect. In just twenty years, the United States went from being the originator of technological breakthroughs and the world's leading producer of electrical and electronic goods to being a major consumer of products made abroad. As with autos and steel, the Japanese postwar policy was to combine licensing technology with limits on foreign direct investment and protection of the domestic market to foster indigenous expertise in consumer electronics. By the late 1950s, Japan was ready to export televisions: it set up an institute to promote exports, monitor them, and ensure quality control and maintained a certification process that inhibited the sale of U.S. televisions in Japan. Japan was very successful in penetrating the U.S. market and replicated this strategy with videocassette recorders in the 1980s. Two top American producers of consumer electronics, GE and RCA, have dropped out of that market altogether—and out of the commodity chips market as well—to concentrate their efforts on military projects, more esoteric high-tech products, and financial services. Many fear that what Japanese industrial policy has wrought in its consumer electronics dominance is soon to come in producer electronics as well.[78]

The machine tool industry is yet another example. Early on, the preference of the air force for special performance characteristics led to the development of a very expensive form of numerically controlled machine tool rather than a simpler variant, one that would have complemented rather than supplanted the skills of machinists. Over time, the continued presence of the U.S. government as a large customer has encouraged a relatively high-cost strategy in the domestic industry.[79] As a result, Japanese companies were able to use the principles of robotics—developed at the expense of the Pentagon—

63

to create a better machine tool, which they then sold back into the U.S. market. Thus, when an autoworker is replaced by a robot, he or she cannot simply find a job making robots—they are imported.

It is not surprising that these industries languished while aerospace and electronics boomed. By the 1960s the aircraft and missile companies alone employed more scientists and engineers on R&D work than did the chemical, drug, petroleum, motor vehicle, rubber, and machinery industries combined.[80] In funding, the gap has been huge and persistent. Aerospace, communications, and electronics garnered over $23 billion in R&D funds from the federal government in 1989, while the steel industry received a miniscule $21 *million* (Table 3.4). In the same year, the ACE complex walked away with almost 82 percent of all federal funding for manufacturing research and development. While the aerospace industry spent only slightly more of its own R&D funds as a percentage of sales than did the average manufacturing firm (3.7 percent compared with 3.2 percent), its total R&D funds as a percentage of sales were a stunning 15 percent compared with less than 5 percent for all manufacturing, the gap being almost entirely due to military subsidy.[81] Over the years, the lopsided pattern of favoritism in federal R&D funds for the ACE industries has ensured their preeminence in both domestic and international markets, especially for military products; steel, petroleum, food, textiles, and other industries, receiving negligible federal subsidies, have been overtaken by foreign competitors.

Furthermore, almost none of the other protections and incentives given to aerospace by the Pentagon are matched by government aid to basic manufacturing. There are no funds for plants and equipment, no low interest rates, no guaranteed markets, only rare cases of bailouts (Chrysler is the outstanding exception), ineffective trade policy, and no adjustment assistance—only weak plant-closing legislation. In short, as the Office of Technology Assessment (OTA) concluded in 1989, "other industrialized nations—particularly in Western Europe and Japan—construct their technology efforts with a greater emphasis on economic development over military development than does the United States." For instance, both Japan and Germany spend about 50 percent more on nondefense research and development as a percentage of GNP than does the United States.[82]

TABLE 3.4

Federal versus Industry R&D Funding for Selected Industries, 1989
(in millions of dollars)

INDUSTRY	FEDERAL FUNDS	INDUSTRIAL FUNDS	TOTAL FUNDS	FEDERAL % OF TOTAL R&D	% OF FEDERAL FUNDS
Total Manufacturing	29,233	59,648	88,871	32.9	100.0
Aerospace[a]	15,647	3,511	19,157	81.7	53.5
Electronics, Communications[a]	7,928	10,618	18,546	42.7	27.1
Rubber Products	313	930	1,243	25.2	1.1
Autos, Trucks, Railroad Equipment (including tanks)[a]	1,982	9,431	11,413	17.4	6.8
Scientific Instruments[a]	991	5,531	6,522	15.2	3.4
Machinery (including computers)[a]	1,669	10,457	12,126	13.8	5.7
Fabricated Metals	73	732	805	9.1	0.2
Iron and Steel	21	601	622	3.4	0.1
Chemicals	381	11,134	11,515	3.3	1.3
Petroleum Products	21	2,068	2,089	1.0	0.1
Food and Beverage	0	1,172	1,172	0.0	0.0
Paper/Pulp	0	1,009	1,009	0.0	0.0
Textiles	0	176	176	0.0	0.0

[a]Military R&D-intensive industries

SOURCE: Aerospace Industries Association of America, Aerospace Facts and Figures, 1989–1990 (Washington, D.C.: AIA, 1989), p. 104, derived from Battelle Corporation data.

Trouble on the Horizon

By 1986, the peak of the Reagan buildup, DOD, NASA, and other government agencies accounted for 75 percent of sales of aerospace products and services, up from 59 percent in 1980. Space-related sales also ballooned in the 1980s, overtaking civilian aircraft sales in 1983. But by 1987 the impact of zero growth in defense budgets was already being felt. Although military aircraft sales reached a record of $43 billion in 1987, up 6.1 percent from the previous year, a number of big weapon system contracts—for the B-1 bomber at Rockwell International, (so-named since 1973, following the 1967 merger of North American Aviation and Rockwell Standard) and the C-5B transport at Lockheed—were drawing to a close. Military aircraft sales, the largest segment of aerospace sales, dropped by more than 10 percent in real terms as a result of the completion of these programs.[83]

Aerospace remains a risky business. Changes in international arenas, shifts in taxpayers' stances, and budgetary crises can instantly cancel, or at least postpone, the big weapons programs that represent billions of dollars to contractors and thousands of jobs to their employees. As pressures to decrease the military budget are felt, big chunks of capacity and pools of workers could be idled. From 1989 to 1991 more than 50,000 jobs are expected to be lost at military aircraft plants, the start of a decline that could last through the early 1990s.[84]

Meanwhile the forecast for military exports looks cloudy. They languished in the 1980s, owing to the slowdown in the world economy, the heavy debt burden of developing countries, a rise in offset and domestic content agreements (where the purchasing country demands that a share of the weapons be made within its borders, or that the seller buy an equivalent amount of its goods). Military exports also stalled because of a decline in U.S. government financing for foreign military sales, and a natural drop-off in sales following a period of heavy defense purchases. In the 1970s, still flush with Vietnam War orders, U.S. manufacturers controlled 79 percent of the world aerospace market, a level they have not matched since. In the post–Vietnam War build-down, this share fell precipitously to a low of 64 percent in 1980. Reagan's initiatives, by generating enormous military orders, pushed the American share back up to 73 percent in 1985. Since then, tapering military orders, Airbus's strong commercial showing, and declining Third World arms orders have caused a dramatic drop, down to 62 percent in 1989.[85] But because U.S. companies still control a very high percentage of the world aerospace market, they will continue to be targets of the national industrial policies of customer nations.

The Gulf War gave new impetus to U.S. military exports, which, according to an aerospace executive, are "the only game in town right now."[86] Signaling that the military's closet industrial policy is still alive and well, the Bush administration, shortly after the hostilities were over in late February 1991, asked Congress to appropriate $1 billion in loan guarantees for overseas customers of U.S. military contractors to help those customers compete in an increasingly crowded market. This was the first time such aid had been requested since the 1970s.[87]

Even the commercial part of the industry, although robust in the early 1990s, faces problems. The United States still leads the commercial aircraft competition, albeit with considerable year-to-year volatility. Particularly in the post–Vietnam War period, the American net trade balance in aerospace products rose consistently, to a peak of around $13 billion in 1980. During the Reagan buildup, the trade balance fluctuated between $10 billion and $12 billion as imports rose faster than exports. Since 1985 a booming commercial demand has increased the surplus once again, to nearly $20 billion, supplemented by more modest gains in arms exports.

But the American share of the world market is sure to continue to erode, even with coproduction and joint ventures, for several reasons. One is the considerable competition mounted by the Europeans and the Japanese, who have explicit civilian industrial policies to nurture aircraft development and sales. Suppliers in particular may suffer as they are displaced by domestic partners elsewhere. Another reason is the limit on air traffic expansion, which is expected to flatten out late in the century. Furthermore, spin-offs from military projects have declined; in both component technologies and airframes, the demands of military missions have increasingly diverged from the requirements of commercial passenger and freight transport.[88]

In addition, the aerospace industry does not promise to create many more jobs. Even with the tremendous commercial aircraft boom of the late 1980s, increases in overall employment are slowing down. The industry's share of manufacturing employment actually *fell* from 6.9 percent to 6.7 percent between 1987 and 1990. While jobs on the civil side were expected to rise in 1990 by 13 percent to 304,000, military, missile, and spacecraft jobs declined by 4 percent to 684,000, resulting in a decline of 2,000 jobs overall and reversing seven years of net growth.[89]

Nor will electronics bail us out. Since 1983 the electronics sector has had a trade deficit, growing to more than $25 billion by the late 1980s. In 1985 the high-tech producer goods segment of this industry swung into deficit, and such products have accounted for more than two-thirds of the increase in the electronics deficit since 1983. Studies of the high-tech industry conclude that it can be counted on to provide only a small share of total employment in the future.[90]

Since the Second World War, the Pentagon has sponsored what many economists have seen as a second industrial revolution.[91] They have contended—and many still believe—that the military sector has been the main source of technical revolution in the past few decades, making it the dynamic factor in the economy. This revolution appears to have run its course. The Gulf War, after a brief spurt to replace matériel, slowed but could not prevent the military budget's decline. The government is still pushing its military-industrial policy. But the shift in the U.S. military role in a multipolar world, the decline in the nation's military-industrial base, and a changing global military market are forcing even the Bush administration to pay more, if grudging, attention to the plight of U.S. commercial industry. Fortunately, the demise of American commercial sectors is not an irreversible fact.[92] Like plants in a garden starved of sun, rain, and food, they have withered, but they are not dead.

4

A Wall of Separation

■

IF the aerospace, electronics, and communications industries have been the big winners from America's closet industrial policy, the big companies that dominate them have profited most of all. It is also these companies—Lockheed, Rockwell, Boeing, General Dynamics, TRW, and others—that have the most to lose from an end to the cold war. The key to successful conversion lies within their corporate borders. In assessing whether or not these giants and the host of subcontractors clustered around them can cope with a shift toward commercial markets, we must know something about the differences between the two markets. What we find is a "wall of separation"—a business culture on the military side that is ill suited to engage in commercial production, and vice versa.[1]

Lockheed: A Military-Industrial Prototype

The history of Lockheed, a company whose original mission was to produce commercial aircraft, offers an excellent overview of the makings and operation of a big cold war weapons producer. For most of its history, the company endeavored to be a big contender in the commercial aircraft world, and it certainly succeeded in being big. In 1982 Lockheed ranked fifty-seventh in the Fortune 500, with sales of $5.2 billion. But in the same year, the company's fiftieth anniversary year, Lockheed was forced to acknowledge defeat in commercial aircraft: its L-1011 had bitten the dust of competitors—Boeing,

McDonnell-Douglas, and foreign firms. In the 1980s, more than ever, Lockheed was tied to the Pentagon and military markets.

Lockheed was started in 1912 by the entrepreneurial Loughead brothers, Allan and Malcolm, who made exhibition flying planes in California. After a number of fits and starts, the company employed 1,200 workers and had sales of $4.5 million by 1936. It appeared to be on the way to commercial success with its all-metal biplane, the Model 10 Electra. By 1941 Lockheed had grown to be the largest aircraft company in the United States, with 53,000 employees; the Second World War's demand for bombers and fighters swelled its ranks to 93,000 by the war's end.[2]

Shrinking after the war was painful. The air force cancelled 600 Lockheed contracts worth $1 billion, and the company's work force plunged to 35,000. Lockheed continued to win contracts for its new jet fighters and trainers, and it tried earnestly to move back into commercial aircraft. But making it in the nonmilitary market was not easy when competing against other firms that had been similarly boosted into major corporate status by the Second World War and also had considerable excess capacity. Increasingly, Lockheed found itself turning toward government markets, which offered substantial advantages not available elsewhere.

Compare the Lockheed entry into missiles and spacecraft, for example, with its attempts at commercial jetliners. In the former field, at its immensely successful Silicon Valley plant, Lockheed enjoyed Pentagon financing, R&D funds, and lucrative long-term contracts. By the 1980s Lockheed could boast that it had designed and built every fleet ballistic missile in the free world's inventory—the Polaris, the Poseidon, and the Trident. Similarly, Lockheed produced almost half of all satellites launched by the United States through the early 1980s. Missiles and satellites brought in $14 billion and $9 billion, respectively, in sales for Lockheed over the first twenty-five years of the cold war.[3] Lockheed has been the nation's principal designer and builder of antisubmarine warfare aircraft, the major supplier of heavy airlifters, and the developer of the fanciest reconnaissance planes, including the infamous U-2 and its successors.

In contrast, Lockheed struggled unsuccessfully for decades to compete in the market for large passenger aircraft. In the early postwar period, both Lockheed and Douglas decided to go slow on long-range jet transport, chiefly because Boeing's 707, used by the air force as an in-flight refueling tanker, appeared to have the world market—then estimated at about 100 craft—sewed up. Instead, Lockheed revamped its Electra turboprop. But after initial success, fatal airline accidents and technical problems in the late 1950s killed commercial sales; the navy continued for decades to buy a version of it.[4]

Again, in the 1970s, Lockheed tried to capture a share of the commercial aircraft market. It had lost the lucrative supersonic transport (SST) contract to Boeing, but now its goal was the high end of the market—a 300-passenger competitor to Boeing's new 747. Banking on its considerable experience in big transport planes, Lockheed poured millions of dollars into the design of what was to become the L-1011 TriStar. The demise of this plane, the last of which rolled off the assembly line in 1983, aptly demonstrates the nightmares of the commercial marketplace for aircraft manufacturers. Lockheed thought it could expect sales of 300 planes, but at a late date Douglas entered the fray, cutting the market in half. Selling a mere 150 planes would not have permitted Lockheed to cover development costs; in addition, at a crucial moment its engine supplier, Rolls-Royce, went bankrupt. Lockheed had to lay off its workers, and production was stalled for a fatal year. The company lost over $2.5 billion in this ten-year effort to regain a foothold in the commercial aircraft market. Reflecting on his firm's experience with what he called "the commercial aviation bug," CEO Roy Anderson concluded that, "in this era, we cannot afford this love affair."[5]

Meanwhile, Lockheed was doing spectacularly well on the military aircraft side. From a position of seventh-largest DOD prime contractor in 1957, it had climbed to number one by 1962, a position it kept on and off for the next fifteen years (for five of those years it placed either second or third).[6] Furthermore, Lockheed became a top NASA contractor, a position it holds to this day.

But big sales in absolute dollars did not always translate into performance and profits. In the early 1970s Lockheed ran into unprecedented problems, beginning with its air force C-5A airplane. The product of a $5 billion program and the largest contract ever written up to that time, each plane was originally priced at $29 million but ended up costing the Pentagon $62 million. (The comparable commercial Boeing 747 cost $23 million in the same year.) The program was plagued by design problems and contract snags, resulting in cost overruns on the order of $1 billion. In 1972 the C-5A suffered major technical breakdowns once an hour for every hour of flight time. Its wings developed cracks. Scrutiny of a randomly selected plane yielded 47 major and 149 minor flaws, according to the General Accounting Office (GAO). Pilots were warned that the landing gear would fail every four hours. A production manager at the Marietta plant revealed that these deficiencies were known by the company, but that it falsified its paperwork to expedite payment. A host of other problems were discovered in the C-5A's instrumentation, automatic pilot, carrying ability, and radar systems.[7]

Corruption has been another endemic issue. Lockheed's was perhaps the most highly publicized case of paying bribes and making other improper payments to foreign military and government officials to procure sales. In the early 1970s Lockheed paid more than $200 million in commissions to agents abroad.[8]

Caught with disastrous results from the C-5A experience, stunned by more military aircraft cancellations, and coping with huge losses from the slowdown of the L-1011 project, the company was on the brink of bankruptcy by 1971. Top management wrote to the deputy secretary of defense, David Packard, that without interim financing of $640 million the company would have to halt work on Pentagon programs. Cong. William Moorehead (D-Penn.) of the House Banking Committee viewed the situation as little more than blackmail, characterizing Lockheed as "an 80-ton dinosaur who comes to your door and says, 'If you don't feed me I will die and what are you going to do with 80 tons of dead, stinking dinosaur in your yard?' "[9] Nevertheless, the government jumped in. In 1971 Lockheed signed an agreement with DOD accepting a $484 million loss on four military contracts and received an emergency loan guarantee through a special act of Congress, raising the company's line of credit to $650 million.[10]

In the 1980s Lockheed's performance problems continued, as just two examples will attest. Since 1977 it had secretly produced its Stealth fighter, which incorporated new technology enabling it to avoid radar detection. But it came before the congressional and public eye when one crashed near Bakersfield, California, in 1986. In the same year, Lockheed was accused of overcharging between $400 million and $500 million for fifty C-5Bs in what the air force called "the largest by far claim of faulty pricing on a single Pentagon program."[11]

None of this has derailed the company from its rank as a top-ten defense contractor; indeed, the bailout helped Lockheed stay in first place through most of the 1970s. Lockheed reaped some $21 billion in government sales from 1970 to 1979, accounting for 67 percent of the company's revenues. As Bankers Trust vice-president Frederick Leary put it in 1976, "The rest of the company is going like gangbusters helping absorb the L-1011 losses, and that way you can carry a sick baby for a long while."[12] International arms sales helped, too, pumping in hundreds of millions of dollars in cash flow. The C-5A, despite its ignominious start, was still reaping profits for Lockheed in the

1980s, after Congress appropriated $8 billion for fifty more. Such long-term success despite the notoriety and congressional wrist-slapping explains why companies like Lockheed are so keen to stick with military markets.

Today Lockheed remains tied to the Pentagon's apron strings. In 1986, at the height of the Reagan buildup, Lockheed made 87 percent of its sales to the U.S. government for military purposes. It continues to win plum prime contracts in the post-Reagan era: an order for fifty Stealth fighter jets, the Milstar program, the F-22 advanced tactical fighter (which is estimated to be worth $64 billion over the next twenty-five years),[13] the new remotely piloted Aquila battlefield "model plane" with lasers and television cameras (anticipated to be a $1.5 billion program), and the job of maintaining the nation's space shuttles. At a prospective $6 billion, the shuttle service contract is considered to be one of the richest deals in the history of the space program.

Lockheed's Trident II program, now being phased out, was a follow-on to a fleet ballistic missile program that has kept the company's enormous Silicon Valley division afloat for twenty-five years. Milstar is expected to carry that division a good twenty years into the future. "Spook work," such as production of the Stealth fighter, will bring in as much as 20 percent of receipts.[14] In space—what Lockheed disingenuously calls its "nondefense" business—the company has the space telescope project in addition to the shuttle service contract and plans to build space structures that will use solar arrays and house people for long periods of time.

Lockheed's attempts to diversify have been superficial. Although it had big plans in the early 1980s for data systems and electronics, most of those efforts have either created more trouble than they were worth or ended up in new defense-dependent divisions. Lockheed hired a former assistant secretary of defense to set up a new division to compete for government computer and electronics contracts, hoping such sales would increase from 40 percent of total revenues in 1987 to 60 percent by 1991. The strategy is working—by 1989, 43 percent of Lockheed's $10.6 billion in sales came from electronics and software products and services. But most of this business is accounted for by Lockheed's acquisition of companies like Sanders Electronics; purchased in 1986, much of Sanders's work is military.[15] Preexisting military operations have not proven to be easily convertible to commercial production.

The company has publicly stated its pessimism about any future commercial ventures. Asked in 1984 whether Lockheed had a policy of making no more ventures into the commercial field, CEO Anderson responded: "Well, in the foreseeable future. I don't think we will ever go as prime contractor. First of all, it takes so damn much money. Secondly, the competition: Boeing, McDonnell-Douglas and Airbus. So where would we step in? It wouldn't be in our interest to try."[16] More recently, in a 1985 interview with us, Steve Chaudet of Lockheed's public relations office put it this way:

> We are dealing here with very, very expensive products, products that require redundancy. . . . Question is, can you take this industry and take this technology base that it has and transfer it to somewhere else? Very few have been successful. Take an example. Rohr got into building cars up there for BART [San Francisco's public transit system]. Disaster! They're too high-cost! They'd have been better off going to some guy in Omaha in a goddamn Quonset hut whose labor costs are low.

By and large, that is the company philosophy. In 1989, despite the looming military build-down, Lockheed decided to sell most of its nonmilitary operations, including its extensive information systems division, to concentrate on its weapons expertise.[17]

Lockheed's story is not all that much different from that of a couple of dozen other large military contractors, the bulk of them in aerospace. Even those whose military division operates within a larger conglomerate umbrella, and even many small, specialized subcontractors, face special demands and circumstances when producing for the military. Over time, they have learned to adapt to this top-heavy market in ways that make adjusting to peacetime and a build-down particularly problematic.

Who's Who in Selling to the Pentagon

Aerospace and its allied industries are dominated by a number of heavy hitters, many of whom are highly defense-dependent. The military side of these industries is surprisingly concentrated, with less than fifty firms that really count. (That is, the government's 1986 report on the aerospace industry cited only fifty firms with establishments primarily engaged in the development and/or manufacture of aerospace products.)[18] Twenty-five of these firms account for 50 percent of all defense prime contracts (Table 4.1).[19] The list was headed in 1988 by McDonnell-Douglas, General Dynamics, General Electric, Tenneco,

TABLE 4.1

DOD Top Military Contractors, 1988

RANK	COMPANY	PRIMES (MILLION $)	% OF DOD TOTAL
1	McDonnell-Douglas	8,003	5.84
2	General Dynamics	6,522	4.76
3	General Electric	5,701	4.16
4	Tenneco	5,058	3.69
5	Raytheon	4,055	2.96
6	Martin-Marietta	3,715	2.71
7	General Motors	3,550	2.59
8	Lockheed Aircraft	3,538	2.58
9	United Technologies	3,508	2.56
10	Boeing	3,018	2.20
11	Grumman	2,848	2.08
12	Litton Industries	2,561	1.87
13	Westinghouse Electric	2,185	1.59
14	Rockwell International	2,184	1.59
15	Unisys	1,380	1.01
16	Honeywell	1,366	1.00
17	Textron	1,276	0.93
18	TRW	1,250	0.91
19	Texas Instruments	1,232	0.90
20	IBM	1,065	0.78
21	LTV	942	0.69
22	FMC	862	0.63
23	Ford	791	0.58
24	Singer	785	0.57
25	ITT	769	0.56
	Top 25 Contractors	68,164	49.74
	U.S. Total	137,049	100

SOURCE: *Aerospace Industries Association of America,* Aerospace Facts and Figures, 1989–1990 *(Washington, D.C.: AIA, 1989).*

Raytheon, and Martin-Marietta. At one time or another in the past decade, Lockheed, General Motors, United Technologies, Boeing, and Rockwell have all been among the top five. The top ten in 1988 walked away with more than one-third of all DOD prime contracts, for a total of $47 billion. While concentration is a trait of American markets generally—in 1975, 111 firms made more than half of total U.S. sales—it is much higher in military spheres than in most, although not all, American industries. Jacques Gansler points out that using the Kaysen-Turner criterion for a heavily concentrated industry (one in which the largest eight firms make at least 50 percent of shipments), subsectors of the defense industry are very highly concentrated.[20]

One group of companies is composed first and foremost of airframe-makers, although they may also do system integration and electronics and communications work; some also make ships and tanks. This group includes Lockheed, Boeing, McDonnell-Douglas, General Dynamics, Grumman, LTV, Rockwell, and Northrop. A second group of companies, also prime contractors and predominantly from the electronics industry, makes smaller unmanned missiles. This group includes Martin-Marietta, Raytheon, Hughes, Unysis, Honeywell, and Allied-Signal. A third group that principally makes propulsion units and aircraft engines includes General Electric, United Technologies, and Westinghouse.[21] Yet other contractors, smaller and less apt to be found among the top twenty, serve as systems integrators (TRW, for example) and makers of specialized communications, guidance, and control equipment and instruments (such as IBM, Tenneco, and Singer).

In addition to DOD contracts, these same companies reap large revenues from sales to NASA (Table 4.2). Although NASA expenditures are small compared with DOD contracts, they still amount to an enormous market: in 1988 they reached only 5 percent of the $137 billion DOD budget, but that amounted to a substantial $7.3 billion in contracts. Rockwell is the top award winner, with a stunning 24 percent of NASA contracts in 1988, followed by Lockheed, Martin-Marietta, McDonnell-Douglas, Boeing, and General Electric.

Conversely, several of the largest aerospace contractors are heavily dependent upon the military and space market. For six of the top DOD and NASA contractors, prime contracts made up more than 50 percent of their sales over the period 1985–88 (Table 4.3). For companies like Grumman and General Dynamics, defense-dependency is severe, but in general dependency rates fell somewhat in the late 1980s, chiefly because big firms diversified into the civilian sector through acquisitions.[22]

Large, second-echelon contractors are also heavily subscribed to military markets. Their dependency is often obscured by their operation of both commercial and military divisions, the latter relying heavily upon Pentagon sales. At Allied-Signal, for instance, 55 percent of its aerospace division sales are to the government. In fact, the aerospace division at Allied-Signal accounts for 40 percent of the conglom-

TABLE 4.2

NASA Top Contractors, 1988

RANK	COMPANY	PRIMES (MILLION $)	% OF NASA TOTAL
1	Rockwell International	1,714	23.56
2	Lockheed	793	10.90
3	Thiokol	423	5.81
4	Martin-Marietta	341	4.69
5	McDonnell-Douglas	299	4.11
6	Boeing	260	3.57
7	General Electric	211	2.90
8	United Space Boosters	191	2.63
9	EG&G Florida	156	2.14
10	Bendix	152	2.09
11	Computer Sciences	151	2.08
12	TRW	143	1.97
13	Ford Aerospace & Communications	137	1.88
14	United Technologies	91	1.25
15	IBM	87	1.20
16	Contel	76	1.04
17	Grumman Aerospace	74	1.02
18	Pan American World Services	70	0.96
19	Planning Research	47	0.65
20	Boeing Technical Operations	42	0.58
21	Teledyne Industries	40	0.55
22	BAMSI	40	0.55
23	Raytheon Service	38	0.52
24	Sverdrup Technology	38	0.52
25	Perkin Elmer	31	0.43
	Top 25 Contractors	5,645	77.59
	U.S. Total	7,275	100

SOURCE: *Aerospace Industries Association of America,* Aerospace Facts and Figures, 1989–1990 *(Washington, D.C.: AIA, 1989).*

erate's overall sales. (The company has other divisions, especially in its materials area, that are also significantly defense-oriented.) Hughes, a division of General Motors, is more than 80 percent dependent upon military dollars.[23] If its military-related sales to other agencies, such as the Department of Energy, were included, the percentage

TABLE 4.3

Military and Space Dependency of Major Defense Contractors, 1985–88

COMPANY	PRIMES (MILLION $)	SALES (MILLION $)	DOD AND NASA PRIMES AS % OF SALES
Grumman	12,057	13,625	0.88
General Dynamics	29,015	35,951	0.81
Martin-Marietta	14,670	20,055	0.73
McDonnell-Douglas	32,205	52,357	0.62
Lockheed	22,094	41,719	0.53
Raytheon	15,301	29,566	0.52
Rockwell International	22,101	48,209	0.46
Litton Industries	7,787	18,538	0.42
Honeywell	7,128	25,830	0.28
Textron	6,413	23,418	0.27
Boeing	16,196	62,294	0.26
Texas Instruments	5,202	21,789	0.24
United Technologies	14,992	65,831	0.23
Unisys	7,454	37,821	0.20
TRW	4,972	25,756	0.19

SOURCES: Aerospace Industries Association of America, *Aerospace Facts and Figures, 1989–1990* (Washington, D.C.: AIA, 1989); *Business Week,* special issues, 1986–89.

of Hughes business attributable to U.S. military demand would be even higher.

These dependency rates are underestimated in that they exclude the many subcontracts that one firm issues to another. Moreover, many companies are exporters of military equipment to parties other than the U.S. government. Military aerospace exports reached a staggering $8 billion by 1987, more than the entire NASA budget. In 1987, for every dollar spent for aircraft equipment by the U.S. government, the aerospace industry received another twenty-two cents in orders from other governments. In addition, illegal sales through private arms traders deepened defense-dependency but are impossible to gauge accurately.

Exports of complete aircraft represented 45 percent of the aerospace trade, chiefly shipments of F-16 and F-18 fighters and E-3A AWACS in 1989. For a company like Lockheed, such sales are a significant share of revenue. In 1984, 10 percent of Lockheed's $8.1

billion in sales came from foreign governments, mainly in the Middle East. For General Dynamics, a single plane, the F-16, can be a major source of profits from exports; as of 1989 the company had sold 1,859 F-16s to the U.S. military and another 1,236 to foreign governments, including the Netherlands, Israel, Turkey, and Belgium. In addition, profits on such exports are believed to be about two and a half times as profitable as military sales to the U.S. government.[24] Throughout the cold war period, such foreign sales have supplemented domestic military demand. From 1949 to 1962, official government arms sales totaled $16 billion; the Pentagon gave away another $30 billion. In a 1986 speech, a Pentagon official claimed that its sales program had yielded $1 billion in profits for American industry and provided 1.2 million man-hours of employment for companies.[25]

It is not just that these companies became big players in the American military market. They became, bred on defense dollars, *enormous* companies. Aerospace began in the 1940s as a small industry with tiny firms; the war boosted them into big ones, but by the 1980s they had reached mammoth proportions. By 1968, 75 percent of the top one hundred contractors were among the *Fortune* 500 firms, and twenty-nine of *Fortune*'s top fifty were major defense contractors. But it took another twenty years to make it to the very top. In 1983 none of the top ten defense contractors ranked among the *Fortune* top sixty.[26] But a few years later, after a steady diet of military contracts and frequent conglomeration and buy-outs of other firms, several had finally made it to the top 25 of the Fortune 500, including Boeing, United Technologies, McDonnell-Douglas, Rockwell, and Allied-Signal.

Government contracts helped keep IBM, General Motors, and General Electric in the top ten of all American companies ranked by stock market value.[27] Such size and asset value made military contractors respectable among the U.S. corporate elite and made it easier for them to generate support for military spending among this group.

It is much harder to trace the size and military dependency of the small contractor sector. Despite many expressions of interest in such data by Congress and the public, the Department of Defense has refused to keep records of subcontractors or require companies to report them. Gansler distinguishes three types of subcontractors: (1) the medium-sized subcontractors and suppliers that are divisions of large firms, often through conglomerate buy-outs; (2) the medium-sized, independently owned firms; and (3) the small businesses operating as subcontractors or even prime contractors.[28]

Over the postwar period, the number of subcontractors appears to have fallen absolutely, with some reversal each time a military buildup occurs. Between 1963 and 1980, the number of suppliers of military electric generators fell from twelve to seven, for instance. In build-down periods, many go under or drop out of military markets altogether.

There is some evidence, too, that subcontractors have become more, rather than less, specialized in military projects, as the "wall of separation" reaches down into their ranks. Although the Pentagon has already launched small-business programs with procurement set-asides, these determine which subcontractors get funding more than they influence the overall level of funds subcontracted.[29] Since the overall share of the military budget going to top corporations has not altered much over the postwar period, it is reasonable to conclude that small businesses have not increased their share either.

Breeding Defense-Dependency

How did it happen that the military market came to be so dominated by a few large corporations, and many of these corporations so dependent upon Pentagon dollars? Many of the great names of aerospace were heavily defense-dependent from the outset because of the extraordinary investment involved and the inadequacy of civilian markets for long stretches of the industry's history. As we saw in chapter 3, the tenacious new aircraft companies turned to government sales to keep alive, especially in the critical period of the Depression, when other competitors—Ford, for instance—dropped out to concentrate on commercial markets. As a percentage of total sales, military purchases accounted for 59 percent of Boeing's receipts from 1931 to 1937, 75 percent of Chance-Vought's and Grumman's, 76 percent of Curtiss's, 79 percent of Consolidated's, 91 percent of Douglas's and 100 percent of Martin's.[30]

Very little of the growth of small firms into corporate giants during the Second World War was financed from traditional sources (retained earnings, stock issue, or bank credit). Some $3.5 billion of capacity additions were paid for by the government, compared with only $420 million financed by the companies themselves. Boeing and Douglas each received thirteen government investment dollars for every one dollar they committed, while North American received fifteen to its one, and Martin twenty to one.[31]

It was also during the war that the enduring relationships between particular suppliers and the competing services were forged. Deliberately, to streamline provisioning and rationalize investment, the services divided up the airframe industry into captive "stables." To the army air force went Bell, Boeing, Curtiss, Lockheed, Martin, and North American; the navy maintained jurisdiction over Consolidated, Grumman, Chance-Vought, and part of Douglas. These arrangements of convenience were to become deep ruts in the postwar period as connections between clients and suppliers persisted. To this day, Boeing and Rockwell (formerly North American) make bombers for the air force, and Grumman, LTV (which absorbed Chance-Vought), and McDonnell-Douglas sell fighters to the navy.[32]

After the war, the aircraft companies scrambled to restructure. Profits plunged, plant capacity shrunk dramatically, and the work force dropped to around one-tenth its former size. Fully half of the sixteen leading aircraft companies identified by President Truman's Air Policy (Finletter) Commission did not show a profit in 1947. Boeing's receipts, for instance, fell from $421 million in 1945 to $14 million the following year; Consolidated's fell from $644 million to $13 million, Grumman's from $237 million to $38 million, and North American's from $400 million to $56 million.[33] The companies and the services were frantic. The commission concluded:

> In a freely competitive economy the number of companies manufacturing a particular product levels off at a point determined by the ordinary laws of economics. In the case of the aircraft industry, however, it would be dangerous to rely only on the operations of these laws. The demand factor fluctuates so violently from peace to war. If a reasonable degree of expansibility is to be maintained for periods of emergency, it is necessary to exercise some industry wide control in the interests of national security. It may even be desirable to keep a few marginal manufacturers in business who might be forced out if the normal laws of supply and demand were allowed to operate.[34]

The firms that flourished under this policy were often virtually set up for—and their experience limited to—the design and production of military weapon systems and related aerospace vehicles, notes Murray Weidenbaum, an economist who has thoroughly studied the industry's rise. Cold warfare pushed thirteen of the top fifty prime contractors to rates of military dependency in excess of 90 percent by the mid-1960s, while another sixteen owed 50 percent or more of their business to government.[35] Some were more diversified than others within military markets. By the late 1950s, for instance, Boeing was making bombers, jet tankers, and missiles, and General Dynamics was producing fighters, bombers, missiles, and submarines.[36] But others, like Grumman, tended to produce mainly one product line for one major service, limiting their flexibility still further.

Over the postwar period, remarkable stability has characterized the ranks of the military-industrial companies. Few have dropped out of the business, and those who have disappeared from the top twenty-five have generally done so through mergers and acquisitions with other companies. Six companies have maintained their top-ten status for over thirty years, from 1957 to 1988—McDonnell-Douglas, General Dynamics, General Electric, Lockheed, United Technologies, and Boeing. Another seven companies stayed within the top twenty-five over the same period—Raytheon, General Motors (and Hughes), Westinghouse, Rockwell, Unisys (and its predecessors Sperry and Burroughs), Textron (with Avco), and IBM. Another six new entrants remained in the top twenty-five once they made it into the cold warrior ranks—Honeywell (1966), Litton (1968), Tenneco (1971), FMC (1979), Texas Instruments (1984), and Singer (1988). The only firms to drop out of the top twenty-five were a handful of oil, chemical, rubber, and shipbuilding companies (General Tire and Rubber, Standard Oil of California, Exxon, GTE, and Newport News Shipbuilding) plus a single aircraft firm, Republic.

What is often lost in the now common contention that military contractors are more diversified than ever before is the fact that they are also more dependent than ever before on defense spending in real terms. The top ten contractors increased their sales in real dollars to the Pentagon dramatically in the 1980s (Figure 4.1). As a group, they boosted sales by 47 percent between 1980 and 1988, a marketing coup that would make any civilian firm drool. Although lower *shares* of their total sales may have been made to the Pentagon, the drop represents diversification through mergers and buy-outs that occurred with retained earnings in the 1980s. Defense divisions of these corporations are now more dependent than ever before on Pentagon spending, making the conversion effort all that more formidable.

These, then are the elite of the ACE complex—a set of large and privileged firms that dominate the private side of the military marketplace. The singularity of the ACE complex and its large, powerful corporate leaders has made it the subject of considerable scrutiny by economists over the postwar period.[37] Remarkably—but consistent with the stability in the industry itself—not much has changed over the decades. Companies have gotten bigger, contract "teaming" has become more common, and international ties have been forged. But by and large, these corporations have been exhibiting the same distinctive behavior for fifty years.

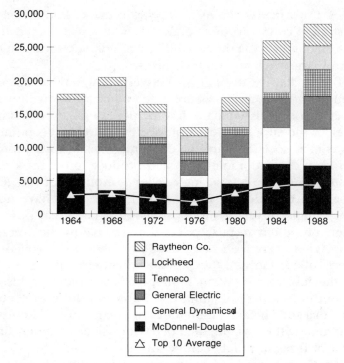

FIGURE 4.1
Military-Space Receipts of Top Contractors, 1964–88 (in millions of 1982 dollars)

Strange Bedfellows

What happens when suppliers are so few in number and so enormous, and sell to such an unusual customer? No analyst disputes that the ACE complex operates in less than a model market. Summing up their research three decades ago, the economists Merton Peck and Frederick Scherer concluded that "a market system exists only in a more or less atrophied form for the weapons acquisition process."[38] The economist Herman Stekler has succinctly summarized the four salient features of the aerospace industry: "a high concentration of sales, the absence of competition, a failure on the buyer's part to impose economic incentives on the sellers, and high entry barriers. One would theorize that the performance of an industry with such a structure would not be outstanding. This, indeed, is the case."[39] These features make the ACE industries distinctly different from commercial industries. In particular, the ACE complex is marked on the one hand by the strange courtship of a single, albeit complex buyer, the U.S. government, and on the other hand by the selling efforts of a limited number of large, military-oriented firms.

Economists like to distinguish between competitive markets, in which many firms compete against each other for many buyers, and imperfect markets, in which a few parties dominate on either the customer or the supplier side. Competitive markets, economists believe, maximize social welfare and consumer satisfaction by forcing all firms to keep costs to a minimum and produce in the most efficient way. In imperfect markets, a single seller or monopolist can get away with charging extortionary prices from buyers, who have no other choice. A single buyer or monopsonist also has great power over suppliers in its ability to push prices down to below the average rate of return. When there are a handful of dominant sellers (oligopolists) or buyers (oligopsonists), the situation is more complex. Collusion among the few can result in monopolistic or monopsonistic outcomes, but only if the colluding few figure out how to circumvent antitrust laws and vigilantly monitor each other's moves. Competition will exist among the few, but their behavior will be strikingly different from that of firms in purely competitive situations.

Scholars have pegged the ACE complex as industries operating in a unique market with a monopsonistic buyer facing an oligopolistic seller.[40] On the demand side, the U.S. government exercises considerable power not only over the growth and decline of firms making weapons but over their entry and exit into the market. Several factors temper its power as a buyer, however. First, no one agent buys weapons, but a numerous and complexly related set of players in the services, DOD, and NASA, and Congress. Weapons purchases were highly decentralized before the Second World War, but with the formation of the Department of Defense in 1947, the creation of the Advanced Research Projects Agency in 1958 to oversee long-term defensewide research centrally, and the development of the Defense Logistics Agency for joint purchases (also in 1958), centralization in DOD increased. In spite of this concentration of buying power, however, there remain intense rivalries between the army, navy, and air force, between groups within each of the services, and between the services and other DOD offices. Furthermore, the nuclear weapons activities of DOE and the space defense activities of NASA remain in separate agencies.[41]

Dozens of controversial conflicts within the government over weapon system priorities have marked the decades since the Second

World War: between the air force and the navy over strategic bombing planes versus aircraft carriers in the late 1940s; between the army and the air force over limited warfare preparedness versus massive retaliation, and for control over missiles in the 1950s; and within the air force between the Strategic Air Command and the Air Defense Command over bombers versus missiles. Nevertheless, with the rise of centralized planning, oversight, and purchasing since Defense Secretary Robert McNamara's tenure in the 1960s, and the limiting of Congress to the late stages of appropriations approval, the monopsonistic characterization remains a fairly good one.[42]

Despite its clout in this market, the government exercises considerable restraint. One reason is that the market is also concentrated on the supplier side, so that no minimum price is revealed through open competition among the aerospace companies. Furthermore, yielding management functions to a group of profit-making defense services firms, upon whom the government is then dependent for procurement advice, makes the few sellers the government faces privy to its urgency and inexperience, lessening its leverage as a monopsonistic client considerably. The government finds it difficult to jawbone suppliers into low-cost, efficient production modes when collusion by the sellers results in the artificial scarcity of technical information and the absence of yardsticks.[43] This situation is all the more ironic when it is remembered that the technical expertise of these firms has been developed largely on government funds.

Over time, the monopsonistic power of the government may have decreased. In 1962 government purchases accounted for over 94 percent of the aerospace industry's total sales, but as commercial spin-offs in aircraft, computing, communications, and electronics built up new segments of the industry, this share fell to 65 percent.[44] These total shares can be misleading, however. Military work is performed almost exclusively in divisions or entire firms dedicated to the military market; for those segments of the industry, continued reliance on the federal government is the only option. Normally, foreign sales are also negotiated through the government, which retains the power to decide what will be sold and at what price.

On the supply side, the aerospace industry is highly oligopolistic: a few dozen firms account for the bulk of prime contracts. Only a small number of sellers compete for any particular weapon system or product line. Many contracts are "sole-source"—Northrop is *the* builder of the B-2 Stealth bomber, for instance. In 1968 the Joint Economic Committee of Congress determined that 58 percent of defense contracts were awarded on a sole-source basis, and another 31 percent were awarded on the basis of purely ritualistic negotiations with alternative sources.[45] Even projects like the advanced tactical fighters had only two teams vying for them at the design stage. Sole-source negotiations and follow-on contracts from original development work result in more than 90 percent of total military dollars being awarded on a noncompetitive basis. Less than 20 percent of military work is formally advertised, and only 10 percent is allocated in an open process.[46]

On an industry-by-industry basis, these oligopolistic features are pronounced. Jacques Gansler computes that in 1967 just four firms accounted for over 93 percent of all contracts in satellites, nuclear submarines, space boosters, fighters, attack aircraft, missile guidance systems, inertial navigation systems, missile reentry vehicles, aircraft fire-control systems, transport and tanker aircraft, helicopters, and jet aircraft engines. Even in products such as data processing systems, radar systems, and communications systems, the top four companies controlled over 50 percent. If anything, these percentages were higher by the late 1980s. Jacques Gansler concludes that "this [oligopolistic] characteristic is perhaps stronger in the defense industry than in any other part of the U.S. economy."[47]

Such concentration is attributable to a number of extraordinary features of the military market throughout this century. Aircraft engineering research and development was wholly funded by the government from 1919 to 1926, limiting the number of firms in that market. Concentration increased with the institutionalization of research and development in airframes and electronics after 1930. In 1942 panic about the prospect of the United States going to war prompted the chairman of the War Production Board, Donald Nelson, to condone the government's dealing with only a few large prime contractors to facilitate administration and enhance speed. After the war, concern about the preservation of an industrial base resulted in the Department of Defense performing a kind of triage—spreading the meager contract dollars around to a few large firms whose success seemed possible. By the late 1940s, although fifteen airframe companies were in business, more than 75 percent of all air force funds for airframe procurement went to just three firms.[48] A 1961 study showed that while the 100 largest DOD prime contractors accounted for 74 percent of that market, the 100 largest manufacturers accounted for only 35 percent of manufacturing sales.[49]

The cold war further solidified the oligopolistic structure of the industry. At first, it increased the number of firms competing: the prospect of contracts for missiles and their automated electronics payload propelled some electronics firms into the fray. The number of prime contractors between 1950 and 1955 rose from nineteen to twenty-six. But as fewer but more expensive contracts were awarded, sales went to the few firms that won out as contractors for large weapon and space systems, while marginal firms became subcontractors or were bought out by the successful companies. The exorbitant cost of facilities—a space laboratory required a minimum investment of $14 million in the 1950s—kept new competitors from other quarters out of the competition. Electronics firms were the exception because of their prior track records and experience in doing subsystems work.[50] Those leaving the market in this crucial early period included Curtiss-Wright, Fairchild, and Bell, all of whom left both airframes and missiles; Martin, which exited airframes but remained in missiles; and General Electric, Firestone, and RCA, all of which left the missile sector.

As the decades wore on, the strange bedfellows became more attached than ever, and more used to each other's company. The firms became increasingly defense-dependent, and the government became increasingly dependent upon them. Some contractors were dependent upon a single large program for long stretches, and even the giants of the weapons business, such as Boeing and General Dynamics, derived most of their sales revenues from three or four programs, giving the companies' operations what Peck and Scherer called "a feast or famine character."[51]

Concentration in the military market increased in the 1980s, despite the huge jump in defense spending. The Center for Strategic and International Studies estimates that the number of military suppliers or subcontractors of all types fell from 138,000 in 1982 to fewer than 40,000 in 1987.[52] The effects of cutting military budgets ripple through the ranks of thousands of small suppliers, who are the first to feel the squeeze. In addition, big contractors often react to budget cuts by bringing work in-house in order to keep their work force, slow the decline in sales, and look more competitive in the race for the big, new, hotly contested weapon systems. The Pentagon has been accused of collaborating in this squeeze on the small firm, and complaints by smaller firms of Pentagon favoritism toward the big contractors have become common.[53]

If the military market is so thinly populated and yet so lucrative, why are there no new firms entering it?[54] Electronics firms did in the 1950s. Others have tried to do so through acquisitions. But in general, few new corporations have managed to enter the top ranks in the entire postwar period. Gansler lists thirteen barriers to entry: they include, in addition to the technological imperatives and high capital costs, the elaborate reporting and accounting demands of the government, political considerations, "brand loyalty" as practiced by the services, security clearance difficulties, and social stigmas.[55]

Power and concentration in the market may be as much a problem for those on one side of the table as for those on the other. The government can withhold crucial information from one firm that it might have gotten from or shared with another. The four-year presidential election cycle can also bring about unanticipated changes, compelling contractors to cope with considerable long-term uncertainty and encouraging them to influence Congress and public opinion. All but the savviest, most adept firms shy away from such vulnerability.

Are the structural features of the military-serving ACE complex inevitable? Walter Adams and James Adams, in a dissenting view, suggest that this highly concentrated structure has been deliberately fostered by the military and the firms involved. They contend that more suppliers could easily be found, increasing the flow of technical information to the Pentagon and lowering costs and improving choice in the long run. In sympathy with this view are Gordon Adams's arguments about the artificiality of the "iron triangle." Seymour Melman points the finger squarely at state managerial capitalism: the state bureaucracy is responsible for shaping the industry and deciding who will get which contracts.[56]

Certainly the postwar stability in rank and membership among the top fifty contractors is remarkable. Already by the 1960s analysts were noting that, from 1940 through 1965, the top fifty contractors accounted for between 57 percent and 67 percent of total prime contracts, while the share of the next fifty ranged between 7 percent and 10 percent. If anything, both concentration and stability increased during the first round of the cold war and during every cycle of boom and bust thereafter.[57] Since then, new entrants have joined the ranks of the top fifty, but most of them did so through mergers: LTV, General Telephone & Electronics, Textron, and Litton. Stability has been assured with the diversification of the biggest companies into several procurement programs and with the Pentagon watching that every firm gets its "fair share." From 1957, the end of the first cold war buildup, to the present, the top twenty-five contractors have maintained a market share of between 45 percent and 57 percent.[58]

The unique combination of a monopsonistic client concerned with performance rather than price and an oligopoly of suppliers leads to another extraordinary feature of the military marketplace. The Pentagon is worried about the long-term, sustained ability of the military-industrial base to supply it in times of both hot and cold wars. Because so few companies supply its long list of crucial items, its awards calculus must include spreading around contracts to ensure supplier survival and vigor, or what James Kurth calls the "follow-on imperative"—the evolved habit of giving big companies "turns" in producing new weapon systems. Even when cost information is available, pure economics will not dictate the government's choice when a more costly system is offered by the next firm in line.[59]

Boeing has been a major beneficiary of such choices. From the Second World War on, it received successive orders for bombers, tankers, and cargo planes, ensuring the firm's success well into the 1960s. After the Vietnam War, when Boeing's SST program was in trouble, the firm received contracts for the E-3 and E-4 aircraft, the AWACS, and trainer aircraft, which eased its crisis. On the other hand, Boeing has often been passed over when other firms were more desperate. The follow-on contract to its Minuteman program went to Martin-Marietta for the MX missile, the KC-135 successor went to McDonnell-Douglas for its KC-10, and the B-52 follow-on went to Rockwell for its B-1.[60]

Most of the other big companies in defense-dependent industries have also benefited from the follow-on imperative. It was generally believed that General Dynamics won the contract in the early 1960s for the F-111, widely considered the inferior candidate, because of losses amounting to $400 million in its Convair division, then teetering on the brink of bankruptcy. Kurth found that follow-on behavior appears to have dictated Pentagon choices in eleven out of twelve major contracts studied between 1960 and 1972. Despite widespread criticism, follow-on operated right through the 1980s, when Fairchild (A-10 trainer), McDonnell-Douglas (C-17, F-18), Northrop (F-18), and Lockheed (C-5) were the major beneficiaries. In a recent update of his analysis, Kurth accurately predicted that Lockheed, widely rumored to be in trouble, would be the next to receive a follow-on. In early 1991 the Lockheed team (the company had joined forces with Boeing and General Dynamics) won the bid for the advanced tactical fighter contract.[61]

The ACE industries, at least the leading firms, are protected in another way. In times of grave financial difficulties, whether their own fault or not, companies enjoy the protection of the federal government. The Lockheed bailout of the early 1970s is the most prominent example, but there have been other, quieter ones. The watchdog attitude of the Pentagon acts as a sort of invisible shield against the pressures of Wall Street. Remarkably few aerospace companies have been the target of hostile takeover attempts in the 1980s, and few such efforts have succeeded. LTV, for instance, failed in its effort to take over Grumman in the early 1980s. After a long hiatus, takeover attempts are now on the rise, especially as aerospace stocks become depressed as a result of forebodings about cutbacks. Martin-Marietta recently staved off a takeover attempt by Bendix, and Lockheed was recently put under siege by Harold Simmons, the Texas drugstore-chain millionaire.[62] The Pentagon makes it known that any change in control of a crucial contractor working on technologically sophisticated and classified work might rouse it into action. The fact that the Pentagon often owns the plants operated by big defense companies also makes takeover less attractive, since these assets are not available for sale.

With the thawing of relations around the world and mounting pressures to cut military spending, further consolidation among American military contractors is likely, and the follow-on imperative will be that much stronger. In the 1990s, General Dynamics, McDonnell-Douglas, Northrop, and Raytheon are expected to dominate, but many of the other big firms will flourish by being major subcontractors or partners. Concentration is likely to increase all the same, leaving fewer and bigger firms in the military-industrial complex. "For military contractors, it will be rag tag, rough and tumble and dog-eat-dog," William Anders, a former Textron official, said in late 1989. "It's going to be a bloodletting and the guy with the most blood will win."[63] Another aerospace executive, whom we spoke to in 1986, direly predicted that the six major military aircraft producers of the 1980s will have been pared down to two by the year 2000.

Why a Wall of Separation?

Success in commercial aerospace markets has generally been incompatible with success in producing for the military; several companies have foundered in the effort to serve both. Some big prime contractors have ended up serving just the Pentagon. Even those who manage to sell to both markets do so by dedicating entirely different divisions to each. Within such companies, the "wall of separation" between the military and commercial divisions permits little exchange of either personnel or product ideas.[64]

Both the structure of the defense industry and the peculiar nature of its product form the foundation of the wall. Military contractors are not selling a finished product, just an idea. In the initial stages of development of a weapon system, when irrevocable decisions are made, firms compete to prove to the military client that their team will come up with the best new round of equipment to meet the desires of top officers. But there is no guarantee that a weapon system will be successful, and even less guarantee of the real cost of its development. Since the weapon system has not yet been produced, its capabilities, performance, and true costs are unproven, and none of these attributes can be used by the government to determine to which company it will award the contract.[65]

In this environment, winning a contract is very different from selling a steel mill a continuous caster with a track record or selling consumers on a product already scrutinized by *Consumer Reports*. First, it requires a powerful lead role for the firm's strategic planners, whose job is to integrate the company's research, design, development, production, financial, and marketing staff efforts, not to mention those of its top subcontractors. The team's job is to convince DOD or NASA that its firm has the most promising approach.

This type of sales job requires a cohesiveness between company divisions not found in other commercial firms. The story of General Electric's efforts to become a prime contractor on complete airborne-accessory power components is instructive. GE had always been firmly committed to decentralized management. In the late 1950s it initiated a pioneering project to put all the power components needed into one package. Its initial difficulties in convincing the Pentagon of the efficacy of its decentralized structure (it lost the first round to RCA) led to internal reorganizations to make its military-related development work more team-oriented and concentrated.[66]

Winning a contract also requires a large marketing team heavily interpenetrated with the same technical personnel who will eventually design and build the prototypes. Design engineers are often the only ones who can explain the product to the naval officer or the air force captain. Marketing groups in these firms are apt to be concerned with meeting the stiff technical specifications of the military customer and communicating those specifications to the rest of the firm.[67] This orientation requires a division of labor in stark contrast to that of a standard industrial corporation, in which operations and marketing are lodged in separate departments.

Selling to their unusual client—the Pentagon—requires that the big defense contractors have marketing teams that are familiar with the inner workings of the Pentagon and the services. No one does this job better than former military men, who are attractive hires for the military-oriented firm. Two types of military recruits are of use: young technical experts—the seven-year men, for instance, who have Air Force Academy engineering degrees and have served their requisite time on air force projects—bring to the company leading-edge information about current equipment and requirements; seasoned middle managers—the newly retired twenty-year men—bring it a lot of institutional knowledge about a particular service and personal connections with top brass. The result is a marketing apparatus riddled with former military men whose highly valued inside information would be of little or no use to a commercial counterpart.

Yet another twist on the way in which firms sell their projects to the Pentagon is a consequence of the follow-on imperative. Since all firms know that the Pentagon and Congress vigilantly monitor the relative strength of the military-industrial base and the leading firms within it, each has incentive from time to time to "cry wolf," to claim that its turn has come. Aerospace firms spend more time than the average industrial company assessing their own strength vis-á-vis competitors and packaging this image for the government's industrial base watchers. They become, in the words of Walter and James Adams, "courtiers of DOD, NASA and AEC [now DOE], functioning in a world of socialized risks and private profit."[68]

The marketing function is aimed not just at the Pentagon but at Congress and the public as well. Companies cultivate important congressional representatives and engineer coalitions of trade unions, chambers of commerce, retired military personnel, and other interested parties to press Congress for continued military contracts and weapons program support.[69] Such "geographical constituency building," as it is called, is rather rare in commercial firms, for which the public sector is not a major customer.

The differences lie not just in the strategic planning and marketing end of the business but in the structure and management of production. In cost-conscious mass production, the structure of the entire firm is geared to produce large volumes at low unit prices. The Second World War clash between Ford, with its millions of auto customers, and Consolidated, with its single government client, illustrates many of the substantive differences in production and management style.

The compulsion for secrecy forms yet another barrier between the two markets. Its role in the split between military and commercial firms dates back to early 1930s, when some industry voices had begun to bridle under the strictures of military clientelism and were urging President Hoover to move government patronage from the services to the Department of Commerce, a maneuver he tried unsuccessfully in 1932. By 1936 much of the work for the military had been pulled behind the veils of secrecy, making it increasingly difficult to apply technologies to commercial craft.[70] Shrouding the nature of the product is essential in projects that are on the leading edge of cold war competition, and this need is reflected in a firm's structure. Personnel must be carefully screened, and internal labor markets are developed to ensure loyalty and longevity. Work must be parceled out so that no one person knows all of the crucial elements of a design.

Contemporary tendencies in industrial restructuring also divide military from commercial firms. Among the latter there has been a marked trend toward vertical disintegration, where firms divest themselves of in-house supply and marketing functions, to capitalize on external economies as a response to a prolonged profit squeeze.[71] But the tendency is just the opposite among the big military contractors: to demonstrate competence to their Pentagon judges, aerospace firms are bringing in or developing in-house capabilities in certain areas, such as composite materials. In general, defense firms throughout the postwar period have performed more work in-house, relative to their sales, than do firms in other industries. For instance, value added over a fourteen-year period from the early 1950s to the mid-1960s was eighteen percent higher in aerospace than in all manufacturing.[72] Aerospace firms are also shutting out independent producers and creating excess capacity, often at taxpayer expense. Their ability to do so is purely a function of the market power of these firms and their dealings with a willing monopsonistic buyer.[73]

The shift away from assembling platforms in favor of electronics and defense services may change this pattern at military-oriented firms somewhat, but then again it may not. A Lockheed spokesman, taking a lesson perhaps from the commercial side of the industry, suggested to us in a 1985 interview that electronics work might be capable of being less vertically integrated. Nevertheless, the separation between military-oriented aircraft and electronics firms has diminished over the decades, as has the distance between the competing defense operations of individual firms. "Teaming"—firms sharing proprietary information in constructing a proposal and mapping out the division of labor that will result—first took root in the 1950s and grew throughout the cold war period.[74]

Nevertheless, the means by which ACE companies and their military-oriented divisions operate and make their money remain profoundly different from those of commercially oriented firms. This wall of separation will be difficult to breach and disassemble.

How Well Does the ACE Complex Perform?

Over the first half of this century, charges of war profiteering and shoddy product were made against many of the major military contractors.[75] In the cold war period, the cast of characters changed but the substance of the charges did not. Writing in the early 1970s, Walter Adams and James Adams concluded that "cost overruns have been enormous, product quality has fallen short of original promise and contracting requirements and . . . profits have in some instances been astronomical."[76] In the 1980s several prominent firms were the targets of criminal investigations, and outstanding cases of equipment failure and cost overruns continued to pepper the front pages.

ACE companies try to meet what they see as a triad of expectations from their military clients: a demand for high-performance equipment, an insistence on rapid development and construction, and a desire for cost-efficiency. Trade-offs among these three criteria are inevitable. In the words of one contractor, "You can get two of these, but not three—it always ends up that the cost factor takes third place." Quality and development time win out time and again over cost. Peck and Scherer found in the 1950s that "maximizing quality was slightly more important in weapons programs than minimizing development time, which in turn was much more important than minimizing development cost."[77] This pecking order of goals has not changed appreciably since then.

Many studies have documented the systematic nature of cost overruns. Peck and Scherer, for instance, found that for twelve large projects in the 1950s and early 1960s, final costs were on average 320 percent of original estimates. Stekler compared defense contracts in terms of degree of competition for them and found that costs in the absence of competition were 25 percent higher and that the gap between military and civilian production was even greater. He found considerable evidence of excessive development and of what he calls "gold-plating" and concludes that costs could be reduced without sacrificing quality.[78]

One problem is that the government's demand is relatively "inelastic": it is not apt to cancel orders or buy fewer weapons if unit costs escalate. Oligopolistic companies dealing with a client with relatively inelastic demand can raise prices considerably above costs without losing business.[79] The Stealth bomber is the latest example of enormous cost overruns. By 1989 it had exceeded estimates by 25 percent; at a cost of more than $500 million per airplane, it was the most expensive bomber ever built. Since 1981, when the first appropriations for the plane were made, the cost of the total fleet of 132 Stealths has escalated from $37 billion to $43 billion. In comparison, the controversial B-1B bombers cost $278 million apiece and could fly farther and carry more weapons.[80] Similarly, in the Hughes-Raytheon AMRAAM (Advanced Medium Range Air-to-Air Missile) program, the cost of a single missile rose to $500,000 from an original estimate of $200,000.[81] Most new weapons programs, in fact, go through a process of continual cost escalation. In 1979 the General Accounting Office found that since 1969 the Defense Department's initial planning estimates were consistently 100 percent below the actual costs of major systems. It failed to turn up a single instance of DOD either accurately estimating or overestimating the cost of any such system.[82]

Seymour Melman argues that this tendency is endemic, a function of "cost maximization." Companies have an incentive to maximize costs because "cost-plus" is the general device for determining profit payments. The higher the costs in the base, the higher the profits in absolute terms. Melman shows that military officers and bureaucrats have an incentive to collude in such cost maximization—their prestige is measured by the size of their programs.[83] The only limits are the political acceptability of military spending to the public and Congress and to a lesser extent, the competition between the services for weapon systems.

Small contractors and suppliers also participate in this oligopolistic profit-taking, though the benefits to them are not always salutary. In many areas of subcontracting single sources prevail, resulting in exceptionally high prices to the government. Indeed, small firms continually try to find a market niche as a strategy for survival; to put it bluntly, they search for a protected position that permits them to charge excess profits. In general, however, small firms have lower profits than the large companies and face much greater risks. In addition, they are under pressure from the large oligopsonistic prime contractors, especially those that have more than one supplier. Sometimes, as a result, small firms are tempted to collude to fix prices. Gansler found that by the 1980s there existed among subcontractors more sole-source contracts, fewer suppliers, rising prices, and lengthening lead times.[84]

Cost escalation is hard on the public purse. Since each generation of weapons costs more, Congress must decide to either cut back the number purchased or up the outlay substantially. Gansler notes that each new generation of equipment costs three to five times as much as the prior one, resulting in lower levels of procurement with higher

costs. The M-1 tank cost three times as much as the M-60 tank it replaced, excluding the effect of inflation. To achieve a one-to-one replacement rate, the nation would have to triple its procurement expenditures, in dramatic contrast with the commercial sector, where costs for new generations of equipment continually fall while the products get better. For instance, prices for nondefense electronics products (excluding inflation) have plummeted over the decades, while the quality of everything from calculators to personal computers to videocassette recorders has increased many times over.[85]

Part of the excess cost to taxpayers consists of unwarranted profits received by the ACE companies. Their profits have historically been high by economywide standards, especially when the relatively low level of risk exposure is considered. (The government supplying much of the plant in which these firms operated has helped to minimize their risk even further.) From 1950 to the early 1960s, the rate of return on assets of the top aerospace companies ranged from 14 to 20 percent, except for three companies (Douglas, General Dynamics, and Lockheed) whose commercial businesses were sustaining heavy losses. These rates were substantially higher than those of nonmilitary manufacturing firms.[86]

In the period immediately after the Vietnam War, the profit record for military contractors was spottier, as it was for many American companies. Rates of return on sales were rather low. But since companies generally take on few risks and often rely upon progress payments instead of operating loans, a better measure of profit is rate of return on invested capital. Using this measure, the studies differ: they yield rated return estimates ranging from a low of 11 percent to a high of 26 percent, compared with a civilian industry rate of 15 percent. Estimates of return on equity are 16.5 percent, compared with 12.9 percent for all industry; moreover, bigger contractors tend to post higher profit rates than do the smaller ones.[87] But in general the immediate post–Vietnam War profit margins were not as remarkable as they were during the periods before.

Nevertheless, since the most recent buildup began, aerospace companies have posted healthier profit rates than manufacturing overall. For ten of the eleven years from 1976 through 1987, the aerospace industry's rate of return exceeded the U.S. manufacturing average. During the deep recession of the early 1980s, the big military contractors were protected by a surge in government orders; they made profits while the rest of the nation's durable goods makers dipped into the red. This was reflected on Wall Street: in 1987 stocks of firms making more than half of their sales to the government averaged a 25 percent annual market rate of return over the previous ten years, 60 percent higher than the average commercial rate of return.[88] Also, the reported rate of return may hide many forms of profit that would not exist without government largess—higher wages and benefits for workers and managers, for instance, or costs of doing business that are really investments in future ventures or other types of perquisites. The available figures on the profitability of commercial versus military sales within individual companies suggest that military work is more profitable. For instance, Boeing's commercial sales accounted for 62 percent of its revenues in 1983 but only 20 percent of its profits, while its military aircraft, missiles, and spacecraft sales, accounting for 43 percent of its sales, provided 78 percent of its profits. Occasionally, as in the late 1980s, pressures on the Pentagon to eliminate excess profits result in some diminution of the gap. The Aerospace Industries Association found in a 1988 study that procurement reforms cut the profitability of a sample of contracts by 23 percent.[89]

Has the militarized ACE complex made up for its extravagance by performing well on quality and timeliness? Not very often. Governmental oversight committees, scholars, and journalists have disseminated horror stories about the failure of many designs and completed weapon systems, and studies confirm that the quality of the industry's products often does not meet the Pentagon's expectations.[90] The B-1 bomber, for instance, turns out to have a number of problems that keep it grounded, including faulty flight controls and flaws in its terrain-hugging radar system, electronic warfare system, and gearbox.[91]

One of the biggest failures has been the x-ray laser, the fantastical weapon that launched the Reagan "Star Wars" program. Devised at the Lawrence Livermore National Laboratory and zealously promoted by Dr. Edward Teller, the lab's aged cold war patriarch, the beam of the x-ray laser turned out to be much less powerful when it was projected, as well as impossible to focus. The director of the lab's x-ray laser program quit in protest that his group's findings were being misrepresented, and several top young scientists followed him. Failure does not seem to have stopped the program. In late 1989 construction began on a building at Livermore to house laser and related research, and the Bush administration continues to request funding for nuclear directed-energy weapons.[92]

Not only is product quality often found wanting, but tremendous waste is incurred in production, and many weapons become obsolete before they are even produced. Such problems are far too frequent to be dismissed as normal error. Between 1954 and 1965 alone, the

United States spent some $12 billion on major projects that either never reached the production stage or were in deployment for a very short period of time.[93] In a study of thirteen major aircraft and missile programs between 1955 and 1972, the Joint Economic Committee of Congress concluded that "less than 40% produced systems of acceptable electronics performance. . . . Two of the programs were cancelled after total program costs of $2 billion were paid. . . . Two programs costing $10 billion were phased out after three years for low reliability." The committee found that the services had spent $4.1 billion on twenty-eight systems that had been abandoned before deployment, and $18.9 billion on fifteen more systems abandoned after they were deployed.[94]

Military contractors have also often had dubious success meeting the timeliness criterion. Peck and Scherer found that the average project they studied ran over its time limit by one-third, and they cite other studies suggesting time overruns of 50 to 60 percent.[95] More recently, Hughes and Raytheon are nearly three years behind schedule in delivering the $12 billion AMRAAM to the Pentagon, and Northrop's "Tacit Rainbow" antiradiation missile is one year behind schedule and has failed early flight tests.[96] Nor are the aerospace industry and the Pentagon anywhere near a "just-in-time" system, which is now so common in commercial industry. Defense Secretary Richard Cheney recently acknowledged that the Pentagon has a $103 billion inventory of spare parts, uniforms, and other supplies, many of them redundant and overstocked. The Senate Budget Committee staff gauged the overstocking at almost 30 percent of the total. Sometimes the outfitting verges on the hilarious. For instance, the navy is hoarding a 13,557-year supply of a type of machine tool used in making a circuit for its F-14 fighter.[97]

Several scholars have pointed out that the disappointing performance of the ACE complex may be structurally unavoidable. The extraordinary uncertainty—from both pressing the limits of technical knowledge and the geopolitical vagaries of demand—under which ACE firms do their planning leads them into the bidding strategy of routinely padding budgets and underestimating costs.[98] In addition, the heavy reliance on cost-plus contracting is the joint product of the bidders' risk aversion and the government's desire to prevent successful firms from making excessive profits, but it leads to a lack of incentives to minimize costs.

The McNamara reforms of the 1960s were intended to address this latter situation. But by and large, the attempt to promote efficiency in aerospace military work has been a failure. Reform has not led to frugality in weapons production and may have exacerbated the tendency to spend extravagantly on large, unnecessary weapons. Indeed, critic James Fallows believes that the attempt to fashion military procurement along "managerial" lines led to an artificial emphasis on machinery over men in military strategy. The "natural legacy of viewing war as a resource transformation process is an over-reliance on technology and an underemphasis on the intangibles of leadership and esprit," an emphasis he deplores because it often results in increasing the combat vulnerability of pilots and soldiers. Fallows shows how the radar-guided missile has forced pilots to stay in a locked pattern that leaves them open to destruction; how the battlefield TOW (Tube-launched, Optically tracked, Wire-guided) missile increases the visibility and mortality rates of gunners; and how the M-16 rifle was responsible for many unnecessary deaths in Vietnam.[99]

Yet not all the performance problems are attributable to the companies themselves. "Gold-plating" may be the result of the procuring agencies' excessive demands for performance rather than cupidity on the part of companies. Among Pentagon top managers being gauged by the change in their military budgets, the incentives to push expensive weapon systems are powerful, especially when service rivalries are involved. During the Reagan buildup, the secretary of the army was judged as successful because despite the eclipse of ground warfare by strategic and tactical air- and sea-borne weapons, his budget rose 30 percent (after inflation), compared with 26 percent for the navy and 40 percent for the air force.[100] This mentality leads, in Fallows's words, to a "culture of procurement in the Pentagon which draws the military toward new weapons because of their great cost, not in spite of it."[101]

The Resilience of the Wall

As we shall see in chapter 8, the responses of defense firms to military cutbacks have ranged from the fearful to the cynical. By now, most of them have failed so many times in commercial efforts that they know their own strengths and weaknesses and are loath to try again. Cultures, business practices, company structure, and work-force specialization constitute great barriers to an easy transition. Moreover, forty years of military boom-and-bust cycles have taught them to believe that they will be rewarded for preserving their high-tech weapon–making capability. In the interim, they are not averse to tempting

Congress and the public by dangling new "defensive" possibilities before their eyes, fantastic and expensive as they are.

Instead of taking the challenge of conversion seriously, the big defense contractors have chosen a strategy of banking on core projects, "diversifying" into military electronics, lobbying the government for commitments to new projects, and acquiring other, unrelated operations with Reagan-Bush–era military profits. The wall of separation may prove even more difficult than the Berlin Wall to tear down.

5

Innovation Goes to War

■

O N 1 July 1976 the National Air and Space Museum opened in Washington, D.C., in time for the American bicentennial celebration. Visitors during that first gala year saw a clever model of the bounty of military-led research for society. In a temporary exhibit on the first floor, visitors were invited to ponder the contribution of their tax dollars to new products. A large Styrofoam structure, lit from within and shaped like a wedding cake, coughed up golf balls from the top, like a volcano. The balls bounced down the sides, where they randomly fell into craters with labels like "gortex," "laminated skis," "insulation material," and so on. The message was obvious—see what wonderful and useful things have been harvested from this extraordinary and pioneering commitment!

In the postwar period, our society has experienced tremendous breakthroughs in technologies for computation, visualization, and communications. These new ways of doing things owe a great deal to the largesse of a government client intent on pursuing a highly automated, deterrent-based cold war. Through long-term, stable financial commitments, human and material resources were combined in hundreds of new and enlarged laboratories across the nation to make the computing, electronics, and communications revolutions that have so dramatically altered the technological landscape. In the process, the government created an impressive set of science and engineering establishments, encompassing the nation's top research universities, the national labs, dozens of military labs, and large cadres of science and engineering personnel in private companies. All of this constitutes a huge, highly specialized, public industrial technology program—a stunning anomaly for a nation so dedicated to laissez-faire.

Science-Based Weapons

Modern warfare has become science-dependent, a fact irrefutably demonstrated to millions of Americans watching on television in early 1991 the deadly accuracy of air-delivered weapons in Iraq. How it became so is a fascinating story, full of big visions, secret experiments, fits and starts, and finally, the slow amassing of an impressive array of permanent institutions dedicated to the harnessing of science and engineering in the interests of war. We have witnessed, in H. L. Nieburg's words, "the emergence of the scientist-technologist into the public cockpit."[1]

In turn, science has become increasingly war-dependent. Already by the 1960s, scientists and engineers working on military projects dominated so much of what went on under the rubric of science that, in Nieburg's view, science had become nationalized.[2] The shift was in area of interest as well as in magnitude. Before the Second World War, government expenditures on research and development, much less on basic research, were quite modest, and more than 40 percent was allocated to the Department of Agriculture.[3]

The A-bomb was the harbinger of the new era of scientific warfare—in more ways than one. It was, of course, the ultimate in manpower-saving lethal technology. It was also the product of an extraordinary collaboration among the most brilliant physicists and scientists of the day. Highly secretive and extravagantly expensive, the Manhattan Project launched in 1942 eventually employed 150,000 scientists and technicians. It was a highly risky affair—the official history of the Atomic Energy Commission admitted that the decision to conduct Enrico Fermi's chain-reaction tests under the University of Chicago's football stadium was "a gamble with a possibly catastrophic experiment in one of the most densely populated areas of the nation."[4] If the yardstick measures potency and deadliness of output, their efforts were highly successful. Indeed, for many, the A-bomb was the ultimate demonstration of the advantages of technological superiority in warfare.[5]

The crafting of the A-bomb demarcates the beginning of a historically new process. Previously, most innovations in equipment for war were adaptations of domestic or industrial technology; with the A-bomb, innovation began to be conducted in taxpayer-sponsored labs expressly devoted to military endeavors. In addition to the A-bomb, many other innovations that made vital contributions to the Allied victory—the proximity fuze, gun sights, missile technology, bomb sights, and developments in radar, echo sounding, and naviga-tion—had emerged from government-science collaborations. Over time, such explorations in weapons innovation became embedded in the many labs of a permanent military-industrial complex.

It was not always so. Before the twentieth century, weapons ad-vances were not primarily the province of specialists.[6] Inventors generally worked on craft or industry problems, often just for the love of inquiry. Occasionally their findings had military value, but rarely were they personally involved in transferring those findings to the military sector. Even late in the nineteenth century, when early aircraft pioneers worried that their experiments might wend their way into military hands, many responded as Alexander Graham Bell did: "I am not ambitious to be known as the inventor of a weapon of destruction, but I must say that the problem, simply as a problem, fascinates me, and I find my thoughts taking more and more a prac-tical form."[7]

The specters of the airplane and submarine as horribly powerful tools of war provoked the federal government to its first serious effort to organize public agencies for research and development. In 1915 President Wilson's secretary of the navy established the Department of Invention and Development. Its job was to research effective counter-weapons to that "new and terrible engine of warfare, the submarine," and he turned to Thomas Edison for help.[8] Also in 1915, Congress created the National Advisory Committee for Aeronautics to promote the growth of aviation in the United States. The challenges of building aircraft for battle—in particular, the tricky problem of hitting an enemy in or from the air with unpredictable visibility and highly angular velocities—demanded considerable contributions from mathematics and physics. Realizing that war was increasingly a matter of scientifically devised destruction, military leaders began to build a system for converting scientific and technological advances into de-signs for production.[9]

The Second World War, especially its code-breaking, aerial bomb-ing, and submarine activities, mobilized scientists as never before. Military commanders added scientific advisers to their staffs. Science and warfare were fused not only in the secret Manhattan Project but also in the many private-sector labs of defense contractors. The notion that warfare is an industrial matter was widely acknowledged; the notion that warfare also poses scientific questions was relatively new, but it was powerfully demonstrated during the war. No longer would superiority in sheer quantity of industrially produced armaments se-cure victory; now, it was equally important to win the quality battles of the arms race. And quality depended upon scientific and engineering expertise.[10]

Supervision and control of military research was for the first time concentrated at the highest levels of government. In 1940 President Roosevelt set up the National Defense Research Committee—which was later merged into the Office of Scientific Research and Development—to coordinate and supervise, under MIT's Vannevar Bush as chair, all scientific research related to warfare, including the Manhattan Project.[11] And in the first comprehensive attempt ever to evaluate new technologies under fire, a strategic bombing survey was designed and carried out with the help of a diverse group of military and foreign policy experts, economists, and businessmen. The survey team recommended an integrated peacetime establishment for the collection of intelligence data and an ongoing, forceful program of research and development.[12]

By the war's end, large cadres of scientists were working in organized settings ranging from company headquarters to national labs to national advisory committees. Among them, a consensus was developing in favor of the permanent institutionalization of the relationship between science and government. Vannevar Bush reported to the president in 1945: "There must be more and more adequate military research in peacetime. It is essential that the civilian scientists continue in peacetime some portion of those contributions to national security which they have made so effectively during the war."[13] Similar ideas were espoused by top military leaders. Eisenhower, in a memorandum to other army officers in 1946, stated it bluntly:

> The armed forces could not have won the war alone. Scientists and businessmen contributed techniques and weapons which enabled us to outwit and overwhelm the enemy. Their understanding of the Army's needs made possible the highest degree of cooperation. This pattern of integration must be translated into a peacetime counterpart which will not merely familiarize the Army with the progress made in science and industry, but draw into our planning for national security all the civilian resources which can contribute to the defense of the country.[14]

Nevertheless, great anxiety about the return of peace, as well as a return to the isolationism that had reigned between the the two world wars, left many players worried that such a conversion to peacetime military science would not take place. But the cold war, with its demands for continual innovation, would ensure that it did.

Creating the Modern Research System

The science writer David Dickson identifies three phases during the postwar period in the evolution of the modern government-dominated research system.[15] First, military initiatives and the rise of the cold war gave the navy, air force, and army research agencies a head start on nonmilitary alternatives, like the National Science Foundation (NSF). By the early 1960s each new weapon system required on average about $1 billion in R&D costs alone and roughly half of the 1.2 million American scientists and technologists were supported by the federal government budget, either directly as civil servants or indirectly through contracts with companies, foundations, or universities.[16] The second stage was the Vietnam War–era shift toward equipping a hot war followed by widespread disillusionment with the military. This era saw a significant hiatus in military-dominated research and expanded support for civilian research and development programs. In the third era, beginning with the Reagan administration and continuing through Bush's, a big new push for high-tech research on military problems filled the coffers of research labs once again.

Immediately after the Second World War, President Truman, believing the need for a continued military presence in scientific research had ended, dismantled the Office of Scientific Research and Development. Fueled by interservice rivalries and competition among groups of scientists, new organizations rapidly appeared after the war to fill the gap, many of them set up by wartime advocates of the military-scientific partnership.

Chief among these was the Office of Naval Research (ONR), established in 1946 by a navy top brass worried that the air force might dominate the military in the coming nuclear age. Even as the bill creating the ONR was signed into law in August 1946, it already had 177 contracts, totaling $24 million, with 81 laboratories, including industrial as well as university labs. The ONR, inheriting many wartime R&D labs, employed 1,000 in-house scientists by 1948. By 1949 it was supporting 1,200 projects in 200 institutions involving 3,000 scientists and 2,500 graduate students.[17] The ONR was the first federal agency to successfully provide long-term funding for *basic* scientific research (the systematic inquiry into the fundamental aspects of phenomena without specific applications in mind, such as the study of subatomic particles or genetic structures).[18] The ONR also established precedents in research management that helped shape the federal scientific research contracting system for the rest of the century. These innovations included the research contract, proposal procedures, peer or merit review, funding patterns, valuative procedures, and other operational modes, many of which were adopted later by other military and civilian agencies. The ONR aggressively funded research in universities and nonprofit organizations, sponsoring far more basic research than any other government agency during the immediate postwar period.[19]

The ONR remained the main military research agency, even after the creation in the late 1940s of the Air Force Office of Scientific Research and the Army Research Office. Its lead, however, was challenged by other models of publicly sponsored research. One, the proposal for the National Science Foundation, was laid out by Vannevar Bush in his famous report, *Science: The Endless Frontier.* Bush proposed that the NSF be responsible for funding most of the basic research in the United States after the war. He stressed that the government should provide long-term support for basic research to independent laboratories based on a merit system, which would guarantee scientists substantial latitude in determining the direction of their own work. The government meanwhile would maintain its access to state-of-the-art research and expertise in research areas relevant to its various needs.

Other visions of a national science agency competed with both the ONR and Bush versions. Sen. Harley Kilgore (Dem. -W.V.), a populist New Dealer, had pushed for a more comprehensive national science foundation in which research would be guided after the war by a broad number of national domestic concerns and research funding would be distributed on more or less democratic grounds. Military needs would be only one of several making claims on this new research institution. Bush opposed Kilgore's proposal vociferously, bolstered by others in the scientific community who feared any form of social control over their work. Bush's coalition won out. On 10 May 1950 President Truman signed the bill creating the National Science Foundation mostly along lines favored by Bush. Unfortunately, by the time of the NSF's birth, the ONR had already taken the lead role in supporting basic research in the nation, and other federal agencies had staked out much of the remaining scientific terrain for their own missions. In 1946 the Atomic Energy Commission was created, taking on the primary responsibility for nuclear energy research, much of it for military purposes. The responsibilities of the AEC were later subsumed, first by the Energy Research and Development Agency (ERDA) in the early 1970s, and then by the Department of Energy established by President Carter. The National Institutes of Health

(NIH), founded in 1930, had become the principal sponsor of bio-medical research.

One final, essential element in the system—again, a cold war product—remained to be incorporated. In 1958, on the heels of the Soviet Union's successful *Sputnik* launch into space, the Pentagon established the Defense Advanced Research Projects Agency (DARPA) to maintain U.S. technological superiority over potential adversaries and to avoid future technological surprises. DARPA displaced the ONR as the Defense Department's lead agency in sponsoring basic and advanced technology research. Its principal mandate was to pursue highly imaginative, innovative research on concepts with potentially significant defense applications. The agency has played a pioneering role in ordnance, aerospace, and computing technologies and in a number of other militarily relevant technology areas,[20] such as directed-energy weapons research (most of which was transferred to the SDI program in 1984).[21] The nation's space program was also initiated under DARPA before being transferred to the newly created National Aeronautics and Space Administration in 1959.

All of this empire building took place during an enormous upsurge in the American economy that permitted considerable elasticity in government spending. Already by 1950 highly speculative guided-missile research demanded the resources of 4,000 armed services members and 11,000 additional employees of contractors and other private organizations. But in a wealthy, expanding economy, such costs seemed insignificant.

A second phase stretches from the mid-1960s through the 1970s; as the space program was bringing NASA into prominence, civilian and military R&D spending claimed roughly equal shares of the total federal budget. NIH grew rapidly as the major sponsor of medical research and a significant force in the nation's medical school system. The Department of Agriculture continued as the major supporter of university and state agricultural experimental stations. The AEC oversaw the expanding development of civilian nuclear energy, as well as nuclear weapons research. The NSF, while still remaining a relatively small player in the nation's total R&D program, became a much more significant supporter of basic research, especially in the universities.

The first phase was a boom time for science, reaching its apogee during the Kennedy administration; the second phase was marked by a real-dollar decline in both federal R&D and basic research support, including military research spending. A slump in the status and prestige of science and a questioning of its consequences ensued. In reaction to public feeling against the Vietnam War, including strong protests against war research from within the science and engineering communities, the government shifted its focus toward using science to address social needs—for instance, tackling major health problems (cancer, heart disease), developing alternative energy sources, and protecting the environment.[22]

With the Reagan presidency, a third phase began in which broad social goals for science were eschewed. Two priorities, military strength and economic competitiveness, dominated the federal government's science and technology program. Federal funding for research and development grew very rapidly, from roughly $30 billion in 1980 to an estimated $66.7 billion by 1990—or roughly half of all R&D spending in the United States today. Most of this increase was due to the rise of military-related research and development. From 1979 to 1986, the defense portion of the federal R&D budget jumped from 49 percent to 70 percent of total federal R&D spending—an annual growth rate, in constant (1982) dollars, of nearly 9 percent. Correspondingly, civilian R&D obligations in constant dollar terms declined at a rate of almost 4 percent each year during this period.

Military R&D spending has since begun a gradual descent owing to mounting budget pressures and the unwinding of the cold war. Nevertheless, it still accounts for over 60 percent—an estimated $41 billion in fiscal 1990—of the total federal commitment to research and development in the nation. These figures include R&D spending by the Department of Energy for primarily nuclear weapons research, about 7 percent of the total. These military R&D spending figures are understated, however, because NASA programs relevant to military missions are rarely included in national defense R&D budget accounts.[23]

From Cradle to Grave

The enormous commitment to high-tech research for military purposes spans the entire invention and innovation process, following a weapons technology "from cradle to grave." The Pentagon sees its research, development, testing, and evaluation (RDT&E) system as a continuous, step-by-step cycle that moves in a structured manner from fundamental science and technology research to the more applied activities (though in reality this process is rarely linear or smooth). At the cradle end are what the Department of Defense calls its science and technology (S&T) programs. These accounted for one-quarter of its total 1991 R&D budget, or about $9 billion.[24]

The Defense Department's S&T programs include three types of activity: basic research, applied research (or exploratory development), and advanced technology development. ("Basic" and "applied" research are commonly used terms throughout the nation's science and technology system, though the boundaries between them are often quite fuzzy. "Exploratory development" and "advanced technology development" are terms that appear solely in the Pentagon's arcane R&D lexicon.) In applied research, the sponsoring agency seeks to gain the knowledge necessary to meet a specific need (such as mathematical algorithms for designing microchips). Advanced technology development involves "proofs of concepts" and demonstrations of specific technologies (such as prototypes of automated target recognition systems). The SDI program falls under this last category. In fiscal 1991, the Department of Defense spent about $1.1 billion on basic research, $2.7 billion on applied research, and $5.2 billion on advanced technology development.[25] It is in these programs that the more fundamental breakthroughs in warfare technology and the economy-shaking innovations have taken place. The other three-quarters of the Pentagon's R&D budget goes to the development, testing, and evaluation of specific systems, which are primarily carried out in private industry.

For the critical, upstream S&T program, the primary research performers are the federal government's in-house laboratories, academic institutions, and industrial research facilities. Universities pursue more of the basic research and in the process train a future generation of scientists and engineers. Industrial labs carry out design and development research aimed at paving the way for future weapon systems that will also, they hope, gel into procurement contracts. In-house labs do much of the research and development on technologies, applications, and systems of specific interest to the different services. Or, to use DOD's own terms, DOD in-house labs performed an estimated 30 percent of its basic research and 39 percent of its exploratory development research in 1990. Industry laboratories and R&D organizations performed 45 percent of DOD's applied research, but only 9 percent of basic research. Academic institutions and nonprofits picked up the rest.[26]

Universities as the Cradle

Universities are the cradle of the Pentagon's overall R&D enterprise. They performed over 57 percent of DOD's basic research in 1990, but only 10 percent of its applied research and under 5 percent of the research in advanced development technology.[27] Among the fruits of this critical early work are fundamental developments in armor and antiarmor technology, propulsion and guidance systems, satellites, surveillance, target recognition, electronic warfare, cryptography, training and war-game simulation, and C³I systems.

The inflow of substantial government money for research and educational support was an entirely new phenomenon for universities in the postwar period, and very much the product of cold war competition. In the 1950s and early 1960s, when defense missions accounted for over 80 percent of all government grants, such grants "provided a vastly greater source of research funding for university physical scientists than ever before had been available."[28] By 1968, ninety-two academic institutions were listed among the Pentagon's top 500 contractors for RDT&E programs.[29] Government support had become a habit.

The rise of military research as a university mainstay did not go unchallenged. Students, faculty, and other critics in the late 1960s opposed the role of university researchers in developing technologies employed by the military in Vietnam, such as night-vision devices, electronic sensors, and chemical defoliants. Social and peer pressure increased the reluctance of researchers to apply for military funding.[30] These protests contributed to a dramatic drop in military support for basic research in the universities. The DOD basic research budget had fallen 25 percent in real terms by 1971, and almost 50 percent by 1975. Other federal research priorities benefited from this defense slump. DOD's share of all federal basic research dropped from 20 percent in 1963 to 9 percent in 1975, while other agencies' research budgets grew. Thanks to this downturn in military support and to the expanded role of civilian agencies such as the National Science Foundation and the National Institutes of Health, universities had substantially reduced their dependency on military patronage by the mid-1970s. Dickson reports that "between 1971 and 1975, the DOD share of funding of university physics departments dropped from 32 to 19 percent, while the National Science Foundation's share increased over the same period from 19 to 35 percent. DOD support for engineering in universities dropped from 46 percent to 28 percent."[31] Ever since then, the largest share of federal research funding to universities has gone to support research in the life sciences.

As the vigilance of critics waned in the 1970s, a third, Reagan-dominated phase set off an upswing in academic defense-dependency. The infusion of "Star Wars" and other new research initiatives dramatically shifted federally funded research once again toward military priorities. Military support for academic research increased by 60 percent between 1980 and 1986, while NSF funding—and that for all agencies combined, excluding DOD—rose only 7 percent during those years.[32] DOD funding fell again after 1986, owing in part to mounting budget pressures, but Congress restored funding levels in 1989 and 1990, reflecting its "support for the early stages of R&D as a means of maintaining U.S. technological advantage."[33] In computer science, DOD had garnered more than 60 percent of all federal funding by 1988, while in engineering its share had risen to 44 percent (Table 5.1). In the 1980s the Pentagon firmly established itself as an acceptable and welcome patron of academic research. The 1991 appropriations bill passed by Congress increased technology base funding by 2 percent in real terms above the fiscal year 1990 level, and 13 percent above the Bush administration's request.

As it poured more money into universities, the Defense Department also sought to cement its academic ties through formal mechanisms whereby university officials and prominent researchers would help to shape the military research agenda consensually. In the early 1980s it created the DOD–University Forum, which brought together periodically, for three years, university presidents from most of the major institutions benefiting from DOD funds and the senior leadership of Pentagon R&D organizations. Richard D. DeLauer, undersecretary of defense for research and engineering at the time, concluded that the forum was "reasonably successful in creating an improved atmosphere of trust" and in reconfirming "the traditional mutual interdependence of the military establishment and the university community in research endeavors."[34] Other Reagan-era initiatives were the Defense University Instrumentation Program, which doled out $25 million a year to universities for the purchase of major scientific instruments in research areas of interest to the military, and the University Research Initiative, which over the 1986–87 period provided $115 million to eighty-six universities, and since 1988 has given out $85–100 million yearly, accounting for almost one-fifth of the Defense Department's academic R&D spending.[35]

Universities perform three tasks for the Pentagon in their nursing of infant technologies. First, they do much of the basic and applied

TABLE 5.1

DOD Support for University Research (in 1990 dollars)

DISCIPLINE	DOD SUPPORT FOR UNIVERSITY RESEARCH (MILLIONS $)		% SHARE OF FEDERAL $ FOR UNIVERSITY RESEARCH (1988)	
	1978	1988	DOD	NSF
Total All Fields	445	785	11	17
Life Sciences and Psychology	56	99	2	5
Physical Sciences	80	102	11	38
Astronomy	5	5	6	37
Chemistry	23	45	14	38
Physics	48	52	11	33
Environmental Sciences	94	99	22	54
Atmospheric Sciences	14	27	22	47
Geological Sciences	12	29	25	48
Oceanography	62	42	25	69
Mathematics	22	36	28	52
Computer Science	39	124	61	26
Engineering	152	321	44	27
Aeronautics and Astronautics	29	46	54	—
Chemical	6	3	5	60
Civil	2	11	26	70
Electrical	57	86	57	37
Mechanical	25	30	37	39
Metallurgy and Materials	32	126	67	13

SOURCE: *Data computed from National Science Foundation,* Federal Funds for Research and Development, Federal Obligations for Research by Agency and Detailed Field of Science/Engineering, Fiscal Years 1969–1990 *(detailed statistical tables) (Washington, D.C.: Division of Science Resources Studies, NSF, 1990).*

research that is critical to new technologies designed to dominate in both cold and hot war arenas. In the most recent buildup, military technologies based on advances in microelectronics and computing in particular were touted by Pentagon planners as "force multipliers"—for offsetting Soviet numerical superiority—and as the basis for a new generation of "smart" weaponry.[36] Consequently, university research programs in these areas gained new prominence and expanded funding. One such program explored VHSICs (very high-speed integrated circuits) to increase the information-processing power of cruise missile and precision-guided munitions. Another was DARPA's Strategic Computing Program, launched in 1983 to create a new generation of high-performance computing systems; this program poured unprecedented amounts of money into artificial intelligence, computer architecture, and microelectronics design.[37] Yet another was the Strategic Defense Initiative.

Not all of this work has been subject to normal academic rules or has remained within ivy-covered walls. Some research labs were set up with an arm's-length relationship with their host institutions. Housed in separate facilities, sometimes off-campus, quasi-academic centers like MIT's Instrumentation Laboratory or Johns Hopkins University's Applied Physics Laboratory sprouted during the postwar period, allowing university faculty and graduate students to work on classified projects with fewer constraints and behind a veil of secrecy.[38] Many Vietnam War–era protests successfully questioned the legitimacy of such secret and military-dedicated work in university laboratories, and several centers had their academic connections severed. The Stanford Research Institute became a separate, nonprofit research corporation in 1970, the University of Wisconsin phased out its administration of the Army Mathematics Research Center in 1970, and MIT spun off its Instrumentation Laboratory to become the Charles Draper Laboratory in 1973. Others kept their academic links, including the Applied Physics Lab at Johns Hopkins and the University of Southern California's Information Sciences Institute.[39]

A second task of universities laboring in the fields of the Pentagon is to provide military planners and contractors with ready access to a reserve labor force of the best scientific and engineering minds in the nation.[40] Since the Second World War many members of the academic research community have lent their expertise to military projects and policy-making bodies as consultants and advisers. Significant numbers of academic faculty have participated on a continuing basis as members or senior advisers to such organizations as the Defense Science Board, the Army Science Board, the Air Force Scientific Advisory Board, and the Naval Research Advisory Committee.[41]

The participation of "independent" university scholars in advisory capacities has also served to legitimize certain military projects, a fact that lies very much at the heart of the recent SDI debate. But not all such experts line up behind the Pentagon. Protests from physicists, mathematicians, and computer scientists about the technical viability, feasibility, rationality, and, not least, the morality of the proposed SDI system played a major role in challenging its credibility before Congress, as in the anti-ABM effort of the early 1970s. Some made personal sacrifices in order to register their protest.[42]

The third, vital task of the universities is educating and training the future generations of scientists and engineers who will staff the military's R&D system. In 1986, toward the end of the Reagan buildup, DOD provided 43 percent, 56 percent, and 33 percent, respectively, of the federal support to graduate students in mathematics, computer science, and engineering.[43] The vast expansion of engineering programs went hand in glove with the institutionalization of military research in the universities over the postwar period. Already by the mid-1960s, the air force alone was providing funding for more than one thousand doctoral candidates and many more at the master's level. Students so funded, as well as their sponsoring professors, were expected to develop their skills along lines of interest to the Pentagon. Over the decades, as this expectation became entrenched, whole subfields of training emerged around specific military technologies.[44]

The Faustian Bargain

The gradual amassing of a Pentagon-funded research establishment presented many individual scientists and engineers with what some have called a "Faustian bargain." As Spencer Klaw puts it, "Unless he is extremely careful about the fine print in the contract, the scientist who accepts government patronage may find himself morally compromised."[45] Once tapped into the Pentagon's contract pipeline, a scientist may have a difficult time disconnecting. Over time, one's research interests and priorities inevitably shift onto terrain congruent with the missions of the military.

Critics argue that excessive DOD sponsorship of academic research skews the direction of scientific research, hinders the free dissemination of knowledge and information, undermines the university's role as a place for the dispassionate and critical study of science and society, and makes universities unwitting accomplices in the immoral actions of the federal government (that is, the military).[46] While anecdotal evidence abounds, consensus about these points has been difficult to achieve, in part because it is, as David Wilson observes, "a matter of alternative histories."[47]

At the broadest policy level, the critics argue that military research and development precludes comparable research investments in vital social needs areas, such as renewable energy and the environment.[48] The academic reflection of these skewed priorities has been the growth of a two-tiered university system: certain of the sciences and engineering have lavish resources at their command and other fields, such as the humanities and many of the social sciences, are impoverished. This lopsided funding pattern and its corrosive effects on academic diversity and salary structure have worsened in the past decade.

A small number of elite universities reap the lion's share of government research grants. Of 3,400 higher education institutions in the United States, the top 100 spent 83 percent of the total federal funds for research and development.[49] This concentration is especially prevalent in DOD's academic R&D program. Pentagon agencies tend to put most of their money into a few "centers of excellence." For example, of the nation's 200 doctorate-granting computer science departments, just *five* received nearly 80 percent of DARPA's academic funding for that field from 1976 to 1989.[50] (This is a significantly greater concentration than exists at other agencies, such as the NSF.)

Within disciplines, too, the lure of generous Pentagon grants can deform the balance of what is researched and taught. Paul Forman argues that not only has military funding pulled the field of physics toward certain problem areas at the expense of others, it has even influenced the theoretical basis of the discipline.[51] Although the Defense Department accounts for only 11 percent of the federal dollars going to the physical sciences (see Table 5.1), it supplies about 30 percent of the federal support to the subfields of condensed matter and atomic physics.[52] In computer science, DOD-favored areas like artificial intelligence have seen their funding levels grow by leaps and bounds, while theory and database systems have gone without.[53] For researchers in some fields, a scientist recently complained, it is like being "homeless in a rich city."[54]

The growing divide between the haves and have-nots creates great temptations to fashion and repackage one's research interests. Scientists are usually loath to admit that the "loosely coupled and complex relationship"[55] they enjoy with their funding patrons has any effect on their choice of problems to work on. Yet federal agencies, especially those in DOD, very consciously try to influence the direction of research in the fields of science they fund.[56] Perhaps the effects are small, but they add up in the long run. J. C. R. Licklider, who was the chief architect of DARPA's computer science program, observed that although

> few are willing to claim a total independence between research goals and eventual result . . . there are many choice points that one passes through research. And if there's just a little shading and biasing of one to the right or to the left, you wind up in a pretty different place after you go through 1,000 more choice points.[57]

At the very least, military sponsorship operates as a force field does on the flow of electrons, guiding the "random motions" of researchers' choices along lines of general interest to that agency. As Richard Abrams observes: "Knowledge is power. . . . That scientific inquiry and intellectual talent should follow the leads of money and politics is in any case hardly new, either in twentieth-century America or elsewhere and at other times in history."[58]

In the Corporate Nursery

Although universities are the critical center of innovation for the nation's R&D system, they account for a relatively small fraction—3 percent—of the total amount spent by DOD on research and development. Private industry is the number-one recipient of such funds, performing approximately two-thirds—$24.7 billion in 1990—of DOD's research and development.[59] Conversely, federal agencies provide approximately one-third of all funding spent on research and development performed by industry in the United States, 82 percent of which, in 1989, came from DOD.[60] These funds are tightly targeted on a small number of firms. If we include military-related NASA and DOE funding for industrial research and development and the unreimbursed portion of independently funded research and development by industrial firms, which is ostensibly related to DOD programs, then more than one-third of all industrial research and development performed in the United States today is military-related. Such patronage reinforces the great wall of separation.

Not surprisingly, aerospace communications equipment and electronics are the ACE industries that have claimed the largest portion of federal R&D awards to industry over the postwar period and are the most dependent on federal support for their R&D activities (see Table 3.4). The biggest military contractors in these industries have also been the greatest beneficiaries of the Defense Department's R&D bonanza. Five contractors—McDonnell-Douglas, Lockheed, Martin-Marietta, Boeing, and Grumman—claimed 32 percent of DOD's total RDT&E awards in 1987, and the top twenty RDT&E contractors received 58 percent (Table 5.2). Although small, inventor-led firms have

TABLE 5.2

RDT&E Awards to Top Twenty Defense
Contractors, 1987

COMPANY*	1987 (MILLION $)	% OF TOTAL
McDonnell-Douglas	1,669	7.7
Lockheed Aircraft	1,631	7.5
Martin-Marietta	1,608	7.4
Boeing	1,224	5.6
Grumman	902	4.1
General Electric	784	3.6
Raytheon	594	2.7
TRW	557	2.6
Rockwell International	494	2.3
IBM	471	2.2
General Motors	395	1.8
Westinghouse Electric	385	1.8
Honeywell	341	1.6
General Dynamics	334	1.5
United Technologies	282	1.3
LTV	253	1.2
Unisys	176	0.8
Ford Motor	172	0.8
ITT	163	0.8
Singer	147	0.7
U.S. Total RDT&E Awards	21,809	
Share of Top 5		32.3
Share of Top 10		45.7
Share of Top 20		58.0

*Listed are only those firms in the DOD's 1988 list of its top 25 prime contractors.
SOURCE: Department of Defense, 500 Contractors Receiving the Largest Dollar Volume of Prime Contract Awards for RDT&E, 1987 (Washington, D.C.: GPO, 1989).

made many of the qualitative breakthroughs in military technology, their share of these funds has been diminishing. In the SDI program, for instance, small firms have received a much smaller share of contracts than their capabilities would warrant.[61]

The big contractors have an inside track on fashioning future military directions through their involvement on DOD and NASA advisory committees. Here contractors are able to discuss and debate, at early stages, projects in which they have a direct private interest. Furthermore, the Pentagon actually pays companies to shape future military programs and explore new technological options. Under two subsidy programs—Bids and Proposals (B&P) and Independent Research and Development (IR&D)— the Pentagon reimburses contractors for expenses incurred in responding to government requests for proposals or in preparing unsolicited proposals directed toward anticipated military needs. It also covers corporate costs for pursuing new directions in research and technologies that might result in new products with military applications.[62]

What makes this R&D activity so attractive to defense firms is that it is enormously lucrative in and of itself. About one-quarter of their sales over the postwar period have consisted of R&D contracts, which incorporate the normal rate of return allowed by the government. This benefit is enjoyed by few others in the private sector. As a result, defense firms engage in abnormally high rates of research and development. The Harvard policy analyst Lewis Branscomb reports that "for the top 78 U.S. military prime contractors, the R&D intensity ratio—meaning the ratio of R&D to sales of their military business—is, on average, 4.9 times that of the civil business of the same companies."[63]

Furthermore, this profit-making carries no risk. Through R&D contracts and "spec" reimbursements, the Pentagon spares industrial firms the sunk costs that are normally associated with the initial stages of new product development. Thus, military contractors have little reason to invest in the development of new products for civilian commercial markets, even if closely related to their military products.

McDonnell-Douglas's difficulties in competing in the civilian aircraft market in the early 1980s dramatically illustrate the seductive draw of military R&D activities. After suffering a serious drop in its commercial sales, the company decided to go for broke on the multibillion-dollar R&D contract for the C-17 military transport rather than invest up to $2 billion out of its own pocket to design a new-model commercial jetliner for a shaky market. Even if McDonnell-Douglas had not been awarded the follow-on contracts for production of the C-17, it could not lose on the DOD-subsidized investment in designing a new transport. Its experience in developing the C-17 might also prove invaluable in winning R&D and production contracts for later, more advanced versions of similar types of military aircraft, and technological spillovers might benefit future efforts in commercial aircraft design.

Winning the competition for R&D contracts for major weapon systems is often the first step toward winning follow-on production contracts. After intensive lobbying by corporate officials and the air force, McDonnell-Douglas's C-17 proposal eventually beat out Lockheed's efforts to get the military to purchase more of its C-5 aircraft. Hence, the Pentagon's targeted R&D policy gives military firms very strong incentives to continue to design, develop, and then sell to the Pentagon—and to Congress—new and ever more exotic weapon systems, with almost all expenses, from research and development to production, paid by the taxpayer.

The Spin-off Slump

The cozy relationship among universities, corporate labs, and the Pentagon has existed for over four decades. In the past, it was by and large accepted by the American public because its fruits—marvelous innovations and a strong economy—seemed so palpable. But that acceptance has begun to evaporate as fewer and fewer grand new technologies have emanated from ongoing, enormous research commitments. As a result, the nation's science and technology policy, and the government's role in it, have become hot new topics of debate in the 1990s.

It is easy to list the commercial spin-offs from military programs in the past—jet aircraft, microchips, computers, satellites, and lasers are a few of the more prominent ones. Bill Thomas argues that "some of the most fundamental products and processes that have made the United States a global industrial power have resulted from military research and development."[64] In addition to direct spin-offs, the ability of the Pentagon to create a large-scale demand for innovative products, such as for the early integrated circuits, has helped boost major new technologies out of the nursery and into commercial production.

The earlier spin-offs were remarkably unplanned. The Pentagon followed, until the 1980s, a laissez-faire policy toward the civilian industrial sector, allowing market forces to determine which technologies would be spawned from military research and development and procurement. Among the only exceptions were an ill-famed air force program during the 1950s to develop a new generation of numerically controlled machine tools, and the more successful entrepreneurial efforts by DARPA to build up the computing field during the 1960s and 1970s.

Military R&D achievements, even over the past decades, are disputed by many. Some organizational analysts believe the services are inveterately slow adopters and poor agents of invention. Over time, they argue, incrementalism silts up the truly innovative impulse. Most of the major inventions that distinguished the nuclear and aerospace age have not been succeeded by others of similarly revolutionary impact, despite the billions of dollars poured into military research. Indeed, the process has become "baroque," in the words of Mary Kaldor—innovations become esoteric and less and less militarily relevant, while performance characteristics outrun the capabilities of soldiers and pilots.[65]

The "depletionist" economists, such as Seymour Melman, Lloyd Dumas, and John Ullmann, argue that military research and development has been a net drain on the U.S. industrial base, diverting vital science and technology resources away from the civilian economy. Furthermore, design and performance incompatibilities between civilian and military uses greatly curtail spin-off. Ullmann, for example, notes that fewer than 1 percent of the eight thousand patents resulting from navy research and available for licensing are actually licensed compared with 13 percent of Department of Agriculture patents.[66]

Judith Reppy, summing up studies of the impacts of military R&D spending on productivity and patents, concludes that they "suggest little or no benefit to the civilian economy from military R&D." She concludes, however, that "we are still in the state, described by Ulrich Albrecht, in which the strongest statements to be made about spin-off are derived from a priori theoretical reasoning rather than from appeal to the evidence."[67] Our own review of the evidence leads us to believe that military research and development has artificially nurtured some technologies and industries at the expense of many others, with a net negative impact on the American economic structure in the long term.[68]

But more to the point, the slump in the stream of spin-offs has alarmed many economy watchers. According to the Office of Technology Assessment, military R&D spending has had less impact on commercial innovation as defense-related technology has grown apart from civilian technology.[69] Jay Stowsky concludes that as defense research and development has become more oriented toward esoteric weapons development, its civilian impact has been neutral to negative.[70] For instance, the circuits designed in the expensive VHSIC (very high-speed integrated circuits) program are only marginally relevant to the needs of commercial semiconductor producers.[71]

In response to the weakening link between high levels of military R&D commitments and commercial vigor in the economy, a new strategy, dubbed "dual-use" technology policy, has come to the fore. It has rapidly become the manifesto of a loose coalition of military and civilian leaders from both the Pentagon and commercial high-tech industry circles. If this marriage of military and high-tech interests succeeds in overcoming the opposition of laissez-faire ideologues in the White House and skeptical officials within the Pentagon itself, it will have major repercussions in the nation's economy and in national security in the years to come.

Dual-Use: The Pentagon's New Tack?

"Dual-use" refers to technologies that promise military superiority and have commercial potential as well. Proponents of dual-use argue that the Pentagon should support research and development that will promote both national security and economic strength for the nation. In the late 1970s the Pentagon embarked upon a series of new high-technology initiatives aimed at the commercial-military intersection. The principal dual-use technologies envisioned by the Pentagon included microelectronics, computers, telecommunications, advanced materials, aeronautical propulsion, communications satellites, airframes, machine tools, robotics, high-definition displays, complex systems engineering, and optics. Recently, even biotechnology and industrial synthetic chemistry have attracted interest.[72]

A major motive force behind dual-use is a growing preoccupation of congressional, Pentagon, and industrial officials with the declining availability of high-tech components and systems for the military. The number of small contractors and suppliers has been steadily shrinking for years. High-tech commercial firms have been moving abroad. Many vital U.S. high-tech industries have suffered stinging losses in global market shares to Japanese and European competitors, weakening them at home as well. New barriers have cropped up to prevent innovative small and medium-sized firms from entering or remaining in the military supplier market.[73]

As the domestic supplier base for critical high-tech products diminished, the Pentagon worried about its growing dependence on foreign suppliers for important defense technologies. In 1988 Avtex, a manufacturer of rayon fibers for the apparel industry, announced it was closing its plant owing to foreign competition in the clothing business. The disclosure "sent shock waves through the DOD and NASA. It was discovered that Avtex was the only producer of fibers that were critical to the production of missiles and rockets."[74]

Military technology, once considered the principal spur to commercial innovation, is now widely perceived to be falling behind its civilian counterpart. Defense analyst Jacques Gansler argues that many civilian high-tech components and systems now perform as well or better than military ones of comparable scale and complexity. They also tend to be cheaper and more reliable and can be developed much more quickly than those developed exclusively for the military.[75] Pentagon dual-use advocates believe that to retain the superiority of U.S. weaponry, the military must be able to rapidly exploit advances in commercial technologies and incorporate them into military systems. Their ambitions for dual-use strategy include strengthening the technological capabilities of suppliers of critical components and tying the nation's science and technology base more closely to military needs, through projects that accelerate the transfer of technologies from the research laboratory to military applications. In many ways, their goal is the polar opposite of spin-off; they are looking to "spin-on"—to move technologies into the military from the more advanced private sector.

What kinds of dual-use technologies are taxpayers paying for? Here one may plunge into a labyrinth of acronyms describing narrow and highly esoteric applications, but a few examples will suffice.

The precursor and model for dual-use projects was the very high-speed integrated circuit program. Begun in 1979, the program's aim is to advance the state of the art of integrated-circuit technologies relevant to military needs and to accelerate their introduction into military systems. Another major motivation, contends Glenn R. Fong, "was the need to reassert Pentagon influence over the development of semiconductor technology." By 1979 military demand accounted for only 7 percent of integrated-circuit production, compared with 70 percent in 1965.[76] Although the success of the VHSIC program has been questioned, it has quickly become a prototype for subsequent government-industry, dual-use high-tech programs.[77] There is now a follow-on to the VHSIC program; the microwave/millimeter wave monolithic integrated circuit (MIMIC) program was initiated in 1987 to develop advanced chips of gallium arsenide for use in sensors and communications. DARPA funded the MIMIC program at $67 million in 1989, $78 million in 1990, and $107 million in 1991.[78] To implement this and other such programs, DOD has forged entrepreneurial, collaborative relationships among government agencies, universities, nonprofit organizations, and private industry, in planning as well as in implementation.

Another big effort is DARPA's Strategic Computing Program, a $1 billion, multiyear program that is the military's, if not the nation's, most ambitious computer R&D effort to date—reputedly a response to Japan's fifth-generation computer program. While the program has not been as successful as had been hoped in developing artificial intelligence applications, DARPA likes to tout its successes in promoting and commercializing a new generation of superfast parallel-processing computers based on its computer architecture effort.[79]

On the commercial front, DARPA has bankrolled the Semiconductor Manufacturing Technology Program. It supports Sematech, the semiconductor industry consortium that was established to restore the commercial competitiveness of the U.S. semiconductor industry. Since 1988 DOD has allocated $100 million each year to this effort, matched by investments from the consortium's membership. Sematech is the largest and best-known example of DOD's foray into the commercial sector to promote dual-use high-tech objectives.

Another major effort of the Defense Department is its Manufacturing Technology (Mantech) Program; with a budget of $311.5 million in 1991, its purpose is to improve technologies, from machine tools to automatic machinery for making military uniforms. There are other dual-use DOD initiatives—too many to be discussed here—that often involve collaborations among the government, industry, and academia, including projects in hypersonic aircraft technology, high-performance turbine engines, advanced composite materials, x-ray lithography, high-definition television, machine tools, optoelectronics, and computer-based manufacturing technologies. *Science* magazine reports that "by the late 1980s, the Pentagon was . . . channeling hundreds of millions of dollars into generic manufacturing technologies likely to have both military and civilian applications." DOD accounts for over 40 percent of the $1.3 billion spent by the federal government on "advanced manufacturing and materials R&D."[80]

The Politics of Dual-Use

These initiatives constitute a deep penetration by the military into almost every critical high-technology development in the United States today; they could have a profound impact on the future and direction of a number of pioneering technologies. The future of dual-use initiatives is in doubt, however, because support for them depends on a fragile coalition of interests.

DARPA plays a leading role. Although all branches of the military R&D establishment have participated, DARPA has established a unique niche as DOD's flagship agency in the fostering and management of dual-use. Dual-use technology policy, in fact, has become "manifest destiny" for DARPA. The agency's documents tout the relevance of its programs to both economic competitiveness and national defense. Some DARPA officials believe that their agency has become the American equivalent of Japan's Ministry for International Trade and Industry (MITI). Indeed, one DARPA program manager has claimed that "MITI was modeled after [DARPA]. . . . It's in that sense that DARPA was started. It is very interested in applying the same sort of strategic thinking and planning for national competitiveness for manufacturing."

Congress has supported DARPA's new industrial policy bid. A small and lean organization—it has only about 160 employees and is noted for its relatively flat hierarchy—DARPA has a reputation within Congress for being one of the most effective organizations in the Pentagon's labyrinthine bureaucracy. Since 1985 it has seen its budget double, reaching over $1.2 billion in fiscal 1990 and rising to nearly $1.5 billion in 1991.[81] Its budget includes a whopping 114.3 percent increase in its spending on high-definition displays ($75 million in 1991), a doubling of support for x-ray lithography ($60 billion), $50 million for a brand new precompetitive technologies initiative, and a $20 million incremental increase in its high-performance computing research. DOD also saw its consolidated manufacturing technologies efforts expand by 84.7 percent (to $314 million) and is providing the funding for the newly formed Critical Technologies Institute ($5 million) in the White House's Office of Science and Technology Policy (OSTP).[82]

Dual-use's other principal adherents include executives in the civilian high-tech sector who are desperate for government help in the global high-tech sweepstakes. Although many either owe their start to the military or still do some business with it, they are now mainly competing against government-business coalitions in Japan and Europe. Since the early 1980s these high-tech leaders have become increasingly vocal about the need for a greater government role in maintaining the U.S. "competitive advantage" in technology.

Ironically, the clarion call for a new high-tech industrial policy was first issued by the President's Commission on Industrial Competitiveness, headed by Ronald Reagan's friend and fellow Republican John Young, the CEO of Hewlett-Packard. Established in 1984 by Reagan, the young commission's purpose was to check the momentum of Democratic calls for a comprehensive industrial policy to address the massive deindustrialization of the nation's industrial heartland over the previous years. The commission's report acknowledged the serious downturn in the U.S. economic position in the world economy and recommended that the federal government exert leadership in sustaining U.S. competitiveness. Although it got a very cool reception in the White House, the report was the precursor for many subsequent studies, all of which repeated its warnings about the rapid erosion of the competitive position of U.S. technology.[83]

What this group of high-tech executives wants, however, is a far cry from DOD's vision. They favor a new industrial policy that will protect the U.S. technological advantage in economically strategic industries. Many would prefer that leadership come from a civilian agency. At least two such vehicles have been pushed: Sen. John Glenn (Dem.-Ohio) has introduced a bill to create a civilian equivalent to DARPA, and though underfunded, the responsibilities of the National Bureau of Standards have been changed to reflect its new name, the National Institute for Standards and Technology.

But the politics look tough. While a civilian agency dedicated to promoting industrial technology may be desirable, many in the high-tech community have concluded that there is currently only one organization in the government that has the resources and experience to play the lead role in pursuing such an industrial policy—the Department of Defense. As Jacques Gansler notes, DOD is "the most politically acceptable and available organization to do it." And as the science policy writer Daniel S. Greenberg observes, "Given the absence of an alternative bankroll, that's where they [industrial technology initiatives] are bound to remain."[84]

The more serious opposition has come from an opposite corner. Despite the impressive array of political and industrial forces behind it, dual-use high-tech industrial policy has attracted strong opposition from within the Bush administration, which insists that government should not be in the business of picking technological winners and losers in private industry. In 1989 the Office of Management and Budget (OMB) tried to order DARPA to stop funding several major high-tech projects, including research on high-definition television and x-ray lithography, because they were too closely linked to civilian rather than military objectives. The OMB reportedly wanted to withdraw its support from the Sematech consortium as well.[85]

Ironically, DARPA's savior has been the Democratic Congress. Calling the elimination of these programs "economic insanity," the late Sen. John Heinz (Rep.-Penn.), Cong. Richard A. Gephardt (Dem.-Mo.), Cong. Mel Levine (Dem.-Calif.), and Cong. Norman Y. Mineta (Dem.-Calif.) sent an angry letter of protest to the White House asserting the importance of DARPA to the nation's high-tech competitiveness.[86] Congress's willingness to continually increase spending for dual-use technology programs reflects its sensitivity to certain industrial groups that no longer benefit from the military's cold war industrial policy. Some congressional leaders—most prominently, Cong. George Brown (Dem.-Calif.), chair of the House Committee on Science and Technology, and Sen. Jeff Bingaman (Dem.-N.Mex.)—appear to be intent on forging a national technology policy, although no single path has been charted. At this point, proponents of a new high-tech policy seem to be content to push their agenda piecemeal. As evidence of a possible thaw in Bush administration opposition, they point to a report on technology policy recently released by the White House and to growing interest in the notion of a critical technologies list to guide future government technology investments.[87] Under the leadership of Alan Bromley, who appears sympathetic to a more active government role in technology research, the White House Office of Science and Technology Policy has also been successful in pushing major new initiatives in high-performance computing, global change research, and math and science education, all of which grew out of studies of cross-agency panels of the Federal Coordinating Committee on Science, Engineering and Technology (FCCSET). Each of these programs is slated to receive significant funding in the White House 1992 budget request. The White House is also sponsoring a number of new studies by FCCSET panels that could lead to future cross-disciplinary research programs.[88]

Meanwhile, coming full circle, some powerful Pentagon officials are also less than enamored with the idea of a new industrial role for DOD. The services are often jealous of DARPA- or OSD- (Office of the Secretary of Defence) led technology-based initiatives, which they feel may challenge their current military mission or their war-fighting doctrine.[89] Opposition to DARPA's entrepreneurial activities prompted Pentagon top management in 1990 to fire DARPA director Craig Fields, perhaps DOD's strongest proponent of dual-use policy. As a result of the Gulf War and shrinking military budgets, many colonels and their generals are likely to call for shifting DOD's R&D funds toward short-term, explicitly military ends and away from investments in long-term generic technologies and commercial high-tech industrial ventures. Eliot Marshall writes that "Pentagon officials have privately expressed resentment at the 'earmarking' of funds by Congress and regard the growing support for industrial projects as a form of pork-barrel politics that must be stopped, particularly at a time when the overall military budget is shrinking."[90]

However, a dual-use technology policy run out of the Pentagon may enjoy renewed impetus from two amendments attached by the U.S. Senate to the 1992 Defense Authorization Act. Both were originally sponsored by Sen. Jeff Bingaman (D.-N.Mex.), a leading technology policy proponent. One of the amendments, formerly *The Advanced Manufacturing Technology Act,* provides for the creation of manufacturing extension programs to help small and medium-sized firms carry out R&D. The other amendment, formerly *The National Critical Technologies Act,* lays the basis for a full-blown dual-use technology policy with the goal of revitalizing the defense-industrial base. If adopted, these amendments will once again extend the Defense Department's influence in the civilian industrial sector.

The Limits of Dual-Use Policy

Given the economic policy paralysis of the Bush administration, not to mention its unwillingness to tackle the nation's myriad social and environmental ills, the call for a high-tech industrial policy may appear to some to be a breath of fresh air. It is a bold assertion that government must act. According to Lewis Branscomb, a former chief scientist at IBM and a proponent of dual-use policy, "The promotion of U.S. industrial technology calls for more sophisticated forms of U.S. public and private cooperation than we have known in the past."[91] He and other proponents of such a high-tech industrial policy envision government forging more effective institutional mechanisms for guiding the nation's economic future. They recommend that S&T resources be devoted to the success of such ventures. The dual-use strategy would redistribute R&D resources toward certain "strategically" important areas in the civilian economy. In Branscomb's view, the technologies targeted by such a policy are actually "multi-use," not just dual-use, in that their utility ostensibly would extend over many facets of social life. A dual-use industrial policy would seem to represent an effective counter to the military's aerospace-centered industrial policy of the past forty years while simultaneously reconciling both military and civilian technology needs.

Yet the high-tech dual-use strategy is seriously deficient in a number of ways. First, it does not address a number of critical national needs—such as protecting and cleaning up the environment, improving public infrastructure, mass transportation, occupational health and safety, and education, and developing renewable energy sources. These efforts will require carefully tailored investments in science and technology. A national industrial policy dominated by the agenda of a relatively small number of military and civilian high-tech industries is unlikely to cover all economically or socially important areas of S&T development. Without a coherent, coordinated federal policy to mediate, the industries advocating it are likely to compete with these other areas for the same resources. For example, major manufacturing sectors suffering a dearth of R&D funding—steel, textiles, and those producing alternative energy and environmental products, for example—are unlikely to be targeted by a dual-use industrial policy.[92]

In addition, the high-tech emphasis on "revolutionary," state-of-the-art innovation diverts attention and resources away from the equally important incremental improvements in process technologies and product design that need to be made; such improvements could have even greater impacts on local and regional industrial development. In the United States there are rigid, if somewhat artificial, distinctions between scientific research and different levels of applied research and development, but the Japanese do not seem to have any difficulty with calling research on process improvements "basic research."[93]

Furthermore, the persistent role of the Department of Defense as the principal federal sponsor of high-tech industrial programs is inevitably a major stumbling block to success, even on its own terms. Not all critical civilian technologies, nor all important areas of scientific inquiry, will necessarily meet the test of military relevance. Despite its intent, dual-use policy may end up hindering the transfer of technologies in precisely those areas of greatest commercial and national need. Given that the DOD has profusely funded the critical dual-use technologies behind semiconductors, supercomputers, superconductors, robotics, airframes and advanced propulsion, and advanced ceramics, it is interesting to contemplate why U.S. commercial industries in these areas are are rapidly losing ground to their Japanese and European competitors. While DOD seeks new applications for more advanced weapon systems, the Japanese and the Europeans invest in civilian and commercial enterprises. The Japanese, for example, are applying their advanced ceramics technology to cutting tools, fuel-efficient engines, power turbines, and many consumer items. Superconductor research is an integral part of Japan's magnetically levitated (Maglev) transportation program.

Ironically, the Sematech consortium may be the exception that proves the rule, though its success in improving the global performance of U.S. semiconductor firms is still unproven. After initial difficulties in working out mutually acceptable arrangements with DARPA, Sematech has been able to maintain its strict focus on commercially relevant technologies. It is unique in that DARPA has purposely remained at arm's length from the consortium, avoiding the kind of micromanagement that has characterized its involvement in most other high-tech programs.

But research and development on transferring new technologies into military systems does not enhance what the Brookings Institution economists Kenneth Flamm and Thomas McNaugher call the "middle-ground" research capabilities of civilian industrial groups, capabilities that are critical to their performance in the marketplace.[94] The technology base per se is not the real crux of the problem in technology transfer, whether to military or civilian applications. Success lies in linking generic R&D activities directly to producers of technology products. Consortia like Sematech are specifically designed to foster such a connection at the so-called precompetitive technology level.

It is at the "middle-ground" level that the divergence between military and civilian interests presents the greatest difficulties. Here, Pentagon-sponsored innovations are guided by military rather than commercial criteria in technology demonstration products. For example, the way DARPA would test a new state-of-the-art parallel-processing computer chip for a "smart" guided-munitions system is not remotely similar to how its potential for desktop or workstation computers should be tested. The lessons learned from the latter process would be much more useful for producers of business and personal computers. As Lewis Branscomb observes, "The closer a technology is to application—that is, to an artifact—the more specific are its requirements and the more unlikely is the spin-off. Guns are almost never good substitutes for butter."[95]

The history of the machine tool industry illustrates the problems with dual-use ambitions. Critics agree that the heavy hand of the military in trying to force innovations in machine tools to meet its specific needs was a major factor in the eventual decline of the commercial machine tool industry in the United States, in comparison with the Japanese and European industries. While U.S. firms concentrated on developing highly specialized and expensive tools for the military market, Japanese and European firms stole the U.S. domestic market with inexpensive, high-quality machine tools geared to the needs of commercial industry. The MIT Commission on Industrial Competitiveness argues that the problem arose out of a mismatch between the needs of the potential DOD user and commercial producers.[96]

In the final analysis, DARPA is a *military* agency, governed by the mandate to create and develop advanced technology for military systems. Although the agency prides itself on the links it has forged with commercial industry, the primary users of its programs' products remain military contractors, the military services, and the intelligence communities. In fact, during the 1980s DARPA came under congressional and internal Pentagon pressure to tie its programs more firmly to military objectives and had to shift more of its budget toward applied research and development. This pressure is most likely to increase as a consequence of the Persian Gulf conflict.

This is not to say that DARPA's efforts will not generate innovations useful to the civilian sector, but rather that most of DARPA's programs are designed primarily to satisfy military needs. It is hard to believe that DOD will be able to change its practices and focus sufficiently to be an effective guardian of the nation's civilian technology base.

In any case, DARPA's dual-use initiatives represent only a small fraction of the massive pool of R&D money at DOD's command; its budget, after all, is only 3 percent of DOD's total R&D expenditures. The serious shortage of resources for domestic technology development exists partly because most federal R&D money does not go either to DARPA or into purely civilian undertakings, but to projects in which military objectives and missions dominate. The dual-use industrial policy being touted today does not solve this fundamental problem—that the military continues to consume most of the federal R&D dollars and to crowd out civilian research.

Yet another major shortcoming of the military high-tech policy marriage is that it restricts participation in S&T policy-making to a very small number of industrial, governmental, and professional interest groups. Current national S&T policy-making offers insufficient mechanisms for public accountability and inadequate channels for input from other major stakeholders in society. Without such input, industrial and federal R&D managers will have little incentive to incorporate into their agendas concerns about, for instance, the environmental and occupational toxic effects of new production or product technologies. Moreover, while high-tech industrial policy gives lip service to the importance of the work force's involvement in technological decision-making to enhance industrial productivity, it makes few provisions for encouraging participation of this kind within industrial settings.

It is especially problematic that dual-use strategy pays no attention to the problems of economic adjustment for workers and communities dislocated by technological change—especially those problems that may be exacerbated by the dual-use policy itself—not to mention by cuts in the military budget. New manufacturing technologies could displace or de-skill large numbers of workers in the United States. Radically new products could render whole industries obsolete. While some workers might benefit in the long term, a dual-use policy makes no provisions for those who are displaced in the interim.

A dual-use policy does not guarantee that American workers and communities will be beneficiaries of taxpayer-funded high-tech R&D subsidies. Many U.S. high-tech firms are notorious for setting up their production facilities abroad. Nor does a dual-use policy adequately address the need to strengthen technical education and training programs for workers and to expand access to these programs to women, minorities, and other currently underemployed people.

It remains to be seen whether today's dual-use advocates will be successful where earlier efforts to promote a U.S. industrial policy failed. At present, their proposals, which are at best piecemeal approaches to the nation's economic ills, are the only publicly discussed alternative to the business-as-usual macroeconomic strategies of privatization and deregulation pursued by conservative economists within and around the Bush administration. But even if dual-use programs are put into place, the nation's pressing economic, environmental, and social problems still will not be adequately addressed. A narrowly conceived, military–high-tech industry S&T agenda cannot build more housing, clean up the environment, improve transportation, and upgrade the nation's infrastructure.

In chapter 9 we will suggest how some of these shortcomings of a dual-use strategy might be rectified. But first we take a look at the people whose knowledge and skills were employed in building the ACE complex—and whose energies we will need to redirect to meet other national goals.

6

Weapons of Paper
and Pen

■

PICTURE the Hughes Aircraft shop floor, where communication satellites are made. The "shop" occupies two high-ceilinged bays in an impressive ten-story building in El Segundo, California, adjacent to the Los Angeles airport. About eight thousand people work in this building, which is classified as a manufacturing facility. Every year the shop turns out between three and five satellites, the majority dedicated to military missions. Each satellite is one of a kind.

On the shop floor are a few white-coated technicians, mostly youngish men, poised around a stationary, half-assembled satellite about ten feet in diameter. They might be wielding a hand tool to mount an essential electronic component. But there are few machines in the shop and none of the assembly-line movement that characterizes most manufacturing plants. The only real pieces of large capital equipment are two simulation chambers into which completed satellites are thrust to see if they can withstand temperatures hundreds of degrees below zero. The chambers were tailor-made on site.

Altogether, about 300 people work on the shop floor. The other 7,700 employees are upstairs at desk jobs—designing satellites, ordering components, lobbying the Pentagon, and complying with government regulations. They are, in the words of one military contractor, wielding competitive "weapons of paper and pen."

The Hughes plant typifies military high-tech manufacturing. "Labor is our most important input" was a refrain we heard again and again from the contractors we interviewed. As a group, defense workers stand out from the rest of the work force: a disproportionate number of them are scientists and engineers. With the rise of cold war, new technical occupations were created in aeronautical engineering, computer science, and nuclear physics. In the blue-collar ranks as well, workers are more skilled, paid better, and assured of greater job security than their counterparts in the private sector.

But while these jobs are good, they are often vulnerable to cutbacks in defense spending. When cuts happen, the wall of separation between military and commercial markets, combined with geographical segregation, makes reemployment difficult. White- and blue-collar workers alike have often migrated long distances from their hometowns to their military-oriented jobs. Whole communities have sprung up to house and service these workers and their families. With cutbacks looming, workers and their communities now are coming face to face with the down side of having specialized skills and living in relatively isolated and concentrated communities.

Defense Job Growth

Overall, some 6 percent of the American work force is directly employed in producing for the Pentagon, not counting those whose work serves the military demands of NASA, DOE, or foreign governments. Numerically, this group is almost exactly as large as it was in 1963, after the first round of cold war buildup. Because the labor force has been growing, however, a smaller percentage of the work force is employed in defense jobs than in 1963, when this group accounted for one in ten jobs.[1] About half of today's defense workers are private-sector employees—compared with 44 percent in 1963—and the rest work for the government either as military or civilian personnel.

In the 1980s the number of workers dependent upon defense jobs jumped considerably over the previous decade. By the mid-1980s, at least 6.7 million Americans were employed in military-related jobs. Of these, 1.2 million had newly come under the defense umbrella between 1980 and 1985, an increase of 22 percent.[2] The armed services themselves received the smallest increase—5 percent, or only 110,-000 jobs. The number of civilian defense workers employed directly by the government climbed by 79,000, an increase of 6 percent. The big winner was the private sector, which gained 993,000 new jobs, an increase of 46 percent. By 1985 there were almost three defense industry workers for every two who had been there in 1980.[3]

The military buildup was a major contributor to American job growth in the 1980s. By conservative measures, it accounted for at least 17 percent of overall job growth, and certainly for a relatively high share of good jobs (gauged by pay, benefits, and working condi-tions). Employees in the manufacturing sector in particular were ben-eficiaries. Defense demand accounted for an estimated 30 percent of the growth in goods-producing industries in the first half of the dec-ade; defense spending is heavily skewed toward industrial output compared with other forms of spending. A stunning 54 percent of all defense-related private jobs created from 1980 to 1985 were in manu-facturing. A tax cut or an increase in social security benefits, in com-parison, would have generated about 20 percent more jobs. Within manufacturing, the ACE complex carried off the lion's share of the bounty; in 1990, 79 percent of DOD procurement outlays went to the aerospace, electronics, and communications industries.[4] This increase in the goods-producing share of military spending occurred twice as fast as during the Vietnam War period.

The buildup played a particularly remarkable role in making over the face of American manufacturing. Military-oriented manufacturing jobs flourished while jobs in civilian sectors were deeply cut. Al-though defense requirements, from both direct and indirect Pentagon demand, created about 600,000 new manufacturing jobs, total manu-facturing employment declined by almost one million from 1980 to 1985. For every job added in defense manufacturing, three were eliminated in nondefense plants. In durable manufacturing, long con-sidered the strongest segment of American manufacturing, total jobs fell by 680,000 despite an increase in defense-related durables jobs of 580,000. (Note that almost all of the net increase in jobs came in the durables industries.)[5] By the end of the decade, a substantial shift in the composition of manufacturing work had taken place in the United States—away from commercial work and toward military projects.

A big chunk of the job gain was concentrated in the five major defense hardware industries—aircraft, shipbuilding, ordnance, mis-siles, and communications equipment. Together, these industries added about 400,000 defense jobs, enabling them to withstand severe losses in commercial markets in the same period. But service indus-tries garnered a large share of the increase, too. For instance, the business services sector increased its military-related jobs by 96,000, up 61 percent. Wholesale trade, hotels, professional services, and the restaurant business also increased their defense-related jobs by signif-icant percentages, as did transportation, education, and repair ser-vices. These service sectors together added almost 400,000 new jobs because of DOD demand.[6]

Soldier, Sailor, Candlestick-Maker?

In the flagship plant of Sundstrand Corporation, a large military con-tractor sited in Rockford, Illinois, hundreds of people labor to make specialized parts for a high-performance fuel-injection system for mili-tary aircraft. Working quarters for white-collar and blue-collar em-ployees are separated by a lengthy corridor running down the middle of the main shed. Visitors walking down this path cannot help but be struck by the differences in the work being conducted on either side, beyond chest-high partitions.

To one's left are the machinists. Each is working at a separate workstation, using precision machine tools to stamp out or hone individual parts. No interactions between people are taking place, only between man or woman and machine. The workers are evenly dispersed across the plant floor. The actual product is clearly in evi-dence, as are carts and dollies for moving the unfinished materials from one workstation to another.

To one's right are the engineers. Their work space is occupied by a sea of desks, each piled high with paper and equipped with a computer terminal. At almost any time, a majority of the desks are unoccupied. Clumps of white-shirted engineers here and there en-gage in vigorous conversation, punctuated with gestures and refer-ences to sheaves of paper. No physical materials other than paper are in evidence, and there would be no room to push even a dolly between the workstations.

What is happening here? On the left, blue-collar workers are mak-ing the actual product that will go into the fighter plane or bomber. Theirs is craftsman's, not assembly-line, work, just as it is for the workers at the Hughes satellite facility. Their work is relatively straightforward; it follows a pattern laid out months or years before by designers and engineers and plant managers. There is little need to discuss the production process, although the workers need consid-erable skill and judgment to turn out quality parts. As a result, inter-action is minimal, and the production side of the plant offers few human conversations to compete with the quiet hum of modern machine tools.

On the right side, in contrast, engineers who are designing and improving new product and production processes are busy confer-ring, consulting, and advising on each of the myriad steps that must be taken. Teamwork is the rule here. Not all the participants in these conversations are engineers; some are managers, and some are technical people, the links backward and forward to the entire, complicated structure that designs, markets, and makes the equipment that the Pentagon wants.[7]

The occupations favored by cold war military spending are special ones. Both in the white-collar and blue-collar domains, relatively skilled people are demanded by the high-performance standards of cold war weaponry. Cold war production has been considerably less blue-collar–intensive than hot war production is. For instance, during the Korean conflict, the ratio of capital outlays to operating expenses, most of which went for labor, was about one to four. During the ensuing cold war buildup, it increased to one to one. But as the missile buildup was completed, and as R&D expenditures increased as a share of output, the white-collar labor component of aerospace began to rise, at the expense of both blue-collar labor and machinery.[8] Images of Rosie the Riveter faded as the defense work force became increasingly white, male, and well-educated.

How the military-industrial work force evolved is a story worth telling. Before the war, in the depression-ridden 1930s, this was still largely a country of farmers, laborers, professionals, and businessmen. When the Second World War began, industrial workers were easily shifted over into defense projects and their numbers grew. Thousands of women and blacks were recruited, for instance, for aircraft plants. But the war's Manhattan Project and its more sophisticated naval and air actions planted the seeds of change. As early as the 1930s, 90 percent of the aircraft industry's labor was skilled or semiskilled; but in response to wartime needs, the aircraft industry called for more highly skilled workers, precipitating conflicts with the automakers' strategy of relying on semiskilled labor.[9] Demand for engineers and certain types of scientists surged, and colleges and universities scrambled to serve the new cold war need. Engineering and science were prestigious as well as lucrative professions. In the late 1940s a college-educated engineer was more than twice as likely as an educator to make it into the higher income ranks, closely followed by scientists. Only law, medicine, and dentistry carried better prospects.[10]

The male engineer on the move was already a prominent phenomenon by 1947. Ernest Havemann and Patricia Salter West found that "the real rolling stones are the graduates who majored in engineering, 59% of whom have left their home states." Physical science majors were in second place with 49 percent, while only 38 percent of all other majors left home. Much of the movement of the college-educated took place from traditional centers toward the South and the West. The East and the Midwest sent more students to college than any other regions; combined, the two regions were home to 70 percent of the graduates surveyed (but only 56 percent of the population). The West accounted for only 10 percent.[11] College graduates went to work not just for industry but for the burgeoning Pentagon establishment. The cold war boosted Pentagon-paid jobs to 3.5 million by 1960—1 million in civilian areas and 2.5 million in military positions. In comparison, the entire Bell System, with its production subsidiary Western Electric, employed only 735,000, and General Motors employed 595,000.[12]

The rise of the cold war created dramatic shifts in the occupational composition of the defense work force. Production workers made up 74 percent of the work force in 1947, but only 54 percent by 1961. Within the engineering occupations, too, shifts began to take place. As electronic warfare gained in stature in the missiles and space era and electronics firms became prime contractors, the percentage of electronics engineers among all engineers began to rise. In the short, heady five years from 1954 to 1959, electronics engineers increased from 16 to 25 percent of all airframe engineering employees.[13]

In parallel fashion, the government also expanded the ranks of its technical personnel. By 1958 the services employed 300,000 military officers, about 11,000 of whom were assigned to R&D and procurement activities. The training of officers had advanced to the point where about 68,000 of them had bachelor's degrees in engineering and physical science, and blue ribbon committees were recommending that future officers, at a minimum, have master's degrees. In 1957 the services also employed about 43,000 civilian scientists and engineers, half of whom were engaged in research and development; another 10,000 civilians served as contract negotiators, price analysts, contract administrators, auditors, and lawyers.[14]

Over the cold war decades, scientists and engineers became relatively more dependent upon defense spending. In the early 1970s the Bureau of Labor Statistics (BLS) estimated that 48–59 percent of aeronautical engineers, 22 percent of electrical engineers, and 23–38 percent of physicists worked on military-related projects. Certain blue-collar jobs became concentrated in the defense sector, too. In 1970, 54 percent of tool and die makers, 25 percent of sheet metal workers, 19 percent of machinists and airplane mechanics, and 14 percent of draftsmen worked in military production. By the late 1970s military missions called for higher proportions of skilled and semiskilled workers—42 percent versus 28 percent—than did the rest of the economy.[15]

The Military "Scientific City"

On the northern fringe of Colorado Springs, Colorado, 1,200 Ford Aerospace employees work in a multistory office building perched on a mesa. These defense industry workers are the polar opposites of Rosie the Riveter. Totally dependent upon government military contracts, and predominantly white, male, and young, they wield no welding tools and wear no overalls. Instead, they labor over piles of paper, stopping frequently to consult and interact with personal computers linked together in a state-of-the-art network, and occasionally with each other. Most of them are working on battle management systems, funded by the SDI program. As described by one company official, they create computer models of a strategic defense system, then simulate a missile attack to test it:

> The Air Force gives team members some basic technical information, such as how quickly a sensor can detect a missile launch and how quickly that information can be sent to the command post. . . . Then systems engineers take over. They combine the weapons systems on space platforms, arrange sensor satellites, set up weapons systems on the ground, create communications structure and establish command posts. Then the nuclear threat is programmed. It can be anything from the accidental launch of a single nuclear missile to a massive attack. The attack scenarios, and possible defenses, get very complex.[16]

All this on desktop computers. Here, "weapons of paper and pen" have been supplanted by the keyboard and screen.

Employees at Ford's Colorado Springs facility are considered service industry workers, not manufacturing workers. But their work is not much different from that of the scientists and engineers in Hughes's El Segundo, California, plant or Sundstrand's Rockford, Illinois, plant. Over the postwar period, large numbers of scientists and engineers were hired by large, specialized contractor firms, where they do research and development as well as produce each successive generation of arms. As with their counterparts in commercial industry, these scientists and engineers constitute what Daniel Bell calls a corporation's internal "scientific city," where technical skill is the overriding determinant of competence for place and position.[17] Compared with managers, whose ability to win contracts and generate profits decides their fates, and blue-collar workers, whose performance requirements are more perfunctory and whose tenure is protected by union-won contracts, defense scientists and engineers face highly varied and uncertain career paths within the military-industrial complex.

Yet among the supporting casts of thousands, the ranks of scientists and engineers have grown at the expense of blue-collar workers. By 1980, the gap between military and nonmilitary manufacturing was quite striking (Table 6.1). Industries with high rates of defense-dependency and/or large defense receipts were heavily represented among those with disproportionately large shares of scientists and engineers in their work force. The missile and spacecraft industry is the most science and engineering–intensive: more than 40 percent of its work force is in these occupations, compared with less than 6 percent for manufacturing as a whole. Computing, scientific instruments, and

TABLE 6.1

Concentrations of Scientists and Engineers in Manufacturing, 1980

RANK	INDUSTRY	SCIENTISTS AND ENGINEERS (% OF TOTAL EMPLOYMENT)
1	Space Vehicles and Guided Missiles	41.19
2	Office Computing Machines	26.70
3	Engineering, Laboratory, and Scientific Instruments	26.45
4	Communications Equipment	21.86
5	Optical Instruments and Lenses	19.80
6	Industrial Organic Chemicals	19.80
7	Aircraft and Parts	18.53
8	Drugs	17.67
9	Petroleum Refining	14.62
10	Measuring and Controlling Instruments	14.14
11	Electronic Components and Assembly	12.84
12	Industrial Inorganic Chemicals	12.65
13	Plastics and Synthetic Resins	11.36
14	Engines and Turbines	10.65
15	Ordnance	10.42
	Total Manufacturing	5.82

SOURCE: *Ann Markusen, Peter Hall, and Amy Glasmeier,* High Tech America *(Boston: Unwin & Hyman, 1986), table 2.5 (based on the 1980 Occupational Employment Survey, U.S. Department of Labor).*

communications equipment follow, each with more than three times the manufacturing average.

The tremendous growth in military research and development spending during the 1980s arms buildup was a major stimulant in the demand for scientists and engineers. Between 1976 and 1986, the ranks of scientists and engineers whose primary work activity was research and development expanded by 100 percent and 90 percent respectively.[18]

Landing a new aerospace contract can result in a big chunk of new scientific and engineering jobs. In a single week of new awards in 1984, Lockheed Missiles & Space Company in Silicon Valley announced that it was hiring 2,600 people to work on the Trident ballistic missile and the MILSTAR communication satellite. Of these, 25 percent were electrical engineers and 16 percent were computer scientists.[19] During the 1980s buildup, professional, technical, and service jobs in defense-related industry increased by 82 percent, compared with only 57 percent for blue-collar precision and craft workers, and 48 percent for the less skilled operators and fabricators.[20]

In some defense industries, especially the more mature ones producing ships and tanks, blue-collar workers continue to predominate. In private shipyards, production workers may account for as much as 80 percent of the work force. In contrast, 55 percent of the employees at Hughes, a large defense electronics firm, are in technical occupations. Over 40 percent of Hughes's work force hold engineering degrees. The mix of blue-collar workers with scientists and engineers also varies with the production cycle. For instance, at Textron's Avco, on Route 128 outside Boston, the movement from the design phase into the production of a missile boosted the blue-collar share of total firm employment from 25 percent to 50 percent in just two years.[21] In the service end of the industry—where computer programmers model "Star Wars" systems, and technical assistance firms aid the installation and operation of equipment—the number of scientists and engineers can be even higher. At TRW's Washington, D.C., area systems house, two-thirds of the 1,500 employees are engineers, and at Ford Aerospace's SDI operation in Colorado Springs, virtually all of the workers are white- and pink-collar.

Occupations, like industries, continue to exhibit skewed rates of defense-dependency, according to recent studies by the Bureau of Labor Statistics (Tables 6.2 and 6.3). In 1986 the highest rates are found in the engineering professions and among aircraft assemblers and other skilled metal and electronics workers. Among scientists and engineers, aeronautical engineers top the list, followed by metallurgi-

TABLE 6.2

Selected White-, Pink-, and Gray-Collar Military-Related Occupations,
1986

OCCUPATION	MILITARY-RELATED (THOUSANDS)	TOTAL EMPLOYMENT (THOUSANDS)	MILITARY SHARE (%)
White-Collar			
Aeronautical and Astronautical Engineers	18.9	51.6	36.6
Metallurgical and Materials Engineers	2.9	17.8	16.5
Electrical and Electronics Engineers	57.0	391.5	14.6
Mechanical and Industrial Engineers	44.2	345.1	12.8
Nuclear Engineers	1.4	13.8	10.0
Purchasing Agents	14.5	184.9	7.8
Chemical Engineers	3.6	51.4	7.1
Mathematicians and Statisticians	2.1	38.2	5.4
Computer Scientists and Systems Analysts	18.7	349.7	5.3
Physicists, Astronomers, and Physical Scientists	2.2	41.7	5.2
Civil Engineers	7.4	193.1	3.8
Economists	1.0	28.9	3.5
Agricultural, Biological, and Forestry Scientists	1.4	107.5	1.3
Urban and Regional Planners	0.2	20.5	0.8
Psychologists	0.3	66.2	0.4
Pink- and Gray-Collar			
Tool Programmers and Numerical Controllers	1.6	8.8	18.1
Procurement, Planning, and Expediting Clerks	27.2	251.5	10.8
Engineering Technicians	65.1	682.9	9.5
Drafters	25.3	333.2	7.6
Guards	53.9	784.8	6.9
Pest Controllers and Assistants	2.5	43.8	5.8
Computer Programmers	25.7	463.6	5.5

TABLE 6.2 *(Continued)*

OCCUPATION	MILITARY-RELATED (THOUSANDS)	TOTAL EMPLOYMENT (THOUSANDS)	MILITARY SHARE (%)
Registered Nurses	4.6	1387.6	0.3
Cashiers	13.9	2122.5	0.7

SOURCE: *Compiled by Ann Markusen from unpublished Department of Labor (Bureau of Labor Statistics) data, 1986.*
NOTE: *We include here all the occupations that show relatively high degrees of defense-dependency in the BLS data, plus a number of occupations with low levels of such dependency for comparative purposes.*

TABLE 6.3

Selected Blue-Collar Military-Related Occupations, 1986

OCCUPATION	MILITARY-RELATED (THOUSANDS)	TOTAL EMPLOYMENT (THOUSANDS)	MILITARY SHARE (%)
Aircraft Assemblers	12.2	24.0	50.8
Electrical and Electronics Assemblers	30.0	170.1	17.6
Machinists, Metalworkers, and Shipfitters	94.8	900.0	10.5
Aircraft Mechanics and Engine Specialists	10.8	105.1	10.3
Machine Tool Operators	99.8	966.1	10.3
Welders, Cutters, Solderers, and Brazers	29.1	283.5	10.3
Inspectors, Testers, and Graders	65.7	689.9	9.5
Metal/Plastic Machine Operators	45.2	586.1	7.7
Data Processing and Electronics Repairers	8.2	109.1	7.5
Millwrights	5.8	86.2	6.7
Plumbers, Pipefitters, and Steamfitters	17.2	343.2	5.0
Sewing Machine Operators	10.9	781.6	1.4
Auto Mechanics	6.8	578.2	1.2

SOURCE: *Compiled by Ann Markusen from unpublished Department of Labor (Bureau of Labor Statistics) data, 1986.*

cal, electrical, mechanical, and nuclear engineers. Some pink- and gray-collar occupations, such as procurement, production, planning, and expediting clerks, are also favored by military outlays. These occupations are employed at rates two to three times the national average; pest controllers and technical writers also have rates in excess of the national average. Cost estimators, employment interviewers, and blue-collar supervisors are net beneficiaries, and vocational education teachers have an extraordinarily high rate of 61 percent.[22] This unique mix of occupations gives the military-industrial conversion problem a special texture.

In reality, defense-dependency rates are much higher than these figures suggest, especially for scientist and engineers. The BLS estimates of defense-dependency (Table 6.2) do not include NASA, DOE, or other non-DOD military projects, nor do they include military work for foreign governments. Adjusting for these omissions would add about 15 percent to the BLS estimates. Furthermore, the proportionality assumptions employed in translating output estimates into employment and occupational estimates undoubtedly skew the results downward.[23] We compared the BLS results for scientists and engineers with estimates generated from the self-reporting of these groups in the Survey of Scientists and Engineers (SSE), a panel study conducted by the National Science Foundation. It tracks a sample of scientists and engineers drawn from the 1980 census. Entrants to the labor force since 1980, predominantly young people, are excluded, although by 1986 they may have constituted as much as 30 percent of the occupational group. Because young workers were probably employed in disproportionately higher numbers in the defense business, their exclusion from the SSE data would have resulted by 1986 in underestimation of their presence in defense-related occupations.

We found systematic differences between the BLS and SSE data, especially at the "high" end (Table 6.4). Aeronautical and astronautical engineers in the SSE study reported a rate of dependency on DOD and NASA funding of 69 percent, compared with the 37 percent estimated by the BLS method. The SSE defense-dependency estimates exceed by four times the BLS estimates for mathematicians, physicists, and other physical scientists and are more than twice as high for electrical engineers and computer scientists. In only five of the twenty-eight occupations do the BLS figures exceed those of the SSE—industrial, chemical, petroleum, and mining engineers and agricultural scientists—and here, except for petroleum engineers, the differences are relatively small. Almost 16 percent of *all* scientists and engineers are defense-dependent, and if we exclude social, psycho-

TABLE 6.4

BLS and SSE Estimates of Occupational Defense-Dependency, 1986

OCCUPATION	BLS (% IN DEFENSE WORK)	SSE (% IN DEFENSE WORK)
Aeronautical and Astronautical Engineers	36.6	68.7
Oceanographers	n.a.[a]	50.0
Physicists and Astronomers	7.4	33.9
Electrical and Electronics Engineers	14.6	31.6
Metallurgical and Materials Engineers	16.5	24.2
Mathematicians	4.8	20.3
Physical Scientists	2.8	19.9
Mechanical Engineers	12.0	17.6
Other Engineers	14.7	17.2
Nuclear Engineers	10.0	15.8
Industrial Engineers	14.4	13.4
Computer Scientists	5.2	13.2
Atmospheric Scientists and Meteorologists	7.4	9.7
Statisticians	6.2	8.9
Civil Engineers	3.8	8.2
Chemists	4.1	7.1
Earth Scientists[b]	3.3	5.0
Chemical Engineers	7.0	5.0
Other Social Scientists	1.1	4.7
Medical Scientists	n.a.	4.3
Economists	3.5	4.3
Biologists	1.5	3.8
Sociologists and Anthropologists	n.a.	3.8
Biochemists	n.a.	3.4
Psychologists	0.4	3.1
Mining Engineers	4.3	2.7
Petroleum Engineers	3.4	0.9
Agricultural Scientists	1.5	0.8
Urban and Regional Planners	0.8	n.a.

[a]*n.a.: not available*
[b]*BLS figure includes oceanographers.*
SOURCE: *Compiled by Ann Markusen from unpublished data from the National Science Foundation's Survey of Scientists and Engineers and from the Department of Labor (Bureau of Labor Statistics).*

logical, medical, biological, and agricultural scientists, the rate reaches 18–19 percent. Even these figures are low estimates because additional scientists and engineers are employed in DOE work, in work associated with arms sales abroad, and in nonreimbursed research and development that companies do in anticipation of future Pentagon sales.[24]

Do defense-supported workers make higher wages than their civilian counterparts? For the scientists and engineers we have the data on, the answer is yes. Overall, regardless of the measure of income used, defense-supported scientists and engineers did better than their counterparts. Three measures of annual income are available in the SSE. The first is an annual salary figure recorded to adjust for academic salaries, which are normally paid on a nine-month basis. The second is total professional salary for the year, across all employers and including periods of unemployment. The third is the salary recorded for the job longest held in the previous year by the respondent. (We believe the second measure, the total professional income variable, best describes the actual earnings of these professionals.) By these measures, defense-supported scientists and engineers earned mean salaries of $46,062, $46,011, and $44,016, respectively. Which measure was used made little difference to the gap between the two groups—in all cases, nondefense salaries were 83–85 percent of defense-funded salaries.[25] The SSE findings corroborate findings from earlier decades. In the 1960s, for instance, a survey of engineering salaries showed that an engineer with ten years of experience was paid $9,300 on average by machinery-producing industries, while the aerospace industries paid $11,500.

The income differential was found to be significant statistically for all three measures, over all three years sampled (1982, 1984, and 1986) over which period it grew dramatically as the Reagan defense buildup took place. All scientists and engineers appear to have benefited, as their incomes on average jumped 44 percent from 1981 to 1985. But defense-supported workers did much better. In 1981 the mean professional income of nondefense workers was 92 percent of the mean for defense workers; in four buildup years, it fell to 85 percent. Apparently, as the demand for personnel in defense-oriented sectors grew, it pushed up wages and salaries to create a larger differential. Thus, despite the fact that younger workers were disproportionately filling new defense-created job slots in the 1980s, tight demand pushed up incomes for older workers who continued to work on defense projects.

These gaps exist within occupations, too. Aeronautical engineers not working on defense-related projects made only 93 percent of what their defense counterparts made in 1981, and this figure had decreased to 84 percent by 1985. Defense-supported aeronautical engineers enjoyed income growth of nearly 50 percent over the four-year period, compared with increases of only one-third among their nondefense counterparts. The gap was widest for mathematicians—those who chose not to work on defense projects made only three-quarters of what defense-supported mathematicians did. Such widening gaps occurred within other defense-oriented occupations in physics, astronomy, electrical engineering, and computer science. Workers in most nondefense occupations—mechanical, mining, or industrial engineers, chemists, biologists, biochemists, and even psychologists—made more on defense projects than on work for other employers.

It also appears that more lucrative graduate school research support and more "interesting" research projects draw many of the best students toward specializations in military-oriented work. One University of California professor of electrical engineering who refused on principle to take military research contracts finds that he must hustle research support for his graduate students from Pacific Bell Telephone Company; otherwise, he would have no students. The glitz associated with big bucks and leading-edge military technologies goes a long way toward explaining why American industrial and civil engineers find themselves on the low end of the totem pole—unlike their counterparts in Japan, where industrial engineering is highly respected.

The Mental Assembly Line

Many young people who majored in science or engineering in graduate school accepted jobs within the military-industrial complex because the work promised to be more interesting, creative, and challenging. For some, that promise has been kept. But for many, the hierarchical pecking order, the endless, minute design changes required by the client, and the restrictions imposed by security arrangements make their work resemble a "mental assembly line," as one former Lockheed engineer commented. Furthermore, it is not that easy to move either up or out.

There are many distinctions in a defense firm's science and engineering hierarchy, both by task and by career path. At the high end, both in salary and prestige, are the research scientists. Next come the "techy" engineers, who work on ideas, prototypes, and computer simulations and are funded by R&D, not procurement, contracts. Then come the production engineers, whose job it is to get the product out, integrating the design and prototype work with the actual assembly. The lines between strata are sometimes fuzzy—a physicist can be working on an applied project, and an electrical engineer can be doing research on basic composite materials. One vice-president distinguished between the "eggheads" at his research lab and the "can-dos" down in the business units. Career paths vary dramatically for the different strata of technical workers.

The Eggheads

Research scientists tend to be relatively immobile; they enter a defense firm as young graduate students and stay for a long time, if not a lifetime. Their work quickly becomes highly specialized and entangled with company and military secrets. To compensate, companies often treat this stratum very, very well. Every year, for instance, Pat Stone, the vice-president of Allied-Signal's Engineering Materials Research Lab in the Chicago area, hires between six and fifteen newly minted Ph.D.s, ages twenty-six to thirty—almost never any older. He searches all over the world. "If I'm a mountaineer, I'll go to Tibet, not to Mt. Whitney," he quips. "Excellence is a top priority—we try to hire as many Edward Tellers as we can." His strategy is to find the progeny of professors with reputations, much as one would look to Native Dancer as a stud for a new generation of racehorses, an analogy he uses.[26]

Defense research operations offer a number of incentives to young researchers. They stress the quality and challenge of the work, as well as the quality of the research equipment; defense firms often have machines that cost more than $1 million apiece and may not be available in universities or other industries. Some firms stress the beauty of their environment—Kaman touts its "gardens of the gods" location in Colorado Springs. Those in less attractive surroundings disparage this attraction. "Top scientists will come to the top lab no matter where it is," rebuts Morton Klein, the vice-president for business development at the Illinois Institute of Technology's Research Institute, a large defense contractor in chemical weapons research. Since most top military research labs have few competitors—two or three at most—recruiting specialized talent is not all that difficult.[27]

There are sticks as well as carrots. One manager reports that he uses the intellectual property rights issue as a deterrent to exits by his researchers. "A fellow can't do his own work if he leaves—he can only go back to college. That's why it's a stable environment here—they know they're coming for life." In his tenure, only three people had left his shop for another job, and in all cases they had had to negotiate an intellectual property agreement. "When you sign on, your rights *are* the company's—you agree to this." A scientist finds it hard to even consult on the side—managers can and do sue both the individual and the company involved.

Depending on their temperament and preference, scientists can often move up within the firm. Such moves usually involve a move to a business unit. "Some Ph.D.s end up preferring the engineering end," reports one manager, "where they can be a big fish in a little pond." As their tenure lengthens, some research scientists turn out not to be very good at the basic research end; others are more restless and want to get their hands dirty. Thus, some show their stripes as true eggheads, and others become can-dos.

Labor hoarding of the eggheads is clearly in evidence. Most defense research managers try hard to keep their scientists for competitive reasons. They do so by trying to approximate university environments. Several expressed great fear of deep spending cuts that would force them to lay off their research staffers. "A big layoff could cost you twenty-five years, two generations," worried Pat Stone of Allied-Signal. "Research labs are like mountaintops—they are slow to grow but can come down fast." Stone cited a competitor's corporate lab which got such a bad reputation from laying off almost 700 people recently that top-quality people are no longer interested in working there.[28] Defense research managers worry that such cuts may spoil their relationships with academics who supply them with students. They aim for a solid record of maintaining both stability and a talented work force to ensure a future stream of researchers. Hoarding labor also enables defense managers to respond rapidly to new opportunities. Lockheed's chairman and CEO, Daniel Tellup, bragged to a *Wall Street Journal* reporter: "At Sunnyvale, we have the Palo Alto research lab, with about a thousand scientists and four operating divisions. When we see an opportunity emerging it is amazing how we can get a program manager, pull a team together and almost overnight have a critical mass attuned to that bid."[29]

Mimicking the university culture, however, sometimes encourages too much independent thinking. A number of top research scientists have been among those who publicly question the arms race. As

Melissa Everett points out in her book about defense defectors, *Break-ing Ranks,* "Former weapons scientists have been a driving force behind the Bulletin of Atomic Scientists, the Federation of American Scientists, the Union of Concerned Scientists and numerous other lobbies and publications opposed to the nuclear arms race."[30] She reminds us that over twelve thousand scientists and engineers signed a pledge not to accept SDI research funds.

Yet most scholars who study the social psychology of military-related scientists conclude that powerful socializing forces make it difficult indeed to question the work that they do. William Broad's research on weapons scientists at the Livermore Lab details a complex set of reasons why young people, even former antiwar activists, work on nuclear weapons design: good salaries and the prospect of making a lot of money from commercialization; the belief that they are con-tributing not only to preparedness but to the creation of something new and better; the extraordinary tools and resources of the lab; intellectual curiosity; the stimulation of bright colleagues; the excite-ment of fierce competition and the prospect of notoriety; even the thrilling aura of danger and risk.[31] Most top defense scientists believe in their work and defend it vigorously. One young weapons scientist told Broad:

> I don't think I fall in that category, of working on weapons of death. We're working on weapons of life, ones that will save people from weapons of death. It's a moral decision and I believe in it very strongly. I can't understand why everybody in the world isn't working on finding ways to eliminate nuclear war. Obviously the decision to build bombs has been there for forty years and we keep getting more of them. Why not find technical solutions to a technical problem?[32]

A special language, part abstraction and part humor, helps to dis-guise the ultimate purpose of the work. Carol Cohn dissects this "technostrategic" language employed by defense intellectuals, who speak of "clean" bombs and Peacekeeper missiles. She argues that referring to the incineration of cities as "countervalue attacks," to human death as "collateral damage," and to nuclear missiles as "dam-age limitation weapons" helps to distance designers from the true aims of their projects, shifting attention to the survival of weapons rather than the survival of human beings.[33] Such abstraction even extends to how scientists refer to themselves—not as bomb makers but as "weapons designers," for instance.[34]

Nevertheless, a few scientists have gone public with their misgivings about the moral implications of their work, often changing careers because of their doubts. Everett chronicles the story of Tom Grissom, an experimental physicist at Sandia, a weapons lab in New Mexico operated on contract by Western Electric. A manager of sixty people developing state-of-the-art nuclear weapon triggers, Grissom resigned in the mid-1980s:

> The present course has become odious and alarming to me, as well as intellectually unsatisfying. I cannot accept the premise that we are any longer engaged in a labor of deterrence, with some measure of moral justification, but rather, it seems to me, merely in the self-serving perpetuation of a military-industrial establishment which by its very nature and staggering enormity must ultimately result in our own destruction. In this I can find no historical solace for my fears.

Grissom had been inspired in part by a close friend and former mentor, Gordon McClure, who had retired from the lab in 1982 and devoted himself to a second career of researching, writing, and speaking out against further weapons development. But Grissom felt isolated in leaving:

> I do not observe individuals straining against their consciences. . . . Instead, I observe people who derive enormous stimulation and personal satisfaction from technically challenging and interesting tasks, and from the exercise of power, content not to examine too closely their own motives and constantly reinforced by other like-minded individuals.[35]

Grissom, according to Everett, "believes that the compartmentalization of an institution like Sandia quite effectively keeps people inside from having to look at the meaning of their work. So does the competitive pace, the hierarchical structure of a lab and the character of an industry in which somebody else is always in charge."[36]

Moral dilemmas have driven some entrepreneurs, and the scientists and engineers who work for them, to shy away from military contracting. As Robert Noyce, a former executive of Fairchild Semiconductor, put it:

> The main reason we stayed clear of military involvement was because I thought it was an affront to any research people to say that you are not worth supporting out of real money. . . . In a sense the military funding made whores out of all the research people. You were dealing with a critic of the research you were doing who was not capable of

critiquing the work. . . . There are very few research directors anywhere in the world who are really adequate to the job . . . and they are not often career officers in the Army.[37]

The Can-Dos

From day one with a military contractor, young engineers are launched on a different trajectory from the one for research scientists. The engineers come out of college or graduate schools with great expectations. They have worked hard and developed concrete skills. In school, they have been impressed by the real-world experience of their professors, many of whom have connections with industrial firms. In a field like aeronautical engineering, these firms are bound to be military contractors. Faculty help to link up their students with summer jobs and entry-level positions, and most do not care very much whether the work is military or not.

But most young engineers are not prepared for the real world of work with a military contractor. Defense engineers face a kind of forced internal mobility, and it is not always upward. Their comparative advantage in state-of-the-art knowledge is soon used up as newer, younger, and cheaper engineers are hired. Based on their superiors' assessments of their talents, engineers soon find themselves pushed in various directions, toward the shortages the firm thinks it has. The luckier ones can make it as generic, technical types doing R&D design. For this work, they must keep up their educations, which the company often pays for, but which requires considerable additional time.

Defense work also entails extensive on-the-job training. Most engineers report learning 90 percent of what they do on the job; this is a higher percentage than for industry generally.[38] This investment by the firm in human capital encourages managers to deploy technical workers where they are most needed, to cut down on the expense of retraining. The ones who demonstrate business acumen and a keen sense of organizational politics can move up into management or supervisory positions. Defense managers report watching carefully to see which engineers demonstrate leadership skills and do not mind being judged as part of a unit and which shun responsibility for others and prefer to be graded as individuals. The former tend to be drawn up into managerial positions with considerable exposure to other operations in the firm, while the latter are encouraged to develop deep knowledge in a narrower field.

Engineers often feel baffled by the internal career ladders at their firms. As new hires, they must figure out the pecking order and politics of the company themselves, and many never do figure it out. Even those who are good at what they do and have honed their skills may end up stuck in jobs they do not enjoy.

Defense managers report considerable difficulty in shifting engineering and science personnel from military-oriented to commercial projects within the company. Those working on defense become narrowly specialized in a particular technology and find it difficult to think in the more pragmatic and wide-ranging way required on the commercial side.[39] Some companies—like Boeing, for instance—have permanent programs to encourage lateral moves from military to commercial divisions and back. But many complain that older, more narrowly specialized engineers have a particularly hard time adjusting.

Nevertheless, a fairly high degree of shifting between defense and nondefense work in the 1980s has been detected by Joshua Lerner in his analysis of the Survey of Scientists and Engineers. The movement appears to have gone in both directions, despite the considerable defense buildup. Of those engineers and scientists who worked on defense projects in 1982, almost one in four—24 percent—sampled had shifted out of defense work by 1986, a surprisingly high share for a period of intense military buildup. The majority of them, however, appear to have shifted projects within firms rather than to have moved from one firm to another. The rate of shifting *into* defense work was slightly higher: 27 percent of those who had been in civilian jobs in 1982 worked in defense in 1986. Furthermore, of those working in defense-supported jobs in 1986, 26 percent had not had such support in 1982. Rates of movement were highest among those concentrated in industries with relatively lower degrees of defense-dependency—computing and electronics, in particular. Low movement rates, on the order of 15–20 percent, were recorded for those in aircraft and ordnance. Younger workers had relatively higher rates of movement from one sector to the other; Lerner found that those who stayed with defense work tended to be relatively older and "plateaued."[40]

Movement outside of the firm, especially to the civilian high-tech sector, is much more difficult. Such movement is fairly high for the youngest engineers, some of whom have deliberately joined up with a contractor who will pay to complete their educations before they move on. But older workers have a harder time making the switch. According to Bill Bradford, executive secretary of the Seattle Professional Engineering Employees Association, "The major problem is keeping up with the state of the art, whether it's aero-astronautic, or computers, or industrial or whatever. For instance, if a man has worked for fifteen years on radar tracking, and a new technology comes along, his skills are obsolescent. He's fifty. This is a bad problem."[41]

According to one engineer, middle-range technical people, even those who have a little juice left to them," have a hard time moving to civilian firms. Even in Silicon Valley, where commercial job openings abound, engineers who have worked for large defense contractors—such as nearby Lockheed Missiles & Space, the single largest Silicon Valley employer with a staff that has fluctuated between 20,000 and 30,000—encounter considerable prejudice in local labor markets. Many could not go to a company like Hewlett-Packard, even when it is hiring like mad.

Civilian firms interviewed by the Center for Economic Conversion in Mountain View, California, report that engineers emerging from defense firms often cannot cope with a more open, cooperative culture.[42] Some prospective employers worry that engineers from big military contractors will quit their new jobs to rejoin their original company once contracts are flowing again. More commercially competitive employers worry that laid-off defense engineers and scientists will be overspecialized and untutored in cost-consciousness.[43] Such firms are looking for young hotshots who are more malleable, who can adjust easily to the commercial culture. As a result, discrimination against the restless military aerospace engineer is strong.[44]

Some defense engineers cast an envious eye at nearby civilian high-tech firms, where management is rumored to be more "enlightened," and work to be more interactive. In the product divisions of some large aerospace firms, engineers in room after room sit at desks lined up row upon row, facing the production manager. Bureaucratic structures within these firms are often carbon copies of the military services and their Pentagon civilian counterparts, created in tandem over the decades. In many defense workplaces, the type of teamwork mythologized in Lockheed's famous "Skunk Works," or observed in Sundstrand's Rockford plant is the exception rather than the rule.

There are several reasons why the work environment of military firms stifles the creativity, autonomy, and job satisfaction of their engineers. First, design changes are frequent in the continual back and forth between the military client and the company, changes over which the average engineer has little say. An engineer may have to make dozens of minor changes in a design, a process that can become quite tedious. Plus, "need to know" security restrictions keep the engineer in the dark about the rationale for such changes and about the end use of the work. One engineer reports that it was not until he read an article in *Aviation & Space Technology* that he understood the nature of the satellite project on which he was working. Making the work even more tedious is the Pentagon requirement that each engineer document thoroughly and continually every move he or she makes. Some engineers envy the degree of interaction that technicians and blue-collar workers seem to enjoy among themselves, and their ability to see their product actually get built.

The degree of specialization also is very great; each engineer is consigned to his or her own niche. Such specialization can mean sudden death when one's skills become obsolete. For instance, one unfortunate fellow at Lockheed spent over a decade developing a horizon-scanning device used in satellite stabilization. When a different technique was developed for the same purpose, he became obsolete and was soon out of a job.

Defense managers sometimes reflect out loud on the "mental assembly line." One characterizes many of his engineers as "closet people, in-and-out human computers." Some of the better ones, he says, have no social skills, ride bikes to work, bring paper bag lunches, and love to play chess. Many do not like people. It could be that these stereotypes, extensions of the image of college engineering students as "nerds," help managers avoid caring about the social environment in which engineers work and about their degree of alienation. Engineers often feel that few people, including their families, ever know or acknowledge the work they have done, a feeling reinforced by the security system that prevents defense workers from talking about their work even with their spouses or children. As a result, the alienation sometimes spreads out of the workplace. In the early 1970s a Silicon Valley psychologist coined the phrase "Lockheed syndrome"—a malaise identified by engineers' spouses who were alarmed at how completely divorced from reality their spouses had become, functioning like cogs in a mental machine.

But for all the disillusionment, most engineers in defense firms consider their work "just a job." While scientists and engineers differ from blue-collar defense workers in many ways, some feel a kinship with them. Many engineers in California firms come from blue-collar or farm families in the Midwest; a top-ranking research scientist at Kaman is a coal miner's son from West Virginia, for instance. Some have formed unions—mostly in the large facilities of companies like Boeing and McDonnell-Douglas—and collectively bargain over salaries and working conditions. Their unions include the Seattle Professional Engineering Employees Association, the Wichita Engineering

Association, the Southern California Professional Engineering Association, and the Engineers and Scientists Guild, all of which belong to the Council of Engineers and Scientists Organizations. These union efforts, however, are few and far between. Defense managers, with the support of the Pentagon, discourage professional unions by pegging salaries to the bargained wage gains of their blue-collar work force and by reinforcing the ideology of professionalism. Engineers are taught to believe that they are part of management, even though few will rise above the supervisory level.

Most engineers therefore are not as shielded from downturns as unionized shop-floor workers or their scientific brethren. In both the early 1960s and the early 1970s, large numbers of engineers found themselves on the streets because of substantial defense cuts. In California a regional recession occurred with defense cutbacks in 1963–64. Some 30,000 engineers were laid off, mostly in Silicon Valley and the Los Angeles basin, and had considerable difficulties finding reemployment.[45] In the Vietnam War build-down, unemployment among engineers increased from 0.7 percent in 1967 to 2.9 percent in 1971, an increase much greater than that for all other professions.[46]

Military-Industrial Managers

Managing military-industrial activities is different from managing an auto or steel firm because of the unusual factors that govern the military market—the peculiar client, the emphasis on technical performance, the continual pressure to innovate and tailor the product. Large military contractors are much less apt than civilian firms to turn to business schools for MBAs, particularly those whose expertise is finance. Instead, managers for military-industrial projects are often drawn from the ranks of engineers.

Engineers working on defense projects report that a considerably greater portion of their time goes to management and administration than is true for their civilian counterparts, who spend more time in production and operations.[47] Top executives encourage engineers with a knack for it to "graduate" into management ranks and sometimes pay for their retooling in MBA programs. Engineers are also drawn into management positions because of their knowledge of the technology, the product, and the production process. "Its easier to train an engineer to be a manager than a manager to understand engineering," states one aerospace engineer. Nevertheless, most of the former engineers in middle-level management at many firms have never received formal education in management, or even much training inside the firm in how to manage people. To change gears in this direction is often difficult. The intricacies of internal bureaucratic politics must be mastered. Engineers also do not often have the temperament to manage other people. As a result, some insiders say, management is often highly uneven in quality.

Some managers in military-oriented corporations are drawn from the ranks of the military itself. Absorption of former officers is common industrywide. Gordon Adams found that, from 1970 to 1979, 1,942 individuals moved between DOD or NASA and the top eight defense companies. Of these, 1,672 went from the government agencies to the companies, while 270 went the other direction. He estimates that about one-third of the civilian transfers involved staff in crucial areas of research and development, and that 24 percent of such moves placed the employees involved in positions with a conflict of interest.[48]

Most of the former officers end up at the top, in public relations, marketing, or personnel positions. At one Colorado Springs firm, 15 percent of the managers we interviewed were former military personnel, many of whom had spent portions of their military careers in the Springs and liked living there. The Washington, D.C., offices of the large contractors have even higher proportions of retired officers. Contractors want the inside information and experience with military systems and paperwork that former military officers have. But they sometimes find officers rigid and unsuited to the management style preferred in high-tech companies, which often eschew the hierarchy and excessive emphasis on formal rank that characterize the military.[49]

The malaise that affects defense engineers often extends to managers as well. Movement to other operations within the company or to other companies becomes increasingly difficult with age and experience; managers also experience a narrowing of skills and deepening specialization. Some continue to climb up the internal job ladder. But even in companies like Boeing, which has large and robust commercial as well as military divisions and a formal program for employee-initiated moves between them, it is rumored that managers must be extra qualified before they are considered for transfer to the commercial side of the business. Pay differentials compensate military-industrial managers for this relative immobility. Executives in defense firms, according to a study by the inspector general, are paid 21 percent more in salaries and bonuses than their counterparts in nondefense companies employed in similar work. In 1982 the top-paid aerospace executive was Harry Gray of United Technologies, who made a salary of $1.5 million, plus stock options of $3 million. The lowest pay for a top defense executive was Sanford McDonnell's salary of $515,000. But he is a member of the family owning a large portion of the company; his salary underrepresents his returns.[50]

The wall of separation between military and civilian industrial management is apparent in the distance maintained between the two when mergers or buy-outs marry a defense-oriented firm with a civilian one. Following the largest such takeover in the 1980s, Hughes's purchase of General Motors, Hughes top management stated that there would be few changes in the way GM did business and that it would remain relatively autonomous. By contrast, recall our account of Ford's effort to tame Ford Aerospace by insisting that the latter's southern California top-management team move to company headquarters in Dearborn, Michigan. The move was a disaster. Ford Aerospace executives kept insisting that they had to "be above the shop" to properly manage their technology-intensive business. Eventually, Ford had to let them return to Newport Beach.[51]

Blue-Collar Defense Workers

Over the years, a scarcity of blue-collar workers has been a big problem for defense employers. In early periods of intensive military demand, extraordinary efforts to recruit labor were undertaken. The major formation of labor pools for the aircraft industry took place under wartime conditions. During the First World War, for instance, the Manufacturers Aircraft Association proposed to the government officials in charge of the military draft that, in light of the industry's need for the equivalent of a small army, certain classes of workmen be either assigned to aircraft companies or held in reserve. Thus, with the government's cooperation, the number of employees in aircraft production rose from 5,000 to 175,000 in the short period of American involvement in the war.[52]

During the Second World War, shortages were so pressing that the government mounted a program to expedite the interregional migration of blue-collar workers. Between 2.5 and 6 million workers were "reemployed" in defense work by 1941; new work, especially in the aircraft industry, was heavily concentrated in Los Angeles, San Diego, and Seattle. The demand for labor set off large streams of migration. San Diego's population, for instance, grew by 20 percent in the twelve months from May 1940 to May 1941. Firms sent scouts to find out-of-state blue-collar labor, and the U.S. Employment Agency, with 1,500 local offices, helped channel labor as well.[53]

Over time, blue-collar workers have tended to reproduce themselves, so that it is now uncommon for employers to have to recruit interregionally or pay for relocation costs. Several contractors reported to us that they simply post job notices and their employees call friends and relatives to apply. Some might come from out of state, but they absorb their own moving costs.

In large part, recruitment practices have changed because the number of blue-collar workers required in military production has fallen over time. Aerospace employment, for instance, after slow but steady growth, leveled off in 1987. But the composition of the work force had changed dramatically over the post–Vietnam War period; the number of blue-collar production workers decreased as the number of white-collar scientists, engineers, and technicians increased. In 1987 there were 40 percent fewer production jobs than there had been in 1968—down to 440,000 from 738,000. Also by 1987, production workers represented only 45 percent of all aerospace employment, down from 53 percent in 1968.[54] This steep decline occurred because each new addition to the arsenal was produced in fewer and fewer numbers. The military budget for aircraft went up 75 percent—and that for missiles 91 percent—between 1980 and 1984. But the actual number of aircraft and missiles produced increased only 9 percent and 6 percent, respectively.[55]

Defense-related blue-collar employment had been declining for some time. A study for the International Association of Machinists and Aerospace Workers (IAM) found that the number of machinist jobs in military industries actually declined by 12 percent between 1975 and 1978, despite the beginnings of a military buildup. As of 1979, only 13 percent of IAM members were working in military production, far fewer than in earlier decades.[56] Because batch manufacturing has dominated defense production, and because Pentagon leaders have required experimental automation in contractor plants, direct labor costs, or "touch labor," make up only about 10 percent of total manufacturing costs, in contrast to 60–70 percent in the indirect activities of planning, scheduling, and controlling operations and people.[57]

Thus, the 1980s buildup did not boost blue-collar employment as much as overall spending hikes would suggest. Nevertheless, some individual blue-collar occupations continue to be unusually military-oriented. As illustrated in Table 6.3, shipfitters are estimated to be 53 percent defense-dependent, while riggers, machinists, tool and die makers, and machine tool operators are three times as apt to be working on military projects as the average American worker. By comparison, very small percentages of sewing machine operators and auto mechanics are dependent upon military spending—1.4 and 1.2 percent, respectively. The occupations shown in Table 6.3 account for almost half a million jobs in military manufacturing, but many other blue-collar workers can be found in industries not included. These rates of defense-dependency are relatively low, but it should be noted that they are underestimated because of the omission of NASA, DOE, and foreign military sales–related work.

Blue-collar defense workers tend to be more highly skilled than their counterparts in civilian industry. Defense companies have almost no automaker-style assembly lines. Workers craft single items and are often experts; they receive a considerable amount of on-the-job training. Some report a pride in working with specialized equipment. Some are restive under the tough security regulations and the rather strict and authoritarian nature of work in defense industries. On the whole, they work under different conditions than do their white-collar coworkers. For one, the production runs for modern weapons create feast-or-famine working lives. Even when commitments are long-term, as they are in five-year shipbuilding plans, changes in policy and budget constraints often result in short-term blue-collar employment swings of large magnitude. Unlike scientists and engineers, production workers are less likely to be "hoarded" when companies experience downturns in their orders. (The only exception appears to be experienced, skilled machinists, who are often in such short supply that firms are reluctant to lay them off temporarily.)[58] Labor turnover rates in military-serving shipyards run as high as 75 percent per year.[59] For another, the enthusiasm of the Pentagon and defense firms for automation introduces great uncertainty and deep blue-collar job cuts into the industry. The Pentagon has been an active proponent of automating technologies in the aerospace industry, despite the small production runs and high degree of craftsmanship involved. The big aerospace companies were among the first to experiment with the "factory of the future," and their experiments were underwritten by DOD.[60] This interest is ongoing. In 1988 Lockheed announced that it was installing in its Burbank, California, plant a $3.5 million computer-aided layout and fabrication facility that will cut the time required to make sheet-metal airplane parts from two months to two days. Completely computer-controlled, the system will run presses and metal cutters on the factory floor from remote workstations, replacing machinists.[61] Many workers also have been displaced by the automation of inventory control and testing procedures throughout the aerospace industry.

Unions ameliorate these problems a great deal. They protect workers from arbitrary layoffs and have pressed for layoff prenotification. Thanks to their unions, blue-collar workers in defense-dependent industries do appear to make better wages than their counterparts in civilian production. In 1988 hourly earnings averaged $11.59 in shipbuilding, $11.31 in ordnance, $12.26 in radio and television communications equipment, $13.60 in aircraft and parts, and $10.08 in engineering and scientific instruments. These wages exceeded the average of $9.29 an hour for workers across all nonfarm industries.[62] Some of this differential may be explained by the relatively higher levels of education and skill among workers in these industries. In addition, firms making military sales appear to be able to pass on higher labor costs to their customers.[63]

Health and safety issues are a special problem for defense workers. Many working in nuclear weapons facilities are at continual risk, and path-breaking work has been done by some unions such as the Oil, Chemical, and Atomic Workers International Union (OCAW) in bargaining for worker protection.[64] At aircraft and electronics plants, where many special materials, metals, and glues are used, exposure to toxic substances is also a serious risk. Here, too, the various unions have taken the initiative. At the General Dynamics M-1 tank plant in Warren, Michigan, several workers passed out over a two-year period from exposure to FC113, a fluorocarbon solvent used to flush out tank hulls. Despite complaints to the company and to the Occupational Safety and Health Administration (OSHA) by the United Auto Workers, another worker died from a similar exposure in late 1983. This event resulted in citations for willful violation by General Dynamics and a criminal investigation by the state's attorney general. Blue-collar workers face physical danger, too. In early 1983, UAW member Russ Joyner was crushed to death while rolling up tank tread at the Aberdeen, Maryland, proving grounds, despite previous warnings by the union that such a tragedy could occur. General Dynamics was again fined by OSHA.[65]

Antiunion attitudes are particularly virulent among managers in military-industrial companies. Many aircraft plants are unionized, dating back to historic bargains struck during the Second World War when firms agreed to let the unions in, in return for a no-strike pledge. Some companies have tried to do an end run around their unions by moving to newer, nonunion sites. Pratt & Whitney, for instance, built a new aircraft engine facility in Maine in 1979, lowering its labor costs by 25 percent and receiving a $2.1 million tax break into the bargain. General Electric relocated engine production to two nonunion sites— Vermont in the 1960s and Kentucky in 1980. The moves were also driven by a desire to avoid work stoppages, which are widely believed to concern management more than wages because of their effect on timeliness and performance. Between 1927 and 1959 there were about 600 work stoppages in the aircraft industry, mostly among West Coast airframe firms.[66] The newer defense electronics firms are less apt to be unionized, and most are militantly opposed to unions. The Pentagon is an active collaborator in union-busting. It has encouraged companies to build new plants or yards in nonunion locales, often at taxpayer expense.

The Pentagon also put considerable pressure on contractors in the 1980s to cut costs. In 1982 Secretary of the Air Force Verne Orr directed his subordinates to make every effort to keep wage increases in line, stating that he was "fully prepared to accept work stoppages in some of our weapon acquisition programs, if that is what it takes."[67] Later that year, Defense Secretary Caspar Weinberger stated that the Defense Department "is not going to be blackmailed" into military weapons contracts with excessive labor costs.[68] Within a year, the air force was threatening to withhold federal contracts from firms that could not demonstrate that they had labor costs under control and called the CEOs of major aerospace companies to a meeting in Washington to discuss the matter.[69] As a result, many large contractors have successfully demanded that their unions accept two-tiered wage systems in which new hires enter their jobs with a lower wage structure than their already employed counterparts. Lockheed was later accused by the government of overcharging because it billed the Pentagon at the original proposal rates, not for the much lower wages it actually paid.[70]

The layoffs that occur after weapons programs are completed or cancelled are a nightmare for blue-collar workers. Many workers are laid off at one time, and the layoffs are concentrated within regional labor markets, decreasing the workers' chances of rapid reabsorption into those markets. The end of the B-1 bomber program alone resulted in the layoff of 12,000 workers.[71] In an area like Los Angeles it is easier to find work with another defense contractor, though not if all firms are experiencing layoffs at once. But often layoffs are concentrated in communities with few other industrial employers, compounding the employment problem. These limited options are evident in the willingness of blue-collar workers to migrate at their own expense to new jobs. In the Vietnam War–era aircraft engine boom of

1964–67, researchers found that 14 percent of the new factory recruits to New England firms came from outside the region—a total of 10,000 blue-collar migrants.[72]

One woman's story, reported recently in *Business Week*, is instructive. Gail Sibley, a thirty-seven-year-old single mother in Montville, Connecticut, was laid off in March 1990 from the local United Nuclear Corporations plant, which makes nuclear submarine reactors, when the navy awarded the work to Babcock and Wilcox in Lynchburg, Virginia. Sibley was making $31,000 a year as a programmer of electronic inspection systems. Almost immediately she had difficulty meeting her mortgage payments and paying her son's medical bills out of a weekly unemployment check of $260. When interviewed, Sibley said she was willing to relocate but there was not much demand for her skills.[73]

For most blue-collar workers, as for most engineers, defense work is not just a job. Many affirm that it is a good job, and some feel they are contributing to their country's defense. Experience with conversion politics shows that workers and their unions are willing to support conversion even though they support a strong defense. As Dan St. Clair, a UAW assembler of missile launchers at an FMC Corporation plant in Minneapolis, puts it: "I'm not ashamed of being a defense worker. We take a great deal of pride in our work. I'm not a pacifist. I believe in a strong defense."[74] But knowing that defense contracts will not last forever, St. Clair has worked for five years on the Minnesota Task Force on Economic Conversion, a group formed to find ways to prevent plants from closing when defense requirements change. At the UAW-organized General Dynamics plant in Warren, Michigan, the union waged a successful campaign to keep the M-1 tank in production, but local union officials say they are interested in seeing if the plant could make bulldozers or prefabricated housing in the future.[75]

Many do worry about producing deadly equipment. In one survey of weapons industry workers, 63 percent expressed ambivalence or moral discomfort with their work.[76] A few have decided to quit. Louis Raymond, a supervisor at the salvage yard of the General Dynamics Electric Boat shipyard in Groton, Connecticut, and a devout Catholic, had become opposed to the nuclear arms race and left his job in 1983 in what he described to Melissa Everett as the major crisis in his life. With no savings and a wife and four children, Raymond fell back on his skills as a carpenter to become self-employed.[77] Tony Mazzocchi, an official with OCAW, says of his members working in weapons plants, "I never met a defense worker who would not rather be working on something else."[78]

Rosie the Riveter and Her Minority Coworkers

Throughout most of human history, war-making has been the job of men. Women have been consigned to roles as camp followers, nurses, hearth watchers, and victims of rape and pillage. What has happened as the labor input into war-making has moved from the front line back into provisioning? Has the new high-tech ability to keep soldiers out of combat led to more women being engaged in defense work?

Many women do work for the defense-related industries. Roughly 232,000 women worked for military contractors in 1985.[79] Because of the paperwork required by Pentagon overseers, defense industries have disproportionately high numbers of clerical workers compared with other manufacturing industries. These jobs are primarily filled by women. In the Los Angeles area, women constitute between 80 and 90 percent of all defense industry clericals, but only 4 percent of professionals and 7 percent of managers.[80]

Overall, because of the high concentrations of scientific, engineering, and blue-collar jobs, defense-related industries employ relatively fewer women than do other manufacturing industries.[81] Although many women worked as "Rosie the Riveters" in the Second World War, the end of hot war and the veterans' return home ejected most blue-collar women from the aircraft industry. On the aerospace shop floor, women are now less evident than they are in many other industries, including autos and consumer electronics.

The same is true in the science and engineering ranks. SSE data from 1986 reveals that women constituted only 9 percent of scientists and engineers supported by DOD or NASA funds, though they accounted for 15 percent of all scientists and engineers generally. Occupation by occupation, women, minorities, and foreign-born workers, underrepresented to begin with, were also more apt in the 1980s to eventually leave defense work than were their white, male, native-born counterparts.[82]

Women's underrepresentation in these defense jobs is in part a product of their low participation rates in science and engineering generally. A number of excellent studies show that discrimination in college and graduate-level funding and in hiring and promotion prac-

163

tices are also major contributors to the gender gap. Over time, however, the number of women receiving degrees and holding jobs in these fields has increased, albeit more in the less defense-dependent fields, such as computer science and life sciences, than in fields like aeronautical engineering or physics.[83]

Another look at the 1986 SSE data reveals that, because women are more apt to be underrepresented among defense-supported scientists and engineers, who are paid more than their nondefense counterparts, the gap between women's and men's salaries is even higher in these occupations than it otherwise would be. Women's earnings in defense-dependent industries like aerospace and communications lag behind men's even more than in the economy as a whole. In the Los Angeles aerospace industry, full-time working women make sixty-one cents for every dollar earned by men, and in the communications equipment industry, they make only 51 percent of what men do. This compares unfavorably with 64 percent for the economy as a whole.[84]

Minorities are also relatively underrepresented in the defense work force: constituting about 18 percent of the working population, they made up 15 percent of defense-supported scientists and engineers in 1982, up from 5.5 percent in 1976. Most of these gains were made by Asians, who accounted for 9.4 percent of defense-supported scientists and engineers; they make up 2 percent of the general work force. Underrepresentation of minorities in defense science and engineering jobs appears to be almost entirely a function of the exclusion of Latinos, African-Americans, and Native Americans from science and engineering occupations generally, in turn a function of both discrimination and relatively poor educational levels.[85] In 1988 only 3 percent of all scientists and engineers were Afro-American, though their rate of participation in the work force was more than three times that figure.

Once a minority person receives training, however, he or she is as apt to be hired by defense employers as by any other. In fact, Asian and black men have slightly higher rates of employment in defense jobs than they do in nondefense ones; women of all races and ethnicities, including Asian, do better outside of defense. Minority men seem to benefit at the hiring stage from government affirmative action practices, which are not as effective in eliminating race and gender discrimination at the prior stage of education and training.

Community groups have complained about the small number of women and minorities in defense industrial jobs, and some have pressed Congress to act more aggressively. One of their points is that people of color are overrepresented in the frontline military service, where the pay is low, but underrepresented on the higher paying industrial side.[86] Recently, the number and percentage of African-Americans recruited into the military services has actually been declining, but there has been no appreciable opening up of new opportunities for them, in either defense or other sectors.[87]

Redeployed Defense Workers—What Are Their Options?

The end of the arms race presents the nation with exciting though difficult choices about how to redeploy the defense work force. A major concern is the shift of resources—plants, bases, and labor—out of one set of industries and product lines and into others. Since military spending is heavily concentrated in certain industries, occupations, regions, and cities, peace threatens considerable displacement and community distress unless a concerted effort to plan and smooth the transition is made.

In 1988, 6,572,000 people worked for the military or for military contractors.[88] Each $1 billion of defense spending generates about 50,000 jobs.[89] With cuts looming, as many as 1 million civilian workers could lose their defense-related jobs between 1989 and 1995, including 830,000 to 1,066,000 in the private sector. The losses would be heavily concentrated by industry: in communications equipment, employment is predicted to decline from 349,600 in 1988 to 213,400 in 1994; guided missiles, from 134,900 to 105,100; and shipbuilding, from 102,300 to 61,700. To that must be added 320,000 to 550,000 active duty military and DOD personnel who are to be shed.[90] Hence, the nation could face structural unemployment comparable to the unemployment of the early 1980s in the industrial heartland.

Can defense-related workers find other jobs if their plants are closed? Many have considerable advantages to bring to new jobs, particularly the skills they have acquired through DOD-financed education and through working on sophisticated designs and weapon systems. On the other hand, they are often overqualified or overly specialized for jobs in the civilian sector. They may be stuck in communities far from the locus of new job generation. They may need new skills—in business management, in marketing, or in technical areas—to move into the best civilian jobs.

Some sense of what is likely to happen to professional workers in a defense build-down can be glimpsed in the responses of Seattle-area Boeing employees when their ranks were depleted in the early 1970s as a result of simultaneous drops in military and civilian orders. The work force fell from 100,000 to 30,000. Engineers showed considerable versatility in responding to the crisis. Some moved into non-defense work at Boeing. Some migrated to other regions, although many were keen on the Seattle area and could not sell their houses in any case. Of these, some started new firms to pursue everything from medical technology to computer-related activities. Still others just pumped gas and waited for the aerospace market to boom again. The wait was long, but the jobs eventually created were lucrative and called on their old skills.

Few studies have been done of the experiences of laid-off military-industrial scientists and engineers. One illuminating survey was done eight months after the cancellation of the Dyna-Soar contract in Seattle in the early 1970s; some 77 percent of the 5,229 employees displaced responded. Of these, 30 percent were still unemployed. Professionals of all occupational groups had the lowest unemployment rate (17 percent) and the shortest unemployment stints (twelve weeks), especially compared with blue-collar workers. But among the reemployed there appeared to be considerable downgrading in the skills needed for their new jobs. The number of men working as professionals was down 30 percent, most noticeably among workers over thirty-five. Younger workers found jobs relatively more rapidly and were more apt to find them outside of the defense sector.[91]

When big cuts do come, as they have in the past, it is the older, more specialized engineers and scientists among the technical staff who have the most difficult time. In the big layoffs at Lockheed in the late 1960s and early 1970s, senior engineers with larger salaries were disproportionately dismissed. Many were shocked to be treated that way—in the good times there had never been any pressure to weed out staff. Some of those laid off were eventually replaced by younger engineers. Some voluntarily left to become teachers and salesmen. Most never found their way back into engineering.[92]

Despite demonstrable ability to find new jobs, at least in the long run, engineers may find displacement to be particularly traumatic. Many have never experienced layoffs or job insecurity. A surprising majority have stayed with the same firm over long periods of time.[93] For instance, among the scientists and engineers who reported working on military projects in 1982, Lerner found that two-thirds had been working for the same employer in 1976. Not as many nondefense workers displayed this degree of firm attachment in 1982. Internal labor markets, rather than external ones, have provided engineers with most of their opportunities to change jobs. But in the future, given the posture of many of the larger defense contractors, movement within a firm may not be as easily accomplished. To the extent that jobs within the same firm are not forthcoming, white-collar defense workers face a tough transition. They may have to accept considerable wage cuts in moving to other jobs, and they may have to uproot themselves as well.

What will make the adjustment particularly difficult in the 1990s is the large-scale nature of the engineering layoffs that are likely to happen. The Institute of Electrical and Electronics Engineers predicts that 55,000 of some 240,000 defense industry engineers could lose their jobs by 1995, on top of the thousands laid off already. Job insecurity could become a more common experience for these workers as they bounce around in a more competitive labor market. Donald Hicks, a defense industry consultant and a former Pentagon and Northrop official, puts it darkly and succinctly: "An awful lot of engineers and scientists will be driving cabs."[94]

The glut of engineers on a depressed labor market could drive many to accept inferior jobs or try new occupations. For some, it has happened already. Bruce Hill, a forty-two-year-old computer systems engineer, was laid off in February 1988 from Lockheed's subsidiary in Austin, Texas. He subsequently worked at Raytheon in Boston, at E-Systems back in Texas, and then for the FMC Corporation in Silicon Valley, where he works on the Bradley armored vehicle. Hill's income has plunged by one-third, and he lost tens of thousands of dollars on his home in Texas when forced to sell it. Hill told a *Business Week* reporter in June 1990 that he has decided to try working for the government as a safety engineer if he is laid off again. The job does not pay well, but it is protected from layoffs.[95] But even jobs with the government may be hard to come by. In early 1990, Defense Secretary Richard Cheney announced a civilian hiring freeze, noting that the Pentagon would probably eliminate more than 50,000 jobs over the next year.[96]

R&D work may be more protected. Outlays for procurement, which had increased 78 percent in real terms, peaked in 1987, falling 9 percent from 1987 through 1990. RDT&E outlays rose 88 percent to peak in 1989; they fell 5 percent thereafter. Gordon Adams reports that there is general support for continuing high levels of funding for defense research and development to maintain the defense technology base and to ensure the retention of the option to produce the next generation of hardware, as a hedge against international change.[97]

Blue-collar workers will face greater difficulties than their white-collar coworkers. Both the more skilled crafts-workers and the less skilled occupations face similar problems. In Marion Anderson's relatively optimistic simulations of the impact on jobs of switching from military to conversion industries, such as solar energy, gasohol, railroad equipment, fishing vessels, and professional and educational services, she found that blue-collar crafts-workers were the only occupation that would still suffer net job loss—6,300 workers for every $10 billion of cuts.[98] And although the defense industry has relatively high numbers of scientists, engineers, and crafts-workers compared with manufacturing as a whole, the bulk of the defense work force is still found in less skilled positions. In 1983 the Congressional Budget Office estimated that 58 percent of the defense industry's work force consisted of assemblers, operatives, laborers, and service, sales, and clerical workers. Blue-collar workers could absorb the bulk of the job cuts as whole weapon systems are cancelled.[99]

Blue-collar adjustment is particularly problematic in a recessionary economy. In past build-downs, relatively robust civilian sectors absorbed excess labor and put people to work. The biggest problem was coping with returning veterans, whose claims on their jobs sometimes put newer workers out on the street. It was this problem that Walter Reuther's famous conversion program was meant to address: "The answer to the problem of postwar employment is not the fighting soldier against the production soldier."[100]

To make matters worse, the aerospace industry has staunchly opposed initiatives at both the state and local levels to pass plant-closing legislation that would give workers and their unions guarantees of early warning of closings and some public resources to cope with the layoffs. As Lockheed's chairman of the board, Roy Anderson, told an interviewer in 1984: "We made up our mind as an industry that we are going to go up there to Sacramento and talk to the Legislature. We haven't really done that. It's our fault. We're dumb. We go back to Washington but we don't go to Sacramento. But we're going to do that."[101]

Today's blue-collar defense workers, the grunts of the cold war, are in danger of becoming our next generation of Vietnam War veterans. While their military brothers and sisters are returning from the hot war in the Persian Gulf with government promises to do better by them this time, defense plant workers worry that no one will help them with their similarly tough adjustment to the end of the cold war, especially given the decline of civilian industries and a recessionary economy. As a result, their political opposition could hamper American adjustment to the end of the cold war. As Michael Closson, the director of the California-based Center for Economic Conversion, puts it:

> Military spending has become a giant and largely sacrosanct jobs program, employing directly and indirectly significant, though declining, numbers of blue collar workers and increasing numbers of technical professionals. . . . Fear of job loss and the attendant economic chaos is used to keep defense workers in line and to thwart efforts to scale back military production or to convert it to socially useful purposes.[102]

Or as Odessa Komer, the head of the UAW's aerospace division, warns: "Without a stronger legislative environment—an industrial policy, no less—isolated attempts at conversion will have a rough time of it. Workers in the U.S., with limited safety nets and hostile employers, have little incentive to support attempts to shift production away from their traditional activities."[103]

Proposals to deal with the displaced defense worker, which some see as the crux of the entire conversion problem, range from strategies focused on the individual worker to those encompassing industrial and technology policy. Retraining must be part of the solution for both white- and blue-collar defense workers. Some have suggested creating a form of GI bill for workers that would permit them to return to school with enough income to maintain their families and homes.

But retraining and education are not enough, especially in a depressed economy. As we shall see, workers, their professional organizations, and their unions have begun to press for much broader and deeper solutions to the problem. If they are not forthcoming, opposition to defense cuts by a majority of the military-industrial work force is likely to grow.

7
Cold War Communities

∎

COLORADO Springs is like a fishbowl. Poised on the abrupt junction where high plains meet the Front Range, the city has an arid climate and majestic views. The predominant hue is a dusty brown. In the winter light, patches of snow give the city an austere and rugged aura. Few trees adorn the angular mesas slumped against the flank of Pikes Peak. Ubiquitous housing subdivisions march over undulating plains, reminding one of a military encampment. This is not an inappropriate image, for "the Springs" is one of the most successful military-industrial communities in the nation.

Sprawled across its margins, and buried deep in the mountain, are the military facilities that form the core of the area's economy. Several sites are key to the city's claim to be the Space Capital of North America. The North American Air Defense Command, the strategic defense nerve center mimicked in the film *War Games,* operates from the depths of Cheyenne Mountain. The new test bed for the Strategic Defense Initiative is being installed ten miles east at Falcon Air Force Station. The newly unified U.S. Space Command operates out of the unprepossessing Chitlaw Building. Fort Carson, a large, combat-ready army base, occupies a mesa on the city's southeast side. To the north, the city's pride and joy, the Air Force Academy, sends its chapel spires up against a foothills backdrop.

These military facilities employed 37,000 people in 1987 and accounted for 30 percent of the region's work force. A few large and many small contractors and subcontractors arrayed around the military facilities do research and advise on, install, and operate top-secret, state-of-the-art equipment. Adding in military construction and procurement contracts, the Pentagon accounts for half of the area's $4

billion economy. With a modest multiplier, this means that at least
two-thirds of the Springs economy is dependent on Pentagon spending, and particularly on atmospherically based cold war.

The Reagan buildup was a boondoggle for the Springs economy.
Jobs grew by more than 5 percent a year in the first half of the 1980s;
but growth has been considerably slower since then, and a speculative real estate market has crumbled. Further reversals, particularly in
the cold war functions associated with the U.S. Space Command,
could plunge the local economy into a severe recession.[1]

Colorado Springs is not an anomaly. Dozens of other installation-
hosting cities and towns across the nation are similarly vulnerable.
Many are not as diversified across functions and missions as the
Springs. Several major metropolitan areas in the nation are also highly
dependent upon defense spending, particularly the Los Angeles and
Boston areas, the Washington, D.C. area as a defense services center,
San Diego as a naval center, and Seattle as a one-company military-
industrial city.

Throughout human history, the pursuit of war, arming for war, and
defending against aggression have all affected human settlement patterns. From the forts and encampments where soldiers were deployed
to the cities where quantities of weapons were made, the business of
war has both dispersed and concentrated populations. In industrial
societies, major industrial cities have been the locus of armament
production for hot wars prosecuted with mass-produced weapons
wielded by human beings. But the peculiarities of cold war altered
that pattern, in both the United States and the Soviet Union. Entirely
new centers of deployment and production developed outside of the
traditional industrial heartlands of each country. In the process, each
nation has financed the erection of whole new communities and
experienced unprecedented shifts in its population centers.

Producing cold war weapons, from bombers to missiles to communication satellites, and their accompanying gear places entirely different demands on the production environment than does traditional
military or civilian outfitting. Factors that drive industrial location in
many other heavy industry sectors—questions of raw materials access, transportation costs of both inputs and outputs (getting to market), and regional capital markets—are unimportant to military-
oriented ACE producers. They have preferred cheap, relatively
depopulated desert areas in particular, rather than existing industrial
centers, for production as well as storage facilities, since cold war
weaponry cannot be stored or stockpiled in urban armories, close to
centers of population. For reasons of scale, experimentation, secrecy,

and security, relatively virgin sites were chosen by the new industries and their military clients as the loci of cold war activity.

Over the postwar period, the Gunbelt emerged—a patchwork of cities and towns strung out along an arc from Alaska to Boston, sweeping down through Seattle, Silicon Valley, and Los Angeles in the West, across the more southerly mountain and plains states, through Texas and Florida, and up the eastern seaboard through Newport News and Long Island to Massachusetts and Connecticut. Three major centers anchor the complex. Los Angeles is the undisputed capital of cold war industrial design and production. Washington, D.C., serves as the defense services capital. And because of the disproportionate share of military R&D funding received by its universities, Boston is the leading military-educational complex. As satellites to these major centers, many smaller cities and towns specialize in a single production line or one type of military installation. Many are highly dependent upon a single service, strategic policy, or weapon system.

In contrast, most of the cities of the nation's industrial heartland, the states surrounding the Great Lakes, were cold-shouldered by the cold war. The industrial culture of the region—plus the fact that during the rise of the cold war its firms and factories were too busy producing consumer goods to meet pent-up postwar demand—appears to have repelled both the military and the new high-tech entrepreneurs who together built the new military-industrial complexes. The spectacular rise of Los Angeles to surpass Chicago as the nation's number-two city is symbolic of this lopsided, cold war–propelled development pattern. In a deeper sense, it is also symbolic of the atrophy of American civilian industries in a policy environment that quietly lavished enormous resources on a select set of military and military-generated industrial sectors.

Politics has also influenced the emergence of this new national defense perimeter. The preferences of top military officers have often been key in the choice of production and deployment sites. The rise of the air force, a conspicuously western-oriented service, and its preferred out-sourcing procurement policy prevailing over the army's arsenal system directed a disproportionate share of activity westward. Postwar presidents, all of whom hailed from the Gunbelt with the exception of the never-elected Gerald Ford, ensured that their local constituencies got good chunks of the defense pie. Congress is a more complicated and mixed story. Congress has not been dispersing military expenditures across the regions that one would have expected, due in part to its broad-based composition. Nevertheless, many members have been instrumental in winning and maintaining military bases in their own districts. Local boosters (such as military affairs committees) have also been effective in selling their towns to the military and to contractors as places to do business.

The rise of the Gunbelt has been a costly event for the nation. Billions of dollars have been spent on building new plants, new infrastructure, and new communities. Millions more have been spent relocating well-educated talent from some regions of the country to others. Of course, no phenomenon of such a massive scale is an unmixed blessing. Defenders of the Gunbelt might argue that its rise improved the regional income distribution by bringing down per capita incomes in the midwestern heartland and boosting southern and western incomes. Or they might point to the role it has had in engendering new centers of high-tech innovation.

On the other hand, it has led to increasing geographical segregation of military-industrial activities from other sectors in the economy, creating communities with pro-military cultures and greater vulnerability to downturns in the military spending cycle. The Gunbelt has altered the geopolitics of the nation and accounts in large part for the extraordinary shift in voting power and congressional representation to the West and the South. The Gunbelt may have created a constituency that, favoring the continuation of cold war and high levels of military spending, may be larger and have fewer options than if military spending patterns had more closely mimicked the regional industrial profile of the nation.

The Cold War Gunbelt

There is some irony in the fact that the rise of the modern aerospace industry, so militarily oriented in its initial decades, marked a return from mass-produced provisioning for hot war to the more highly crafted, small-batch type of production that characterized preindustrial warfare manufacturing. What is equally fascinating about the rise of military aircraft production is the industry's rejection of the older industrial sites in the heartland for the new "greenfield" cities on the periphery of the nation. Despite the midwestern origins of many of the early aviation pioneers, and despite the early lead of older industrial states like New York in aircraft production, California had by the 1930s begun to dominate the new industry.

The Los Angeles aircraft complex was virtually founded on military contracts. While a couple of firms were started by locals, many of the major aerospace firms were originally transplants, brought to the area by extraordinary boosterism and with the blessings, and dollars, of the military. Donald Douglas, for instance, was the first to succeed in the southern California aircraft business. Educated at MIT and Annapolis, Douglas moved to Los Angeles in the early 1920s to start his own company, with vigorous support from the *Los Angeles Times* publisher, and a notorious booster, Harry Chandler, and contracts for three $40,000 navy torpedo planes. Follow-on naval contracts and army contracts for its World Cruiser, which made the first around-the-world flight in 1924, secured his company's future there. North American Aviation also moved from Baltimore to Los Angeles in the mid-1930s with a key government contract in hand.[2]

Aircraft manufacturing was more regionally concentrated by 1940 than all manufacturing employment; 32 percent of its workers were in California. Production clustered in newer and relatively smaller urbanized areas, many of them on the outskirts of then medium-sized cities such as Los Angeles or Seattle. By 1939 only 7 percent of aircraft workers were employed in cities of more than half a million, and 62 percent worked in communities with populations of less than 25,000. In contrast, 33 percent of auto workers and 43 percent of machine tool workers were in the nation's largest cities.[3]

Nevertheless, the principal sites of military manufacturing during the Second World War—for instance, sites for shipbuilding and the new auto industry, which produced trucks and tanks for war—continued to be places where both commercial and military production could take place. The shift in the locus of defense spending from the industrial heartland to the perimeter after the war reflects the shift in military war-fighting emphasis from hot war to cold war. For instance, in 1951, a hot war year, prime contracts were heavily concentrated in the same regions that accounted for the bulk of commercial manufacturing—the Northeast and Pacific regions (Table 7.1). As cold war supplanted hot war, the distribution of contracts shifted markedly away from the East North Central and Middle Atlantic regions and into most other regions, although New England increased its relative share and the Pacific region maintained its relatively high level of military contracts.

Some states within these regions showed even more remarkable differentials by the mid-1980s (Figure 7.1). The per capita prime contract spending rate in Massachusetts climbed to over twice the national average, and California increased its already considerable share. The spending rates in Illinois, Indiana, Michigan, Ohio, New York, and New Jersey, however, dropped rapidly. Other states, such

TABLE 7.1

Index of Regional DOD Prime Contracts, 1952–89

REGION	1952	1952–56	1957–61	1962–66	1967–71	1972–76	1977–81	1982–86	1987–89
New England	136	156	169	180	176	202	228	216	228
Middle Atlantic	125	119	104	96	94	94	86	83	75
East North Central	133	89	63	64	65	49	48	50	49
West North Central	79	76	84	90	99	103	112	109	110
South Atlantic	53	61	69	82	87	83	86	95	106
East South Central	23	29	25	38	59	73	60	53	61
West South Central	49	70	81	76	126	81	97	88	84
Mountain	20	37	102	104	63	75	64	72	113
Pacific	179	223	234	205	164	192	179	174	146

NOTE: Awards of $10,000 or more for fiscal years 1952–81, of $25,000 or more for fiscal years 1982–89. If a region's per capita receipts matched the national average, the index is 100. A higher figure, for instance 136 for New England in 1952, means that that region's receipts were 136 percent of the national average, or 36 percent higher. A lower figure, for instance the Mountain region's 20 in 1952, indicates that that region's receipts were only 20 percent of the national average per capita.
SOURCE: U.S. Department of Defense, Prime Contract Awards by State, (Washington, D.C.: USGPO, 1953–1990.)

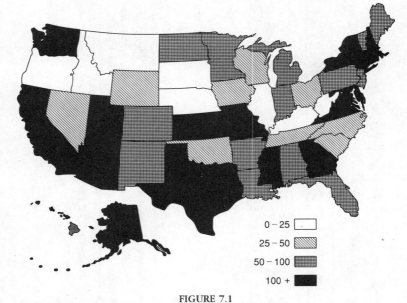

FIGURE 7.1

Military Prime Contracts per Capita as a Percentage of the U.S. Average, by State, 1984

as Arizona, Utah, Mississippi, Virginia, and New Hampshire, had minuscule numbers of contracts in the early 1950s but saw their share of awards shoot up over the cold war decades. Much of the change occurred in the 1950s—the seminal decade for the displacement of hot war by cold war.

Regions benefiting from R&D and procurement expenditures (which tend to move together) and those favored by military facilities also differ dramatically. Based on each region's per capita receipts divided by the national per capita expenditure for 1983, R&D outlays are heavily concentrated in New England and the South Atlantic and Pacific regions, while the mountain, South Atlantic, and Pacific states benefit from large shares of military base and government office operations.[4] The role of R&D funding as a long-term investment strategy favoring the Gunbelt over the industrial heartland is seen in the large gap between the Pacific and New England regions' receipts, which in 1983 were 175 percent and 157 percent of the national average, respectively, and those of the East North Central region, which had only 14 percent of such receipts.[5]

On a state-by-state basis, military prime contracts for research and development are even more concentrated. Those given to business firms are most heavily concentrated in California, whose firms garner over 40 percent of the total. Thanks to Boeing, however, the state of Washington enjoys higher per capita corporate R&D receipts than California. On a per capita basis, firms in Colorado, Massachusetts, Utah, and Missouri also receive a disproportionate share of R&D contracts.[6] In awards to educational institutions, Maryland and Massachusetts top the list in absolute dollars as well as in per capita receipts, with 60 percent of all university-based military R&D prime contracts between them. Maryland's high ranking is due almost entirely to the Applied Physics Lab at Johns Hopkins University; Massachusetts benefits from university-connected facilities, such as MIT's Lincoln Lab, as well as from large research shops run by professors. Massachusetts also leads in R&D awards to nonprofit institutions, many of them spin-offs of MIT, such as the Draper Lab in Cambridge. Together, Massachusetts and California dominate 75 percent of all such nonprofit receipts.[7] These distributions of military funding to corporate and university laboratories have been very stable over the postwar period. They have benefited the host regions by building up pools of scientific and engineering skills and stimulating considerable commercial spin-off.

By weapon system and industry group, the military procurement map is even more highly differentiated. Military aircraft contracts, which constitute about one-third of all prime contracts, are highest, on a per capita basis, in the New England, Pacific, and West North Central regions. Although the Pacific region wins the highest proportion of receipts in absolute-dollar terms (26 percent in 1984), New England has the highest per capita spending, with more than three times the national average. New England makes most of the military aircraft engines; airframe production is heavily concentrated in southern California, Seattle (Boeing), St. Louis (McDonnell-Douglas), and Wichita (Boeing).

In missiles, the Pacific region dominates in both absolute dollars and per capita receipts, with 42 percent of all such contracts in the 1980s. The Pacific, New England, and mountain regions are the only ones with missile contract receipts in excess of the national per capita average; the Pacific region's receipts are three times that average. The big Pacific missile-makers include Boeing in Seattle and General Dynamics, McDonnell-Douglas, Lockheed, Rockwell, and Hughes in California—mostly airframe firms that successfully made the move into unmanned missiles. Those in the mountain states include Martin-Marietta in Denver and Unisys, Thiokol, and Hercules Powder in Utah. New England, whose missile contracts had by 1982 nearly matched the Pacific region's levels, has a number of firms, such as Raytheon, making small and medium-sized missiles.

In shipbuilding, military patronage has also favored the few at the expense of the many. Although it has hundreds of shipyards in coastal areas of the United States, the navy has concentrated its work in a small number of them. In the mid-1970s, only eleven of four hundred private shipyards in the country were working on new navy orders.[8] Shipbuilding prime contracts are heavily concentrated in New England—which won awards in the 1980s in excess of 500 percent of the national average—with smaller concentrations in the Pacific, Middle Atlantic, South Atlantic, and East South Central regions.

As we might expect, the location of military electronics and communications contracts follows closely the expenditure patterns for aircraft and missiles. Many of the airframe producers successfully shifted into electronics and communications work with the rise of the cold war; by the early 1960s, five of the top eleven military airframe manufacturers had diversified into electronics, generally on nearby sites.[9] New England and the Pacific region have boasted shares of electronics and communications activities well above the national average since the early 1960s, and both regions had increased their shares to over twice the national average by 1982. The rise of these new high-tech military-industrial complexes came at the clear expense of the Middle Atlantic region, whose per capita share dropped from more than 200 percent of the national average in 1962 to just above it in 1982; its absolute receipts dropped from 39 percent to 19 percent over the same period. And in what appears by now to be a distinct pattern, nuclear weapons prime contracts are also a New England and Pacific specialty, although these were once concentrated in the Northeast and Midwest. California has gradually come to dominate the industry—accounting for 13 percent of prime contracts in 1962, but 57 percent of all such contracts by 1982.

The only category in which the East North Central region excels is tank and truck prime contracts, for which it receives more than three times the national per capita average. These contracts are heavily concentrated in three states—Michigan, Ohio, and Indiana. But over the postwar period, both New England and the Pacific region have increased their share in these industries as well, at the Midwest's expense. By the early 1980s, both regions received more than an average share.[10]

Many of the most successful regions in the postwar period, especially those celebrated in the "new industrial districts" literature, are those that have been major recipients of defense procurement funds.[11]

Top-ranking counties at the height of the buildup included Los Angeles, Santa Clara (Silicon Valley), San Diego, and Orange in California, Middlesex in Massachusetts, and King (Boeing) in Washington (Table 7.2). Southern California is the center of the Gunbelt: more than $23 billion in prime procurement contracts were concentrated in the three counties of Los Angeles, Orange, and San Diego in 1984, accompanied by considerable additional expenditure for military facilities.

The rise of the air force as the third, and leading-edge, cold war service has left its imprint on the Gunbelt, especially during the initial key decade of the 1950s. After the Second World War and before the missile buildup, both the air force and its parent, the army, concentrated their purchases in the three industrialized regions—the Northeast, Midwest, and Pacific. The Southeast and the mountain states

TABLE 7.2

DOD Prime Contracts by County, 1984

RANK	COUNTY	TOTAL CONTRACTS (MILLION $)
1	Los Angeles (California)	13,762.9
2	St. Louis (Missouri)	5,852.2
3	Santa Clara (California)	4,661.2
4	Orange (California)	3,715.7
5	Nassau (New York)	3,661.7
6	Middlesex (Massachusetts)	3,642.1
7	Tarrant (Texas)	2,942.4
8	King (Washington)	2,421.5
9	San Diego (California)	2,155.6
10	Cobb (Georgia)	2,122.2
11	Sedgwick (Kansas)	2,077.0
12	Essex (Massachusetts)	1,945.9
13	Hartford (Connecticut)	1,845.6
14	Jackson (Mississippi)	1,761.9
15	New York (New York)	1,663.5
16	New London (Connecticut)	1,571.0
17	Fairfield (Connecticut)	1,548.0
18	Suffolk (New York)	1,399.8
19	Dallas (Texas)	1,397.6
20	Baltimore (Maryland)	1,372.8

SOURCE: *Department of Defense,* Prime Contracts by County, 1984 *(Washington, D.C.: USGPO, 1985).*

were not yet important for defense-related production. Cold war policies of the 1950s changed that geography as army and air force contracts tilted toward the South, the West, and New England. When the army's share of expenditures rose during hot wars—during the Vietnam War, for instance—the industrial Midwest did relatively better than other areas. By the early 1980s, the air force had become a solidly Gunbelt-oriented service, its contracts concentrated in the West and along the northern Atlantic seaboard. In the 1980s, with the shift in nuclear capability toward submarine-based missiles, the navy as well as the air force received a disproportionate share of new contracting authority, which further favored the Gunbelt regions.

Particularly because of its close association with the rise of the air force and its preferences for privately contracted atmospheric weaponry, the Pacific region came to be the center of cold war production par excellence. But perhaps the more remarkable region is New England, whose diversity as a major producer of aircraft engines, missiles, defense electronics, military communications, and nuclear weapons is quite pronounced, as is its status as a key basic R&D center for the Pentagon. New England alone among the older industrial regions managed to catapult itself into being a military-industrial center in the postwar period. As we shall see below, this had a great deal to do with its craft and precision-machining traditions—so unlike the mass-production model dominating the newer regions to the west of it. Its disastrous regional economy in the key period of the 1950s also played a part, as did its considerable congressional and presidential clout over the decades.

As the investment that prime contracts represent shifted toward the Gunbelt, so did the center of military-industrial employment. In Figure 7.2, the darkest states have concentrations of military-related jobs within manufacturing in excess of the national norm; those with no cross-hatching have shares of defense-related employment less than 25 percent of the nation's, and those with diagonals have 25–50 percent. The map shows how heavily defense-related jobs are concentrated in an arc from New England through Florida, Texas, selected plains and mountain states, to California. It also shows what a patchwork the Gunbelt really is; a number of states do not join in the spoils of their regions, most notably, Alaska, Nevada, Arkansas, and North and South Carolina.

Not surprisingly, the states that have enjoyed the lion's share of military prime contracts and R&D expenditures have posted the best records for manufacturing job growth in the past several decades. Despite a net loss in industrial jobs nationally from 1972 to 1986,

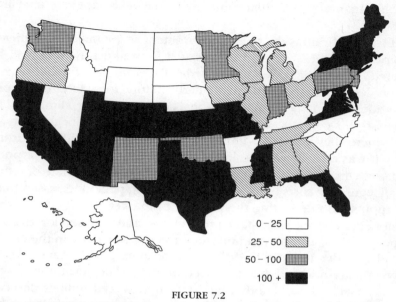

FIGURE 7.2

Military Manufacturing Job Shares as a Percentage of the U.S. Average, by State, 1983

California, Washington, and the rest of the defense-oriented mountain states experienced growth in excess of 30 percent; most of the older industrial heartland states endured losses in excess of 20 percent. Defense spending helped stem job loss in otherwise troubled states, such as Massachusetts and Missouri, and boosted growth in Virginia, Georgia, and Florida.[12] Defense spending, particularly in the procurement and R&D categories, stimulated growth in personal income and manufacturing employment from 1976 to 1985 in those states with relatively large military receipts.[13]

How the Gunbelt Came to Be

Why this dispersed patchwork of military-industrial centers developed is a matter of considerable complexity. Two sets of players were involved: the private-sector decision-makers who decided where plants would be built and at which ones weapon systems would be designed and constructed, and public-sector decision-makers—military officers, Pentagon officials, members of Congress, and local boosters. Both groups engaged in a very different locational cost calculus than that forced on company managers competing in civilian markets.

How significant is the role of government as the major customer in determining where defense dollars will flow and how jobs will be created? Given the way in which the Department of Defense and its predecessors operated, particularly before the McNamara cost-conscious era, many normal locational constraints were eliminated by the cost-plus contract, which freed up contractors to locate more or less where they pleased within the continental United States. Ironically, it was actually profitable to locate far from existing labor pools and government users, since a contractor could charge a rate of return on all legitimate costs of recruiting and moving personnel, assembling the inputs, and delivering the product to market.

Strategic concerns, military preferences, and interservice rivalries appear to have also played important roles, particularly in the crucial decades of the 1940s and 1950s, in determining the location of the new military-oriented plant and equipment. The locations of key military facilities was another factor. Congressional politics deserves less credit, in contractors' accounts, than the layperson is led to believe. Our evidence for these conclusions comes from the dozens of interviews we conducted with defense contractors across the country between 1986 and 1989, probing their past and present location decisions, as well as from data from secondary sources. (Regrettably, the quality of the data from our project does not permit us to determine definitely how other hypothesized locational factors—such as climate, the presence of universities and skilled labor—stack up against the government's role).[14] In what follows, we show how these factors joined to shape the rise of the Gunbelt.

Location Theory When Government Is the Market

In traditional location theory, the cost of overcoming the "friction of distance" is considered the major determinant of industrial location.[15] Industries locate, it follows, at sites that minimize the sum of the cost of assembling the inputs to production and the cost of reaching the market, all else being equal. The model can also accommodate the differentials of the prices of inputs themselves varying across production space, and market demand being sensitive to location. But what happens when the market consists of a single, large, public-sector institution—the U.S. government?[16]

The straightforward argument for market-oriented location becomes relatively unimportant. Since the military-industrial complex has traditionally awarded cost-plus contracts, it is unlikely that sensitivity to delivery costs matters much in the siting calculus of defense contractors. Nor is demand "distance-elastic"—the government has no incentive to favor nearby suppliers over more distant ones, with one exception. The Department of Defense has a "buy America" policy that discourages the importation of military material. Thus, defense contractors may limit themselves to domestic site choices far more than their commercially oriented counterparts do. Of course, as foreign governments become bigger customers of defense contractors, as they have in the past decades, the pressure to locate production facilities overseas might be expected to increase. Growing demands for coproduction agreements—in which companies promise to produce some portion of their product in the purchasing country—are evidence of this.

In the meantime, however, the location of the customer is also incidental because the actual physical site of defense demand is hard to pin down. The final design and appropriation of funds are carried out in Washington, D.C.; a certain amount of private-sector design and lobbying activity is thus clustered around the nation's capital. But the bulk of the product is not delivered there. It goes instead to numerous facilities around the country, even around the globe. These destinations vary as the locations of key military bases shift, so that they cannot always be predicted by contractors in advance. Some defense industry products are stockpiled and stored for future use elsewhere. Some receptacles, such as missile silos and launchers, are dispersed, secret, or even mobile.

The very term "mobilization" suggests another trait of military-related output that diminishes the significance of market-oriented siting. Many of the big-ticket items, such as ships, aircraft, and trucks, literally move themselves to market; hence, they have a built-in ability to minimize the "friction of distance." This is not the case, however, with missiles, communication satellites, space shuttles, and other major assemblies.

Other, more subtle market influences affect the location of military-industrial plants. First, military installations themselves, as the users of industrial output, offer to firms certain attractions that can minimize their costs and increase their chances of being awarded contracts. Certain key facilities, at which one-of-a-kind weapon or communications systems are deployed, serve as critical testing sites for these systems as well as for newly innovated aircraft. Moving production facilities close to the site might help a firm to quickly work out bugs in its product, facilitate its fit with an in-place system, permit timely completion of contracts, and thereby maximize performance. The costs of testing and evaluation can be lowered through the free use of military airstrips and other facilities.

Access to information and a labor pool favors locations near either the end-user or the chief decision-makers in Washington. By permitting its employees to have daily contact with military end-users, a firm heightens its chances of winning future contracts. Proximity gives the firm's management and engineering staff early warning of new generations of technical problems or of shifts in strategy and weaponry requirements—to which they may then devote themselves with a head start. Similarly, proximity permits firms to hire former military personnel—whose knowledge is invaluable in marketing and design—when they exit the services.

Strategic concerns are yet another contribution to the shape of defense-oriented production patterns. The Pentagon's worry that certain key plants might be extraordinarily vulnerable to particular types of aggression, be it long-range bombers, nuclear first strikes, or terrorism, leads it to prefer certain regions and locales over others. The desire to have more than one source for a particularly critical product has led the Pentagon to require "second-sourcing" from contractors: building a second, duplicate branch plant.

More directly, the government builds its own plants: GOGOs (government-owned, government-operated facilities) and GOCOs (government-owned, contractor-operated facilities). For these plants the government must have an explicit locational strategy based on strategic as well as labor supply and other conventional locational concerns.

Finally, individual and group preferences within the government figure in contractor locational choice. There is, of course, the notorious pork-barreling process in Congress, whereby some members cash in their "chits" for certain priorities, which may be military facilities or contracts. Some members of Congress devote their careers to military affairs, in the process engineering base openings, forestalling closings, and lobbying for big prime contracts in their home districts. But there are many other less visible decision-makers along the path from mission idea to execution. Middle managers in the services, who must plan for and operate the various commands located around the country, and their bosses in the Pentagon might be expected to have geographical preferences that matter a great deal in contract or facility location.

Plants producing for both commercial and military markets exhibit locational tendencies similar to nonmilitary plants. In addition, locations often vary between industrial segments that produce for hot wars and those that are cold war–oriented. When the mission is arming, feeding, clothing, transporting, and directing large numbers of troops, then weaponry, matériel, and transports are demanded in large quantities and are mass-produced in more or less the same sectors and cities that turn out autos, machine tools, and consumer goods in peacetime. But if the mission is to create ever newer generations of deterrents, the resulting small-batch, technology-intensive weapons are more apt to be crafted at sites relatively free of cost-minimizing pressures, where a very different business culture prevails. The army's need for military goods–producing capacity has partly given way over the postwar period to the air force's industrial requirements for relatively automated atmospheric warfare, paralleling the geographical shifts in defense output by service.

In extensive interviews, contemporary contractors reported that the *cost* of delivery of product to market is indeed not an important locational determinant. Even if delivery is cumbersome and expensive—as it is in transporting a Cape Canaveral–bound satellite through the Panama Canal, or strapping a shuttle onto the back of an airliner—no one has ever suggested that for this reason the assembly plants be located closer to the user end, not even during the cost-conscious McNamara era. As far back as the 1930s the government not only has been willing to sanction locations far from the East Coast concentration but has also funded in its contracts the construction of new plants in faraway sites. Contracts for weapons research provided taxpayer dollars for Kaman's move from Albuquerque to Colorado Springs in the 1950s; more recently, McDonnell-Douglas moved its Hughes helicopter operation to Mesa, Arizona. The Pentagon is not only indifferent to locations far from the "market," but it is willing to fund such moves, even at rather hefty costs.

Camp Followers

An exception to this pattern is the way in which contractors cluster around strategic military planning or deployment centers. Defense services are dispersed to the South and the West because military installations are to be found there. Key military facilities have often operated as a locational lure for defense contractors. Before the First World War, the army (and later the navy) concentrated its air training activities in San Diego, influencing the move of Consolidated from Buffalo in 1934. Similarly, early military flight fields in Nassau County on Long Island drew a number of New York airplane companies in the 1910s, including the precursors of Republic and Grumman.[17]

In these early decades, communities vied to be the home of the new aircraft industry, and many of them pinned their hopes on the attractiveness of their existing military air facilities. For instance, business leaders in San Antonio, Texas, which became an air training center in 1913, also wanted to attract aircraft manufacturing. The town's military affairs committee offered local government land for bases to train the new expanded branch of the army, while simultaneously offering industrialists who built aircraft plants contacts with officers whose needs would stimulate orders for their factories. Although it was ultimately unsuccessful, their effort was characteristic of a pro-military philosophy and attitude common in ambitious western cities, whose military affairs committees often sought to attract both military bases and military-industrial plants in tandem.[18]

In the postwar period, military installations continued to attract contractor activity. With the cold war emphasis on the performance and precision of weaponry and defense systems, contractors have been more beholden than they are during hot wars to their clients' requirements and oversight. Defense products are often but one element in an intricate system of detection, decision-making, response, and guidance functions, so that proximity to the user is necessary to ensure a fit with upstream and downstream equipment. Many sequential tests with interspersed trips back to the drawing board favor proximity to the military client. In addition, more and more of the contract work resides in design and development stages, favoring agglomeration around defense planning centers.

All these factors lead to the "camp follower" phenomenon, the name a TRW executive gave it in an interview with us. He was referring to TRW's setting up shop in 1953 at southern California's Edwards Air Force Base. TRW is a systems integrator; its work necessarily brought it next door to the client. Key facilities like the Edwards and Vandenburg air force bases and the air force's western procurement offices, especially its Ballistic Missiles Division, anchored the aerospace industry in Los Angeles in the 1950s. The government installations offered advantages for both testing and maintenance functions, as well as information synergy. Defense company managers not so well situated complain that remoteness from military centers has hampered their ability to increase their government contracting. Dr. Richard Herring of Ball Aerospace in Boulder, Colorado, reflected that although TRW, Hughes, and Ball began their satellite and instrumentation businesses at about the same time, the first two companies benefited from their proximity to the Los Angeles military, an advantage not shared by Ball.

Many companies relocated in the 1950s, often in "infant industry" stages, in tandem with new missions at existing military bases or with the opening of new military facilities. Radiation Corporation (ancestor of Harris) set up shop in Melbourne, Florida, in 1950, drawn by Cape Canaveral, which was established in the same year.[19] Branch plants are the more common camp follower; they have been built around cold war centers such as the Air Defense Command in Colorado Springs, the Redstone Arsenal at Huntsville, Alabama, and the Cape Canaveral–Kennedy Space Center in Florida. Martin-Marietta set up its Orlando facility, devoted to army missile and defense electronics work, close to Cape Canaveral in the mid-1950s. McDonnell-Douglas set up shop in the neighboring Titusville area in 1970 to work on the Dragon precision-guided missile and, by 1980, on the cruise missile. Both Huntsville and Colorado Springs have grown dramatically in the postwar period, almost entirely owing to facility-drawn branch plants of major contractors. The Washington, D.C. area has boomed in the last decade as most contractors have expanded their planning, development, and lobbying functions there.

Much of the new clustering is due to branch operations of anywhere from ten to two hundred people who install and service the systems on bases. Some of these businesses are small "storefront" operations that companies set up near the principal military commands, especially those with high-tech cold war missions. Many companies reported that only in Colorado Springs could they keep their eyes and ears close enough to the ground to get the information required for future planning of their parent firms' space defense bids. Storefronts are also scattered around the Pentagon's highly decentralized procurement offices, stretching from the Air Force Electronic Systems Division at Hanscomb Field, in Massachusetts, through the Air Development Center in Rome, New York, Florida's Eastern Space and Missile Center at Patrick Air Force Base, and the Air Force Space Division in Los Angeles.

A more subtle role in defense activity siting has been played by the government's lead in getting engineering and technical labor accustomed to noncosmopolitan communities. Government R&D activities, particularly in the national lab system, are distributed much further away from both the East Coast and the industrial heartland than commercial research and development.[20] The labs in particular—Los Alamos, Sandia, Livermore—drew high-powered personnel, beginning in the early 1950s. When firms spun off from the labs (which happened more frequently early on than now), scientists and their families would often prefer to stay in relatively remote locations. For instance, the siting of Kaman's move from Albuquerque to Colorado Springs was heavily influenced by the newly acquired preference for the western landscape of its managers and personnel, all former Sandia Labs employees.

Defense installations also act as a potential labor pool. Technical and professional military personnel exiting the service can often be more easily recruited at the site of their last assignment, where many have invested in housing because they like the location. Skilled mechanics and technicians with similar preferences are also available at military bases; moreover, the spouses of enlisted personnel have often proved to be an underappreciated and underutilized work force. In Colorado Springs, the presence of both white- and blue-collar labor was a drawing card for the major contractors locating branch plants there.

The Geography of Strategic Fears

Strategic concerns have also left their mark on the domestic manufacturing landscape. These were most significant in the 1940s and 1950s, first during the Second World War, when aerial bombing by Japan was a possibility, and later when cold war fears of long-range bombing and intercontinental ballistic missiles were on the rise. Because initial defense contracts were terribly overconcentrated—45 percent went to just eight industrial areas—the Plant Site Board was established by the federal government in 1941 and given the task of accepting or rejecting new production site proposals. The board was particularly concerned with reducing labor migration and allocating defense work where there were concentrations of the unemployed.[21] The board also strove to interiorize war-making capacity whenever possible, chiefly away from the West Coast, and to decentralize the war-making capacity of major industrial nodes. Many new government-financed plants were required to be located away from their parent plant, especially if the latter was on the Pacific coast.

The geographically concentrated aircraft industry was a special target of this wartime effort at dispersal. Reluctantly, many firms complied. Almost all the aircraft companies were one-city operations in 1939, and at the war's outset, approximately 60 percent of airframe manufacture took place in the Pacific region. By the war's end, government directives had produced a far-flung set of branch plants in places like Wichita, Omaha, Marietta, Georgia, Oklahoma City, St. Louis, Tulsa, and Forth Worth. While many branch plants closed after the war or were converted to other uses, others remained aircraft centers, often at government insistence. Boeing, for instance, was strong-armed by the Pentagon to continue its military aircraft operations at Wichita, and McDonnell stayed in St. Louis, where it had set up a new aircraft plant in 1945.[22]

In spite of compliance from some aircraft firms, many other companies vigorously resisted dispersal. James Douglas, son of the founder of Douglas Aircraft, told us that although the government wanted the company to expand inland, it refused and settled in Long Beach, California, instead. In congressional hearings, government officials concluded that decentralization efforts had worked much better with government-financed plants than with private ones. At the war's end, the Plant Site Board dispiritedly acknowledged that it had failed in its effort to produce a more evenly distributed regional military-industrial base: it had affected only about 8 percent of the nation's manufacturing capacity. Particularly regrettable, in the board's view, was its failure to locate defense facilities in those areas of the South that had suffered heavy losses in cotton and tobacco export markets. A shift of 8 percent, however, is quite substantial, especially for being accomplished in less than six years. In fact, this shift represents a discontinuity in growth patterns that we believe permanently altered the regional balance of industrial power.[23]

The second major era of strategic concerns affecting locational patterns occurred immediately after the Korean War. Fearing Soviet development of the long-range bomber and ICBMs, Pentagon decision-makers again argued for decentralization and for second-sourcing. For instance, Sundstrand Corporation, the only military supplier of constant-speed drives for aircraft in 1955, was required by the air force to build a duplicate plant at least one thousand miles from its headquarters in Rockford, Illinois. It chose a site in Denver. So did Martin-Marietta when, as part of a lucrative Titan missile contract, the Pentagon required that it set up an alternative to its Baltimore plant in the mid-1950s.

It is difficult to know how much decentralization of manufacturing capacity resulted from cold war initiatives by the Pentagon. Unlike the siting of key military facilities in the interior, which yielded some important new military-industrial complexes (Colorado Springs, the Titusville-Melbourne-Orlando corridor, and Huntsville), the second-source demand tended to produce isolated branch plants in dispersed locations. These branch plants sometimes induced modest industrialization in the surrounding communities—particularly in parts of Colorado and the South Central states—but no dynamic new agglomerations appeared. Nevertheless, such plants were pioneers in the decentralization of skilled assembly, metalworking, and parts production, helping to convince civilian manufacturers that they too could spin off more routine functions from the industrial heartland.

Arms Geography and the Make-or-Buy Decision

Early interservice rivalries were also decisive in the rise of the Gunbelt. Historically, the victory of the air force, which preferred out-sourcing to private companies, over the army, the champion of in-house missile production, was key to promoting southern California as the military-industrial capital of the nation. The two services struggled for dominance in developing missiles in the 1950s. The army sponsored a massive effort at the Huntsville Redstone Arsenal, where Werner von Braun labored with his team to produce ballistic missiles. The air force fought back by developing a competing ballistic missile with teams of private-sector players: Convair in San Diego, North American Aviation in Los Angeles, and General Electric in New York. To oversee the effort, the air force opened the Western Development Division in the Los Angeles area in 1954 and promoted the formation of a new Los Angeles–based team, Ramo-Wooldridge (later TRW), to integrate R&D and production activities. (Nuclear warheads, however, were to be made at Los Alamos.)[24]

Huntsville, Alabama, was far from any existing center of aircraft production, though close to the atomic research and plutonium-producing facilities at the national lab in in Oak Ridge, Tennessee. It was also distant from the point of final weapons assembly in Los Alamos. Choosing it as a missile development site reflected the army's traditional emphasis on production in its own arsenals; its leaders argued that arsenals offered real advantages in objectivity, stability, and the development of expertise. The Redstone Arsenal was also linked to regional production partners—such as Martin in Orlando, Florida, which manufactured its Jupiter and Pershing missiles—as well as to its auto industry partners to the north.[25]

The Los Angeles coalition of air force and private contractors won out, largely because of politics. Mutual interests were strong:

> If the Air Force was interested in excluding the Army from missile and space missions, the airframe industry was equally desirous of eliminating the competition from the automobile industry and liquidating the competition emanating at the time from the Redstone Arsenal missile engineering team. They also wished to discredit the concept of weapons development implicit in the Army's arsenal system.[26]

By eschewing any in-house capacity, the air force developed a large, well-heeled constituency of scientists, organized labor, and industry, while its impeccable free-enterprise credentials removed most of the stigma from the surge in public spending that was involved.[27] In the process, the center of the aerospace industry moved irrevocably to the West Coast.

The relative strength of aerospace centers over naval centers owes much to a similar struggle immediately after the Second World War between the navy on the one side and the army and emerging air force on the other. The army and the air force favored a unified command to be lodged in the new Department of Defense and viewed air power as the key to the country's defensive future; the navy, whose supercarriers were in competition with the air force's strategic bombers, opposed a new tripartite DOD. The navy lost the battle—as well as its position as the first line of military security—to the air force, whose strategic bombers functioned best in a western-oriented, decentralized base and production structure. Ironically, the navy's position was enhanced in the 1980s when the undetectable submarine-based missile became the most powerful deterrent weapon—a boon to coastal shipyards.

Another example is the recent struggle within the air force between the Strategic Air Command (SAC), headquartered in Omaha, and the emerging Space Command—charged with space-based defense systems and much of the responsibility for the Strategic Defense Initiative—in Colorado Springs. In the late 1970s SAC won its battle to have the warning system in Colorado Springs moved to Omaha, thereby mixing defensive with SAC offensive functions. Colorado Springs was stripped to the minimum—just the NORAD communication center in Cheyenne Mountain remained. But by 1983, those in the air force who wished to segregate, once again, defensive from offensive missions won their battle to bring the warning system back to Colorado Springs. That decision was the key to anchoring SDI operations there, as well as new clusters of defense R&D and production facilities.

Cold-Shouldered by the Cold War

The massive geographical shift, underwritten by military patronage, in the leading-edge industries cannot simply be attributed to a "cowboy" culture that lured a disproportionate number of officers and early aircraft pioneers to the West. It also was caused by the industrial heartland's failure to nurture the aircraft pioneers who first emerged from its bicycle, auto, and machining industries. Though midwestern cities provided home bases for many of the earliest aircraft inventors and entrepreneurs—the Wright brothers, Alexander Graham Bell, Glenn Curtiss, Henry Ford—the aircraft production ventures of these pioneers had all disappeared by the 1950s. Because of profound differences in business culture and unfortunate timing, Dayton, Detroit, Buffalo, and other inland cities lost out to the newer airframe centers on the coasts.

To be sure, pockets of military-industrial activity still exist in the heartland. Minneapolis, with its defense electronics and computers, and St. Louis, with its McDonnell-Douglas and General Dynamics contracts, are important exceptions to the rule—as is New England, the stunning counterfactual case. Why did that aging industrial region manage so successfully the transition into defense production and research? At the critical juncture, during the 1950s, its human and physical resources were similar to those of the Midwest: excellent engineering schools, a strong machining tradition, heavily unionized and skilled blue-collar labor, and hotly contested partisan politics.[28]

John Mollenkopf argues that, in general, conflictual municipal politics has induced private-sector firms to migrate to the Sunbelt. But for defense activity, the tendency appears not to be true in the aggregate, especially for New England. But in the 1950s the business culture and economic prospects of New England were dramatically different from those of the Midwest. Its factories were not flush with pent-up postwar demand. Many of its industrial mainstays—textiles, shoes, apparel—faced permanent low-cost competition from the South and from overseas; by the 1950s these New England industries had already lost their market dominance. During that decade, many volumes were written on the depressed New England economy. The recovery of the region became a major public policy priority, and searching for new markets preoccupied the region's leaders.[29]

During the war, the production of a huge range of goods—automobiles, electric refrigerators, vacuum cleaners, sewing machines, electric ranges, washing machines, radios, phonographs, all mainly midwestern products—had been prohibited. After the war, households with forced savings clamored for these goods; satisfying the demand required the total dedication of midwestern factories. Thus, in the 1950s, the decade most critical for developing aerospace capacity, the Midwest had neither time nor incentive to go after government defense markets, while New England did.

The Midwest had developed a distinctly different economic mission as well. With its unusually egalitarian agricultural hinterland, the "Third Coast" had developed the mass market and the mass-production technology to serve it, epitomized by Henry Ford's Model T and by Sears catalog sales. Efficient mass production required standardized commodities and enormous plants with relatively routinized labor. In contrast, New England remained a predominantly craft-oriented economy, with smaller plants and market niches in certain precision-machining sectors. Such firms moved easily into the small-batch, innovative, and superprofitable product lines that the cold war economy favored.

The Midwest also had a distinctly different business culture, which prejudiced its chances with the defense establishment. It was the region of big, powerful oligopolies—from the steel giants of Pittsburgh to the automakers in Detroit and the farm machinery plants in Illinois.[30] These corporate monoliths controlled their markets, were preoccupied with fighting their unions, and eschewed risky investments in new technologies. Midwestern ways of producing and selling were better pitched to the housewife than the Pentagon colonel. Selling to the military had been a hassle during the Second World War, and midwestern firms were glad to be done with it.

Their New England counterparts, however, had no choice but to learn the new customs associated with peddling to the military and defending their goods before Congress. (They learned well, and not for the last time—Richard Barff and Prentice Knight show that the timing of New England's employment turnarounds has been closely associated with defense buildups.)[31] Supporting casts of universities and politicians busied themselves with defense-generated economic activity in New England, whereas the midwesterners were too busy with commercial industry demands. In retrospect, it is not hard to see why the easterly portion of the nation's old industrial quadrant strove to revitalize itself through government largesse, while the then-booming Midwest was indifferent if not hostile to such overtures.

Pork-Barreling: The Pentagon versus the Politicians

Between and within the branches of government—the services, the Pentagon, the White House, and Congress—conflicts frequently surface over the geography of military spending, particularly the highly publicized tensions between the "pork-barreling" Congress and the mission-oriented Pentagon. The perception is widespread that pork-barreling—the notion that a certain proportion of expenditures in any given year are spread around in ways that will benefit the constituencies of certain members of Congress—explains why defense spending does not follow an evenhanded, population-based expenditure pattern. Yet both our contractor interviews and empirical studies show that neither congressional defense committee leadership nor voting patterns on military questions is correlated with defense expenditure.[32] On the other hand, the motivations and discretion of other government players, from bureaucrats to generals, are often quite significant and underappreciated.

Representatives and senators are assumed to have "chits" that they use to direct certain spoils their way. These might indeed be spent on defense contracts. Evidence for this idea is usually anecdotal—citations of the number of military bases in Mendel Rivers's (Dem.-S.C.) district, for instance, or the flashy maps Rockwell produced in the early 1980s to show how almost every congressional constituency stood to gain a chunk of business from the B-1 bomber. But there are a number of problems with this line of reasoning. First, it ignores other government players. By the time a program reaches the appropriation stage, it has gestated for a number of years, and executive branch managers generally have in mind specific contractors at specific sites as the producers of what they need. Expertise and facilities, especially in the more innovative cold war procurement categories, are where they are and cannot easily be moved, even at the behest of a member of Congress.

Buttressing this view of congressional power over sitings is the contention that Congress wields greater power over facility closings than over openings. U.S. Air Force Gen. John Herres, for instance, believes that

> the military is the dog that gets wagged by the tail when it comes to base closure. . . . Operating base structure is expensive as hell. You don't win wars with base structure, but with weapons systems. We always want to close more bases than we can get away with. But we always get zinged by the political community.[33]

In plant or base closings, members of Congress are accountable to an existing constituency of firms and jobholders, rather than the potential constituency an opening evokes. In addition, it is easier to keep funding an existing activity than to insist that a new activity be created from scratch in one's district. For instance, a newcomer to the Illinois Defense Technology Association occasionally suggests that it try, with congressional help, to convince a big defense contractor to relocate to Illinois. The rest of the members then teach the newcomer about the ludicrousness of such a proposal. Better to fight for more contracts to existing area firms and to keep the Great Lakes Naval Station open.

Second, the argument confuses defense expenditures with plant siting. Most annual expenditures are for incremental projects, replacement parts, a new or modified generation of fighter plane, or similar equipment that will almost surely come from one of a few existing suppliers, minimizing locational choice. De facto evidence of congressional impotence in defense plant siting is the simple fact that defense manufacturing capacity is quite concentrated in the United States— and remained so even in the geographically competitive 1980s, when defense spending was booming. Even when plant relocation is possible or planned, congressional politics plays a minor role. When United Technologies' Pratt & Whitney division wanted to relocate an operation, politics was its lowest-ranked criterion for doing so among eight, far behind cost and availability of labor, access to highways, site features, and infrastructure. No contractors reported in our interviews that congressional politics loomed large in their locational calculus.

This is not to say that isolated instances of congressional sway do not distort patterns of defense contracting. Donald Potter of Stewart-Warner argues that "the politics stuff is grossly overrated" but nevertheless believes that it could matter in the big contracts, "not [contracts] in the millions, but in the billions." Another industrial manager thinks there is a certain amount of horse-trading on the big projects— you can have this airplane if we can have this military facility. To win the larger new weapon programs, concessions must sometimes be made to individual members of Congress.

Geographical Constituency Building

Of greater significance in anchoring the Gunbelt is "geographical constituency building." This is an exercise institutionalized within the Pentagon: a group of staffers analyzes the political distribution of defense sentiment and then tries to mobilize enough votes on important new projects by pointing out to individual members of Congress the jobs and firms in their district potentially affected. Rarely, however, does this work its way back into the procurement planning process. Placating Congress may be a minor irritant for defense contractors, but not a serious concern. While one or two long-time defense industry executives could recall an instance in which congressional clout mattered, most said they could not, claiming that expertise and track record, as well as Pentagon connections and strategic concerns, are what count. The Pentagon's "geographical constituency building," in fact, sends influence in the opposite direction: to get the weapon systems it wants passed, the Pentagon makes sure that Congress knows what dollars will be spent in particular districts. One congressional staffer asserted that it takes the potential creation of only a few jobs or small businesses to convince a member that he or she should vote for a certain defense appropriation.

Congressional configurations, as well as presidential preferences, do appear to be more important in explaining military facility location than the location of defense manufacturing and service capacity. The infamous role of Sen. Lyndon Johnson in establishing Houston's space center and Sen. John Stennis's (Dem.-Ala.) role in Huntsville's growing arsenal are but a few of the many suspected instances.

But some members of Congress from defense-oriented districts turn out not to be "hawks" and refuse to support every weapon system that has any impact on their districts. George Brown (Dem.-Calif.) of Los Angeles, Ron Dellums (Dem.-Calif.) of Oakland, and Joseph Kennedy (Dem.-Mass.) of Boston are just a few of those members whose records on defense have consistently reflected their preference for cutbacks. One labor union leader told us about the response of Congressman Dellums to a plea that he support a contract for a naval ship that might be landed by Oakland's navy yard. Dellums said that he was absolutely opposed to the program, but that if it should pass, he would do his best to see that the Oakland yard got a fair deal in the competition.

The lack of correspondence between the locus of military spending and the votes of members of Congress is good news; it suggests that principles, not just pocketbooks, still count for a great deal. Yet as high-tech warfare assumes a more permanent role in the U.S. economy, and as "privatization" cuts into other areas of government activity, it becomes increasingly tempting for members of Congress to treat military spending as a pot of jobs and income for the folks back home.

The Pentagon therefore often engages in highly visible campaigns to convince Congress to spend on particular weapon systems. Congressional *support* of a program is important, though Congress has much less to do with *how* program monies are spent. Companies often mobilize local people to support weapons programs, hiring the biggest advertising and public relations firms in the country and targeting publications, communities, and opinion-makers. In initiatives to "keep the B-1 sold," Rockwell set up a speaker's bureau and had its employees speak with publishers and government personnel around the country. It made glamorous films about the B-1's features. It organized an effective letter-writing campaign among plant employees. Between 1975 and 1977, Rockwell spent $1.35 million to mobilize employees, stockholders, communities, and mass organizations to support the B-1 bomber, the space shuttle, and a California referendum, over $900,000 of which was deducted from pretax income as a cost of doing business.[34]

Gunbelt Boosterism

Another difficulty with the pork-barreling argument is that it views members of Congress as independent agents with no connections to local politics or the military-industrial complex. But members, at least those most likely to end up on military committees and to lobby for more military activity in their home districts, are often creatures of a distinctively pro-military, local business elite rather than creators of it. In Colorado Springs, military enthusiast, Cong. Ken Kramer (Rep.-Colo.) and his predecessors and successors are much more the product of a rising defense-oriented entrepreneurial culture than builders of their local defense complex. The same is true of the heavily defense-dependent house seats in Rockford and Joliet, Illinois. The winners' campaigns are often bankrolled by defense interests, and those elected return the favor by assiduously working on winning defense dollars and spending their chits for bases and contracts back home.

Military affairs committees—which have been around since the turn of the century—have lobbied hard for military bases and defense manufacturing in their towns. San Diego, Los Angeles, and San Francisco all competed to be the West Coast naval headquarters; the historian Roger Lotchin found that successful boosterism had much to do with San Diego's victory.[35] Similarly, in the postwar period, new military-industrial complexes were erected in places like Colorado Springs, Huntsville, and Titusville-Melbourne in part because of the special efforts of western and southern military affairs committees. In contrast, Massachusetts and Chicago did not spawn such local boosters until the 1980s.

Although military affairs committees often arranged for cheap or free land packages for both plants and military installations, it was not so much their ability to lower the cost of doing business that won them their sought-after prizes—it was their success in promoting their area's pro-military climate. Generals with discretionary power and new entrepreneurs with defense contracts in hand looking for a greenfield site found the welcome mat out in these western and southern cities. In contrast, they received, at best, ambivalent responses to their proposals from the major manufacturing centers of the industrial heartland—Detroit, Buffalo, and Chicago.

Local boosterism, however, appears to explain which communities *within* regions were designated as defense growth centers by the Pentagon, rather than the overall national pattern. Strategic concerns would often dictate that installations be located in one broad region of the country over another—as, for instance, in the interior siting of air and space defense functions, or in the West Coast siting of new naval facilities. Within each region, cities and towns vied for the jobs and facilities; only a lucky few won out over the many competitors. Thus, mounting a boosterist effort did not in itself guarantee success, as the story of San Antonio shows. But both Lotchin's research on California and our own on Colorado Springs suggest that high-quality boosterism can make a big difference.

Long-term, successful boosterist coalitions have helped create distinctive military-oriented enclaves, which in turn have elected pro-military politicians. Members of Congress from such places can be expected to prefer positions on committees important for military appropriations and to cash in their chits for this type of assignment. In contrast, a member representing the more diversified and commercially oriented Midwest is more likely to be willing to trade a vote for a base in a southerner's district for a vote for urban renewal funding or farm price supports. Thus, through "logrolling," rather than pork-barreling, geographical concentrations of defense-oriented activity remain that way.

The Benefits of the Gunbelt

To those who created it, the Gunbelt has been successful. Its new cities, lifestyles, and real estate markets are highly praised by its partisans. The people who built the Gunbelt feel strongly that it is a good place to live, to work, and to do business. But has the Gunbelt been good for the whole country? One argument is that it has contributed to the narrowing of disparity in American regional incomes. Since the 1940s, per capita incomes in the South and the Southwest have risen from below 75 percent of the national average to close to the national norm, while per capita incomes in the Middle Atlantic and Great Lakes states have fallen from well above the national norm to levels much closer to it.[36] The growth of well-paid defense industry jobs helped to reverse the traditional disparity in standards of living between the industrial heartland and the South.

But how much can overall equalization be ascribed to defense spending? First, in addition to raising per capita incomes in some regions, Pentagon largesse has kept per capita incomes in New England and the far West securely above the national average throughout this century. Military spending appears to have insulated these regions from the general downward pressure exerted by wage equalization and out-movement of industry in other parts of the country. Also, the contribution of defense to higher regional incomes is a very spotty phenomenon: a close look at the distribution of jobs and incomes by city, suburb, and county shows that military procurement has had a very uneven impact even in the regions garnering the lion's share of it.[37]

Of course, many other forces shaped regional income differentials over the decades. The narrowing of the gap between incomes in the industrial heartland and the South is in large part a result of the migration northward of poor rural blacks and whites from the Cotton Belt and the Appalachians. Displaced by mechanization from their agricultural and coal-mining jobs, large numbers of southerners were drawn in the 1930s through the 1950s to the booming factories of

Detroit, Chicago, and Cleveland, only to be displaced again by dein-dustrialization in the 1970s and 1980s. The funneling of military pro-curement dollars away from the industrial heartland played no small role in this process. As the aerospace industries supplanted consumer goods industries as the major manufacturing job generators of the postwar period, the dislocation problems of recent migrants to the heartland were compounded. Meanwhile, a reverse migration of edu-cated northerners into southern defense-based communities—Oak Ridge, Huntsville, Titusville-Melbourne—helped to boost average southern per capita incomes.

A second case for the Gunbelt—made not only by its builders and boosters but by independent analysts—is its ability to generate di-verse new industries. The areas where high-tech defense dollars have been concentrated—Boston, Los Angeles, Silicon Valley, Seattle, Min-neapolis, Dallas-Fort Worth—are among those lauded for engender-ing new high-tech industries in the postwar period. From aerospace to electronics, communications equipment, and computers, Pentagon dollars were almost always crucial to the founding of these new industrial districts, either through direct R&D funding or by ensuring a market for sales. Most accounts of Silicon Valley, Orange County, and resurgent, high-tech New England celebrate the creation of new labor pools, the predominance of small new firms, and the creation of new types of business services that specialize in serving youthful, innovative industries such as computers and semiconductors.[38] The suggestion is that without these virgin (or regenerated) locations, the nation would not have advanced so far in developing such technolo-gies. This is a debatable speculation. Although in the older industrial heartland entrepreneurs found it difficult to sell their ideas and to compete in the shade of the large, long-established, oligopolistic, commercially oriented firms that dominated both the consumer and capital goods markets, in most European countries military produc-tion facilities are physically more closely integrated into older com-mercial regions.

Gunbelt Drawbacks

The rise of the Gunbelt has nevertheless had its costs, not only for the nation but for the regions it dominates. Throughout the postwar period, the Gunbelt's emergence has made regional economies—both those dependent on defense and those that are not—more vul-

nerable to idiosyncratic economic cycles that do not reflect national
trends. This is exacerbated in each region to the extent that it special-
izes in certain technologies or weapon systems. Political cycles of
defense buildup and build-down do not correspond very closely to
business cycles as we know them. Indeed, military spending cycles
tend to be countercyclical. If defense industries were more consistently located next to commercial ones, then we might expect some
relief for the unemployment problems associated with a downturn in
one or the other sector.

When the major military supply industries were located in the
industrial heartland, there was a high degree of such convertibility
between industries. The enormous diversion of resources into and out
of defense production before and after the Second World War was
handled quite easily; Detroit retooled auto plants into bomber factories, and Illinois retooled tractor plants into tank factories. But as
defense production shifted away from the heartland, both old and
new regions lost this flexibility. One became more dependent on
mature civilian sectors, the other on military contracts.

This is underlined by recent experience. In the past decade the
United States has experienced a remarkable divergence in regional
growth rates. From 1979 to 1986, when defense procurement awards
rose rapidly in real dollars, jobs in New England and the South Atlantic, mountain, and Pacific regions grew in excess of 15 percent; in the
Great Lakes states they declined by some 65,000.[39] In the early 1980s,
recession was displacing workers from auto and steel plants in Michigan and Illinois. But no recession-proof aerospace jobs were nearby
to take up the slack.

The investment of billions of tax dollars in new industrial centers in
the Gunbelt has added two new problems to those faced by industries
in the older industrial regions: a lack of basic investment in regional
infrastructure, and a loss of vital creative talent. Considerable tax
resources have gone into the construction and maintenance of the
new aerospace-oriented communities in the Gunbelt; while older
plants in the Midwest have been shuttered and mothballed, new
plants have been built in the South and the West. New cities and
suburbs have sprouted around them, often with considerable national
taxpayer support for the construction of sewers, water pipes, highways, and other types of infrastructure. The Pentagon also pays "impact aid" to school districts and local governments, compensating for
the tax base they lose through the presence of tax-exempt government property.

Billions of dollars have been spent over the postwar period on such communities. This social investment would not pose a problem if infrastructure everywhere was fully employed. Over the same period, older industrial regions experienced industrial decline and dramatic out-migration, emptying plants, houses, and school districts. Infrastructure utilization rates fell and local tax receipts shrank, making it difficult to maintain or modernize community facilities. When new federally funded schools, plants, and utilities are built in Los Angeles or Dallas, at tax payers' expense, and serve groups who have benefited from such facilities elsewhere, this process constitutes a net waste of societal resources. If new military production had been located in existing population centers, the same funds could have been spent to better house our lower-income population, cut taxes, lower deficits, or improve our quality of life in many different ways.[40]

In constructing the Gunbelt, American taxpayers have also financed one of the most impressive population redistributions in history. Generations of scientists and engineers have been recruited to Gunbelt locations at federal expense. Whether an engineer from Boeing in Seattle or a college graduate from the University of Illinois, new employees of Rockwell in Los Angeles have their moving expenses paid for by the company and charged to the government on existing contracts. Estimates of the cost of such moves range between $5,000 and $20,000. Over the postwar period, entirely new labor pools have been formed in this manner. Midwestern engineering schools, many of them among the best in the nation, have routinely shipped a majority of their graduates out of state immediately upon graduation, predominantly to defense contractors. Although not designed as a population resettlement program, this process has nevertheless operated as one. To the social tally for new infrastructure must be added the cost of defense-related moves—a not inconsiderable sum that might have been spent more productively.

The removal from their regional economies of large numbers of the most highly skilled and creative people—who were educated with corporate and personal tax dollars from within the region—handicaps the ability of those regions to compete in increasingly competitive international markets. No abundance of cross-fertilizing ideas flows through the regional business community. It is true that the large auto, steel, consumer electronics, and machine tool firms are mainly responsible for their own disappointing performance—particularly through their oligopolistic domination of their markets. Nevertheless, their workers and host communities are doubly debilitated by the lack of high-tech alternatives, such as those nurtured in the new military-industrial complexes.

Gunbelt Politics

The rise of the Gunbelt has had dramatic geopolitical consequences as well. It has shifted political power south and west, toward regions that are markedly more conservative and Republican than the industrial heartland. Not all regions that have shared in the military buildup are conservative—Massachusetts is an example. (Massachusetts, however, has not experienced a major population increase; indeed, it has suffered net out-migration over the postwar period, and even in the 1980s, the defense buildup had no effect on its relatively low population growth rates and continued out-migration.) Decade after decade, redistricting has given greater power in the electoral college and in Congress to voters from the newer defense-dependent districts. By and large, white-collar employees of defense industries vote much more strongly Republican than do their counterparts in the rest of the economy. It is no coincidence that southern California is a safe constituency for pro-military conservatism, or that Colorado Springs consistently elects "hawks" and votes 70 percent Republican. Similarly, the emergence of new military-industrial centers in the South may have contributed to the recomposition of the southern electorate and its shift toward Republican presidential candidates: while white, Republican professionals moved south, rural, black Democrats went north.

Nowhere is this change more apparent than in the presidential vote. Indeed, the three states of California, Texas, and Massachusetts account for no less than five of the nine postwar presidents. Each of these states has reaped a disproportionate share of the nation's defense contracts. Of the postwar presidents, only Ford and Carter came from states whose per capita shares of prime contracts were less than the nation's (although Georgia ranks exceptionally high in military facilities). In presidential races, the defense-dependent southern and western voters show greater preference for Republican candidates who promise a strong defense and are staunchly committed to major weapon systems.

The physical separation of the defense-oriented aerospace industry from other industrial regions and the concentration of defense-dependent voters in new regions may also have had a positive effect on the level and geographic distribution of defense expenditures. Members of Congress from nondefense regions are less interested in defense matters and tend to shun committees that make the major defense decisions, preferring instead to serve on other committees, such as agriculture, interior, labor, or social services. (Of course, there are important exceptions, including Cong. Les Aspin [Dem.-Wisc.] and Sen. William Proxmire [Dem.-Wisc.]—both of whom, however, have been more critical of Pentagon practices and requests than their Gunbelt colleagues.) These members surrender the playing field to their more concerned colleagues, who specialize in the intricacies of defense spending and are in a better position to funnel it to their home districts.

Thus has the Gunbelt become self-sustaining: the different regional levels of participation in the procurement decision-making process reinforce and expand the imbalances that first emerged in the 1950s.

A Post–Cold War Gunbelt?

Overall, then, the existence of the Gunbelt sustains the pressure to keep up military spending and to continue pursuing military-oriented foreign policy. Within the military a constituency exists for supporting current levels of military spending on purely economic grounds. Over half of all defense jobs are in just ten states, often heavily concentrated in certain locales. For instance, one in five workers in the Norwich–New London labor market of southeastern Connecticut works in a defense-related job, and many more are in service, transportation, and commercial jobs that serve the defense industry. The Bath Iron Works, which builds navy ships, is Maine's largest employer, drawing workers from a thirty-mile region.[41]

When a single sector, be it a military base or a defense contractor, looms so large in a regional economy, its significance is not missed by others in the community. The salaries and wages earned by workers at these plants and installations cycle through the local economy, supporting the employment of many more people. Because of this multiplier effect, the true dependency of certain areas is often underestimated. Estimates of the defense-dependency of Los Angeles in the 1960s placed it at about 40 percent of the work force after defense spending had rippled through the regional economy.[42]

Significant cuts in defense spending will have the greatest effect on places where absolute levels of spending are high and where the local economy is relatively defense-dependent. In the past, the Los Angeles and Seattle economies have demonstrated considerable vulnerability to military spending cycles, each enduring periods of considerably higher than average unemployment. For example, in 1968 Boeing accounted for 19 percent of the Seattle-area work force. The dovetailing of commercial and military setbacks over the next three years resulted in a drop in Boeing employment from 100,000 to 38,000. Area unemployment shot up to 12 percent—double the national average—for a sustained period.[43]

California, as the greatest beneficiary of the 1980s military buildup, is perhaps the most vulnerable, at least in absolute terms. Already by the late 1980s, layoffs were increasing. Jobs in aerospace instruments fell by 11 percent in 1989 alone and were expected to fall another 5.5 percent in 1990 and 2 percent in 1991. Missile and spacecraft jobs declined 1.2 percent in 1989, with larger declines of 3.3 percent and 5.3 percent, respectively, expected over the next two years.[44] California is relatively diversified, however, in other sectors—commercial high-tech, tourism, entertainment, apparel, oil, and agriculture. These industries will help cushion the impact of military cutbacks. But individual California cities and communities will still be badly hurt.

What defense cutbacks represent, especially in light of the Gulf War, is a major shakeout and restructuring of the military market. Part of the restructuring is a response to the growing globalization of the military-industrial base: the Pentagon is increasingly forced to buy from foreign suppliers the high-tech components and subsystems that domestic producers cannot, or no longer know how to, make. The driving force behind the cutbacks, however, is a shift in military doctrine from one based on strategic war-fighting capability—aimed at the Warsaw Pact countries in Europe—to one prepared for what Michael Klare calls "mid-intensity conflict" against Third World powers like Iraq.[45]

The new military strategy will entail some changes in the types of armaments and technologies that the Pentagon requires from its manufacturers. Instead of relatively small numbers of large-scale strategic nuclear weapon systems and platforms, such as M-X missiles and Trident submarines, the new military will need greater numbers of small-scale yet still powerful weapons that are rapidly deployable and highly mobile, flexible, and precise for use in tactical combat situations. These weapons will include new advanced tactical fighter aircraft and advanced mobile missiles, artillery, and rockets. The new military strategy will also rely more on advanced transport and sealift capabilities and on more integrated, "intelligent" C³I systems.

Both defense industries and Pentagon procurement offices have started to adjust to this new market context. The SDI program is trying to shift its mission emphasis from strategic long-distance defense to tactical medium-range defense, and a Lockheed-led contractor team (including Boeing and General Dynamics) recently beat out a McDonnell-Douglas–Northrop bid to develop the new advanced tactical fighter, the F-22—winning a $64 billion contract if all 648 planes are built.[46]

Clearly there will be new winners and losers in this shakeout, even though the Pentagon will try to employ its closet industrial policy to keep the core of the military-industrial complex intact. On the heels of the Gulf War, the Bush administration supported new export credits for U.S. arms-makers.[47] And the Pentagon will pursue, if grudgingly, its dual-use, high-tech R&D programs. But some sectors, firms, and towns will lose. The decision to go with the F-22 at Lockheed could herald a drastic reduction in the number of military fighter, bomber, and attack aircraft manufacturers, from seven in 1980 to two or three.[48] Similarly, the pressures are growing to close "wasteful" military bases.[49]

In the past, defense-dependent businesses and communities could count on new market booms following periodic declines in military spending. Although the new military strategy will provide the rationale for continued military spending, its emphasis on a leaner, meaner, mobile military force will not suffice to keep the Pentagon's budget at cold war levels. As David J. Wheaton, General Dynamics vice-president for planning, observes, "The difference now is that we don't see what would bring [spending] up again."[50]

It is too early to know what the impacts of this sea change will be on Gunbelt industries and communities. Firms and communities that are heavily reliant on antiquated strategic weapon systems and the research and development underlying them will obviously face the greatest threat. Military bases near air or sea ports from which ground units can be speedily deployed will be favored over those in more remote locations.[51] The nation's nuclear weapons labs—Livermore, Los Alamos, Sandia—are already undergoing extensive reevaluation of their long-term missions, with hopes of switching some of their work to civilian objectives. But no overall adjustment policy has been developed to help communities weather the storm of military cutbacks. Economic development assistance and job retraining aid, both of which were passed in the House defense appropriations bill of 1990, are steps in the right direction. But the examples of other communities hit by plant closings in the 1980s are not reassuring. If no new source of economic activity is identified, such funds will be squandered and retrained workers will still be unemployed. Some guarantee of new jobs is required.

Facility reuse is a more pro-active approach to the problem. The state legislatures of many of the more defense-dependent states have passed or are considering legislation to support alternative use planning for their military plants and facilities.[52] As a concept, alternative use planning is attractive but has a long way to go before becoming politically acceptable, as we will see in the next chapter.

8

Scaling the Wall of
Separation

■

THE lights in the ballroom dimmed. On the dais, the spotlights flooded four bright red Soviet flags with their yellow hammers and sickles. Silhouetted against them were the sturdy profiles of retired U.S. Navy Rear Admiral Stanley Fine and Harvey Gordon, the director of government relations for Martin-Marietta Corporation. As the Soviet national anthem boomed out, none of us in the room could help but marvel at the changes this occasion represented. Moments later, the Soviet ambassador, Yuri Dubinin, and the governor of Ohio, Richard Celeste, flanked by the peace activist and academic critic John Ullmann and by Robert Buffenbarger of the Machinists' Union, faced each other in front of four symmetrically placed American flags while dozens of defense contractors in the audience hummed "The Star-Spangled Banner."

What followed on that winter day in 1990 at the Governor's Conference on Economic Transitions for Ohio's Small-Business Defense Contractors (23–24 January) was a stunning speech by the Soviet ambassador. Dubinin announced that the Soviet Union was attempting to cut military spending by 42 percent from 1988 to 1992, with troop reductions of 500,000. The prosperity, stability, and reconstruction of the Soviet economy, he noted, depended upon the reallocation of Soviet resources; to date, expertise, R&D funds, and machinery had been in the service of Soviet defense. In 1989 Mikhail Gorbachev's government drafted a new five-year conversion plan for 1991–95 and sent it on to the Council of Ministers. It proposed a dramatic process of conversion of military-industrial capacity, centered on 420 heavily defense-dependent enterprises. Production of tanks would fall by 52 percent, helicopters by 60 percent, ammunition by 20 percent, and combat aircraft by 20 percent. In their stead, civilian output of stereos, videocassette recorders, personal computers, refrigerators, vacuum cleaners, and the machinery to make them would increase. The Soviets, Dubinin claimed, would invest nine billion rubles in this process, but it would be an efficient investment: financed by a savings of twelve billion rubles in direct government spending, it would release seventeen billion rubles worth of untapped resources for future development.

In his closing comments to the Columbus audience, Dubinin gently told them that when Soviet citizens hear the word *Ohio,* they think of a nuclear submarine. Such is the legacy of the American practice of naming warships after the fifty states. He hoped that in the future the word *Ohio* would come to mean something quite different. For his part, he would bring back news to his people that the governor of Ohio and a large number of his state's small-business managers were serious about reorientation to a peacetime economy.

Whether a "peace dividend" will come about in the United States is a very big question, particularly in light of the Persian Gulf War. The 1990 Ohio conference illustrated the schizophrenia of American leadership on the question. While most participants were palpably excited about the prospects for peace and cooperation, many of the military contractors, and even the government people, were seriously worried, even panicked, about their survival in the post–cold war world. Governor Celeste himself gave a speech that reflected these tensions. For two-thirds of it, he waxed enthusiastic about the historic changes taking place and the great opportunities they might afford for industrial revitalization. At the end, however, he reverted to a tedious recital of existing Ohio programs for local economic development assistance, programs that include helping Ohio contractors learn to bid on Pentagon projects.

Meanwhile, there was murmuring in the hall. Dozens of military contractors who had never met before were swapping horror stories about government red tape and Pentagon fickleness. Between the laments were sandwiched tips on how to approach one's congressional representative, who in Congress was most receptive to defense industry interests, and how to master the Pentagon bidding process. Everyone wanted to know what was really happening—how soon, and how deep, the cuts would come. Few discussed conversion. Some of us wondered whether this conference might not have counterproductively strengthened the resolve of the state's defense contractors to stick with their affluent military customer.

Big Business and the Present Build-down

Significant exit barriers—their degree of defense-dependency, the unique nature of military contracting, its profitability, and the "wall of separation" between the military and commercial sectors—make it difficult for the big defense firms to fashion new commercial products using their existing facilities and expertise. Like Lockheed, which scrambled in the late 1980s for alternatives to help it weather deep defense budget cuts, the big ACE firms have capital equipment that is often inflexible and outdated, and their expensive overhead would not be tolerated in the commercial market. Their heavy debt burdens make it hard for them to raise capital for other ventures. Ongoing R&D contracts for future weapon systems keep them hooked in.[1]

In the late 1980s, despite fair warnings of a military build-down, the big military contractors directed most of their energies toward finding market niches within the still huge Pentagon budget. These "safe harbors" included moving ahead on new generations of high-tech weapons; lobbying for maintenance of high defense budgets; peddling recycled weapon systems to foreign governments; and putting together stock buy-backs, mergers, and acquisitions to make their financial balance sheets stronger or more diversified. There is no sign that this basic approach will change in the 1990s without a dramatic shift in the defense industry's business culture.

One favored strategy of the big aerospace contractors is to position themselves in particular military niches where their expertise is dominant and assured. Those with a foot in the door on fancy new weapon systems have a head start. Martin-Marietta is strengthening its role as lead contractor for the production of expendable launch vehicles, and General Dynamics is nurturing its lead in submarine, missile, and aircraft programs. Hughes, betting that simulated field training for troops will be crucial, is aggressively expanding its work in that area; TRW and Martin-Marietta are just as aggressively pursuing "verification technologies" for monitoring compliance with arms control treaties.[2]

Those companies that specialize in avionics and communications have a better shot at future military markets than the weapons platform makers. Producers of weapon systems appropriate to the military's new strategy of preparedness for "mid-intensity conflicts" will also be favored.[3] Platforms—ships, aircraft, tanks—are long-lived products and sitting ducks for budget cutters and arms negotiators. The future, some believe, is in the gadgets that go on the platforms.

Martin-Marietta's vice-president and chief financial officer, Marcus Bennett, reports that his company is planning on "improving the Air Force without buying new airplanes" by selling them fancy upgraded gear.[4]

Of all the defense firms, General Dynamics is perhaps the master of this market niche strategy. In the mid-1980s it decided against taking on any new risky or experimental military projects; it is taking what CEO Stanley Pace calls a "stick-to-the-knitting approach" by diversifying among all branches of the service and by specializing in heartland weapons—bread and butter armaments that might survive in the post–cold war era. In the opinion of General Dynamic's Stanley Pace, "We feel the government will maintain heartland programs at some level. . . . That makes us more insulated from the cuts than our competition."[5] The company, 85 percent of whose $9.5 billion in annual sales comes from government contracts, has a foot in every field, selling M-1 tanks to the army, Seawolf attack submarines to the navy, and F-16 fighter planes to the air force.

Making more foreign sales is another traditionally successful strategy for dealing with cutbacks. After the Vietnam War, overseas markets were lucrative for American aerospace companies. When U.S. government purchases dropped from $44 billion in 1968 to $17 billion in 1975, foreign military sales took up much of the slack, albeit with some lag. In 1976, the last trough in the domestic military spending cycle before the current one, 70 percent of the missiles purchased by the Army Missile Command were bound for foreign countries, and in that same year foreign sales accounted for a larger share of U.S. military aircraft production than did domestic military demand.[6]

But foreign sales will offer less relief to the beleaguered military contractor in the 1990s. Several of the world's key industrialized and industrializing nations have greatly expanded their arms exports, creating stiffer competition for the once dominant Soviet and U.S. arms traders. Even China and North Korea, once dependent on Soviet weapons themselves, are getting into the act.[7] The U.S. market share is bound to deteriorate. Yet as long as there are Third World hot spots, and a U.S. government willing to subsidize its own arms exports rather than make efforts to slow the worldwide proliferation of weapons, U.S. manufacturers will struggle to maintain market share, even if the returns are meager.

Diversification through buying up nondefense companies is another strategy that defense-dependent aerospace firms use to cope with a tightening military market. Lucrative returns from the Reagan buildup were translated into new acquisitions that magically lowered corporate defense-dependency rates. In just fifteen months, from January 1987 to May 1988, fifteen major mergers and acquisitions were fashioned, absorbing $6.1 billion in cash.[8] Such buyouts have had a major impact on the defense-dependency rates of some corporations. From 1985 to 1988, Lockheed's defense-dependency rate fell from 62 to 41 percent, and Rockwell's from 65 to 32 percent.

The fruits of such mergers, however, have been disappointing. Take the GM-Hughes deal, the biggest merger involving two defense contractors during the 1980s. By 1990 Hughes Aircraft was rumored to be worth $2 billion less than the $5.2 billion GM paid for it in 1985. Hughes, still about 80 percent dependent upon military spending, has suffered from high costs, the loss of several critical contracts, and stiff penalties on its naval satellite radar operations. Yet GM has continued to pour money into Hughes, including another $700 million to acquire smaller firms that produce corporate satellite systems and flight simulators.[9]

Nor has Hughes expertise been used to make better GM cars. GM had hoped that Hughes's radar and satellite technology would be applicable to the car of the future. But only a trickle of gadgetry ended up in GM's cars, such as the fighter-style "head-up display" that projects the car's speed on the windshield. One analyst said, "I don't know what GM has gotten out of Hughes that they couldn't have gotten by putting an ad in the newspaper and hiring 100 engineers."[10]

What holds for GM is true of the domestic auto industry as a whole. All of the Big Three automakers spent heavily in the early 1980s to build or expand their defense holdings, in anticipation of the Reagan buildup. Yet in early 1990 both Ford and Chrysler announced that they were selling their defense divisions to concentrate on autos. In retrospect, they would have been better off using their capital to defend their position in the domestic auto industry against vigorous competition from foreign firms.

Straying even further from their manufacturing missions, some of the big ACE companies are raising new funds by closing up shop and cashing in on the land underneath them. Plants once located on the urban periphery, like those in El Segundo near Los Angeles or on Long Island in New York, are now occupying very expensive real estate. Grumman plans to bulldoze its runways and some facilities in Bethpage, Long Island, and redevelop two hundred of its five-hundred-acre headquarters into an office, shopping center, and hotel complex, hoping to raise $1 billion in the process. Such a diversification would instantly transform Grumman from an aircraft manufacturer into a land development services company.

But company diversification, whether through acquisitions or through land development, will not staunch the tide of defense plant closings with their adverse consequences for workers and communities. If the defense cutbacks continue and foreign sales languish, only commercial product development can take up the slack. Switching into new product lines is a riskier strategy for the big contractors facing DOD spending cutbacks.

Companies like Boeing, GE, and McDonnell-Douglas, which have booming commercial aircraft markets to serve, have had the most success at it. Both Boeing and McDonnell-Douglas have lowered their defense-dependency rates dramatically in the 1980s—from 41 to 19 percent for the former, and 79 to 55 percent for the latter—thanks in large part to a coincidental, though perhaps short-lived, boom in commercial aircraft sales at the end of the decade. The commercial route is viable only for those firms with long experience in the commercial aircraft market. The boom has not been much help to Lockheed, Hughes, Rockwell, Northrop, or Grumman. Lockheed anticipated that in 1990 it would pick up $100 million in subcontracts from heavily backlogged commercial aircraft firms, but that is a drop in the bucket given the company's total sales of $9.9 billion. It is not unlikely that one or more of the big aircraft-makers, Grumman or perhaps Northrop, will disappear from the ranks in this decade.[11]

The history of the efforts the big ACE firms have made to get into new product lines is instructive about both the causes of their failure and the lure of continued DOD contracts. After the Vietnam War, a few companies did manage to shift gears. In 1963 Kaman coped with the helicopter competition by applying its vibration technology to high-quality, fiberglass-laminated acoustical guitars. It took much longer than management expected to turn a profit—until 1972—because penetrating the musical instrument market proved quite difficult. Getting into the guitar business and acquiring bearings and other nonmilitary business helped Kaman lower its defense-dependency rate to below 50 percent by 1977.[12]

But in each successive build-down period, there have been fewer and fewer such stories. Surveying the history of product conversion efforts, the economist Murray Weidenbaum found that aerospace firms have tried many new product lines, but that, "with one major exception (aircraft), these diversification attempts have each been relatively small in comparison with military equipment. . . . The list of abandoned commercial ventures is a long and constantly growing one."[13]

In two of the more spectacular and oft-cited cases, Rohr and Boeing-Vertol failed at their entry into the mass-transit market. Hamstrung by sluggish demand and numerous technical problems, they were unable to match foreign competitors' quality within the time frame adopted by their top managements.[14] These failures were not foregone conclusions. If the companies involved had taken a long-term view, and if the government had supported their pioneering efforts in this new sphere, they might well have succeeded. Instead, financial support and procurement commitments were suddenly withdrawn when the federal Urban Mass Transit Program abruptly shut down at just the critical infant-industry stage.

Over time, the big defense contractors began to articulate the heart of the conversion dilemma—no other product area offered the guarantee of federal commitment, public resources, and luxuriously long lead times that producing defense hardware did. In testifying before Congress in 1970, Boeing's chairman put it bluntly:

> The company has examined many of the civil systems markets during the past five years. These have included in-depth studies of surface transportation, water management, waste disposal and security systems. We find that each of these have elements consistent with our technical and systems management capabilities. However, we do not see either established national goals in these areas, consistent commitment to adequate funding, reasonable-size contracts of adequate duration, or contracting modes consistent with these [civilian markets].[15]

They also discovered that, to make matters worse, commercial initiatives might not merely fail but weaken the company's position in future military markets. In the 1970s Grumman aggressively responded to the Vietnam War build-down with a plan to move half its sales into commercial products. It tried buses, solar energy, refrigerators, incinerators, and a new lightweight canoe. Most of these efforts fizzled out, and the divisions pursuing them were closed down. Ironically, when the 1980s military buildup began, Grumman was saddled with a heavy debt load and had trouble competing for new military contracts.[16]

Contractors seem to believe that there are two lessons in the long history of defense busts and booms: efforts to pursue new products are doomed to failure, and defense will always come back to bail them out. This has been the pattern throughout the twentieth century. After the First World War, Boeing, its contracts cancelled, tried to build sea sleds, a "flying boat" for passenger and mail service, and furniture to keep its workers employed, all unsuccessfully. What really bailed out

Boeing was an order to recondition fifty De Havilland 4s for the army. After the Second World War, Douglas lost money on an aluminum rowboat, and Ryan Aeronautical tried making stainless-steel caskets. Some ventured into new spheres, such as plastics—Martin brought out its Marvinal, a polyvinyl-chloride coating for shower curtains. North American's Dutch Kindleberger and Lee Atwood combed the Sears Roebuck catalog in search of products his company could make but with the rise of the cold war, decided to stick to aircraft.[17]

In the 1990s most of the big military-oriented companies remain committed to selling to the Pentagon. They are still living off highly profitable, established programs. Some are proud of it. CEO Stanley Pace of General Dynamics put it this way: "We're a pure play in aerospace and defense and we intend to stay that way. There will always be a strong defense budget. Even if it goes down, it will still be substantial."[18] Many believe that the government will eventually come through for them, as McDonnell-Douglas found in its long wait for the C-17 contract. This attitude may not bode well for the future: appraising the big contractors' unwillingness and inadequacy in entering the new era, Wall Street discounted aerospace-defense industry member stock by 40 percent in 1988, when the build-down began—taking them back to immediate post–Vietnam War levels.

The big ACE contractors are leery of conversion: they do not know how to do it very well, and they have not seen many success stories. In previous build-down periods, defense firms that "reconverted" to a type of production they had engaged in before did much better than those that never converted from civilian to military production in the first place. A Stanford Research Institute study for the Defense Department in 1964 noted that "a larger share of defense production today is performed by highly specialized defense contractors, many of whose products bear little resemblance to any civilian items and who have had little experience outside defense production."[19] In fact, as the cold war has carried weapons production farther and farther from the mass-production model, few military-dedicated plants remain that have *ever* made anything else. This lack of experience makes conversion a much more formidable task. Military-industrial firms have developed a culture that is geared to the military market, and they find it hard to break out of its strictures.

The lack of any effective conversion program—with technical assistance and financial aid for transition—and R&D support for new, speculative commercial technologies forces the big contractors to bank on the continuation of weapon programs. The stakes are much higher than they were after the Vietnam War. McDonnell-Douglas,

General Dynamics, and Lockheed, for instance, have seen their sales to DOD and NASA more than double in *real* terms since the mid-1970s. Furthermore, the latest build-down dovetails with a rather severe recession in the American economy, limiting possibilities in other markets. The wall of separation is indeed difficult to scale in this environment. It is no wonder that the current business strategy of big contractors has convinced the Pentagon and Congress that there are future security threats from many and often far-fetched quarters.

Smaller Firms: Headed Underwater

It is not just the large firms that have found diversification difficult. Many small firms dramatically increased their dependency on military sales in the 1980s as the Reagan buildup covered up flagging industrial performance in other sectors. Not only did they have to cope with the ups and downs of abrupt changes in military specifications, but many struggled to cope with the dichotomous demands of working for both the civilian and military markets. Concluding that their commercial markets in metals or machinery or infrastructure had dried up forever, many switched permanently to military work. Other firms were founded in the thick of military markets, without a clue about commercial alternatives.

Most of the smaller military-oriented firms subcontract for the big firms, to which their fortunes are tied. As our Lockheed informant puts it, "The aerospace industry is just one big job shop. Here in the San Fernando Valley, you could drive out and find thousands of shops that do precision work for us on demand. They suffer when things are bad. If we go in the tank, they're underwater."

The several speakers at the 1990 Ohio Governor's Conference—James Blackwell of the Center for Strategic and International Studies, Howard Etchell, president of Bowen Machine Products, and Ray Franks, president of High Tech Castings—articulated the difficulties not encountered by the big ACE firms that small contractors must confront. One reason so many are in trouble is that the large prime contractors are dealing with the build-down by cutting back on the number of vendors they use. So is the government itself. The rationale is that using fewer vendors will reduce paperwork and the proportion of supplies that have to be rejected. Hardest hit are the small firms that cannot meet stiff government regulations on quality, especially the demand for statistical quality control. Another difficulty for small firms is that many of their sales are made in the "after-market"—for instance, making replacement parts for aircraft that are already in service. As the services cut back on training and exercises, they require less maintenance work and fewer spare parts. The air force, for instance, is flying about 25 percent fewer hours now than in the mid-1980s. As a result, fighter and bomber plane parts last longer, causing a drop in orders.

For companies formed in response to the enormous Reagan buildup, many with assistance from the government, the cutbacks now present a frightening prospect. Some posted astronomical profits only to see their fabulous infancy turn into troubled adolescence as military sales growth faltered in the late 1980s. High Tech Castings is an example. Formed in 1984 by two ambitious Ohio engineers who were convinced that they could make high-quality aluminum castings to military-aerospace standards, High Tech Castings thrived at the outset. With sales of $700,000 in the first year and $3.2 million four years later—principally to the big firms, McDonnell-Douglas, Boeing, and Rockwell—the company was almost entirely dedicated to big weapon systems, such as the B-1 bomber, the F-15, and the F-18. But by 1990 its sales dropped 40 percent, and it was forced to lay off forty workers. Ray Franks thinks the commercial aircraft market, with between fifteen and twenty domestic competitors and many more worldwide, is too tough for his youthful firm.

For both new and older small defense firms, their expertise in government red tape is useless in commercial markets, and their lack of marketing skills is an outright liability. Bowen Machine Products of Bedford, Ohio, is a perfect example. In 1990 Bowen's sales of machined components and assemblies for military tanks and other army hardware were almost completely supported by military contracts, as they had been since the company's founder split off from General Electric in 1953. When military spending began to dry up in the late 1980s, Bowen tried to find a commercial product that would keep its fifty employees working. It found it was hampered by its utter lack of a marketing program—indeed, it had no sales people at all, having always depended upon its military-related customers to come to it. In the end, according to its president, Howard Etchell, Bowen decided to stick exclusively with its government client and struggled to increase its share of a shrinking pie. By 1990, when prime contractors were cutting back on the number of their subcontractors, this strategy was failing: Bowen had lost two-thirds of its 1985 peak sales of $4.4 million and had dropped from fifty employees to eighteen.

Not all small firms are done in by cutbacks. There are a few stunning cases of successful commercialization. At a 27 October 1989 conference held at the Hofstra University School of Business and sponsored by the Long Island Alliance to Prevent Nuclear War ("The Shrinking Defense Industry on Long Island: Options for Structural Readjustment"), Greg Frisby of Frisby Airborne Systems of Long Island described how his company took the risky road of internal product development. To maintain profitability as the late 1980s build-down took shape, Frisby sought to reduce its reliance on military contracts by marketing its hydraulic equipment to commercial airframe-makers. It succeeded, reducing its defense-dependency rate from 95 percent in 1985 to 35 percent by 1990.[20]

Unlike Frisby, however, most small firms respond to the threat of cutbacks by following the lead of their larger brethren—knocking on the public's door. Consider the Blaw-Knox Foundry, a large steel-casting facility dating back to 1911 in East Chicago, Indiana, with a venerable history of producing for both commercial and military markets. As a result of two takeovers in rapid succession, the foundry became increasingly dependent upon military contracts for a single product, the M-60 tank, which was slated to be replaced by the newer, fancier M-1 tank. Rejecting the alternative product recommendations in a study initiated by a community-union coalition, management pressured the union and Indiana politicians to campaign for an extension of the M-60's life. Model letters to politicians drafted for employees included the following:

> I believe in the American dream that if you work hard for a living, the rewards will come. But I feel as if my country is letting me down when the government says thanks for your efforts, but we no longer need you. . . . I need your involvement in helping to keep the doors of Blaw-Knox open with continued production of the M-60 tank. Your sincere efforts with regards to my plea for help may restore my concept of the "American way."[21]

The company also drafted model taxpayer letters conjuring up the Soviet threat and arguing for the superiority of the M-60 over the M-1. The campaign was nearly successful. Indiana senators and representatives did indeed push for more tank orders, and the Army Matériel Command responded by recommending the purchase of 210 more tanks. But the command's order was overturned by the undersecretary of the army, James Ambrose, and never reached Congress. Its efforts squandered on this single-track strategy, Blaw-Knox closed its doors permanently in 1986, laying off the final contingent of about eight hundred workers, more than 70 percent of whom were semiskilled.[22]

The depressing result of the threat of military market losses combining with the formidable challenge of already crowded commercial markets is that many small defense contractors are afraid of peace and its implications. "Peace is breaking out all over!" Nathaniel Smith, president of Ver-Val Enterprises of Fort Walton Beach, Florida, noted with alarm at the Ohio Governor's Conference, as he outlined the tough issues confronting his firm, a munitions-handling equipment company formed in 1979. One of the nation's most successful black-owned contractors, Ver-Val loads missiles and bombs and transports bombs from maker to deployer. Despite a recent layoff of 100 people out of 267, Smith notes that many of his top managers favor a strategy of "staying right where we are"—in military markets. Over and over, participants in Governor Celeste's historic conference echoed this thought. Maybe, one panel member concluded, we don't *want* to diversify. Maybe, said another, we don't know how!

The wall of separation, then, while it may not be as high for small contractors, especially those with some commercial market experience, is nevertheless difficult to breach. Given the follow-on imperative, given the Pentagon's preference for working with the big ACE firms, and given the streamlining now under way, small contractors may suffer disproportionately from budget cuts. Many are located in the traditional industrial heartland, which has already lost a large share of its commercial business and is encumbered with overcapacity and relatively high levels of unemployment. With no assistance available to small firms, the result will be permanent plant closures and the waste of facilities and human resources.

Converting the Company May Not Convert Jobs

When companies do successfully convert or diversify, the results may not produce jobs for laid-off defense workers or jobs in existing communities. Those ACE companies with preexisting commercial markets, like Boeing and McDonnell-Douglas, may be able to move some personnel from one division to another, but for the most part their commercial work is done in separate facilities and with dramatically different work styles. For instance, Boeing is trying to compensate for post–cold war losses in its military aircraft division by marketing jumbo jetliners to the Soviets. But even if Soviet jet orders help keep Boeing on its feet, they will do little for many of the workers in its old military and aerospace divisions. In 1990 Boeing planned to reduce its Puget Sound work force by 5,000.[23]

Completely new product lines are even less apt to spell new jobs for a company's workers. Raytheon, for instance, terminated eight thousand employees while adapting its microwave technology for home use, and few were retrained for the commercial operation. Kaman moved less than thirty workers from its old wooden rotor-blade shop into its new guitar production line, which in any case never employed more than one hundred workers.[24]

Company success often does not translate into new jobs because management decides to locate new lines in new areas of the country. For instance, the success of Frisby Airborne Systems has not translated into corresponding jobs for Long Island–area workers. In making the switch from the military to a commercial market, Frisby decided to open a new factory in North Carolina.[25] Grumman, also located on Long Island, has an explicit relocation strategy as part of its struggle to survive defense cuts. Grumman vice-president Jake Bussolini claimed at the 1989 Long Island conference that to remain competitive, Grumman must put 40 percent of its costs into regions that are less expensive than Long Island.

This relatively poor reemployment record, even when companies manage to thrive in commercial product lines, tends to pit management against workers in their visions of conversion. Employees want assurances that new efforts will produce jobs for those threatened. They have pushed for participation in alternative use planning and in establishing criteria for the selection of initiatives that will reemploy existing skills and sites. Companies, on the other hand, resist employee participation, guarding their management prerogatives, protecting proprietary rights to information, and insisting on the primacy of stockholder returns in their strategic calculus. This antagonism clouds the conversion issue and hampers cooperation in the pioneering efforts at commercial activity.

Labor: Reconsidering the Benefits of Cold War

Military contractors are not the only ones caught between a rock and a hard place when military spending is cut. Labor unions face related dilemmas. Although blue-collar workers are potentially more "convertible" than either companies or plants, they fear long bouts of unemployment and, even worse, the possibility that no jobs will be available in their communities after their own personal investments in retraining. Without a support system for coping with conversion, many unions succumb to the more certain route of lobbying for more military spending. As a union official at FMC's Silicon Valley plant, where four thousand workers make tanks, put it: "We used to love farm equipment, now we love tanks."[26]

Yet since the Second World War, the United Auto Workers (UAW) and the International Association of Machinists and Aerospace Workers (IAM), both with tens of thousands of workers in defense plants, have consistently taken strong stands in favor of an activist conversion program. In many ways, their ideas have been more visionary than those of their employers. After the Second World War, the UAW's Walter Reuther rebutted the claims of Henry Ford II that plants like Willow Run were "as expendable as a warship." "The pay-off must not be the layoff," Reuther retorted. He argued that six million people could be put to work manufacturing high-quality, low-cost housing in idled airframe plants and updating the nation's railroad stock by producing lightweight modern cars in old tank and electrical factories. To do this, the nation would need a peace production board, with laborers, farmers, and consumers as members, as well as government and management representatives. His Willow Run local envisioned a workers' cooperative to run the housing factory and housing cooperatives in major cities to market the plant's output.[27] This vision was obviated by the enormous surge in postwar auto demand that absorbed the blue-collar work force. During the following decades, as the auto and machinery industries began to implode, the IAM and the UAW continued to press Congress for a comprehensive conversion program that would include alternative use committees in the workplace, community-based planning committees, and a national conversion commission. (The UAW, for example, adopted a resolution to this effect at its twenty-ninth constitutional convention, held 18–23 June 1989.)

The leaders of the American Federation of Labor and Congress of Industrial Organizations (AFL-CIO) have not been solidly behind such visions. They have been successfully threatened by what William Winpisinger, past president of the IAM, calls "job blackmail." In their pitch to organized labor, the Pentagon and military contractors are quick to stress the new jobs created with new weapons programs, but they are silent about the parallel losses when cuts come. In Winpisinger's view, no other segment of the labor force is subjected to such brutal economic determinism:

> The reality is that in an economy that features planned and chronic high unemployment, in many communities military production may be the only game in town. And if that's all there is, then it's damned difficult to tell those military production workers that a particular weapon they're working on ought to be curtailed or scrapped.[28]

Until recently, the top leadership of the AFL-CIO consistently supported both cold war postures and hot war forays, for ideological as well as material reasons. But in the last few years, organized labor has begun to show signs of cooling toward military Keynesianism. Dick Greenwood, who was IAM's point man on conversion for many years, notes a "slow acceptance" of the need for conversion "on the part of the cold-warriors who are in the policy-making positions." As he puts it:

> The concept of conversion was ridiculed over the years—it was politically painted as being sort of red-tainted, so we have that psychological barrier to overcome. But people realize that we do have an opportunity to transfer resources from the military side of the ledger to the civilian side, and they also realize we're going to have to do this to keep "competitive."[29]

This shift is in large part the product of thirty years of disappointing returns. Despite the huge military buildup of the 1980s, the number of skilled, semiskilled, and unskilled workers employed in military production has been steadily decreasing, in both absolute and relative terms, owing to the automation of military production and the increased attention to R&D activities. Studies done for organized labor show that more workers would be employed if spending went to civilian rather than military production. One study in the early 1980s, for instance, showed a net gain from reoriented spending of 34,000 jobs, most of them blue-collar.[30] As it becomes clearer that losses in civilian industries are the result of a closet industrial policy that nurtures the ACE complex, the opportunity costs of a pro-military stance are harder and harder to justify.

Convincing rank-and-file workers of the desirability of conversion, however, is often difficult. Take the situation at Textron-Lycoming in Stratford, Connecticut, where UAW Local 1010 members build and repair M-1 tank engines. Despite a new, state-of-the-art, automated materials delivery line and first-class machine tools—which the workers are proud of—some 60 percent of the unionized workers, many of whom have been with the company for thirty to forty years, face being laid off during the current defense build-down. "Wednesdays are layoff days," says Joseph Zikaris, the chairperson of Local 1010's Skilled Trades Council and a speaker at the 15 June 1990 gathering in Chicopee, Massachusetts, "Economic Conversion: A Conference for Labor." "My people are worrying, waiting. One guy, he's got a wife with multiple sclerosis and lots of medical bills. He's anxious every week that it's going to be his turn—he's lowest on the totem pole."

The sorry state of the Bridgeport area's economy makes the layoffs especially painful. For blue-collar workers, the best option is looking for employment at Sikorsky, another defense contractor facing similar cutbacks. "We're like another branch of the armed services," Zikaris points out, "but we don't have job security, and we don't get many of the benefits." Zikaris's view is that defense contracts have failed to incorporate the hidden costs of dislocation in contractors' bids. He thinks that if such costs were recognized, the Pentagon would be less apt to pay for building new facilities elsewhere while existing plants are idled. Zikaris also believes that blue-collar workers would be much better off if the same sort of planning that goes into defense buildups were used to help transfer and retrain workers and generate new job opportunities.

Many other union leaders have spoken out on the willingness of their workers to convert, and some have actively engaged in conversion planning. A Boeing IAM official claimed that "a tool or die maker, a journeyman machinist or a machine operator could move to anything: railroad cars, plastics, airplanes—it would make no difference." A colleague from the same Seattle lodge backed him up: "We are already prepared for mass transit. Our people have the exterior and interior fabrication skills, the machinists, the fibre glass parts fabricators, the painters, people in wiring and people with electrical skills."[31]

While many union locals are notably loath to give up defense work, those labor leaders active in conversion assert that workers are stereotyped in the press and with the public as gung-ho pro-military supporters. Winpisinger protests:

We're treated as if we are the lumpen proletarian, interested only in our own economic existence, incapable of discerning the issues in guns vs. butter or contributing to the dialogue of disarmament, ending the arms race and peace. Nevertheless, I've never met a worker making weapons of kill and overkill, who wouldn't rather be making implements of peace and prosperity.

223

What Zikaris, Winpisinger, and many of their fellow labor leaders want is recognition of the responsibilities of the nation to defense workers. In their view, the society owes its defense plant workers alternative means of making a living with no loss in income or dignity.[32]

To that end, they have targeted three goals to incorporate into national legislation: prenotification of military plant closings, worker adjustment assistance, and alternative use planning. The first and last of these are opposed by big and small contractors alike; the second is palatable to them, depending on the price. But workers want jobs, and that is why the alternative use concept is so central to their efforts. Lance Compa, a staffer at the United Electrical, Radio, and Machine Workers of America (UE) argues that corporate opposition to worker-initiated conversion is a mistake. As he puts it, "The notion that economic conversion will happen of its own accord sells short the insights and planning capabilities of workers, unions and community supporters. Employees' experience provides a rich store of ideas for new product lines and new production methods."[33]

Whether this is true or not, the disparate situations faced by management and labor when cutbacks come create a difficult arena for conversion. Companies pursue their methods of diversification while workers push for alternative use planning and facility conversion. In the absence of any third party—be it public or private, national, state, or local—the different aims of these two key parties lead inevitably to a standoff. Once blocked in their more creative endeavors, the unions as well as their employers inevitably return to the old standby of lining up behind the military spending lobby. If attitudes and behavior are to improve enough to get the country out of this morass, a third-party catalyst is essential.

What seems clear is that company-led conversion efforts will not be adequate to the task of providing stability for workers and communities. Nowhere is the popular call to "let the market do it" less applicable than in the defense market, which has been dominated and deformed by the public sector. Three alternatives—not mutually exclusive—to company-led conversion have been tried in the 1980s, often with third-party support: converting workers, converting the local economy, and converting facilities. Each has lessons for the future of conversion.

Converting Workers

Retraining workers and trying to find jobs for them on an individual basis is one way of coping with defense cutbacks. This is more or less the strategy embodied in the 1990 conversion legislation, which set aside millions of dollars for such retraining, funneled through the Pentagon and the Department of Labor. This strategy accepts the scrapping of plants and the wholesale exit of defense companies from communities. In their wake, it offers workers interim support, retraining, and placement services. Such federal programs resemble those provided for other special classes of workers. For example, the Trade Readjustment Assistance (TRA) program, available since 1974, provides income support—including extended unemployment benefits—and money for training and relocation expenses to workers who lose their jobs because of competition from imports.

These programs have received mixed reviews. On the one hand, they offer immediate relief and permit workers and their families a breathing space while they look around for other livelihoods. On the other hand, income support programs have been quite expensive and do not guarantee jobs in the long run. "Positive" adjustment programs, which provide support for job searches, instruction, job clubs, or retraining, have done somewhat better, although they have not resulted in placement success rates much over 50 percent.[34]

Much of the failure of these programs stems from the unrealistic timetables imposed upon them. Many occupations in today's growth industries require a relatively high degree of analytical competence. It is not that easy to retrain a semiskilled worker to be a computer-programming machine tool operator. Workers' basic literacy is surprisingly low, and long-term remedial work is often necessary. For higher paid jobs, intensive college-level education may be required. To address this problem, Tony Mazzocchi of the Oil, Chemical, and Atomic Workers International Union has proposed a "superfund" for structurally unemployed workers, modeled on the GI bill and the Environmental Protection Agency's Superfund. Company contributions to the fund would enable displaced workers to return to school long enough to reeducate themselves for the new, computerized world of postmodern production.

Technical and professional employees have also received special forms of adjustment assistance. In the early 1970s the Technology Mobilization and Reemployment Program (TMRP), a federal effort aimed at engineers and scientists, offered career counseling, job search grants, on-the-job training, and relocation assistance. An innovative effort to place former aerospace engineers in professional jobs in state and local government, the program was relatively unsuccessful, mainly because workers were reluctant to relocate and state and local funds were inadequate. At a cost of $28 million, TMRP helped 34,000 engineers and scientists—a small percentage of those displaced—find new work.[35]

Worker adjustment strategies attempt to "convert" the defense worker into a civilian worker. They work best when job vacancies exist in area labor markets, and when the skills called for in emerging sectors match well those previously employed in military production. But if military cutbacks are substantial and take place in a recessionary climate, all the training and job counseling in the world will not create new jobs. Worker conversion strategies belong to a venerable tradition of social service programs that divorce "social" problems, such as unemployment, from the economic and budgetary planning process. Decisions on the economy or the military are made in isolation, with no regard for their displacement effects, and the social service agencies try to clean up the resulting mess. On their own, such efforts are unlikely to provide the impetus needed to substantially retrack our defense-dependent economy along more vibrant commercial lines.

Converting the Local Economy

From the Pentagon comes another strategy for coping with defense-related closings: to palliate Congress, which is always distressed when pork-barrelled jobs are eliminated, the Pentagon's Office of Economic Adjustment (OEA) packages federal economic development assistance, channeling it through local economic development agencies. When a disgruntled congressman balks at cuts for a base or plant in his district, the Pentagon refers him to the OEA, which dutifully prescribes the alternatives for the affected community. The local economic base is at the center of OEA's agenda, not workers or specific facilities. Planners attempt to replace the lost military dollar with other activities, sometimes reusing the site of the shuttered military base or plant. Although alternative activities are introduced into the community, the idea, once again, is that a base or plant closing is inevitable and desirable.

The OEA believes it has been relatively successful, especially with military base closings. Some 100 military bases closed over the past 25 years have been successfully converted into schools, businesses, housing, and other facilities, with a net civilian job gain of 50,000 nationwide. Not replaced were 85,402 military jobs, whose ripple effect on local economies has not been assessed. If the OEA figures are correct, they suggest that the average community with a shutdown plant or base is somewhat smaller than before, but that no significant numbers of civilian personnel have been displaced. There is no way of knowing, however, who occupies the new jobs created, or whether the income levels and benefits approximate those of the previous defense jobs. No independent audit has been carried out to determine the effectiveness of the OEA program. One OEA staffer, when we asked about the reliability of the data, quipped, "Well, you know what they say around here: 'Shoot anything that flies, count anything that falls.' "[36]

The economic development plans supported by the OEA are not much different from those pursued by most small and medium-sized cities. Wichita's adjustment is considered exemplary. Following a drop in Boeing's employment from 35,000 in 1956 to 4,200 in 1971, Wichita business leaders used taxpayer dollars to build the Kansas Coliseum, a new zoo and park, an art museum, the Indian Cultural Center, and 86 miles of bike paths to attract tourists and improve the quality of life for residents. Presumably in response, some large companies, such as NCR and Metropolitan Life Insurance, moved there in the mid-1970s. When Boeing threatened to leave the city altogether in 1976, Wichita city officials waived the company's taxes for 20 years and helped provide financing to modernize its plant. With these incentives in place, Boeing decided to stay.[37]

Public-private partnerships, financial deals, and face-lifting projects like Wichita's form the backbone of most economic development strategies. Community conversion through economic development schemes employs familiar techniques and runs into predictable problems. It relies on a strictly "professional" development approach— that is, it banks on improving the business climate and on government incentives to private business to revitalize the community. By investing in its infrastructure and the quality of life for its residents, Wichita city government apparently did lure new employers into the area. But did former Boeing mechanics and engineers find new jobs at RCA or Metropolitan Life? Furthermore, providing tax breaks for Boeing may have sapped the city's ability to further invest in its amenities, trading current for future growth.

Community economic development is more likely to replace lost jobs and incomes than strategies based on converting the company or converting workers. Especially when the existing facilities are reused and efforts are made to match skills and workers with the new jobs created, the organized third-party intervention of local government and the OEA can go far to ameliorate the negative consequences of defense cuts. Of course, as with worker conversion, such strategies work only where new lines of business can be attracted. Many of the big military-industrial cities—Boston and Los Angeles, for instance—are handicapped by the high cost of doing business; smaller communities that benefit from defense spending are often remote and sometimes heavily polluted from having hosted military missions. During a major build-down, relying upon economic development approaches is simply not enough.

Converting Facilities

Dissatisfied with all of these approaches, a number of communities have experimented with yet another conversion possibility—converting plants through a joint community-labor-management effort. This strategy assumes that management either cannot or will not tackle facility conversion on its own and must be jawboned into accepting the participation of workers and community groups and outside technical assistance. To date, such efforts have originated outside the plant—with the workers, the community, the peace movement, or the local government. But in the future, advocates of this course envision both financial support and cooperation from plant management.

At the heart of the facility conversion strategy is alternative use planning. As proposed in recent congressional legislation, mandatory alternative use planning would be paid for by companies (and would presumably be recoverable for them from government contracts) and conducted by committees made up of management, labor, and community representatives. These committees would have access to company data, to outside consultants, and to marketing help in drafting a new business plan. The proposed planning structure would be a decentralized one, eschewing the creation of another Washington bureaucracy. The federal government would pitch in with funds for retraining, transitional income support, and coordination via a national economic conversion commission. A version of alternative use planning is contained in the bill introduced by Cong. Ted Weiss (Dem.-N.Y.), currently before Congress; it was a major bone of contention during the congressional debates on conversion in the summer of 1990.[38] The bill, subsequently passed, confines its remedies to worker and community aid, eschewing alternative use mandates.

Across the country, a number of spontaneous efforts to institute alternative use planning were mounted in the 1980s. All incurred the opposition of the company management in question, but several went far toward building a cooperative coalition, sometimes with plant managers involved, and toward identifying alternative uses. Although to date no successful conversion has been completed, many conversion efforts have aroused favorable public opinion and some have resulted in new initiatives at the state and local level.[39]

Four conversion efforts from the 1980s stand out for their innovativeness and political significance: at the General Dynamics Quincy Shipyards, near Boston, Massachusetts, where thousands of workers made navy vessels; at the McDonnell-Douglas Aircraft plant in Long Beach, California, where thousands of workers construct commercial jetliners and air force transports; at the Blaw-Knox Foundry in East Chicago, Indiana, where hundreds of workers made heavy castings for the army's M-60 tank; and at the Unisys plant in St. Paul, Minnesota, where hundreds of workers manufacture military computer systems.[40] The four cases cover all three major services, an array of military systems, and widely different regions of the country. A further look at what happened at each facility casts considerable light on the potentials and pitfalls for facility conversion.

Quincy Shipyards

Just south of Boston, Quincy Shipyards was a 180-acre facility belonging to General Dynamics, the largest purely military conglomerate in the nation. It employed more than 5,000 workers as recently as the mid-1980s. In 1982 its future looked grim when its effort to make liquefied natural gas (LNG) tankers for the commercial market failed and competition for military contracts quickened. One navy officer likened the competition among shipyards for secondary contracts to "a pack of hungry wolves chasing a few rabbits."[41] Employment had dwindled to 1,100, and the shipyard seemed destined to be smaller and more defense-dependent than ever.

At that point, a group of activist rank-and-file workers in Local 5 of the Industrial Union of Marine and Shipbuilding Workers of America (IUMSWA) formed the South Shore Conversion Committee, a coalition with local peace activists. Without management, outside consultants, or local government involved, they researched alternative uses and proposed that the shipyard pioneer in making an ocean thermal-energy conversion plant–ship, developed at Johns Hopkins University, to produce electricity at sea.[42] They identified other new products that would not require major investment, including oil rigs, railcars, and bridge spans. The committee hoped to link up shipyard workers nationally with the peace effort, redirecting the industry toward civilian activities.

The Quincy group ran into a number of organizational problems. The local community, reeling from a $20 million adverse tax settlement with General Dynamics, was in no position financially to support alternative use planning. Most rank-and-file union members were either indifferent or hostile, as was the union leadership. But most significant was the vigorous opposition of General Dynamics itself. The company claimed to have researched alternatives such as drill rigs, pressure vessels, and barge-mounted chemical processing plants without finding a viable product.[43] Moreover, it had just terminated the financially disastrous commercial venture of building LNG tankers; it had sold only ten of the planned two hundred vessels. Top management decided to refocus its efforts on getting new navy contracts.

In 1983 it was successful, winning a $409 million contract for cargo ships for the navy's rapid deployment force. This soon swelled the Quincy Shipyards work force to nearly six thousand. The new contracts were a kiss of death for the conversion effort, despite the fact that they were to be short-lived. In 1986 the entire shipyard was closed, and all six thousand workers lost their jobs. In the final six months, revived interest in the shipyard's future led the state of Massachusetts to commission a study, which concluded that any kind of shipbuilding was financially impractical. The price that General Dynamics was asking for the site precluded a worker buy-out, something the union was considering. In a final ironic twist, General Dynamics managed to sell the site to the state Water Resources Department for $50 million, which, in effect, gave the company a bonus for exiting. The state was willing to purchase the site for storage and sludge treatment, but not for productive reuse. At the state's expense, not the company's, dislocated workers received aid and retraining money from both JTPA (Job Training Partnership Act) and Trade Adjustment Assistance Act funds. As of 1990 the state was using the site for storing and shipping barge equipment and hoped to have a secondary sludge treatment facility under construction by 1991. Other parts of the shipyard are used to store vehicles, and a seventy-acre section has been set aside for the IUMSWA to put to a shipbuilding use if it creates a plan considered viable by the state. No such plan is presently under way.

The South Shore Conversion Committee did not enjoy the support of management, and its plans for conversion were never tried. Nor did it bear much fruit in the larger movement toward conversion planning, although one of its important members, Jon Brandow, did go on to work on the Philadelphia Naval Shipyards conversion effort. If anything, the Quincy Shipyards experience appears to have convinced Boston-area peace activists interested in conversion to concentrate on the demand side—to work with certain groups, such as teachers and housing activists, to push for changes in federal spending priorities rather than targeting the point of production. To its credit, however, the South Shore Conversion Committee's attempt to convert Quincy Shipyards was one of the pioneering conversion efforts.

McDonnell-Douglas Aircraft

In the early 1980s the long-standing financial difficulties of the former Douglas Aircraft Company in Long Beach, California, came to a head.[44] Once the leader in commercial aviation, the company never recovered from Boeing's entry into the jet airliner market in the late 1950s, nor had it recouped its development costs from the DC-8. In 1967 McDonnell Aircraft of St. Louis had stepped in to "rescue" the larger Douglas. Unfortunately, the merger did not return Douglas to its former profitability or production levels. In the Long Beach plant that had employed thirty-three thousand workers at its peak in the late 1960s, employment plunged sharply over the intervening years. By the early 1980s the plant was operating at about 20 percent of capacity. Between 1980 and 1982 alone, UAW-member employees fell from over twelve thousand to under five thousand, while the engineering, scientific, and technical work force was cut in half from its previous level of seven thousand.

McDonnell had always been more heavily defense-dependent than Douglas. Under McDonnell's tutelage, the Douglas operation's business was radically altered from a mix of 70 percent commercial and 30 percent military to 70 percent military and 30 percent commercial. McDonnell-Douglas chose to do nothing about the continued attrition of its Long Beach plant commercial work. Instead, the company was banking on a C-17 cargo carrier contract, even though it had yet to be approved by Congress.

Although management seemed to be ignoring Douglas's commercial prospects, the workers were not so indifferent. After a rash of 1982 layoffs, UAW Local 148 (with ten thousand members, one of the UAW's largest locals) sought alternatives for reemploying its members. The Los Angeles Coalition Against Plant Shutdowns (LACAPS), a broad-based coalition of labor, community, and religious activists, met with union leaders to discuss conversion planning. LACAPS then brought in the California Department of Economic and Business Development's Economic Adjustment Unit, a state agency set up to deal with early warning of and intervention into plant closings. In turn, the state representative engaged the Mid-Peninsula Conversion Project (MPCP) (now known as the Center for Economic Conversion, based in Mountain View, California) as a consultant to the UAW on conversion prospects for the plant.

The UAW's goals were to reemploy its workers and rebuild its strength in the plant. An ad-hoc planning group that included the union, the state representative, MPCP, outside experts, and an unofficial representative of the engineers' union at Douglas identified several feasible alternatives for the plant, including light-rail transit assembly, a cogeneration project, and commuter aircraft production. The transit work was particularly attractive. A transportation expert identified potential rail vehicle assembly work on two upcoming projects: the California Department of Transportation's (CALTRANS) San Francisco–San Jose line, and light-rail and rapid-transit cars for Los Angeles County rail projects, partially funded by federal moneys. The CALTRANS contract had been awarded to Sumitomo of Japan, but the vehicles had to be assembled in the United States under a domestic content provision.

By this time, Douglas management had also become interested in the transit work. Management and the union, working together with MPCP and the state as technical assistants, began exploring the possibility of setting up a labor-management committee to oversee the development of new product ideas. Both labor and management felt they had stakes in the effort, and the involvement of a state representative facilitated their working together.

What then went wrong? First, Douglas did not act fast enough on the Sumitomo subcontract; the assembly project went to a northern California plant. Second, a contentious strike for better wages and benefits sidetracked the effort. When the labor-management committee was being set up, Local 148 launched a 113-day strike against a proposed two-tiered wage system and cuts in other benefits. It is unclear whether the strike affected the transit project, although Douglas representatives were willing to continue to negotiate with the union about new products even in the heat of the strike. Most significant, however, was the apparent antagonism of top McDonnell-Douglas management in St. Louis toward the effort. It had earlier rejected Douglas's attempts to move into new product lines and continued to stress military work. Although the Douglas plant management remained interested up to the eleventh hour, the transit project was abandoned when Congress approved the C-17 for Douglas Aircraft Company.

In retrospect, the decision not to pursue alternative products development was shortsighted. Although the Douglas facility boomed for several years during the Reagan buildup, the company today faces massive retrenchment. In 1990 the layoffs again numbered in the thousands, with no new military projects in sight.

Blaw-Knox Foundry

Blaw-Knox Foundry of East Chicago, Indiana, was an eighty-three-year-old maker of heavy castings when it closed in 1986.[45] For most of the century, the plant produced huge castings for the steel industry and even constructed entire steel mills. During the Second World War, besides making castings for ships, power plants, and mining equipment, it produced military tank hulls, turrets, and related equipment. Intermittently, it continued its tank business, but as recently as 1968, at the height of the Vietnam War buildup, tank sales still accounted for only 15 percent of production. For decades, the plant employed about 1,400 workers steadily.

In the 1970s new plant management quietly switched its allegiance to the military market, capitalizing on the foundry's production of the M-60 tank for both the army and foreign governments, especially in the Middle East. By the late 1970s the plant was making four or five tanks a day, working three shifts, and employing 2,500 workers. Meanwhile, its steel business languished as foreign competitors with higher quality products and access to inexpensive financing, especially the Japanese, made considerable inroads into the steel mill market. But Blaw-Knox's new conglomerate owner, White Consolidated, did not seem to care—it had a lucrative, cash-generating government customer that by then accounted for 85 to 95 percent of its output.

Blaw-Knox ran into trouble in the mid-1980s when the M-1 tank displaced its staple, the M-60. The M-1 did not require the castings that were a Blaw-Knox specialty. As related previously, the company's major response to impending doom was to put all of its energies into lobbying for extension of the M-60's lifetime. But not all those with a stake in Blaw-Knox chose to follow management's lead. In 1984 Tom DuBois, a former steelworker and a researcher at the Calumet Project on Industrial Jobs, a nearby, community-based anti–plant closing group, spotted a notice in the trade press suggesting that the plant might be either sold or closed. He notified the president of the United Steel Workers of America local at the plant, who issued a call for a meeting, at which the Blaw-Knox Steering Committee was born.

The committee consisted of representatives from the union, management, the community, and local and regional economic development agencies. They commissioned a study by A. D. Little, Inc., which recommended that the plant be retooled—at a cost of $20–24 million—to produce smaller commercial castings. The investment was crucial because, despite twenty years of profitability and lucrative military contracts, Blaw-Knox had not received an ounce of new equipment since it was taken over by White in 1967. Instead, White had focused on its plants that made consumer appliances, milking cash from the foundry to pay for expansion in that area.

The foundry needed a lot of upgrading—a new $12 million machine tool center, for instance, needed to be installed. The U.S. government would have to put up $4–7 million toward the cost to make it work, but that would be more than paid back within two years by savings in the social costs that would be incurred if the plant were shut down. The social cost calculus showed that, owing to a multiplier effect, a total of 1,334 jobs and $30.9 million in personal income would be eliminated, costing $12 million in lost tax revenue and $7.8 million in higher government unemployment benefit payments.[46] The alternative use plan was never implemented, and the plant closed down in 1986 after White sold out to yet another buyer, NESCO. A former manager confided to researcher Bruce Nissen that the new CEO of NESCO had directed top plant managers, "from day one," to "run the armor work out to the end, and then dump the joint."[47]

Not all of the difficulties in the Blaw-Knox effort were management's fault. There were serious cleavages within the committee itself. The union local refused to take a leadership role, and the international union was preoccupied with the collective bargaining issues involved in a potential closing. Into the power vacuum stepped the professional economic developers, who would not take on the company at the crucial moment. The community groups—the Calumet Project and the United Community Organization—had the right vision but little clout. As a result, the economic development professionals and the Indiana politicians, including the state's two senators, Dan Quayle and Richard Lugar, both Republicans, and the local congressman, were persuaded to support the company's losing strategy of begging for more tanks. The union local and the community groups tried unsuccessfully to generate support for a public jobs authority and the use of eminent domain.

The Blaw-Knox effort did not save jobs. But it has borne fruit in the continuing efforts of the Calumet Project to avert plant closings and facilitate management turnover of endangered plants. In late 1989 the project published a much-quoted retrospective study of Blaw-Knox and more than a dozen other closings in the area, concluding that many of them, including Blaw-Knox, could have been averted had certain public policies and institutions been in place. Its ongoing efforts include a project to create and fund a public jobs authority, modeled on the Pittsburgh area's Steel Valley Authority (see chapter 9), to operate an advance warning system of plant closings, provide "one-stop shopping" to plants in trouble, give technical assistance, and assist in management turnover, using eminent domain if necessary.[48]

Unisys Defense Computer Systems

Unisys Defense Computer Systems was created in 1986 when the Sperry and Burroughs corporations merged, combining their military work into a single division in the St. Paul area with five thousand workers.[49] Shortly thereafter, Unisys was caught bribing consultants for bid-related information; its suspension from bidding on navy contracts for several months caused it to lose ground to competitors. When the navy—which accounts for more than 70 percent of the company's $2.4 billion in annual military sales—announced it was shifting from military to commercial specifications for its systems components, Unisys military sales slumped even further. The company began a long series of layoffs and seemed to have no desire to convert its military-oriented facilities to other uses.

As early as 1985, concerned members of the International Brotherhood of Electrical Workers (IBEW) Local 2047, representing a predominantly female work force, contacted the AFL-CIO and the State Task Force on Economic Conversion to ask for help in challenging these layoffs.[50] A new working group, the Alternative Use Project, was formed with members from the IBEW local, the state AFL-CIO, the Working Group on Economic Dislocation (an anti–plant closing group), and Jobs with Peace. With technical and financial assistance from the state's Department of Trade and Economic Development and the city of St. Paul's Department of Planning and Economic Development, the group hired an independent consultant, Jamie Markham, to produce an alternative use plan. The result was an analysis of over forty new product ideas, including pollution-monitoring devices, automobile computers, home security systems, "smart" irrigation, low-power electronic lighting ballasts, adaptive technologies for the physically disabled, light-rail transit controls, and monitoring systems. All could be manufactured, the study contended, with little or no change to equipment, and with the existing work force.

The company, however, remained adamantly opposed to alternative use planning. It refused to meet with the project, rejected a request for a six-month moratorium on layoffs, and claimed that Unisys was already a "converted company" because it had other divisions producing for commercial markets. The company spokesman belittled the alternative use study, suggesting that management had access to better engineering and new product talent—which it was unwilling to disclose or share. In an interview with us, he likened the union's attempt at input to a stranger coming into a university department to tell it what to do. Because the company would not cooperate, additional funding for alternative use planning could not be provided by the state legislature since it required the participation of management.

To date, the Unisys project has not been a success at retaining jobs. Compared with the preceding cases, however, it still has some chance of success in this narrowly construed sense, and the solid coalition continues to recruit advocates and amass technical assistance, chiefly because of the high caliber of its leadership and its broad base. During a major layoff of 151 workers in January 1990, Governor Rudy Perpich and Mayor Jim Scheibel of St. Paul were at the plant gates to welcome the fired workers and walk the picket line—the first union picket for economic conversion.

Efforts like the Alternative Use Project at Unisys have prompted interest on the part of state and local governments in passing conversion legislation to entice or require companies to do alternative use planning. State representative Karen Clark (Dem.) of Minnesota continues to push legislation that would mandate alternative use committees for defense companies, reserving state development assistance for complying firms. The St. Paul effort represents "best practice" in mounting a conversion effort. The fact that it did not achieve its ultimate goal underscores the depth of the structural problems hampering conversion.

Lessons from Conversion Efforts

Because of management lack of interest and opposition, in none of the cases surveyed were the conversion plans advanced by other parties actually implemented. Nevertheless, each effort demonstrates a remarkable willingness on the part of communities, peace activists, and sometimes labor to explore new forms of production. Certain ingredients appear to be necessary—though not alone sufficient—for a successful conversion effort, especially one initiated by groups other than management.

Labor participation and unity is particularly crucial to mounting a successful conversion. Where a rank-and-file dissident group lacked full-scale union support, as at Quincy, or where a willing local with an indifferent international took the lead role, as at Blaw-Knox, management felt no need to take the effort seriously. But where the union took an active role, as at Douglas, management was more responsive. At Unisys, where local union leadership was backed up by both the international and the state AFL-CIO, support from politicians and the public sector was easier to generate quickly. Larger trade union offices can fund feasibility studies and have research and legal departments to help out. Unions also bring with them an activist tradition; they know how to use strikes and pickets effectively for generating public support and media coverage.

The Unisys case demonstrates, too, that potential divisions between community activists and trade unionists can be bridged successfully. Community activists demonstrated their commitment to taking care of those most adversely affected by the demilitarization of the economy, while trade unionists came out strongly in favor of the peace dividend. As the IBEW Local 2047 president told us, "We have taken the leadership to demonstrate that the cuts to the military budget do not have to cause job loss. . . . Our people are extremely talented and can make many useful and profitable products."

In each case, top management adamantly refused to cooperate in alternative use planning, although plant managers and engineers were sometimes quite encouraging. In addition, evidence of management incompetence or dishonesty in some cases made the firm more vulnerable to protest. Research uncovered failures to maintain and upgrade equipment, making commercial competitiveness difficult (Blaw-Knox), or outright corruption, damaging the plant's reputation with the Pentagon (Quincy, Unisys). The facilities involved were often the subjects of recent mergers (Unisys) or buy-outs (Blaw-Knox) and were hypothesized to be of relatively minor importance to their conglomerate owners, who could reap tax benefits and "facility termination costs" from the government for closing them. But even where managements have clean and competent records, cooperation with the new, more open style of alternative use planning is not easy to achieve.

The obstinacy of management is a legacy of its adversarial relationship with labor; management is partly clinging to what it sees as its proprietary right to do the planning, and partly responding out of ignorance and a fear of the unknown. Instead of considering a new set of practices, which might be badly needed in the face of severe military cutbacks, companies have gone out of their way to disparage conversion efforts and to oppose mandatory alternative use planning in the current debate on conversion legislation. Their stance is reminiscent of similar stands taken against plant-closing legislation and environmental regulations—a reminder that the forces business uniformly opposes do not always lose.

The case studies all reveal, in varying degrees, deficiencies in the technical expertise available to community and union initiators of conversion efforts. To accomplish social cost accounting, new product assessment, marketing studies, and financial feasibility and business plans, coalitions have turned to academics or outside consultants. Sometimes plant managers and engineers have been supportive and willing to help anonymously. But even friendly managers are often at a loss about designing or marketing entirely new products. Although it is an appealing notion that workers have good ideas for new products and know the capabilities of their workplaces, in fact, most of them are not well qualified to tackle the entrepreneurial tasks of business restructuring.

In no case did a coalition come up with a complete business plan or get as far as proposing a worker or community buy-out, although over time groups have demonstrated more awareness that this alternative is viable. After more than ten years of massive plant closings in their industries, some unions, such as the United Auto Workers and the United Steelworkers, have learned that worker buy-outs can be successful, but that outside professional help, at a price, is required. Whether privately or publicly provided, financial help in purchasing such services must be found if worker or community buy-outs are to succeed. The efforts at McDonnell-Douglas and Unisys enjoyed capable third-party intervention from the state, which worked with both management and labor.

Getting technical assistance in a timely fashion is crucial because not all plants and facilities *should* be saved. Some are simply too old, have no redeeming characteristics, are too expensive to refurbish, or are polluted with chemicals, nuclear contaminants, or metals residues. Workers and communities should get assessments of the prospects for such plants as soon as possible, to avoid delays in the retraining and other forms of adjustment assistance that will be necessary when jobs evaporate.

Proposals for state conversion legislation have reflected the experience of local organizing efforts. The proposed Minnesota legislation mandates the creation of alternative use committees at every defense-related facility, reflecting the needs articulated by the Unisys workers. While few states have passed effective conversion legislation, many states have conducted studies on military spending and conversion and are considering proposals. Historically, state legislation has been a precursor for national legislation: for example, the national plant-closing legislation borrowed heavily from state legislation.[51] Including alternative use planning mechanisms in state legislation may lend authority to the controversial Weiss conversion bill in its effort to mandate alternative use committees for all defense firms.

It is too soon to tell whether or not the lessons of these cases can be applied to the increasing number of military-related plant closings. Nevertheless, the progress these conversion groups have made in increasing their sophistication and cooperation is heartening. In 1990 a number of new initiatives cropped up around the country, including conversion efforts at the Bath Iron Works (Maine), the Oak Ridge (Tennessee) nuclear facilities, the Burlington (Vermont) General Electric Gatling Gun plant, western Massachusetts machine tool makers, Long Island–area aircraft plants, and several Connecticut engine and machining factories. Groups in several cities and states, including St. Louis, Seattle, Baltimore, the Naugatuck Valley, Orange County, and Cambridge, have initiated public-sector or nonprofit conversion efforts designed to monitor, cajole, and act when military plant closings occur. In each such effort, workers and communities are restating their commitment to socially useful production.

At the Cold War Crossroads

A sobering aspect of this account of company, worker, and community responses to the challenge of dismantling the cold war arsenal is the mix of fear, confusion, and bumbling that is revealed in the actions of the major players. In this sense, the United States is not that different from the Soviet Union, which faces such great challenges in its new attempts to participate in commercial markets. Here, forty-plus years of cold war have cultivated a set of business institutions and practices that are rigid, if sophisticated, and tailor-made for serving the unique Pentagon client. Changing basic business cultures and converting military-dedicated labs and engineers to new frontiers will not happen overnight. A Battelle Memorial Institute study, for instance, concluded that creating conversion planning offices within companies is not effective because conversion within one to two years is not cost-effective.[52]

It is not that plants, their managers, and their work forces *cannot* be converted to commercial uses, but that a huge attitudinal shift must take place if they are to convert in a way that conserves resources and communities. Companies *can* do it in the right environment and with incentives. They need training in conversion, and they need time for the transition. During the transition, the role of the government as a defender of the public interest and as a conservator of the nation's economic resources comes into play. Without the government's participation, it is simply too easy for companies, workers, and communities to go back to feeding out of the military trough.

To build such a support system for conversion—to give companies and workers incentives for making bold new moves—the public will have to accept the unique nature of the defense industry, its nonmarket character, and the argument that the nation owes the military-industrial community some help in adjusting to a post–cold war world. As Claudette Munson, the former vice-president of the St. Paul IBEW local that has been fighting the closing of the Unisys plant, said at the Chicopee conversion conference in 1990, "Peace shouldn't be a hardship for anybody!"

9
Dismantling the Cold War Economy

■

LOOKING out his window at the Chicago skyline, the Illinois Institute of Technology Research Institute's vice-president for business development, Morton Klein, thought for a bit when asked what he and other Chicago defense contractors might do if there is a serious military build-down. "Well," he said, brightening up and reflecting on the dozens of chemists and chemical engineers in his heavily defense-dependent lab, "we wouldn't need to be the Illinois Defense Technology Association. We could be the Illinois Waste Treatment Association!" Such remarks illustrate the interest of some private-sector managers in the adjustment problem and offer glimmers of hope for a post–cold war economy.

Unfortunately, managers like Morton Klein do not represent the mainstream of the military contracting world. More typical is the attitude of Stanley Pace, CEO of General Dynamics, who believes that his corporation's only recourse in the face of threatened budget cuts is to hunker down, lay off workers, and wait. He has faith that military spending inevitably will pick up again. Such a strategy may help to frighten communities and Congress into holding the reins on defense cuts. But in the end it is a losing strategy for the nation.

There will be no peace dividend without a coordinated and highly visible alternative to the military-based economy. Many industries, along with their workers and communities, badly need some form of help in making the transition. Given the risks associated with change, however, firms are stonewalling and workers and communities are scared. Meanwhile, scientists and engineers and academics worry that if they bite the hand that feeds them, no other source of funding for research and development will materialize. The military-industrial complex is paralyzed by inertia. As the laissez-faire paradigm dissolves under the weight of economic recession and financial crisis, only the piecemeal and limited dual-use technology policy has been put forward as an attempt to fill the void.

Until an effective adjustment strategy is found and the Pentagon is no longer the primary supporter of innovation, the nation is not likely to move forward on the domestic economic front. It is just too costly to bail out savings-and-loans and banks, pay for higher unemployment benefits, and continue to spend $300 billion a year on military preparedness. Unless one or more of these federal commitments changes, there will simply be no money left for new initiatives. Morton Klein may have to wait a long time for his waste treatment research contract (and communities around the country will continue to wrestle with a growing waste disposal crisis).

Toward a Nurturing Economy

Public denials aside, the United States has had an industrial policy for fifty years. The policy has accomplished a great deal. It has ensured that the U.S. military is technologically the strongest on the globe. In either cold war or hot war confrontations, American missiles, aircraft, computers, and satellite-based intelligence and guidance systems can count on dominating. With its military might, the U.S. government has been able, when it so wishes, to unilaterally play the role of the world's cop—as it did exceptionally well in the Gulf War of 1991.

The closet U.S. industrial policy has created whole new industries that stock the military arsenal—the aerospace, communications, and electronics complex. Hundreds of billions of defense dollars, year after year, have gone into constructing an American advantage in these industries, both in direct arms production and in commercial products such as aircraft, computers, and telecommunications. Hefty export sales in these industries are the fruits of years of public-sector cultivation, both in the R&D greenhouse and in the deep and reliable furrows of government sales.

Yet the assembling of this very special and deep expertise, nourished at public expense, has not helped to stave off a slow stagnation in the American economy. Why has the harvest been so lean? First, the closet industrial policy has been very expensive, adding to the budget deficit and absorbing capital that might have been used elsewhere. Second, it has undermined older sectors as it nurtured new ones.

Third, radical but selective technological change has created new problems of worker retooling and displacement and artificially rapid obsolescence of plants and equipment. Fourth, it has created new forms of environmental degradation that pose high costs to the present and future economy. Finally, it has permitted other players in the international economy, particularly foreign companies backed by their governments, to capitalize on the "free" basic research available in the United States and to adapt it to commercial uses, outpacing U.S. firms.

Perhaps most important, though, is that the price for our military preeminence has simply grown beyond our ability to pay. The bulk of the nation's debt is attributable to the defense buildup of the 1980s. Deficits are not necessarily bad; if they are invested in areas such as infrastructure and education, they contribute to the nation's future productivity. But spending borrowed money to fashion ever more deadly and baroque weaponry does nothing for the productivity of American manufacturing industries. Regardless of the nation's foreign policy track, all parties agree that the military budget will have to be cut by at least 20 to 50 percent.[1] If the U.S. economy continues to be sluggish, and with tax revenues faltering, demands for civilian industry revitalization and safety nets for the marginalized will compete for the same precious public funds.

It will not be easy to get the economy back on track. Companies, workers, communities, and whole industries have become addicted to military infusions. Decades of selective and lavish public spending on the military have erected a wall of separation between the civilian and military-industrial segments of the economy. Defense-dependent sectors have a hard time changing course. And because of the geographical concentration of such spending in the Gunbelt, military budgets on the order of $300 billion annually have deepened the dependency of large pools of workers, both white- and blue-collar, on inflated military budgets. Their communities worry that there will be no substitute for the Pentagon gravy train, especially when the same government ruthlessly pursues free trade, deregulation, and privatization policies in every other realm of the economy.

Creative, sometimes strenuous efforts have been made to cope with the specter of military cuts. Companies have begun research and development on large transportation systems, hoping to switch from military aircraft to mass transit. Unions have pushed for worker retaining and alternative use planning. Communities have attempted to convert some military bases and defense plants. But for the most part, the results have been disappointing. Piecemeal approaches, lacking the kind of powerful integrated framework provided by the Pentagon's cradle-to-grave financing, have not been able to replicate the performance of the military-industrial system. As a result, many contractors continue to pursue military markets and lobby for funding, while closing plants and displacing workers. Often, the defense work force and defense-dependent communities act as if they are held hostage to the same future.

What America needs is a systematic economic development strategy aimed at delivering a healthy environment rather than at honing the weapons in the arsenal of destruction. We do not mean simply the physical environment of grass, rocks, rivers, and air, but all living and working environments, from housing to factories and offices, to recreational and wilderness spaces. An economy devoted to personal and public health, a clean and sustainable physical environment, and the stabilization of community and workplace life would be more productive and would achieve a higher standard of living for everyone. Its benefits need not be limited to Americans but could be spread throughout the globe. At the risk of sounding corny, we would put our chips down on a nurturing economy, rather than a destructive one.

Competitiveness Is Not the Answer

It is clear that military expenditures in massive amounts did create a number of spectacular technologies that have become major features of contemporary life. Few modern Americans could imagine a world without personal computers, automated banking, television shows, and weather reports by remote satellite. Such achievements demonstrate that publicly funded industrial policy "works." But why have these landmark technologies, and the industries bred by them, failed to ensure the healthy performance of the overall economy?

Part of the answer is that these technologies occupy a narrow niche in the universe of opportunities. Tailored as they were for the specific military missions of delivering as well as detecting manned, and later unmanned, deadly projectiles to and from remote sites, they spawned a selective set of innovations that took the economy down a certain path. Many of these innovations have turned out to be quite socially useful; others have verged on the frivolous, and still others have been downright dangerous. What is more difficult to see, but equally as significant, are all the forgone breakthroughs in health and safety, environmental protection, housing, transportation, and personal well-being that might have evolved had we devoted our resources to different ends.

Technology transfer is another part of the answer. As military-directed research gets increasingly esoteric, its commercial spin-offs become fewer and fewer. Military innovation can no longer be counted upon to drive commercial technology advances. Rather, the reverse is now true. To stay current, the military must increasingly look to the commercial sector for the latest state-of-the-art technologies. This fact explains the enthusiasm of both civilian corporate executives and military officials for a dual-use strategy that targets specified "critical" technologies for government support.

But dual-use supporters are also more generally concerned about what they have labeled "the competitiveness problem." Despite the glitzy technologies produced by four decades of massive military investment, and despite the relatively robust performance of the ACE complex, the U.S. economy continues to stagnate and lose ground compared with other industrialized economies.

Economists have long welcomed competition as a means to an end—the end being the satisfaction of needs and wants of people in society. In the past, they have argued that other socially important goals, such as income redistribution and economic stability, are also legitimate areas for economic policy-making. Social concerns have fallen by the wayside, however, in the panic over competition from firms in other countries.

Popular understanding of the role of competition, and of the role of past military spending in shaping it, has been distorted by the hysteria over competitiveness. In a rather bizarre twist of logic, the concept that an individual firm must be competitive to survive, and that it must channel scarce resources toward maximizing consumer satisfaction, has been promoted to an economywide imperative. The adjective *competitive* has been transformed into the very unpoetic noun *competitiveness*. It alludes none too subtly to the drama of the arms race. At one time the American economy strove to stay one step ahead of the Soviet Union in launching a better missile or getting to the moon first. Now the "enemy" who must be bested is Japan.

But gone is the vision that sets the goal for the race. The decline of competitiveness is not the problem; it is a symptom of the problem. The goal is not to keep pace on some vaguely defined competitive treadmill, but to ensure the people of the world good food, a clean environment, sound housing, excellent and critical education, and lots of leisure time. The real problem is that public spending and science and technology policies have been diverted from the goal of meeting these general needs. It is time to take our eyes off our feet and to look ahead, past the heels of the guy in front of us, toward the place we ultimately want to go. If we just follow in Japanese and German footsteps, we may end up in a place we do not want to be.

The problem with the remedies proffered for healing the competitiveness ailment is that they concentrate narrowly on the supply side of the economy. In the conservative laissez-faire prescription, only the macroeconomic policy of manipulating the money supply and interest rates would be employed, along with generous support for "basic" research and some tax incentives, ostensibly to create a better environment for private investment. The military-industrial policy would continue, albeit at a reduced level. In the middle-of-the-road dual-use technology strategy, the government would reduce capital costs, subsidize research and development as well as capital, relax antitrust and other regulations (including health and safety and environmental protections), enact protective trade restrictions, and use tax incentives to reward firms for innovation. In a third scenario, liberals envision infrastructure being publicly paid for, workers being trained at public expense, and certain industries being targeted for special treatment— all for the chimeric outcomes of productivity and profitability.

In our view, none of these policies go far enough. An economy that sacrifices health, the environment, jobs, and community stability for higher productivity and profits in selected sectors and firms is not an economy that "works." What we need is a new economic order in which firms, workers, and communities have a common sense of where they are going. *New,* because it would supplant the old military-led industrial policy and sidestep the many shortcomings of the emerging dual-use strategy. *Economic,* because it would face head-on the structural problems in the economy and address the formidable task of repairing and shepherding our precious labor and both our human-made and natural resources. *Order,* because it is impossible to do business, plan for a future, or rear children in a society that has no vision of the future beyond developing a Stealth fighter or beating Japan in developing a new semiconductor chip.

Having a vision of the economy's future—an unfashionable idea in the 1980s, when *deregulation* and *markets* were the key words—is not just a nice idea. Visions have been very successful in driving entire economies and establishing the rules for their organization. In the United States, the visions of military security and of conquering outer space were both powerful forces in shaping U.S. technological expertise and in boosting the ACE complex to prominence. Visions of an environmentally sound, healthy, and stable society could be equally powerful in shaping the next round of investment and technology development.

A National Economic Development Strategy

To achieve a new economic order, vague exhortations to competitiveness should be superseded by a national economic development strategy. We call it an economic rather than industrial development strategy because its goals should be more expansive than picking winners and losers, choosing electronics over steel. The point is not to save the steel or electronics industry, but to conserve resources, put people to work productively, and provide the goods and services that society needs.

Putting forward an economic development strategy for the United States may seem odd—"economic development" used to be pursued by Third World countries only. But in the final decades of this century, the countries that have done well—Germany, Italy, Japan, Korea, or Singapore—have done so primarily because they have undertaken concerted economic development policies based on a vision of where their economies ought to be in the long term.

State and local governments across the United States are already in the vanguard on economic development. A decade of structural change—with both farms and factories folding in unprecedented numbers, and no help forthcoming from the federal government—forced governors, mayors, legislatures, and city councils to act. They felt they had no choice—they had to stop the hemorrhaging of jobs by anchoring existing industries in their communities and encouraging new ones to start up. Publicly funded economic development services proliferated, and bold new experiments in industrial retention, technology transfer, and entrepreneurial aid began.

But these efforts must be nurtured with federal help. State and local governments do not have the resources to fund large-scale industrial turnover, alternative use planning efforts, major R&D initiatives, and large new infrastructure projects—especially when the nation faces new rounds of defense plant and military base closings. Never before has the need for a coordinated national initiative been so pressing.

The substance of a new economic order for the United States can be neatly captured under three main rubrics: environment, health, and community stability. These are the major concerns of the American people going into the troubled 1990s. The environmental vision of a new economic order should encompass a healthy living environment for all, including other species. Clean air, clean water, a protected biosphere, preservation of wilderness, and judicious use of scarce natural resources, from agriculture to industry to households, are its goals. Both a massive amount of careful scholarly research and public sentiment clearly favor a new set of rules governing the interaction between people and nature. The content and effectiveness of these rules will be largely determined by economic considerations—by how much new research, new investment, and new regulation can be devoted to creating a healthier environment.

Human health is another crisis arena. A much smaller share of the population is now covered by health insurance than was true fifteen years ago. Diseases, whether new ones like AIDS or old ones like cancer, have proliferated. Infant mortality is widespread. Mental illness still claims many victims, and stress and depression are on the rise. Occupational health and safety gains have been made in the older industries, but new workplace hazards have arisen with the chemical-intensive processes used in high-tech industry and the eye- and muscle-straining machinery in offices.

Compared with the environment, health has received massive public support, both for research and development and to procure health services for the elderly and poor. But as in defense, these resources have been poured into private and nonprofit sectors without much accountability, resulting in an overemphasis on costly, esoteric technologies and drugs rather than on preventive care. More doctors than ever before favor a national health system like Canada's, and more corporations than ever before are lining up behind the notion of national health insurance. Most important, more people than ever before are fed up with the cost and quality of the health care they receive.

Community stabilization is the third pillar of a new economic order. Champions of the market and rapid capital mobility ignore the destructive effects on workers, households, local governments, and regional businesses when a local economic environment suddenly changes. More subtle but just as important as the external costs—lost incomes, plunging property values, and shrinkage of local clientele— are the losses in well-being from the economically forced out-migration of family members and the breakup of neighborhoods and communities. Excessive displacement accompanied many plant closings in the industrial heartland in the 1980s. It now threatens defense-dependent communities in this defense build-down period.

Economic stabilization has a long, venerable history as a public policy goal. Since the 1930s, governments all over the world have accepted the need to monitor market economies and to intervene when they deviate too much from the desired, generally modest, path of growth. In the 1930s the Tennessee Valley Authority was authorized to rebuild the battered South Central economy. During the Second World War, government planners were concerned about disrupting the settlement patterns of the country and tried to match new defense plants with pools of unemployed workers. In the 1960s the Kennedy administration targeted Appalachia as a region of distress and out-migration, which it attempted to stem by encouraging growth and stabilization in a number of key cities. In the 1970s the Nixon administration redistributed federal funds to suburbs, and later in the same decade, President Carter launched a national urban policy to reverse the fiscal crisis and decline of many cities. Despite their critics, most of these projects were successful to some degree. The Tennessee Valley today, with its new Japanese auto plants and diversified agriculture, is quite a success story, and cities across the nation have revitalized their downtowns, albeit without eliminating inner-city poverty.

Environment, health, and community stability—these areas must compete with national security as a major national priority. For fifty years, Americans have devoted the lion's share of their surplus to pursuing national security above all else, with disappointing results for the economy and growing environmental, health, and community crises. Today, it can be argued that resolving environmental, health, and economic crises is an essential dimension of any meaningful definition of national security. Moreover, unlike expenditures on costly MX or Patriot missiles, gains in these three areas would boost productivity in the economy as a whole. Much less wastage of human resources occurs when healthy, happy citizens are working and living in clean and stable environments. In such a world, precious public funds need not be spent only on cleaning up the messes left behind from current practices.

Building the New Economic Order

Putting forth a vision of change is one thing. Getting there is another. The purpose of a book like this is not so much to map out a specific roadmap but to point in the right direction. The first step is to shift the discourse on industrial policy and economic conversion away from the preoccupation with competitiveness and toward economic development, to encourage citizens and policymakers alike to entertain new possibilities.

What might a new national economic development strategy look like? First of all, it would survey the nation's economic assets, including the stock of capital, labor, and land now devoted to superfluous military activities. During the Reagan-Bush years, national intelligence on the state and stock of our national resources, industries, and infrastructure has deteriorated badly. Many public data sources have been terminated, and some are now available only to high-paying corporate clients. Even data on the military-industrial base is deficient—a series on subcontracting begun in 1979, for instance, was discontinued early in the Reagan years.

Second, savings from military cuts would be judiciously distributed across competing priorities—deficit reduction as well as public investments in the environment, health, and community stability. These priorities would be determined through public debate and the established channels of democratic decision-making. Decisions to invest in overlapping priority areas, such as public infrastructure, transportation, and energy, would be guided by the extent to which such investments contribute to a cleaner environment, a healthier population, and economic stability. Expenditures with long-term economic payoffs would be treated as investments and distinguished from ongoing operating expenditures. Such "demand pull" forces would carry the economy much farther into a new future than would uncertain military high-tech spin-offs or the opportunistic pursuit of narrow technologies like high-definition TV.

Third, nonspending initiatives, such as regulation and incentives for cooperation and planning, would bolster the economic development strategy. Establishing rules for attaining environmental quality, from recycling schemes and minimizing industrial pollutants to cutting allowable auto emissions, will automatically boost interest in finding ways to use recycled materials, make plants cleaner, and explore electric and other nonpetroleum-fueled cars. Companies, assured by the rules of a future market, will invest in the new technologies to attain these ends, creating new jobs at the same time. The market will be the means for testing competing products.

Fourth, the distribution of federal R&D dollars would be guided by this more pluralistic set of goals, creating a robust science and technology base to buttress the economic development strategy. This would include major new science and technology initiatives keyed to these goals. For example, support would be given to R&D programs on new high-tech manufacturing processes that are nontoxic to workers and pollution-free. R&D funds would continue to be disbursed through the relevant agencies whose missions match the call for innovation. If necessary, new agencies would be created, such as the proposed national institutes for the environment or the civilian advanced technology agency called for by many officials in government and industry.[2] In this way, the nation's R&D resources would be weaned from the military and more efficiently directed toward achieving societal goals in the 1990s.[3]

Fifth, an effective economic development strategy would include facility-based planning for alternative uses. To ensure participation and solutions appropriate for specific locales, federal funding could be limited to support for ongoing local and regional conversion efforts. As in the Second World War, new initiatives would be matched with existing labor pools and underutilized capacity in order to stabilize communities and minimize resource wastage. Conversion should be aimed at plants and industries on both sides of the military-industrial divide. After all, the deterioration of many commercial industrial facilities is indirectly the product of cold war hoarding of resources inside certain sectors. Conversion should also be pro-active and long-term, preparing firms, workers, and communities for transition rather than thrusting them rudely into a whirlwind of sudden change.

Finally, macroeconomic and trade policies should be coordinated with the economic development strategy and its conversion efforts. Trade policies that help to manage transition—instead of letting it expose workers and communities to instant economic death—would be implemented. Trade negotiations with every nation should include safeguards that extend the wages, benefits, and environmental protections of U.S. workers to those in other countries, rather than allowing exploitative conditions there to drive down the domestic quality of life in the name of competitiveness. Domestic content rules, similar to those that now guide defense expenditures, would ensure that local businesses and workers are reemployed in such projects, as well as encourage technology transfer back into the United States. Macroeconomic policies that keep real interest rates low and demonstrate a concern for unemployment, not just inflation, would also be pursued.

Any skeptic will immediately question the cost of a new economic development strategy. Our answer to that is simple. We would shift the "peace dividend," in whole or in part, into this broad agenda of environment, health, and stability. The peace dividend is moderately estimated to be nearly $150 billion a year, achievable by the end of the decade.[4] Proponents of the new economic development strategy would have to compete with those who favor using the peace dividend solely for deficit reduction or for bailing out failed financial institutions. In a stagnating economy, Congress will simply have to choose to stimulate the economy through either more military spending or a shift to civilian priorities. It will, of course, require considerable political mobilization to achieve the latter.

But an economic development strategy is not solely a spending program; it is aimed at leveraging comparable spending from the private sector. Take the environmental crisis. Citizens and businesses alike are increasingly willing to accept the need for a concerted attack on environmental degradation. Despite the corporate world's campaign against regulation, environmental restraints have been adopted and complied with, creating new equipment and technology needs. But it is going to take some extra help to get the economy over the hump. Government aid can take the form of low-cost incentives to design and develop new environmental technologies and preventive plans. Similarly, incentives and seed grants can go a long way toward enabling entrepreneurs to respond to new market opportunities in the alternative energy area. For example, an embryonic renewable energy industry in California got a significant boost during the late 1970s and early 1980s from favorable state and federal programs. Counties and cities throughout California also passed ordinances and gave other incentives to businesses to promote conservation and the use of renewable energy sources.

Reinvesting the Peace Dividend

Striving for a new economic order constructed around environmental, health, and stabilization goals is the only way to ensure that the nation's increasingly problematic military-led industrial policy will be transformed. Only with explicit commitments to a new vision of an economic future will the nation be able to remove the exit barriers that now keep firms and communities inside the military-industrial complex and dependent upon further rounds of extravagant spending.

A national economic development strategy is, in the broadest sense, an economic conversion strategy. It would help to overcome the obstacles to conversion, creating effective demand for new socially desirable products, providing R&D resources that enable firms to design and build internationally competitive products, and offering technical assistance for planning and financing conversion efforts. It would create institutional mechanisms that facilitate worker and community involvement in all these activities. To assist workers of all types in making the transition, it would initiate educational and job training programs, along with various other adjustment programs.

As currently practiced, economic conversion has come in for much criticism as a viable economic and political strategy. Year after year, comprehensive conversion legislation has been introduced into Congress. Each time, the preventive remedies, especially alternative use planning, have been dropped for more conventional efforts to help workers and communities cope. As we described earlier, without public-sector support, the many plant, community, and state conversion efforts that have been initiated in piecemeal fashion across the country have met with limited success.

The winding down of the arms race has given economic conversion a new lease on life. In 1990 conversion became a regular subject of news stories and articles in the mainstream press for the first time in decades. Dozens of advisory panels, task forces, and conferences sprang up to address the prospect of military cuts and their economic consequences. In 1990 Congress also passed a much more ambitious, if watered-down, economic adjustment bill, with large appropriations for worker retraining and community adjustment assistance. The Soviet Union, our former adversary, has taken economic conversion very seriously as a necessary part of its economic restructuring. Regardless of what happens in the Middle East and in other skirmishes around the globe, U.S. military spending will have to be curtailed, especially if the nation is going to confront its many looming economic, environmental, and social problems.

Preparing for those cuts, and making the political climate more favorable for them, will require a number of adjustment policies for preventing the dislocation to which workers and communities are vulnerable. The scientific and engineering communities in government, industrial, and academic laboratories will also feel the pinch. Those labs that are heavily dependent on military support will be especially vulnerable to cutbacks in military spending, dual-use R&D policies notwithstanding. The health of the nation's science and technology base will be threatened if no alternative projects are fashioned and funded.

Past conversion efforts, despite their modest achievements to date, offer a number of lessons for a national economic development strategy. Alternative use planning is a novelty and has not yet won the trust of managers oriented toward the long-term Pentagon customer.

Under certain conditions, usually at a time of crisis, management has been relatively more open to worker participation. Such openness may be increasingly required in the future. In coping with the threat of plant closings in nonmilitary industries, workers and communities have had a number of successes in reorganizing management and production, often with the active participation of former plant managers.

To date, there have simply not been the resources, technical assistance, and legislative support needed for these efforts to succeed. Some states—Minnesota, Connecticut, and Washington, for instance—have provided technical assistance. But states cannot possibly ameliorate the scale of the problems that will be caused by the Pentagon cutting tens of billions of dollars over the coming decade. If powerful national conversion policies had been in place, the conversion efforts at Blaw-Knox, Quincy Shipyards, and even McDonnell-Douglas—not to mention corporation-initiated conversion attempts by Boeing, Rohr, and Grumman—might have had a better chance. Ironically, the United States demonstrated in 1991 that it is better at helping to resettle displaced Kurds in a distant land than at aiding those displaced by budget cuts at home.

Conversion planning and job-linked worker retraining programs would eliminate the barriers that defense-dependent facilities face in switching to civilian modes of engineering and production. But planning is not enough. If there is insufficient demand for socially useful products in the domestic and international markets, and if there are not adequate R&D resources for helping firms achieve what Seymour Melman calls "productive competence," then many military-industrial firms will continue to have a difficult time converting their facilities, even if they are willing to engage in alternative use planning.

Recall again the McDonnell-Douglas case: in the early 1980s the company chose to accept a large military R&D contract for the C-17 cargo plane rather than invest in a new commercial aircraft design. The lopsided expected paybacks just made the military contract too attractive to pass up. The company also had little incentive to pioneer in the production of environmentally preferable mass-transit vehicles, even at the modest level of a small-scale assembly operation, because it had no experience in designing such products and, perhaps more important, because the domestic market for mass-transit vehicles in the United States was extremely small. Imagine the difference if McDonnell-Douglas could compete for contracts in an environment of new national commitment to mass transit, whether for design work, direct procurement, or infrastructure improvement.

Let's consider another example. An environmentally benign renewable energy policy coupled with investments in large-scale product development—such as the ocean thermal-energy platform suggested as an alternative product for the Quincy Shipyards—would provide options for converting military shipyards or aircraft facilities. If linked to environmental and other demand pull goals, conversion legislation will enjoy better odds for success in Congress.

Not all facilities would be converted under such scenarios. But many more would enter second lives than under present practices. Both the neglected and the overstimulated industries and regions of the country would be encompassed by the new economic development strategy, which would spread R&D infusions more evenly and redirect more wisely the defense-dependent resources concentrated in the Gunbelt. The strategy's goals would be to achieve relatively stable regional economies, to narrow regional growth differentials, and to eliminate boom and bust in certain industries and occupations, creating a more diversified economy with greater resilience to downturns in any one sector. Included in the strategy would be a more carefully crafted technology policy that does not lead to feast or famine for workers and communities.

Negotiating the Strategy

In constructing a national economic development strategy, all interested parties should participate. Taxpayers, consumers, business, labor, minorities, environmental and peace groups, the unemployed, retirees—all have a stake in the pursuit of an agenda on health, the environment, and community stability. If all are involved, trade-offs can be worked out to the satisfaction of all concerned; too often, one small group has controlled the agenda, with adverse consequences for others.

Broad participation is particularly crucial in the science and technology arena. We live in a technological age whose greatest challenge is developing and employing the knowledge and tools needed to make the material world run in an efficient yet humane and environmentally benign way. Although taxpayers fund an enormous amount of highly technical research, decisions about the direction of that research are hidden deep within bureaucracies. Frank Press, president of the National Academy of Sciences, laments: "It is astounding but true that nowhere in the federal budget-making process is there an evaluation of the complete federal budget for science and technology and its overall rationale in terms of national goals."[5] To accomplish this end, a much greater degree of social accountability and control over the uses and production of science and technology is essential. Whether it be nuclear power, nuclear weapons, toxic wastes, or industrial decline, at root the critical issue is, who controls technology, and for what ends.

Negotiated agreements on the direction of a national economic development strategy would clarify those areas in which the public interest requires some amount of collective restraint on individual behavior. For instance, few companies voluntarily make "front-end" investments in preventive technologies that cut down on pollution in their production processes or on occupational hazards in their workplace; doing so might place them at a competitive disadvantage. A joint environmental planning process could negotiate a set of rules to mandate such investments. Firms, environmentalists, and labor could decide together which occupational health and environmental standards should guide R&D investments in, for instance, new microchip manufacturing processes, the production and use of advanced composite materials in aircraft production, and video display terminals. Such negotiating teams could also recommend selective federal incentives for private-sector research and development and investment, helping to "level the playing field" for environmentally conscious and health-promoting firms.

The innovation cycle is rarely a simple linear path from research to final product. Usually, clusters of small innovative steps are taken, and any one innovation depends on or is fueled by complementary innovations in related technologies. These developmental paths, however, are shaped as much by the potential demand for the ultimate product as by the objectives of the designer or any technological imperative.[6] An economic development strategy instituted through a democratic planning process would therefore lead to a very different pattern of innovation—one more directly linked to social needs and goals than that resulting from the elite military and high-tech industrial policies now practiced by the Pentagon.

Getting There

Inside the beltway, the debate about competitiveness is bearing meager fruit—a free trade pact with Mexico, more funding for DARPA.

The challenge is to forge a political base strong enough to promote a solid economic development program while successfully countering the dual-use coalition and the White House laissez-faire ideologues. Leadership needs to be exerted by a new coalition of many different interest groups, including professional societies, public-interest groups, labor unions, academia, business, and government. Prototypes of such a coalition have been springing up all over the country in the last decade to work on ambitious new projects at both the local and national levels.

For instance, the plant-closing movement has grown in size and sophistication in recent years. It consists of several dozen coalitions of labor, community, religious, and local government groups trying to prevent plant closures and promote economic alternatives. Most have joined a new national organization, the Federation for Industrial Renewal and Retention (FIRR), to link their local organizing efforts and to promote a national industrial policy. For instance, the Tri-State Conference on Steel, a FIRR member organization, has successfully formed a regional coalition to pioneer a new institution, the Pittsburgh-area Steel Valley Authority, which is a public entity with eminent domain powers and technical resources that it uses to prevent plant closings. Among other initiatives, the Tri-State group is now working on a major demonstration project for a regional Maglev rail system, its components to be built in the area.

Plant-closing coalitions have matured into economic development organizations. The Steel Valley Authority is involved in another interesting project that, according to the economist Bennett Harrison, "exemplifies the kind of university-business-government partnership that is so important for revitalizing Rust Belt urban areas."[7] RedZone, a Pittsburgh-based company newly spun off from DOD-sponsored research at Carnegie-Mellon University, makes robots to clean up toxic waste sites and contaminated nuclear facilities and to find buried pipelines and wiring without digging. Components used in the company's robots will be made by blue-collar workers in small machine shops in the Monongahela River Valley, one of the centers of massive layoffs of steel workers in the early 1980s. The Steel Valley Authority is helping RedZone to find suppliers in the valley towns and to obtain financing for its projects.

Experiments in worker involvement in technology design have been going on in Europe for several years, especially in the Scandinavian countries. In the United States, increased worker involvement has begun to gain currency as well. The Massachusetts Center for Applied Technology has attempted to provide technical assistance to small and medium-sized businesses on the condition that they include "nonexploitive" work-force participation. Several labor unions have also made initiatives in the technology and employment area. For example, the Machinists' Union proposed and lobbied hard, if unsuccessfully, during the early 1980s for a "technology bill of rights" for workers. It has also built a well-equipped education center outside Washington, D.C., to train its members in technology issues. Other unions, such as the United Auto Workers and the Communication Workers of America, have promoted collective bargaining responses to the impact of technological change on employment. They have convinced their companies that workers will accept work-altering innovations as long as they are guaranteed job security.

Workers and communities are not the only potential coalition members engaged in such experiments. Palo Alto–based Computer Professionals for Social Responsibility (CPSR), the nation's largest public-interest organization of high-tech professionals, held a conference in 1989 on participatory design, bringing together Europeans and Americans to share views on worker participation in technology development. CPSR is spearheading a far more ambitious effort, called the 21st Century Project, to reorient public support toward using science and technology to solve some of the nation's most critical problems. The project aims to build a broad coalition of experts, policymakers, scientists, technologists, public-interest organizations, professional societies, and citizens concerned about the environment, jobs, the quality of public infrastructure, and education. A related effort, the Coalition for Science and Technology in a New Era, includes representatives from the Association for Computing Machinery, the American Physical Society, the Institute for Electrical and Electronics Engineers, and a number of other professional societies from several disciplines, including the "hard" sciences, the life sciences, social sciences, and engineering. In a separate initiative, Economists against the Arms Race, with five Nobel Prize winners on its board, has begun to study and promote discussion on alternative economic development strategies.

Environmentalists have also been busy. Some are behind the efforts to create a national institute for the environment within the federal government. Another coalition of environmentalists hosted an international conference, called EcoTech, in November 1991 in Monterey, California, to explore both how technology contributes to environmental problems and how technology might be used to solve them.

One effort that exemplifies the blend of goals in a national economic development strategy is the Campaign for Responsible Technology (CRT). A coalition of environmental and labor groups, CRT works on the environmental and health implications of the microelectronics industry. It has been particularly active in challenging the practices of the Sematech consortium as the centerpiece of a national high-tech industrial policy. In 1990, CRT approached, and has since met with, Sematech to discuss pollution prevention, local community relations, and national research priorities. This includes a proposal for expanding its R&D agenda to include environmental and occupational criteria. CRT believes that "funding Sematech is good industrial policy only if the consortium redesigns its research program to provide good jobs for American taxpayers and . . . develops technologies to reduce the risk of worker illness and environmental degradation."[8]

The business community also has many advocates of a nonmilitary-led economy policy. Business Executives for National Security (BENS) has consistently taken a critical view of the Pentagon's domination of both research and development and procurement. Quite a few high-tech entrepreneurs and small businesses across the nation have refused to accept military contracts and have participated in advisory and political groups organized around nonmilitary economic development strategies.

Even former military officers have played an important role in questioning the impact of our military commitments on the economy. The Center for Defense Information, for instance, regularly reports on areas in which the defense budget could be cut without damaging national security.

Peace groups, too, have been active in merging the concerns of their constituencies with those of people whose jobs and communities are in jeopardy from cutbacks. On the West Coast, Palo Alto's Center for Economic Conversion surveys conversion efforts, offers technical assistance, and publicizes "best practices." In Washington, D.C., the National Commission for Economic Conversion and Disarmament has conducted a number of studies of conversion and has been active in crafting and promoting conversion legislation.

Despite these many encouraging initiatives, we are a long way from enjoying the cohesive and effective political leadership needed to achieve a national strategy. DARPA, the dual-use strategists, and the corporate skeptics have a head start in pushing their agenda. Nevertheless, the growing weakness of the U.S. economy—not to mention the nation's mounting social and environmental problems, which existing strategies so far have failed to reverse—may demand a forceful change of course toward a truly new economic order. The state of the economy and the thawing of the cold war present opportunities to both the United States and the world. Bold new initiatives, guided by a strong, democratic leadership and backed by a committed, well-informed public, are required. We have our work cut out for us.

Notes

■

Chapter 1: An Economy at War

1. Greg Bischak, *Building the Peace Economy* (Lansing, Mich.: Economic Research Associates, 1990), p. 10.
2. Michael Klare, "Behind Desert Storm: The New Military Paradigm," *Technology Review,* 94, no. 4: 28–36; William Hartung, "Breaking the Arms Sales Addiction," *World Policy Journal* VIII, no. 1 (Winter 1990–1991): 1–26.
3. David Henry and Richard Oliver, "The Defense Buildup, 1977–1985: Effects on Production and Employment," *Monthly Labor Review* (August 1987): 3–4; Gordon Adams, "Economic Adjustment to Lower Defense Spending," testimony before the Senate Armed Services Committee, 4 May 1990 (Washington, D.C.: Defense Budget, Project, 1990), p. 3.
4. Marion Anderson, *Converting the Work Force: Where the Jobs Would Be* (Lansing, Mich.: Employment Research Associates, 1983), pp. 6, 9.
5. Robert Eisner, "Macroeconomic Consequences of Disarmament" (paper presented at the Economists against the Arms Race Conference on Economic Issues of Disarmament, University of Notre Dame, 30 November 1990, Notre Dame, Indiana) shows that unemployment is correlated with cuts in defense spending, and Lawrence Klein and K. Mori, "The Impact of Disarmament on Aggregate Economic Activity" (in Bernard Udis, ed., *The Economic Consequences of Reduced Military Spending* [Lexington, Mass.: Lexington Books, 1983], pp. 59–77) shows that short-term unemployment can be expected from military cuts.
6. Robert Hale, "The Outlook for the Peace Dividend" (paper presented at Conference on Economic Issues of Disarmament).
7. Bischak, *Peace Economy,* p. 10.

Chapter 2: The Rise of Postmodern Warfare

1. Lauren Holland and Robert Hoover, *The MX Decision: A New Direction in U.S. Weapons Procurement Policy?* (Boulder, Colo.: Westview, 1985), p. 1; Joshua M. Epstein, *The 1988 Defense Budget* (Washington, D.C.: Brookings Institution,

1987), pp. 26, 31; Tom Gervasi, *America's War Machine: The Pursuit of Global Dominance* (New York: Grove, 1984), p. 93.

2. Defense Budget Project, *Major Weapon System Terminations: Fiscal Years 1991–1993* (Washington, D.C.: Defense Budget Project, 7 February 1990).

3. Murray Rubinstein and Richard Goldman, *To Join with the Eagles: Curtiss-Wright Aircraft, 1903–1965* (Garden City, N.Y.: Doubleday, 1974), p. 162.

4. David MacIsaac, *Strategic Bombing in World War II* (New York: Garland, 1976), p. 5.

5. Michael Sherry, *The Rise of American Air Power: The Creation of Armageddon* (New Haven: Yale University Press, 1987), p. 2; Irving B. Holley, Jr., *Ideas and Weapons: Exploitation of the Aerial Weapon by the United States during World War I* (New Haven: Yale University Press, 1953), pp. 25–27; Martin van Creveld, *Technology and War From 2,000 B.C. to the Present* (New York: Free Press, 1989), pp. 185–87.

6. MacIsaac, *Strategic Bombing,* p. 4, citing the Smuts memorandum of 17 August 1917.

7. Sherry, *Rise of American Air Power,* pp. 17, 12, 8.

8. Ibid., pp. xii, 3; J. F. C. Fuller, *Armament and History* (New York: Scribner's, 1945), p. 8.

9. Van Creveld, *Technology and War,* pp. 188, 196, 229.

10. Alfred Hurley, *Billy Mitchell: Crusader for Air Power* (Bloomington: Indiana University Press, 1975), p. 24; van Creveld, *Technology and War,* p. 188; MacIsaac, *Strategic Bombing,* p. 16.

11. Holley, *Ideas and Weapons,* pp. 64, 153.

12. Mary Kaldor, *The Baroque Arsenal* (New York: Hill and Wang, 1981), pp. 12–13.

13. Ibid., pp. 25–26; MacIsaac, *Strategic Bombing,* p. 5; James Fallows, *National Defense* (New York: Vintage, 1981), p. 35.

14. Sherry, *Rise of American Air Power,* p. 20; Kaldor, *Baroque Arsenal,* p. 14; van Creveld, *Technology and War,* pp. 280–81.

15. Matthew Evangelista, *Innovation and the Arms Race: How the United States and the Soviet Union Develop New Military Technologies* (Ithaca: Cornell University Press, 1988), p. 60.

16. Quoted in Sherry, *Rise of American Air Power,* p. 10. Sherry notes that the high fatality rate among early military pilots—one out of every four of the first contingent of flying officers died in training—also justified disproportionate outlays on safer aircraft development and experimentation (pp. 17–18).

17. Ronald Powaski, *March to Armageddon: The United States and the Nuclear Arms Race, 1939 to the Present* (New York: Oxford University Press, 1987), pp. 19–20.

18. William White, *U.S. Tactical Air Power: Missions, Forces, and Costs* (Washington, D.C.: Brookings Institution, 1974), p. 5; Jack Manno, *Arming the Heavens: The Hidden Military Agenda for Space, 1945–1995* (New York: Dodd, Mead & Co., 1984) pp. 139–40; van Creveld, *Technology and War,* pp. 280–81.

19. Quoted in Fallows, *National Defense,* pp. 56–57.

20. White, *U.S. Tactical Air Power,* p. 5.

21. Kaldor, *Baroque Arsenal,* p. 11.

22. Ibid., pp. 12, 25; van Creveld, *Technology and War,* pp. 230–31

23. Van Creveld, *Technology and War,* p. 267.

24. Neville Jones, *The Origins of Strategic Bombing* (London: William Kimber, 1973), p. 20.

25. Van Creveld, *Technology and War,* p. 237; Kenneth Flamm, *Creating the Computer: Government, Industry, and High Technology* (Washington, D.C.: Brookings Institution, 1988), p. 33.

26. Van Creveld, *Technology and War,* pp. 237–40; Fallows, *National Defense,* p. 43. The history of military patronage of early computing research is documented in Flamm, *Creating the Computer,* ch. 3.

27. Manno, *Arming the Heavens,* p. 2.

28. Fallows, *National Defense,* p. 52. See also Manno, *Arming the Heavens,* p. 45, and Van Creveld, *Technology and War,* pp. 243–44, 279.

29. Van Creveld, *Technology and War,* pp. 269–71; M. J. Armitage and R. A. Mason, *Air Power in the Nuclear Age* (Urbana: University of Illinois Press, 1983), p. xii.

30. Quoted in Evangelista, *Innovation and the Arms Race,* p. 222.

31. Fallows, *National Defense,* p. 35. Fallows also argues that high technology has not significantly increased either flexibility or pilot safety and has actually decreased efficiency and potency and heightened pilot vulnerability in many cases (p. 23).

32. Van Creveld, *Technology and War,* p. 227; Evangelista, *Innovation and the Arms Race,* pp. ix, 60. Van Creveld traces qualitative arms competition back as far as 1860 (pp. 223–24).

33. This point was made as early as the Second World War by Fuller, *Armament and History,* p. 20.

34. Van Creveld, *Technology and War,* p. 218; Morris Janowitz, *The Professional Soldier: A Social and Political Portrait* (New York: Free Press, 1960), pp. 22–31.

35. Powaski, *March to Armageddon,* pp. 13–15; Evangelista, *Innovation and the Arms Race,* pp. 64–65.

36. Eugene Lewis, *Public Entrepreneurship: Toward a Theory of Bureaucratic Political Power* (Bloomington: Indiana University Press, 1980), chs. 2 and 3: *Evangelista, Innovation and the Arms Race,* pp. 60, 65–67.

37. A good introduction to the various views can be found in Powaski, *March to Armageddon,* especially chs. 1–6.

38. Evangelista, *Innovation and the Arms Race,* p. x.

39. Ibid., pp. 54–57.

40. See, for example, Michael Piore and Charles Sabel, *The Second Industrial Divide: Possibilities for Prosperity* (New York: Basic Books, 1984); Michael Storper, "The Transition to Flexible Specialization in the U.S. Film Industry: External Economies, the Division of Labour, and the Crossing of Industrial Divides," *Cambridge Journal of Economics* 13, no. 2 (1989): 273–305; Michael Storper and Richard Walker, *The Capitalist Imperative* (New York: Basil Blackwell, 1989); Annalee Saxenian, "The Origins and Dynamics of Production Networks: The Silicon Valley" (paper presented at the Conference on Networks of Innovators, May 1990,

Montreal); Erica Schoenberger, "From Fordism to Flexible Accumulation: Technology, Competitive Strategies, and International Location," *Environment and Planning D: Space and Society* 6, no. 3. (1988): 245–62; Allen Scott, "Flexible Production Systems and Regional Development: The Rise of New Industrial Space in North America and Western Europe," *International Journal of Urban and Regional Research* 12, no. 2 (1988): 171–86.

41. Henry Ford with Samuel Crowther, *Today and Tomorrow* (Garden City, N.Y.: Doubleday, Page and Co., 1926), pp. 205–9; David Burgess-Wise, *Ford in the Air* (Detroit: Ford Motor Co., Corporate History Office, 1988), pp. 1–2; Allan Nevins and Frank Ernest Hill, *Ford: Expansion and Challenge, 1915–1933* (New York: Scribner's, 1954), p. 64.

42. Burgess-Wise, *Ford in the Air,* pp. 44, 46–47; Nevins and Hill, *Ford: Expansion and Challenge,* pp. 240–42; Owen Bombard, "The Tin Goose," *Dearborn Historical Quarterly* 8 (1958): 1–2; Douglas Ingells, *The Tin Goose: The Fabulous Ford Trimotor* (Fallbrook, Calif.: Aero, 1968), pp. 85–87; Robert Lacey, *Ford: The Men and the Machine* (Boston: Little, Brown, 1986), pp. 390–92; Allan Nevins and Frank Ernest Hill, *Ford: Decline and Rebirth, 1933–1962* (New York: Scribner's, 1962), pp. 179, 190–92.

43. Quoted in Lacey, *Ford,* p. 393.

44. Nevins and Hill, *Ford, Decline and Rebirth,* pp. 191–92.

45. Murray Weidenbaum, "The Transferability of Defense Industry Resources to Civilian Uses," in James Clayton, ed., *The Economic Impact of the Cold War* (New York: Harcourt, Brace & World, 1970), pp. 98–100; Fuller, *Armament and History,* p. 179.

46. Van Creveld, *Technology and War,* pp. 195, 262. Some critics argue that weaponry is not a more flexible product, owing to military turf fights and organizational distortions in the procurement process. See Kaldor, *Baroque Arsenal,* ch. 1, and Fallows, *National Defense,* ch. 1, for discussions of those problems.

47. See also Daniel Todd, *Defense Industries* (London: Routledge, 1988).

48. Powaski, *March to Armageddon,* p. 7.

49. Fallows, *National Defense,* pp. 12, 35, 49–50; van Creveld, *Technology and War,* p. 278. Fallows argues that the Trident, because it is a bigger submarine and we have fewer of them, is more vulnerable to discovery and that our reliance on it reduces the number of hiding points on which missiles are dispersed (p. 20).

50. Fallows, *National Defense,* pp. 24, 57.

51. Ibid., pp. 20–21.

52. Malcolm Browne, "Invention That Shaped the Gulf War: The Laser-Guided Bomb," *New York Times,* 26 February 1991, pp. C1, C8.

53. James R. Kurth, "Aerospace Production Lines and American Defense Spending," in Steven Rosen, ed., *Testing the Theory of the Military-Industrial Complex* (Lexington, Mass.: D. C. Heath, 1973) pp. 135–56; James Kurth, "The Follow-on Imperative in American Weapons Procurement, 1960–1990" (paper presented at the Conference on the Economic Issues of Disarmament, University of Notre Dame, 30 November 1990, South Bend, Indiana); Evangelista, *Innovation and the Arms Race,* p. 219.

Chapter 3: The Aerospace Industry Comes of Age

1. Martin van Creveld, *Technology and War From 2,000 B.C. to the Present* (New York: Free Press, 1989), p. 282.

2. Herman O. Stekler, *The Structure and Performance of the Aerospace Industry* (Berkeley and Los Angeles: University of California Press, 1965), p. 31.

3. International Metalworkers Federation, *IMF Guide to World Aerospace Companies and Unions* (Geneva: IMF, 1987), p. 3.

4. Merton J. Peck and Frederick W. Scherer, *The Weapons Acquisition Process* (Boston: Harvard University, Graduate School of Business Administration, 1962), pp. v, 97; Mary Kaldor, *The Baroque Arsenal* (New York: Hill and Wang, 1981), ch. 1.

5. United Auto Workers, *U.S. Aerospace Industry Review* (Detroit, Mich.: UAW Research Department, April 1988), p. 1.

6. Aerospace Industries Association of America, *Aerospace Facts and Figures, 1989–1990* (Washington, D.C.: AIA, 1989), p. 23.

7. U.S. Congress, Office of Technology Assessment, *Holding the Edge: Maintaining the Defense Technology Base* (Washington, D.C.: U.S. Government Printing Office, April 1989), p. 28. See the instances cited in Daniel Todd and Jamie Simpson, *The World Aircraft Industry* (London: Croom Helm, 1986), pp. 58, 102–3.

8. David Henry and Richard Oliver, "The Defense Buildup, 1977–1985: Effects on Production and Employment," *Monthly Labor Review* (August 1987): 3–11. Henry did the industry estimates, and Oliver contributed those for employment, based on Henry's industry totals. See also David Henry, "Defense Spending: A Growth Market for Industry," in U.S. Department of Commerce, *U.S. Industrial Outlook* (Washington, D.C.: U.S. Government Printing Office, 1983), pp. xxix–xlvii.

9. Faye Duchin, "Economic Consequences of Military Spending," *Journal of Economic Issues* 17, no. 2 (June 1983): 548, table 2.

10. Henry and Oliver, "Defense Buildup," p. 7.

11. Ibid., pp. 5–6.

12. Ibid., pp. 6–7.

13. Ibid., p. 7.

14. G. R. Simonson, ed., *The History of the American Aircraft Industry: An Anthology* (Cambridge, Mass.: MIT Press, 1968), p. 23; Alex Roland, *Model Research: The National Advisory Committee for Aeronautics, 1915–1958* (Washington, D.C.: U.S. Government Printing Office, 1985); John Rae, *Climb to Greatness: The American Aircraft Industry, 1920–1960* (Cambridge, Mass.: MIT Press, 1968), p. 2; Ann Markusen, Peter Hall, Scott Campbell, and Sabina Deitrick, *The Rise of the Gunbelt* (New York: Oxford University Press, 1991), ch. 3.

15. Howard Mingos, "The Rise of the Aircraft Industry," in Simonson, *History of the American Aircraft Industry*, pp. 47, 28. See also Benjamin S. Kelsey, *The Dragon's Teeth: The Creation of United States Air Power for World War II* (Washington, D.C.: Smithsonian Institute, 1982), pp. 35, 43, and Rae, *Climb to Greatness*, p. 3.

16. Mingos, "Rise of the Aircraft Industry," pp. 48, 47.

17. Stekler, *Structure and Performance of the Aerospace Industry,* p. 4.

18. Mingos, "Rise of the Aircraft Industry," pp. 50–54.

19. Elsbeth Freudenthal, "The Aviation Business in the 1930s," in Simonson, *History of the American Aircraft Industry,* pp. 88, 92.

20. Freudenthal, "Aviation Business in the 1930s," p. 84; Almarin Phillips, *Technology and Market Structure: A Study of the Aircraft Industry* (Lexington, Mass.: Lexington Books, 1971), p. 1; Stekler, *Structure and Performance of the Aerospace Industry,* p. 6.

21. Freudenthal, "Aviation Business in the 1930s," pp. 100–101.

22. Mingos, "Rise of the Aircraft Industry," p. 20.

23. William G. Cunningham, *The Aircraft Industry: A Study in Industrial Location* (Los Angeles: Morrison, 1951), p. 25.

24. Kelsey, *Dragon's Teeth,* pp. 15–16, 20–22; Stekler, *Structure and Performance of the Aerospace Industry,* pp. 8–12.

25. Stekler, *Structure and Performance of the Aerospace Industry,* pp. 12–15.

26. Ronald Fernandez, *Excess Profits: The Rise of United Technologies* (Reading, Mass.: Addison-Wesley, 1983), pp. 155–57.

27. Michael H. Armacost, *The Politics of Weapons Innovation: The Thor Jupiter Controversy* (New York: Columbia University Press 1969), p. 27; Edmund Beard, *Developing the ICBM: A Study in Bureaucratic Politics* (New York: Columbia University Press, 1976), p. 49.

28. Stekler, *Structure and Performance of the Aerospace Industry,* pp. 15–17, 36, 39.

29. Ibid., pp. 18–24.

30. James Clayton, ed., *The Economic Impact of the Cold War* (New York: Harcourt, Brace & World, 1970), p. 281.

31. David Burgess-Wise, *Ford in the Air* (Detroit: Ford Motor Co., Corporate History Office, 1988), pp. 10, 16, 23.

32. Henry Ford with Samuel Crowther, *Today and Tomorrow* (Garden City, N.Y.: Doubleday, Page and Co., 1926), pp. 204–6; Allan Nevins and Frank Ernest Hill, *Ford: Expansion and Challenge, 1915–1933* (New York: Scribner's, 1954), pp. 240–45; Allan Nevins and Frank Ernest Hill, *Ford: Decline and Rebirth, 1933–1962* (New York: Scribner's, 1962), p. 170; Burgess-Wise, *Ford in the Air,* pp. 33–35, 44, 46–47; Owen Bombard, "The Tin Goose," *Dearborn Historical Quarterly* 8 (1958): 19–20; Douglas Ingells, *The Tin Goose: The Fabulous Ford Trimotor* (Fallbrook, Calif.: Aero, 1968), pp. 85–87; Thomas Sciever, Alma Horvath, and Bessmer, *History of Ford Air Transportation Department: 1901–1979* (St. Louis: VIP Printing, 1980), pp. 6–7.

33. Bombard, "Tin Goose," pp. 19–20, 35; Nevins and Hill, *Ford: Expansion and Challenge,* pp. 245–46; Ford, *Today and Tomorrow,* p. 205.

34. See Markusen, Hall, Deitrick, and Campbell, *Rise of the Gunbelt,* ch. 3, for an extended discussion of the army–air force competition.

35. Peck and Scherer, *Weapons Acquisition Process,* pp. 228–29; Armacost, *Politics of Weapons Innovation,* pp. 89n, 137, 136, 156.

36. Charles Bright, *The Jet Makers: The Aerospace Industry from 1945 to 1972*

(Lawrence: Regents Press of Kansas, 1978), pp. 184–85; see also Stekler, *Structure and Performance of the Aerospace Industry,* p. 101.

37. Robert Lacey, *Ford: The Men and the Machine* (Boston: Little, Brown, 1986), p. 393.

38. Authors' interviews with Bob Isom, Director, Corporate History Office, Ford Motor Company, and Walter Hayes, Vice-President, Ford Motor Company, 12 October 1988, Dearborn, Michigan; Ford Aerospace, undated (1988) memorandum, Arlington, Virginia.

39. Kenneth Flamm, *Creating the Computer: Government, Industry, and High Technology* (Washington, D.C.: Brookings Institution, 1988), pp. 16, 33; Richard Levin, "The Semiconductor Industry," in Richard Nelson, ed., *Government and Technical Progress: A Cross-Industry Analysis* (New York: Pergamon, 1982), p. 26; Senate Committee on Governmental Operations, Subcommittee on Reorganization and International Organizations, *Coordination of Information on Current Federal Research and Development Projects in the Field of Electronics,* Cong., Sess., 1961, S. Rept., p. 138.

40. See the discussion in Ann Markusen, *Profit Cycles, Oligopoly, and Regional Development* (Cambridge, Mass.: MIT Press, 1985), pp. 1109–13; Annalee Saxenian, "Silicon Chips and Spatial Structure: The Semiconductor Industry and Urbanization in Santa Clara County, California" (Master's thesis, Department of City and Regional Planning, University of California at Berkeley, 1980), pp. 117–18; Michael Borrus and James Millstein, "Trade and Development in the Integrated Circuit Industry," in Laura Tyson and John Zysman, eds., *American Industry in International Competition,* (Berkeley: Institute for Governmental Studies, University of California, 1980), p. 24; Flamm, *Creating the Computer,* p. 16; Ernest Braun and Stuart MacDonald, *Revolution in Miniature: The History and Impact of Semiconductor Electronics,* 2d ed. (Cambridge: Cambridge University Press, 1982), p. 98.

41. Stekler, *Structure and Performance of the Aerospace Industry,* pp. 29 n. 24; 31.

42. Ibid., pp. 29, 48, 98 n. 7, 102.

43. Department of Commerce, *1990 U.S. Industrial Outlook* (Washington, D.C.: U.S. Government Printing Office, January 1990), pp. 33–42.

44. Flamm, *Creating the Computer,* p. 68.

45. Ibid., pp. 29, 33, 43, 63–64, 205; Sarah Kuhn, *Computer Manufacturing in New England: Structure, Location, and Labor in a Growing Industry* (Cambridge, Mass.: Harvard-MIT Joint Center for Urban Studies, 1981).

46. Flamm, *Creating the Computer,* p. 68; Kenneth Flamm, *Targeting the Computer: Government Support and International Competition* (Washington, D.C.: Brookings Institution, 1987), pp. 96–97.

47. Flamm, *Creating the Computer,* p. 23; Flamm, *Targeting the Computer,* pp. 42–43, 65–68, 81–82, 108–10.

48. Frances Seghers, "How Do You Chase a $17 Billion Market?: With Everything You've Got," *Business Week,* 23 November 1987, pp. 120–22.

49. Ann Markusen, "Defense Spending: A Successful Industrial Policy?" *International Journal of Urban and Regional Research* 10, no. 1 (1986): 105–22.

50. Todd and Simpson, *World Aircraft Industry,* pp. 255–59.

51. Seymour Melman, *The Permanent War Economy* (New York: Simon and Schuster, 1974), p. 42; Jacques Gansler, *The Defense Industry* (Cambridge, Mass.: MIT Press, 1980), pp. 54–55, 288 (n. 8). Gansler reports that the army, relying on the Army Arsenal Act of 1853, still does much of its work in-house, whereas the air force favors the private sector for manufacturing but uses its own laboratories and repair depots extensively.

52. Clayton, *Economic Impact of the Cold War,* p. 129.

53. Peck and Scherer, *Weapons Acquisition Process,* p. 25; National Science Foundation, *Science and Engineering in American Industry: Report on a 1956 Survey* (Washington, D.C.: U.S. Government Printing Office, 1958), pp. 48, 65.

54. AIA, *Aerospace Facts and Figures, 1989–1990,* pp. 100–101, 104.

55. Gordon Adams, *The Iron Triangle: The Politics of Defense Contracting* (New York: Council on Economic Priorities, 1981), pp. 165–71.

56. Melman, *Permanent War Economy,* p. 43; Gansler, *Defense Industry,* p. 89; Todd and Simpson, *World Aircraft Industry,* pp. 1855–57.

57. Clayton, *Economic Impact of the Cold War,* p. 51.

58. AIA, *Aerospace Facts and Figures, 1990–1991.* This does not include $20 billion of sales of "Related Products and Services," a large portion of which are military-related.

59. Todd and Simpson, *World Aircraft Industry,* pp. 59, 187; Robert Reich, *Minding America's Business* (New York: Vintage, 1983), p. 236.

60. Adams, *Iron Triangle,* pp. 155–61.

61. AIA, *Aerospace Facts and Figures, 1989–1990,* pp. 8–18; Aerospace Industries Association of America, "1989 Year-End Review and Forecast: An Analysis" (mimeograph, 1990), pp. 5–6, tables I, II, V, and VI.

62. U.S. Congress, Office of Technology Assessment, *Paying the Bill: Manufacturing and America's Trade Deficit* (Washington, D.C.: U.S. Government Printing Office, June 1988), p. 68; AIA, "1989 Year-End Review and Forecast," table VI; AIA, *Aerospace Facts and Figures, 1989–1990,* p. 164.

63. AIA, *Aerospace Facts and Figures, 1989–1990,* pp. 26–34; AIA, "1989 Year-End Review and Forecast," table V; UAW, *U. S. Aerospace Industry Review,* pp. 1–2.

64. David Mowery and Nathan Rosenberg, "The Commercial Aircraft Industry," in Nelson, *Government and Technical Progress,* p. 131; U.S. Congress, Office of Technology Assessment, *Making Things Better: Competing in Manufacturing* (Washington, D.C.: U.S. Government Printing Office, February 1990), p. 75.

65. National Science Foundation, *Federal R&D Funding by Budget Function, Fiscal Years 1989–1991,* NSF 90–311 (Washington, D.C.: NSF, 1990), pp. 14, 96–97.

66. Phillips, *Technology and Market Structure,* pp. 1, 127.

67. See Flamm, *Creating the Computer,* p. 27.

68. Braun and MacDonald, *Revolution in Miniature,* pp. 8, 159.

69. OTA *Paying the Bill,* pp. 39–40; Ann Markusen, "Steel and Southeast Chicago: Reasons and Remedies for Industrial Renewal" (report to the Mayor's Task Force on Steel and Southeast Chicago, Center for Urban Affairs and Policy Research, Northwestern University, 1985).

70. OTA, *Paying the Bill,* pp. 2, 67.

71. Ibid., pp. 15, 36.

72. A number of scholars have written eloquently from the "depletionist" camp, including Seymour Melman, *Profits without Production* (New York: Knopf, 1983), and *Permanent War Economy;* Lloyd Dumas, *The Overburdened Economy* (Berkeley and Los Angeles: University of California Press, 1986); Lester Thurow, "How to Wreck the Economy," *New York Review of Books,* 14 May 1981, pp. 3–8; David Noble, *Forces of Production* (New York: Oxford University Press, 1984); Robert Reich, *The Next American Frontier* (New York: New York Times Co., 1983), pp. 189–93; Robert DeGrasse, Jr., *Military Expansion, Economic Decline: The Impact of Military Spending on U.S. Economic Performance* (Armonk, N.Y.: M. E. Sharpe, 1983); Kaldor, *Baroque Arsenal;* Michael Dee Oden, "Military Spending Erodes Real National Security," *Bulletin of Atomic Scientists* 44, no. 5 (June 1988): 36–42. See also Ann Markusen, "Military Spending: Cold War Economics," *Bulletin of Atomic Scientists* 45, no. 1 (January-February 1989): 41–44, and "The Militarized Economy: Deforming U.S. Growth and Productivity," *World Policy Journal* 3, no. 3 (Summer 1986): 495–516. For a dissent from this position, see Gordon Adams and David Gold, *The Impact of Defense Spending on Investment, Productivity, and Economic Growth* (Washington, D. C.: Defense Budget Project, 1990).

73. Melman, *Profits without Production,* p. 154; Dumas, *Overburdened Economy,* pp. 211–12.

74. Melman, *Profits without Production,* p. 150; Dumas, *Overburdened Economy,* pp. 219, 223; Pat Choate and Susan Walter, *America in Ruins: Beyond the Public Pork Barrel* (Washington, D.C.: Council of State Planning Agencies, 1981), p. 1.

75. Candace Howes, *The Cost of Maturity: Foreign Direct Investment in the Auto Industry* (mimeograph, Project on Regional and Industrial Economics, Rutgers University, 20 July 1990), pp. 6–10; Todd and Simpson, *World Aircraft Industry,* p. 17; Melman, *Profits without Production,* pp. 184–87; Richard Cohen, "Iacocca's a Symbol of an Industry's Fall," *Philadelphia Inquirer,* 12 December 1989, p. 15.

76. Jonathon Hicks, "Value of a USX Spin-off Is Disputed," *New York Times,* 17 April 1990, p. D6.

77. Markusen, "Steel and Southeast Chicago," and "Planning for Communities in Decline: Lessons from Steel Communities," *Journal of Planning Education and Research* 7, no. 3 (1988): 173–84; Melman, *Profits without Production,* pp. 188–99; Reich, *Minding America's Business,* pp. 155–68.

78. Susan Walsh Sanderson, *The Consumer Electronics Industry and the Future of American Manufacturing* (Washington, D.C.: Economic Policy Institute, 1989), pp. 3, 9, 13, 18; Reich, *Minding America's Business,* pp. 169–80.

79. Anthony DeFilippo, *Military Spending and Industrial Decline: A Study of the American Machine Tool Industry* (Westport, Conn.: Greenwood, 1986).

80. Murray Weidenbaum, "The Transferability of Defense Industry Resources to Civilian Uses," in Clayton, *Economic Impact of the Cold War,* p. 98.

81. AIA, *Aerospace Facts and Figures, 1989–1990,* pp. 104–5.

82. OTA, *Holding the Edge,* pp. 10, 21; Council on Competitiveness, *Competitiveness Index, 1990* (Washington, D. C.: Council on Competitiveness, 1990), p. 8.

83. UAW, *U.S. Aerospace Industry Review,* pp. 3–4, 8.

84. Eric Shine, "Defenseless against Cutbacks," *Business Week,* 14 January 1991, p. 69.

85. Aerospace Industries Association of America, Aerospace Research Center, "U.S. Aerospace Recovers Market Share Lost in '70s," *Facts and Perspective* (June 1988): 1–3, and "U.S. Aerospace Market Share Declines," *Facts and Perspective* (April 1990): 1–3.

86. Quoted in Charles Lane et al., "Arms for Sale," *Newsweek,* 8 April 1991, pp. 22–27, 23.

87. Clyde Farnsworth, "White House Seeks to Revive Credits for Arms Exports," *New York Times,* 18 March 1991, p. D6.

88. David Mowery, "Joint Ventures in the U.S. Commercial Aircraft industry," in David Mowery, ed., *International Collaborative Ventures in U.S. Manufacturing* (Cambridge, Mass.: Ballinger, 1988), pp. 71–110; MIT Commission on Industrial Productivity, "The U.S. Commercial Aircraft Industry and Its Foreign Competitors," in *The Working Papers of the MIT Commission on Industrial Productivity* (Cambridge, Mass.: MIT Press, 1989), pp. 16–17; OTA, *Making Things Better,* p. 75.

89. AIA, *Aerospace Facts and Figures, 1989–1990,* pp. 136–39; AIA, "1989 Year-End Review and Forecast," p. 7, table IX.

90. Sanderson, *Consumer Electronics Industry,* pp. 5–6; Ann Markusen, Peter Hall, and Amy Glasmeier, *High Tech America* (London: Allen & Unwin, 1985), ch 1, 2; Richard Riche, Daniel Hecker, and John Burgan, "High Technology Today and Tomorrow: A Small Slice of the Employment Pie," *Monthly Labor Review* (November 1983): 50–58.

91. John Clark, "The New Economics of National Defense," in Clayton, *Economic Impact of the Cold War,* pp. 7–26.

92. Sanderson, *Consumer Electronics Industry,* pp. 36–44; Steven Cohen and John Zysman, *Manufacturing Matters* (New York: Basic Books, 1987); Philip Shapira, *Modernizing Manufacturing* (Washington, D.C.: Economic Policy Institute, 1990). See also Joel S. Yudken and Michael Black, "Targeting National Needs: A New Direction for Science and Technology Policy," *World Policy Journal* 7, no. 2 (Spring 1990): 251–88.

Chapter 4: A Wall of Separation

1. The term is widely used—for instance, by James Blackwell of the conservative Center for Strategic and International Studies, who used it in a speech at the Governor's Conference on Economic Transitions for Ohio's Small-Business Defense Contractors, 23–24 January 1990, Columbus, Ohio.

2. Roy Anderson, *A Look at Lockheed* (New York: Newcomen Society, 1983), pp. 8, 11, 20, 23, 28–30.

3. Ibid., p. 9.

4. Ibid., 40.

5. Ibid., pp. 11, 45–46; see also Michael Harris, "Lockheed: Debriefing Roy Anderson," *California Business* (April 1984): 95–110.

6. Calculated from published data on prime contracts by company, Department of Defense, *Prime Contracts over $25,000 by State, County, Contractor, and Place* (Washington, D.C.: U.S. Government Printing Office, 1957–1978).

7. Seymour Melman, *The Permanent War Economy* (New York: Simon and Schuster, 1974), pp. 44–47; Anderson, *Look at Lockheed,* 43–45.

8. Gordon Adams, *The Iron Triangle: The Politics of Defense Contracting* (New York: Council on Economic Priorities, 1981), pp. 333–36.

9. Quoted in Adams, *Iron Triangle,* pp. 309–10.

10. Anderson, *Look at Lockheed,* pp. 44–45.

11. Tim Carrington, "Air Force Is Said to Buy Fifty Stealth Jets, But It Isn't Seen Purchasing Any More," *Wall Street Journal,* 25 August 1986, p. 15; John Cushman, Jr., "U.S. Says Lockheed Overcharged by Hundreds of Millions on Plane," *New York Times,* 29 August 1986, p. 1.

12. Quoted in Adams, *Iron Triangle,* p. 312.

13. Steven Pearlstein, "Other Bidders Settle for Smaller Bites of the Aerospace Pie," *Washington Post,* 29 April–5 May 1991, national weekly edition, p. 11.

14. Edward Kolcum, "Cutback Brings New Strategy for Use of Factory, Workers," *Aviation Week & Space Technology,* 28 March 1988, pp. 36–38.

15. Bill Sing, "Reliance on Pentagon Worries Lockheed," *Los Angeles Times,* 19 May 1983, p. 1D; International Metalworkers Federation, *IMF Guide to World Aerospace Companies and Unions* (Geneva: IMF, 1987), p. 126; Stewart Toy, "Why Lockheed Is Locking in on Electronics," *Business Week,* 29 September 1986, p. 84; Stewart Toy, "Lockheed's New Top Gun Comes out Blazing," *Business Week,* 5 September 1988, pp. 75, 78; George Melloan, "Lockheed's Exciting Life on the Technological Frontier," *Wall Street Journal,* 16 May 1989, p. A15; Bruce Smith, "Lockheed Expects Steady Growth of Defense Electronics Revenues," *Aviation Week & Space Technology,* 5 December 1988, pp. 91, 93.

16. Quoted in Harris, "Lockheed: Debriefing Roy Anderson," p. 103.

17. George Wilson, "The Only Thing Visible about Stealth Is Its Rising Cost," *Washington Post,* 23–29 May 1988, national weekly edition, p. 31; "Lockheed to Sell Most Nonmilitary Lines," *New York Times,* 5 April 1989, p. B1; Toy, "Lockheed's New Top Gun Comes out Blazing"; Roy Harris, Jr., "After Its Slump, a Risk-Averse Lockheed Concentrates on U.S. Defense Contracts," *Wall Street Journal,* 17 May 1983, p. 60.

18. Department of Commerce, Bureau of the Census, *Current Industrial Reports: Aerospace Industry (Orders, Sales, and Backlog)* (Washington, D.C.: U.S. Government Printing Office, July 1987), p. 3.

19. Other analysts have focused on the top fifty companies; see William Baldwin, *The Structure of the Defense Market, 1955–1964* (Durham, N.C.: Duke University Press, 1967), pp. 16–17.

20. Jacques Gansler, *The Defense Industry* (Cambridge, Mass.: MIT Press, 1980), pp. 36, 43.

21. This breakdown is adapted and updated from Herman O. Stekler, *The Structure*

and Performance of the Aerospace Industry (Berkeley and Los Angeles: University of California Press, 1965), pp. 46–49. See also Baldwin, *Structure of the Defense Market,* pp. 60–61; he identifies twenty-one major aircraft and propulsion companies and nineteen major electronics companies doing defense work.

22. See also Adams, *Iron Triangle,* p. 12, and Gansler, *Defense Industry,* p. 41.

23. United Auto Workers, *U.S. Aerospace Industry Review* (Detroit, Mich.: UAW Research Department, April 1988), p. 1.

24. Bureau of the Census, *Current Industrial Reports: Aerospace Industry,* p. 3; UAW, *U.S. Aerospace Industry Review,* p. 7; IMF, *IMF Guide to World Aerospace Companies and Unions,* p. 126; Thomas Hayes, "FSX: Icing on the Cake for General Dynamics," *New York Times,* 2 May 1989, pp. 1, 34; Gansler, *Defense Industry,* p. 89.

25. Jack Raymond, "The Growing Threat of Our Military-Industrial Complex," in James Clayton, ed., *The Economic Impact of the Cold War* (New York: Harcourt, Brace & World, 1970), pp. 245–57.

26. Daniel Todd and Jamie Simpson, *The World Aircraft Industry* (London: Croom Helm, 1986), p. 86; Gavin Kennedy, *Defense Economics* (London: Duckworth, 1983), p. 156; UAW, *U.S. Aerospace Industry Review,* p. 1.

27. "The Business Week 1000," *Business Week,* 13 April 1990, p. 159.

28. Gansler, *Defense Industry,* p. 128. Gansler believes that the similarity of the three types gives them a common set of structural characteristics.

29. Gansler, *Defense Industry,* pp. 129–61; Baldwin, *Structure of the Defense Market,* pp. 28, 31–33. In his 1967 work, Baldwin concluded that DOD procurement policies influenced which small businesses got contracts more than it did the volume or nature of work subcontracted. He also found that subcontracting fell as a percentage of prime from 55 percent in 1957 to 48 percent in 1963.

30. Irving B. Holley, Jr., *Buying Aircraft: Matériel Procurement for the Army Air Forces* (Washington, D.C.: Department of the Army, Office of the Chief of Military History, 1964), p. 22.

31. Stekler, *Structure and Performance of the Aerospace Industry,* pp. 10–11.

32. Ronald Kucera, *The Aerospace Industry and the Military: Structural and Political Relationships* (Beverly Hills, Calif.: Sage Publications, 1974), p. 34; Roger Beaumont, "Quantum Increase in the MIC in the Second World War," in Benjamin Cooling, ed., *War, Business and American Society: Historical Perspectives on the Military-Industrial Complex* (Port Washington, N.Y.: Kennikat, 1977).

33. Stekler, *Structure and Performance of the Aerospace Industry,* p. 15.

34. Finletter Commission, "Survival in the Air Age," in Carroll Purcell, ed., *The Military-Industrial-Complex* (New York: Harper and Row, 1972), pp. 184–85, 195.

35. Murray Weidenbaum, "The Transferability of Defense Industry Resources to Civilian Uses," in Clayton, *The Economic Impact of the Cold War,* p. 98, and Baldwin, *The Structure of the Defense Market, 1955–1964,* 75, Table IV-12.

36. Baldwin, *Structure of the Defense Market,* p. 14.

37. Many of the best studies, covering a thirty-year period beginning in the early 1960s, are cited throughout this chapter. In particular, see the citations for works

by Merton J. Peck and Frederick W. Scherer, Murray Weidenbaum, Herman O. Stekler, William Baldwin, Almarin Philips, Walter Adams and William James Adams, Seymour Melman, Jacques Gansler, Barry Bluestone, Peter Jordan, and Mark Sullivan, and Daniel Todd and Jamie Simpson.

38. Merton J. Peck and Frederick W. Scherer, *The Weapons Acquisition Process* (Boston: Harvard University, Graduate School of Business Administration, 1962), p. 56.

39. Stekler, *Structure and Performance of the Aerospace Industry,* p. 204.

40. For recent characterizations of how doing military business differs from serving commercial markets, see Daniel Todd, *Defence Industries: A Global Perspective* (London: Routledge, 1988); Jacques Gansler, *Affording Defense* (Cambridge, Mass.: MIT Press, 1989); and Anthony DeFilippo, "How the Military-Serving Firm Differs from the Rest" (briefing paper no. 10, National Commission for Economic Conversion and Disarmament, Washington, D.C., December 1990).

41. Stekler, *Structure and Performance of the Aerospace Industry,* p. 49; Peck and Scherer, *Weapons Acquisition Process,* pp. 69–84; Baldwin, *Structure of the Defense Market,* p. 100.

42. Stekler (*Structure and Performance of the Aerospace Industry,* p. 49) rejects the notion that the Pentagon acts as a monopsonist, claiming that interservice rivalry renders the aerospace customer more an oligopsonist; Peck and Scherer share this view to some extent.

43. Walter Adams and William James Adams, "The Military-Industrial Complex: A Market Structure Analysis," *American Economic Association, Papers and Proceedings* 62 (May 1972): 281; Stekler, *Structure and Performance of the Aerospace Industry,* p. 55.

44. Stekler, *Structure and Performance of the Aerospace Industry,* p. 49.

45. Cited in Adams and Adams, "Military-Industrial Complex," p. 282.

46. Todd and Simpson, *World Aircraft Industry,* pp. 90–91.

47. Gansler, *Defense Industry,* pp. 165–66.

48. Almarin Phillips, *Technology and Market Structure: A Study of the Aircraft Industry* (Lexington, Mass.: Lexington Books, 1971), pp. 21, 116; Baldwin, *Structure of the Defense Market,* p. 13; Stekler, *Structure and Performance of the Aerospace Industry,* p. 15 (n. 33).

49. Baldwin, *Structure of the Defense Market,* p. 57.

50. Barry Bluestone, Peter Jordan, and Mark Sullivan, *Aircraft Industry Dynamics: An Analysis of Competition, Capital, and Labor* (Boston: Auburn House, 1981), p. 55; Peck and Scherer, *Weapons Acquisition Process,* p. 195; Stekler, *Structure and Performance of the Aerospace Industry,* pp. 97, 105, 152, 201.

51. Peck and Scherer, *Weapons Acquisition Process,* p. 53.

52. Cited in Richard Stevenson, "New Jet Fighter: Risks Are High," *New York Times,* 27 December 1987, p. D1.

53. Calvin Sims, "Limits Sought on Contracts from Navy," *New York Times,* 13 February 1989, p. 19; Calvin Sims, "G.A.O. Says Navy Contract Unfairly Favored IBM," *New York Times,* 23 June 1989, pp. 25, 30.

54. The debate continues to rage, in fact, over whether or not concentration is

unavoidable in the military-oriented aerospace industry. See the differences between the analyses of Peck and Scherer, *Weapons Acquisition Process,* pp. 53–54, 58, 60; Phillips, *Technology and Market Structure,* p. 2; and Baldwin, *Structure of the Defense Market,* pp. 15, 89.

55. Gansler, *Defense Industry,* pp. 46–48.

56. Adams and Adams, "Military-Industrial Complex," pp. 280–81; Adams, *Iron Triangle,* pp. 155–61; Melman, *Permanent War Economy,* ch. 3.

57. Baldwin, *Structure of the Defense Market,* pp. 9–11, 47; Gansler, *Defense Industry,* p. 11.

58. Peck and Scherer, *Weapons Acquisition Process,* p. 50; Gansler, *Defense Industry,* p. 32.

59. James R. Kurth, "Aerospace Production Lines and American Defense Spending," in Steven Rosen, ed., *Testing the Theory of the Military-Industrial Complex* (Lexington, Mass.: D.C. Heath, 1973), pp. 135–56; Adamas and Adams, "Military-Industrial Complex," pp. 283–84.

60. Kurth, "Aerospace Production Lines and American Defense Spending," pp. 149–54; James Stubbing, *The Defense Game: An Insider Explores the Astonishing Realities of America's Defense Establishment* (New York: Harper and Row, 1986), pp. 184–90; Todd and Simpson, *World Aircraft Industry,* pp. 100–102.

61. James Kurth, "The Follow-on Imperative in American Weapons Procurement, 1960–1990" (paper presented at Conference on Economic Issues of Disarmament, University of Notre Dame, 1 December 1990, Notre Dame, Indiana).

62. Richard Stevenson, "Why Lockheed Is Under Siege," *New York Times,* 13 March 1990, pp. D1, D8.

63. Quoted in Leslie Wayne, "Arms Makers Gird for Peace," *New York Times,* 17 December 1989, p. F3. See also Rick Wartzman, "Defense Contractors Gird for Warming of the Cold War," *Wall Street Journal,* 11 November 1989, p. A8; and John Stodden, "Earnings Outlook Prompts Wall Street to Discount Aerospace/ Defense Stocks," *Aviation Week & Space Technology,* 30 May 1988, pp. 40–45.

64. Weidenbaum, "Transferability of Defense Industry Resources to Civilian Uses," p. 41; U.S. Congress, Office of Technology Assessment, *Holding the Edge: Maintaining the Defense Technology Base* (Washington, D.C.: U.S. Government Printing Office, April 1989), pp. 229–30.

65. Adams and Adams, "Military-Industrial Complex," p. 282; Stekler, *Structure and Performance of the Aerospace Industry,* pp. 58–59.

66. Philip J. Klass, "Aircraft Avionic Firms' Differences Fade," *Aviation Week,* 12 October 1959, pp. 70, 72.

67. Weidenbaum, "Transferability of Defense Industry Resources to Civilian Uses," p. 100.

68. Adams and Adams, "Military-Industrial Complex," p. 284.

69. Melman, *Permanent War Economy,* p. 50.

70. Phillips, *Technology and Market Structure,* pp. 121–22.

71. Michael Storper, "The Transition to Flexible Specialization in the U.S. Film Industry: External Economies, the Division of Labour, and the Crossing of Industrial Divides," *Cambridge Journal of Economics* 13, no. 3 (1989): 273–305; Bennett

Harrison, "The Return of the Big Firms," *Social Policy*, vol. 21 (September 1990): 7, 13.

72. Baldwin, *Structure of the Defense Market*, pp. 38–39. In 1977 a Rand Corporation analysis concluded that vertical integration had been a consistent trend in the industry over the past few decades. Genesse Baumbusch and Alvin Harman, *Peacetime Adequacy of Lower Tiers of the Defense Industrial Base* (Santa Monica, Calif.: Rand Corp., November 1977).

74. Stekler, *Structure and Performance of the Aerospace Industry*, pp. 112–13.

75. For "merchants-of-death" theories and congressional hearings, especially in the 1930s, see Ann Trotter, "Development of the Merchants-of-Death Theory," in Cooling, *War, Business and American Society*, pp. 93–104; H. C. Engelbrecht and F. C. Hanighen, *Merchants of Death: A Study of the International Armament Industry* (New York: Dodd, Mead and Co., 1934); and Philip Noel-Baker, *The Private Manufacture of Armaments* (New York: Oxford University Press, 1937).

76. Adams and Adams, "Military-Industrial Complex," p. 280.

77. Peck and Scherer, *Weapons Acquisition Process*, p. 293. They model this three-way trade-off formally, arguing that improvements can be made along one axis only by making sacrifices along one or both of the other two.

78. Peck and Scherer, *Weapons Acquisition Process*, p. 21; Stekler, *Structure and Performance of the Aerospace Industry*, p. 196.

79. Baldwin, *Structure of the Defense Market*, p. 82.

80. George Wilson, "The Only Thing Visible about Stealth Is Its Rising Cost," *Washington Post*, 23–29 May 1988, national weekly edition, p. 31.

81. Eric Schine, "GM and Hughes: Is the Marriage Fizzling?" *Business Week*, 12 February 1990, pp. 54–55.

82. Cited in Gansler, *Defense Industry*, p. 91.

83. Melman, *Permanent War Economy*, p. 32.

84. Gansler, *Defense Industry*, pp. 85, 148.

85. Ibid., pp. 17, 83; Ann Markusen, *Profit Cycles, Oligopoly, and Regional Development* (Cambridge, Mass.: MIT Press, 1985), chs. 8 and 9.

86. Stekler, *Structure and Performance of the Aerospace Industry*, pp. 94, 158–62.

87. See the extended discussion in Gansler, *Defense Industry*, pp. 85–89.

88. "No Business Like War Business," *In Brief*, summary edition of *Defense Monitor* 16, no. 3 (1987):2.

89. John Stodden, "Earnings Outlook Prompts Wall Street to Discount Aerospace/Defense Stocks," *Aviation Week & Space Technology*, 30 May 1988, p. 40; "Defense Firms Made Money in Recession," *American Metals Markets*, 20 August 1985, p. 4.

90. See Stekler, *Structure and Performance of the Aerospace Industry*, p. 198; Seymour Melman, *Profits without Production* (New York: Knopf, 1983), ch. 11; Louis Nemeth and Kukula Kapoor Blastris, *Defective Defense: How the Pentagon Buys Weapons That Do Not Work* (Washington, D.C.: Center for the Study of Responsive Law, 1989); and James Fallows, *National Defense* (New York: Vintage, 1981).

91. See Molly Moore, "Oops! There's Yet Another Glitch in the B-1 Bomber," *Wash-*

ington Post Weekly, 13–24 July 1988, national weekly edition, p. 3; and Andrew Rosenthal, "Lack of Lubricant Is a Bomber Flaw," *New York Times,* 5 April 1989, p. 16. See also the cases cited in Melman, *Permanent War Economy,* pp. 48–49.

92. William Broad, "Crown Jewel of 'Star Wars' Has Lost Its Luster," *New York Times,* 13 February 1990, pp. C1, C8.

93. Milton Leitenberg, "The Dynamics of Military Technology Today," *International Social Science Journal* 25, no. 3 (1973): 344.

94. Cited in Melman, *Permanent War Economy,* p. 43.

95. Peck and Scherer, *Weapons Acquisition Process,* pp. 21–23; A. W. Marshall and W. H. Meckling, "Predictability of Costs, Time, and Success of Development," in Richard Nelson, ed., *The Rate and Direction of Inventive Activity: Economic and Social Factors* (New York: National Bureau of Economic Research, 1963), pp. 461–75.

96. Schine, "GM and Hughes: Is the Marriage Fizzling?"; David Jefferson, "Northrop Posts Fourth-Quarter Loss of $876.1 Million," *Wall Street Journal,* 16 February 1989, p. B2.

97. Steven Holmes, "Cheney Concedes Huge Inventories," *New York Times,* 6 February 1990, p. A22.

98. Stekler, *Structure and Performance of the Aerospace Industry,* pp. 60, 198.

99. Fallows, *National Defense,* pp. 18–19, 23, 34, 76–95. Nevertheless, two recent studies tackle the question of procurement management with creative suggestions about its improvement; see Donald Pilling, *Competition in Defense Procurement* (Washington, D.C.: Brookings Institution, 1989), and J. Ronald Fox, *The Defense Management Challenge: Weapons Acquisition* (Cambridge, Mass.: Harvard Business School Press, 1988).

100. Richard Halloran, "An Enduring Leader with a Low Profile," *New York Times,* 3 January 1989, p. 8.

101. Fallows, *National Defense,* pp. 18–19, 57.

Chapter 5: Innovation Goes to War

1. H. L. Nieburg, *In the Name of Science* (Chicago: Quadrangle Books, 1966), p. 124.

2. Ibid., p. vii.

3. Milton Leitenberg, "The Dynamics of Military Technology Today," *International Social Science Journal* 25, no. 3 (1973): 337.

4. Quoted in Ronald Powaski, *March to Armageddon: The United States and the Nuclear Arms Race, 1939 to the Present* (New York: Oxford University Press, 1987), p. 6; Warren Davis, "The Pentagon and the Scientist," in John Tirman, ed., *The Militarization of High Technology* (Cambridge, Mass.: Ballinger, 1984), p. 153.

5. Martin van Creveld, *Technology and War From 2,000 B.C. to the Present* (New York: Free Press, 1989), p. 227; J. F. C. Fuller, *Armament and History* (New York: Scribner's, 1945), pp. 17–19.

6. John Nef, *War and Human Progress: An Essay on the Rise of Industrial Civilization* (Cambridge, Mass.: Harvard University Press, 1950), p. 44. Many inventions, however, were created only under the demands of war and military service. See

Waldemar Kaempffert, "War and Technology," *American Journal of Sociology* 46, no. 4 (January 1941): 431–44.

7. Quoted in Robert Bruce, *Bell: Alexander Graham Bell and the Conquest of Solitude* (Boston: Little, Brown and Co., 1973), p. 363.

8. Cited in Nieburg, *In the Name of Science*, p. 130.

9. Irving B. Holley, Jr., *Ideas and Weapons: Exploitation of the Aerial Weapon by the United States during World War I* (New Haven: Yale University Press, 1953), pp. 103–5, 112, 154; van Creveld, *Technology and War*, p. 266; Michael Sherry, *The Rise of American Air Power: The Creation of Armageddon* (New Haven: Yale University Press, 1987), p. 20.

10. Kenneth Flamm, *Creating the Computer: Government, Industry, and High Technology* (Washington, D.C.: Brookings Institution, 1988), p. 2; Fuller, *Armament and History*, p. 16.

11. James R. Killian, Jr., *Sputniks, Scientists, and Eisenhower: A Memoir of the First Special Assistant to the President for Science and Technology* (Cambridge, Mass.: MIT Press, 1977), p. 58; Powaski, *March to Armageddon*, p. 5.

12. David MacIsaac, *Strategic Bombing in World War II* (New York: Garland, 1976), p. 146.

13. Vannevar Bush, *Science: The Endless Frontier: Report of the President on a Program for Postwar Scientific Research* (Washington, D.C.: U.S. Government Printing Office, 1945, pp. 1–2.

14. Quoted in Seymour Melman, *Pentagon Capitalism: The Political Economy of War* (New York: McGraw-Hill, 1970), pp. 231–34.

15. David Dickson, *The New Politics of Science* (Chicago: University of Chicago Press, 1988), pp. 16–18.

16. Matthew Evangelista, *Innovation and the Arms Race: How the United States and the Soviet Union Develop New Military Technologies* (Ithaca, N.Y.: Cornell University Press, 1988), p. 54; Nieburg, *In the Name of Science*, pp. 20, 122.

17. Cited in Edward Gerjuoy and Elisabeth Urey Baranger, "The Physical Sciences and Mathematics," in David A. Wilson, ed., "Universities and the Military," *Annals of the American Academy of Political and Social Science* 502 (March 1989): 58–81 (p. 59, n. 2 and n. 3).

18. David A. Wilson, "Consequential Controversies," in Wilson, "Universities and the Military," pp. 40–57. See also Chandra Mukerji, *A Fragile Power: Scientists and the State* (Princeton: Princeton University Press, 1989).

19. Mukerji, *Fragile Power*, pp. 52–61; David Allison, "U.S. Navy Research and Development since World War II," in Merritt Roe Smith, ed., *Military Enterprise and Technological Change: Perspective on the American Experience* (Cambridge, Mass.: MIT Press, 1987), p. 297; Flamm, *Creating the Computer*, p. 42.

20. Ronald G. Havelock and David S. Bushnell, *Technology Transfer at the Defense Advanced Research Projects Agency: A Diagnostic Analysis* (report to DARPA from the Technology Transfer Study Center, George Mason University, Fairfax, Va., December 1985), p. 3; Flamm, *Targeting the Computer*, p. 73.

21. Dickson, *New Politics of Science*, pp. 31–32.

22. American Association for the Advancement of Science, Intersociety Working

Group, *Research and Development FY 1991*, AAAS report no. 15 (Washington, D.C.: Committee on Science, Engineering and Public Policy (COSEPUP), AAAS, 1990), tables I–1 through I–7, pp. 47–54.

23. To the authors' knowledge, there has been no systematic study made of the DOD-NASA relationship, and the degree to which their programs overlap and influence each other. The NSF's annual breakdown of the federal R&D budget by budget function does not include NASA in the defense R&D figures. See National Science Foundation, *Federal R&D Funding by Budget Function 1989–1991*, NSF 90–311 (Washington, D.C.: NSF, 1990).

24. Department of Defense, Office of the Comptroller, *Department of Defense Budget for Fiscal Years 1992 and 1993, RDT&E Programs (R-1)* (Washington, D.C.: DOD, 4 February 1991).

25. DOD Office of the Comptroller, *DOD Budget for Fiscal Years 1992 and 1993, (R-1)*.

26. National Science Foundation, *Federal Funds for Research and Development, Fiscal Years 1988, 1989, and 1990, vol. 38*, NSF 90–306 (detailed statistical tables) (Washington, D.C.: NSF, 1990).

27. NSF, *Federal Funds for Research and Development, Fiscal Years 1988, 1989, and 1990*; Department of Defense, Office of the Comptroller, *Department of Defense Budget for Fiscal Year 1991, RDT&E Programs (R-1)* (Washington, D.C.: U.S. Government Printing Office, 29 January 1990).

28. Gerjuoy and Baranger, "Physical Sciences and Mathematics," p. 59; Richard M. Abrams, "The U.S. Military and Higher Education: A Brief History," in Wilson, "Universities and the Military," pp. 15–28 (p. 24).

29. Abrams, "U.S. Military and Higher Education," p. 23.

30. Dickson, *New Politics of Science*, p. 123; Richard D. DeLauer, "The Good of It and Its Problems," in Wilson, "Universities and the Military," pp. 130–40 (p. 134).

31. Dickson, *New Politics of Science*, p. 126.

32. National Science Board, *Science and Engineering Indicators—1989*, NSB 89–1 (Washington, D.C.: U.S. Government Printing Office, 1989), appendix table 5–5, pp. 300–301.

33. Defense Budget Project, *Final Congressional Action on the Fiscal Year 1991 Defense Budget: Authorization and Appropriations* (Washington, D.C.: 7 November 1990), p. 2.

34. DeLauer, "The Good of It and Its Problems," p. 136.

35. Office of Assistant Secretary of Defense for Public Affairs, "DOD Announces Awards of University Research Instrumentation Funding" (news release, 11 August 1988); Office of Undersecretary of Defense for Acquisition, "The Department of Defense University Research Initiative Research Program Summaries," May 1987. See also DOD Office of the Comptroller, *DOD Budget for Fiscal Year 1991, (R-1)*.

36. For discussion of the "technological imperative" driving new weapons programs, particularly the centrality of computer-based military technologies to DOD, see Gary Chapman, "The New Generation of High-Technology Weapons," David

Bellin and Gary Chapman, eds., *Computers in Battle: Will They Work?* (New York: Harcourt Brace Jovanovich, 1987), pp. 61–100; Paul N. Edwards, "A History of Computers and Weapons Systems," in Bellin and Chapman, eds., *Computers in Battle,* pp. 45–60.

37. Joel S. Yudken and Barbara B. Simons, "Federal Funding in Computer Science: A Preliminary Report," *SIGACT News* 19, no. 1 (Fall 1987): 54–63, and Joel S. Yudken and Barbara B. Simons, *A Field in Transition: Federal Funding of Academic Computer Science—Current Trends and Issues* (final report of the Project on Funding Policy in Computer Science, Special Interest Group on Automatic and Computability Theory [SIGACT] Association for Computing Machinery [forthcoming]).

38. Abrams, "U.S. Military and Higher Education, p. 23.

39. Walter S. Baer, "The Changing Relationship: Universities and Other R&D Performers," in Bruce L. R. Smith and Joseph J. Karlesky, eds., *State of Academic Science,* vol. 1, *Summary of Major Findings* (New Rochelle, N.Y.: Change Magazine Press, 1977), 2:78; Gerjuoy and Baranger, "Physical Sciences and Mathematics," p. 74; Yudken and Simons, *Field in Transition.*

40. For a discussion of this point from a critical perspective, see Mukerji, *Fragile Power,* pp. 3–21.

41. DeLauer, "The Good of It and Its Problems," p. 133.

42. For discussions of scientific legitimation of the DOD mission, see Mukerji, *Fragile Power,* pp. 21, 62–84; and Gerjuoy and Baranger, "Physical Sciences and Mathematics," p. 71.

43. Gerjuoy and Baranger, "Physical Sciences and Mathematics," p. 68, table 1.

44. W. J. Price and L. W. Barr, "Scientific Research and the Innovative Process," *Science* 163 (16 May 1969): 802–6.

45. Spencer Klaw, "The Faustian Bargain," in Martin Brown, ed., *The Social Responsibility of the Scientist* (New York: Free Press, 1971), pp. 3–19 (p. 3). Robert Rosenzweig, president of the Association of American Universities, also used this term at the panel "Federal Funding and Academic Physical Sciences" (American Association for the Advancement of Science Annual Meeting, 17 January 1989, San Francisco, Calif.).

46. See, for example, Dickson, *New Politics of Science;* Daniel S. Greenberg, *The Politics of Pure Science* (New York: New American Library/Plume, 1971); Stanton A. Glantz and Norman V. Albers, "Department of Defense R&D in the University," *Science* 186 (22 November 1984): 706–71; Clark Thomborson (formerly Thompson), "Military Direction of Academic CS Research," *Communications of the ACM* 27, no. 7 (July 1986): 583–85.

47. Wilson, "Consequential Controversies," p. 54.

48. See John Holdren and F. Bailey Green, "Military Spending, the SDI, and Government Spending on Research and Development: Effects on the Economy and the Health of American Science," F.A.S. *Public Interest Report* 39, no. 7 *Journal of the Federation of American Scientists* (September 1986): 1–17; Nathan Rosenberg, *Inside the Black Box: Technology and Economics* (Cambridge: Cambridge Uni-

versity Press, 1982), p. 236; Joel S. Yudken and Michael Black, "Targeting National Needs: A New Direction For Science and Technology Policy," *World Policy Journal* 7, no. 2 (Spring 1990): 251–88.

49. National Science Board, *Science and Engineering Indicators—1989*, p. 10.

50. Yudken and Simons, *Field in Transition*.

51. Paul Forman, "Behind Quantum Electronics: National Security as a Basis for Physical Research in the United States, 1940–1960," *Historical Studies in the Physical and Biological Sciences* 18, no. 1 (1987): 149–229, cited in Wilson, "Consequential Controversies," p. 54.

52. Gerjory and Baranger, "Physical Sciences and Mathematics," p. 69.

53. Yudken and Simons, *Field in Transition*.

54. Statement from the floor at the panel "Federal Funding and Academic Physical Sciences" (1989 AAAS annual meeting).

55. For an elaboration of this notion, see Edward Hackett, "Funding and Academic Research in the Life Sciences: Results of an Exploratory Study," *Science and Technology Studies* 5, no. 34 (1987): 134–47.

56. See Glantz and Albers, "DOD R&D in the University."

57. Quoted in Dwight B. Davis, "Assessing the Strategic Computing Initiative," *High Technology* (April 1985): 41–49.

58. Abrams, "U.S. Military and Higher Education," p. 28.

59. NSF, *Federal Funds for Research and Development, Fiscal years 1988, 1989, and 1990*.

60. Data derived from National Science Board, *Science and Engineering Indicators—1989*, appendix table 6–2, p. 351.

61. Jacques S. Gansler, *Affording Defense* (Cambridge, Mass.: MIT Press, 1989), pp. 257–263; Rosy Nimroody, William Hartung, and Paul Grenier, *Star Wars Spin-offs: Blueprint for a High-Tech America?* (New York: Council on Economic Priorities, 1988), p. 57.

62. U.S. Congress, Office of Technology Assessment, *The Defense Technology Base: Introduction and Overview—A Special Report,* OTA-ISC-374 (Washington, D.C.: U.S. Government Printing Office, March 1988), pp. 17, 48.

63. Lewis M. Branscomb, "The Case for a Dual-Use National Technology Policy," *Aspen Institute Quarterly* 2, no. 3 (Summer 1990): 41.

64. Bill Thomas, "Military Spin-offs: Engines of Change," *Best of Business Report* 9, no. 1 (Spring 1987): 45.

65. Holley, *Ideas and Weapons,* pp. 175–76; Mary Kaldor, *The Baroque Arsenal* (New York: Hill and Wang, 1981), pp. 5, 20–22.

66. John E. Ullmann, "Economic Conversion: Indispensable for America's Economic Recovery" (briefing paper no. 3, National Commission for Economic Conversion and Disarmament, Washington, D.C., April 1989), p. 17. See also Seymour Melman, *Profits without Production* (New York: Knopf, 1983), and Lloyd J. Dumas, *The Overburdened Economy* (Berkeley and Los Angeles, Calif.: University of California Press, 1986). For a view countering the depletionists, see David Gold, *The Impact of Defense Spending on Investment, Productivity, and Economic Growth* (Washington, D.C.: Defense Budget Project, February 1990).

67. Judith Reppy, "Technology Flows between the Military and Civilian Sectors: Theory and Evidence" (paper prepared for the panel "Defense Spending as Technology Policy for the U.S.," AAAS, 1989 annual meeting). Her citation is taken from Ulrich Albrecht, "Spin-Off: A Fundamentalist Approach," in Philip Gummett and Judith Reppy, eds., *The Relations between Defense and Civil Technologies* (Dordrecht, Germ.: Kluwer, 1988), pp. 38–57.

68. Ann Markusen, "The Military Industrial Divide," *Society and Space* 10, no. 1 (forthcoming in 1992).

69. U.S. Congress, Office of Technology Assessment, *Commercializing High-Temperature Superconductivity,* OTA-ITE-388 (Washington, D.C.: U.S. Government Printing Office, June 1988), pp. 21, 39, 97–98.

70. Jay Stowsky, "Beating Plowshares into Double-Edged Swords: The Impact of Pentagon Policies on the Commercialization of Advanced Technologies" (Berkeley [Calif.] Roundtable on the International Economy, April 1986).

71. Leslie Bruechner and Michael Borrus, "Assessing the Commercial Impact of the VHSIC Program" (BRIE working paper, Berkeley [Calif.] Roundtable on the International Economy, December 1984), p. 5.

72. OTA, *Defense Technology Base,* p. 8. See also Branscomb, "Case for a Dual-Use National Technology Policy."

73. OTA, *Defense Technology Base,* p. 4; U.S. Congress, Office of Technology Assessment, *Holding the Edge: Maintaining the Defense Technology Base,* OTA-ISC-420 (Washington, D.C.: U.S. Government Printing Office, April 1989), pp. 33–37.

74. OTA, *Holding the Edge,* p. 28.

75. See Gansler, *Affording Defense,* pp. 215–38 and endnotes for evidence and discussion of these points.

76. Glenn R. Fong, "The Potential for Industrial Policy: Lessons from the Very High Speed Integrated Circuit Program," *Journal of Policy Analysis and Management* 5, no. 2 (1986): 264–91 (n. 13).

77. For discussions of this, see Bruechner and Borrus, "Assessing the Commercial Impact of the VHSIC Program"; Fong, "Potential for Industrial Policy."

78. DOD Office of the Comptroller, *DOD Budget for Fiscal Years 1992 and 1993,* (R-1).

79. Defense Advanced Research Projects Agency, *Strategic Computing: Fourth Annual Report* (Arlington, Va.: DARPA, November 1988). For discussion of DARPA's computer research programs, see also Kenneth Flamm, *Targeting the Computer: Government Support and International Competition* (Washington, D.C.: Brookings Institution, 1987), pp. 51–75; Terry Winograd, "Strategic Computing Research and the Universities," in Jonathon P. Jacky and Douglas Schuler, eds., *Directions and Implications of Advanced Computing,* vol. 1 (Norwood, N.J.: Ablex, 1989), pp. 18–32; Jonathon Jacky, "The Strategic Computing Program," in Chapman and Bellin, *Computers in Battle,* pp. 171–208; Mark Stefik, "Strategic Computing at DARPA: Overview and Assessment," *Communications of the ACM* 28, no. 7 (July 1985): 690–704; Yudken and Simons, *Field in Transition.*

80. Eliot Marshall. "Beating Swords into . . . Chips?" (box in "U.S. Technology Strategy Emerges"), *Science* 252 (5 April 1991): 22.

81. DOD Office of the Comptroller, *DOD Budget for Fiscal Years 1992 and 1993, (R-1)*.

82. David P. Hamilton, "Technology Policy: Congress Takes the Reins," *Science* 250 (9 November 1990): 747.

83. For a more extensive discussion of the rise of the high-tech industrial policy "movement" and the subsequent coalition between its adherents and military dual-use proponents, see Yudken and Black, "Targeting National Needs."

84. Gansler quoted in Daniel S. Greenberg, "Casting the Pentagon as Guide for U.S. Industry Begs for Calamity," *Los Angeles Times,* 10 January 1989.

85. "The Future of Silicon Valley: Does the U.S. Need a High-Tech Industrial Policy to Battle Japan, Inc.?" *Business Week,* 5 February 1990, pp. 54–60.

86. OTA, *Holding the Edge,* p. 47.

87. Marshall, "U.S. Technology Strategy Emerges."

88. Joseph Palca, "It Ain't Broke, but Why Not FCCSET?" *Science* 251 (15 February 1991): 736–37. See also "Science Initiatives in the 1992 Budget," *Science* 251 (25 January 1991): 376–77.

89. John Markoff, "Cuts Are Expected for U.S. Financing in High-Tech Area," *New York Times,* 16 November 1989.

90. Marshall, "Beating Swords into . . . Chips?"

91. Branscomb, "Case for a Dual-Use National Technology Policy," p. 38.

92. For an elaboration of these and many other points raised throughout this chapter, see Yudken and Black, "Targeting National Needs."

93. Branscomb, "Case for a Dual-Use National Technology Policy," p. 51.

94. Kenneth Flamm and Thomas L. McNaugher, "Rationalizing Technology Invest-ments," in John D. Steinbrunner, ed., *Restructuring American Foreign Policy* (Washington, D.C.: Brookings Institution, 1989), p. 135.

95. Branscomb, "Case for a Dual-Use National Technology Policy," p. 50.

96. For discussions of this development in the U.S. machine tool industry, see David Noble, *Forces of Production* (New York: Knopf, 1984); Melman, *Profits without Production;* Michael L. Dertouzos, Richard K. Lester, Robert M. Solow, and the MIT Commission on Industrial Competitiveness, *Made in America: Regaining the Productive Edge* (Cambridge, Mass.: MIT Press, 1989). For a different view of the causes of the machine tool industry's problem, see David Gold, *Impact of Defense Spending on Investment, Productivity, and Economic Growth,* espe-cially pp. 45–60.

Chapter 6: Weapons of Paper and Pen

1. Joseph Fulton, "Employment Impact of Changing Defense Programs," *Monthly Labor Review* (May 1964): 508.

2. David Henry and Richard Oliver, "The Defense Buildup, 1977–1985: Effects on Production and Employment," *Monthly Labor Review* (August 1987): 7. We be-lieve these to be low estimates; see Ann Markusen and Scott Campbell, "Defense Spending and the Occupational, Industrial, and Regional Distribution of Economic

Activity" (paper presented at the Regional Science Association meeting, 10 November 1990, Boston, Mass.).

3. Henry and Oliver, "Defense Buildup, pp. 7–8.

4. Ibid., p. 8; Charles Schultze, "The Economic Effects of the Defense Budget," *Brookings Bulletin* 18, no. 2 (1981): 4.

5. Henry and Oliver, "Defense Buildup," p. 8.

6. Ibid, p. 9.

7. For a rich depiction of the nature and frequency of interactions among working engineers, see Robert Zussman, *Mechanics of the Middle Class* (Berkeley and Los Angeles: University of California Press, 1985), pp. 33–58. On teamwork, see Pravin Varaiya, "Productivity in Manufacturing and the Division of Mental Labor," in Ake Andersen, David Batten, and Charlie Karlson, eds., *Knowledge and Industrial Organization* (Berlin: Springer-Verlag, 1990).

8. Murray Weidenbaum, "The Impact of Military Procurement on American Industry," in J. A. Stockfisch, ed., *Planning and Forecasting in the Defense Industries* (Belmont, Calif.: Wadsworth, 1962), pp. 135–74; William Baldwin, *The Structure of the Defense Market, 1955–1964* (Durham, N.C.: Duke University Press, 1967), pp. 84–85.

9. William Cunningham, *The Aircraft Industry: A Study in Industrial Location* (Los Angeles: Morrison, 1951), p. 21.

10. Ernest Havemann and Patricia Salter West, *They Went to College* (New York: Harcourt, Brace and Co., 1952), p. 149.

11. Ibid., pp. 234–35, chart 2, and p. 233.

12. Merton J. Peck and Frederick W. Scherer, *The Weapons Acquisition Process* (Boston: Harvard University, Graduate School of Business Administration, 1962), p. 94.

13. Herman O. Stekler, *The Structure and Performance of the Aerospace Industry* (Berkeley and Los Angeles: University of California Press, 1965), pp. 96–97 (n. 2), 100.

14. House Committee on Armed Services, special subcommittee no. 6, *Hearings on Investigation of the National Defense Establishment, Study of Procurement and Utilizations of Scientists, Engineers, and Technical Skills*, 85th Cong., 2d sess., 1958, H. Rept., p. 150; Peck and Scherer, *Weapons Acquisition Process*, pp. 85–87.

15. See Max Rutzick, "Skills and Location of Defense-Related Workers," *Monthly Labor Review* (February 1970): 11–16; Richard Dempsey and Douglas Schmude, "Occupational Impact of Defense Expenditure," *Monthly Labor Review* (December 1971): 12–15; Richard Oliver, "Employment Effects of Reduced Defense Spending," *Monthly Labor Review* (December 1971): 3–11; and the synthesis of these findings in Faye Duchin, "Economic Consequences of Military Spending," *Journal of Economic Issues* 17, no. 2 (1983): 546–47, and Robert DeGrasse, Jr., *Military Expansion, Economic Decline: The Impact of Military Spending on U.S. Economic Performance* (Armonk, N.Y.: M. E. Sharpe, 1983), pp. 14–15.

16. Dale Seastrom of Ford Aerospace, quoted in Phil Witherow, "Spring Team at Core of SDI," *Colorado Springs Gazette Telegraph*, 26 December 1987, p. A5.

17. Daniel Bell, *The Coming of Post-Industrial Society* (New York: Basic Books, 1973), pp. 127, 358, and ch. 3.

18. National Science Foundation, *Science and Engineering Personnel: A National Overview,* Special Report, NSF 90-310 (Washington, D.C.: National Science Foundation, 1990), p. 6.

19. "Lockheed to Hire 2,600 in 1984," *Oakland Tribune,* 31 January 1984, p. 1.

20. Henry and Oliver, "Defense Buildup," p. 10.

21. Jacques Gansler, *The Defense Industry* (Cambridge, Mass.: MIT Press, 1980), p. 192; and our interviews with Hughes and Avco employees.

22. Department of Labor, Bureau of Labor Statistics, unpublished data supplied to us by Richard Oliver and compiled by Ann Markusen; Congressional Budget Office, *Defense Spending and the Economy* (Washington, D.C.: U.S. Government Printing Office, 1983), table A-11, appendix A.

23. See the fuller discussion of this problem in Markusen and Campbell, "Defense Spending and the Occupational, Industrial, and Regional Distribution of Economic Activity."

24. For a fuller discussion of these discrepancies, and of potential sources of error in both data bases, see Markusen and Campbell, "Defense Spending and the Occupational, Industrial, and Regional Distribution of Economic Activity." See also Lloyd Dumas, *The Overburdened Economy* (Berkeley and Los Angeles: University of California Press, 1986), pp. 209–11, and DeGrasse, *Military Expansion, Economic Decline,* p. 80. For similar work on the impact of defense spending on British labor markets, see John Lovering, "The Impact of Defence Spending on the Market for Scientific and Technical Labor" (draft proposal, School for Advanced Studies, University of Bristol, 1987).

25. See Seymour Melman, *Our Depleted Society,* excerpt reprinted in James Clayton, ed., *The Economic Impact of the Cold War* (New York: Harcourt, Brace and World, 1970), pp. 82–92.

26. Interview, 7 October 1987.

27. Interview, 2 October 1987.

28. Interview, 7 October 1987.

29. George Melton, "Lockheed's Exciting Life on the Technological Frontier," *Wall Street Journal,* 16 May 1989, p. A15.

30. Melissa Everett, *Breaking Ranks* (Philadelphia: New Society, 1989), p. 5.

31. William Broad, *Star Warriors: A Penetrating Look into the Lives of the Young Scientists Behind our Space Age Weaponry* (New York: Simon and Schuster, 1985), pp. 212–17.

32. Quoted in ibid., p. 47.

33. Carol Cohn, "Nuclear Language, and How We Learned to Pat the Bomb," *Bulletin of Atomic Scientists* (June 1987): 17–24, and "Sex and Death in the Rational World of Defense Intellectuals," *Signs: Journal of Women in Culture and Society* 12, no. 4 (1987): 687–718.

34. Broad, *Star Warriors,* p. 51.

35. Everett, *Breaking Ranks,* pp. 107–8, 118, 120.

36. Ibid., p. 122.

37. Quoted in Ernest Braun and Stuart MacDonald, *Revolution in Miniature: The History and Impact of Semiconductor Electronics,* 2d ed. (Cambridge: Cambridge University Press, 1982), p. 143.

38. Zussman, *Mechanics of the Middle Class,* pp. 62–68.

39. National Research Council, Office of Scientific and Engineering Personnel, Panel on Engineering Labor Markets, *The Impact of Defense Spending on Nondefense Engineering Labor Markets* (Washington, D.C.: National Academy Press, 1986), pp. 81–82; Linda Levine, "Defense Spending Cuts and Employment Adjustments," Congressional Research Service report for Congress no. 90–55E (Washington, D.C.: Library of Congress, 27 June 1990), p. 9.

40. Joshua Lerner, "The Mobility of Corporate Scientists and Engineers between Civilian and Defense Activities: Evidence from the SSE Database" (discussion paper no. 90–02, Science, Technology, and Public Policy Program, John F. Kennedy School of Governemnt, Harvard University, August 1990), p. 22.

41. Quoted in Marion Anderson, *Converting the Work Force: Where the Jobs Would Be* (Lansing, Mich.: Employment Research Associates, 1983) p. 6.

42. Michael Closson, "Forging an Alternative Path," *Plowshares Press* 13, no. 3 (1988): 3–7.

43. Levine, "Defense Spending Cuts and Employment Adjustments," p. 9.

44. Several analysts have noted that there are really two separate labor markets for defense engineers—one for new graduates and one for experienced workers. See Trevor Bain, "Labor Market Experience for Engineers during Periods of Changing Demand" (final report) (Washington, D.C.: Office of Research and Development, Manpower Administration, Department of Labor, 1973); and Rutzick, "Skills and Location of Defense-Related Workers," p. 11.

45. R. P. Loomba, "A Study of the Re-employment and Unemployment Experiences of Scientists and Engineers Laid off from Sixty-two Aerospace and Electronics Firms in the San Francisco Bay Area during 1963–1965" (Manpower Research Group, Center for Interdisciplinary Studies, San Jose State College, 1967).

46. Bain, "Labor Market Experience for Engineers during Periods of Changing Demand," p. 1.

47. Lerner, "Mobility of Corporate Scientists and Engineers between Civilian and Defense Activities," p. 13.

48. Gordon Adams, *The Iron Triangle: The Politics of Defense Contracting* (New York: Council on Economic Priorities, 1981), p. 13.

49. For discussions of professional structures and behavior in the military, see Morris Janowitz, *The Professional Soldier: A Social and Political Portrait* (New York: Free Press, 1960); and Samuel Huntington, *The Soldier and the State: The Theory and Politics of Civil-Military Relations* (Cambridge: Mass.: Belknap Press of Harvard University Press, 1957).

50. Cited in United Auto Workers, *U.S. Aerospace Industry Review* (Detroit, Mich.: UAW Research Department, April 1988), p. 7.

51. Ann Markusen, Peter Hall, Sabina Deitrick, and Scott Campbell, *The Rise of the Gunbelt* (New York: Oxford University Press, 1991), ch. 4.

52. Howard Mingos, "The Rise of the Aircraft Industry," in G. R. Simonson, ed., *The*

History of the American Aircraft Industry: An Anthology (Cambridge, Mass.: MIT Press, 1968), p. 37.

53. Scott Campbell, "From Dust Bowl to Defense Buildup: Labor Migration and Regional Development During the Second World War," *Annals of Regional Science* (forthcoming in 1992).

54. UAW, *U.S. Aerospace Industry Review*, p. 8.

55. International Metalworkers Federation, *IMF Guide to World Aerospace Companies and Unions* (Geneva: IMF, 1987), p. 121.

56. Marion Anderson, *The Impact of Military Spending on the Machinists Union* (Lansing, Mich.: Employment Research Associates, 1979), pp. 1–2.

57. Tom Schlesinger, "Labor, Automation, and Regional Development," in John Tirman, ed., *The Militarization of High Technology* (Cambridge, Mass.: Ballinger, 1984), p. 187.

58. Barry Bluestone, Peter Jordan, and Mark Sullivan, *Aircraft Industry Dynamics: An Analysis of Competition, Capital, and Labor* (Boston: Auburn House, 1981), p. 135.

59. Judith Reppy, "The United States," in Nicole Bell and Milton Leitenberg, eds., *The Structure of the Defense Industry: An International Survey* (New York: St. Martin's Press, 1983), pp. 21–49, and Gansler, *Defense Industry*, p. 174.

60. David Noble, *The Forces of Production* (New York: Knopf, 1984); Bluestone, Jordan, and Sullivan, *Aircraft Industry Dynamics*, pp. 116–19, 137; Schlesinger, "Labor, Automation, and Regional Development," pp. 183–85.

61. Barton Crockett, "MAP Pilot Pays off for Lockheed," *Network World* 5 (30 May 1988): 1, 8.

62. Levine, "Defense Spending Cuts and Employment Adjustments," p. 6, based on Bureau of Labor Statistics, employment and earnings data, March 1989.

63. Thomas Karier, "A Note on Wage Rates in Defense Industries," *Industrial Relations* (Spring 1987): 198. The UAW had approximately 84,000 workers represented in the aerospace industry as of 1988. UAW, *U.S. Aerospace Industry Review*, p. 10.

64. Fox Butterfield, "Trouble at Atomic Bomb Plants: How Lawmakers Missed the Signs," *New York Times*, 30 November 1988, pp. 1, 12.

65. Howard Kurtz and Michael Isikoff, "General Dynamics under Fire," *Washington Post*, 12 February 1984, pp. 1, 12; United Auto Workers, "General Dynamics: Danger in the Workplace," *News from the UAW* (1984): 5–6. See also Owen Bieber, president of the UAW, "Statement on General Dynamics Corporation" (testimony before the House Committee on Education and Labor, Labor-Management Relations and Health and Safety subcommittees, 20 June 1984).

66. Bluestone, Jordan, and Sullivan, *Aircraft Industry Dynamics*, pp. 107, 153.

67. Verne Orr, memo to Russell Hale, Assistant Secretary of the Air Force for Financial Management, 15 April 1982, cited in Herbert Coleman, "USAF Seeks Industry Wage Limits," *Aviation Week & Space Technology*, 16 May 1983, pp. 16–17.

68. Quoted in Clark Mollenhoff, "Labor Pact Blackmail Is out: Weinberger," *Washington Times*, 20 August 1982, p. 1.

69. Bureau of National Affairs, "Air Force Trying to Impose Wage Cap, Aerospace

Unions Maintain," *Current Developments,* 1 August 1983, p. A-2; Dave Elsila, "The Pentagon's War on Workers," *Solidarity* (August 1983): 11–13.

70. John Cushman, Jr., "U.S. Says Lockheed Overcharged by Hundreds of Millions on Plane," *New York Times,* 29 August 1986, pp. 1, 26.

71. UAW, *U.S. Aerospace Industry Review,* p. 11.

72. Bluestone, Jordan, and Sullivan, *Aircraft Industry Dynamics,* pp. 140–141.

73. "Who Pays for Peace?" *Business Week,* 2 July 1990, p. 64.

74. Quoted in Dave Elsila, "War, Peace, and Jobs," *Solidarity* (November 1989): 9.

75. Ibid., p. 11.

76. Patience Stoddard, "Plowshares into Swords: Thoughts on the Balance between Prophetic and Pastoral Ministry and the Dilemma of the Defense Worker" (Ph.D. dissertation, Harvard Divinity School, 1986), cited in Everett, *Breaking Ranks,* p. 154.

77. Everett, *Breaking Ranks,* pp. 145–57.

78. Tony Mazzocchi, speech before the Other Economic Summit, 7 July 1990, Houston, Texas.

79. Marion Anderson, "Military Spending Creates Few Jobs for Women," *Plowshare* 10, no. 3 (1985): 10.

80. Ann Markusen, Garrett Clark, Charmaine Curtis, Sabina Deitrick, Gary Fields, Anne Henny, Eric Ingersoll, Jeff Levin, Wendy Patton, Jean Ross, and Judy Schneider, "Military Spending and Urban Development in California," *Berkeley Planning Journal* 1, no. 2 (1985): 62; Katherine DeFoyd, "Rosie the Riveter Revisited," *Plowshare* 10, no. 3 (1985): 1.

81. Karier, "Note on Wage Rates in Defense Industries," p. 198.

82. Lerner, "Mobility of Corporate Scientists and Engineers between Civilian and Defense Activities," p. 22.

83. Betty Vetter and Eleanor Babco, *Professional Women and Minorities,* 5th ed. (Washington, D.C.: Scientific Manpower Commission, August 1984), p. 37; National Science Foundation, *Science and Engineering Overview,* NSF 85–302 (Washington, D.C.: National Science Foundation, 1984), pp. 53–54; Shirley Malcolm, *Women in Science and Engineering: An Overview* (prepared for the National Academy of Sciences) (Washington, D.C.: American Association for the Advancement of Science, September 1983), pp. 27, 37; Lilli Hornig, "Women in Science and Engineering: Why So Few?" *Technology Review* (November-December 1984): 40. See the summary of this work and others in U.S. Congress, Office of Technology Assessment, *Demographic Trends and the Scientific and Engineering Work Force* (Washington, D.C.: U.S. Government Printing Office, December 1985), pp. 114–21.

84. Markusen et al., "Military Spending and Urban Development in California," p. 62.

85. See the discussion in Bluestone, Jordan, and Sullivan, *Aircraft Industry Dynamics,* pp. 125–126.

86. "Coalition Targets Military Contractors," *Minority Trendsletter* (August 1988): 10.

87. Congressional Budget Office, *Social Representation in the U.S. Military* (Wash-

ington, D.C.: U.S. Government Printing Office, October 1989); Bennett Harrison and Lucy Gorham, "What Happened to Black Wages in the 1980s?" (working paper no. 90–1, School of Urban and Public Affairs, Carnegie Mellon University, June 1990).

88. Department of Defense, Office of the Comptroller, *National Defense Budget Estimates for Fiscal Year 1988–1989* (April 1988), cited in Jonathan Feldman, Robert Krinsky, and Seymour Melman, *Criteria for Economic Conversion Legislation* (Washington, D.C.: National Commission for Economic Conversion and Disarmament, December 1988), p. 2.

89. Seymour Melman and Christina Files, "Are the Defense Cuts Real?" (mimeo, National Commission for Economic Conversion and Disarmament, Washington, D.C., 23 November 1989).

90. Gordon Adams, *Potential Impact of Defense Spending Reductions on the United States Economy and State Employment* (Washington, D.C.: Defense Budget Project, 2 May 1990), p. 7; Linda Kravitz, "The Wages of Peace" (review draft, summary and findings) (Washington, D.C.: Office of Technology Assessment, August 1990), p. 10.

91. Murray Weidenbaum, "Measures of the Impact of Defense and Space Programs" (paper presented at the annual meeting of the American Statistical Association, September 1975), pp. 8–9.

92. Carl Rittenhouse, *The Transferability and Retraining of Defense Engineers,* (Menlo Park, Calif.: Stanford Research Institute, November 1967), p. 41; cited in Robert DeGrasse, Alan Bernstein, David McFadden, Randy Schutt, Natalie Shiras, and Emerson Street, "Creating Solar Jobs, Options for Military Workers" (report of the Mid-Peninsula Conversion Project [now Center for Economic Conversion], November 1978), p. 30.

93. Lerner, "Mobility of Corporate Scientists and Engineers between Civilian and Defense Activities," pp. 22, 27.

94. Quoted in Rick Wartzman, "Defense Contractors Gird for Warming of the Cold War," *Wall Street Journal,* 11 November 1989, p. A8.

95. "Who Pays for Peace?" *Business Week,* 2 July 1990, p. 67.

96. Stephen Engelberg, "Pentagon Imposes a Hiring Freeze That Could Eliminate 50,000 Jobs," *New York Times,* 13 January 1990, pp. 1, 11.

97. Gordon Adams, "Economic Adjustment to Lower Defense Spending" (testimony before Senate Armed Services Committee, 4 May 1990 (Washington, D.C.: Defense Budget Project, 1990), pp. 3, 13.

98. Anderson, *Converting the Work Force,* p. 3.

99. Congressional Budget Office, "Defense Spending and the Economy" (Washington, D.C.: U.S. Government Printing Office, 1983).

100. Walter Reuther, "Are War Plants Expendable? A Program for the Conversion of Government-Owned War Plants to the Mass Production of Modern Railroad Equipment and Low-Cost Housing" (pamphlet by Willow Run Local 50, UAW-CIO, Ypsilanti, Michigan, 4 July 1945), p. 16.

101. Quoted in Michael Harris, "Lockheed Debriefing: Roy Anderson," *California Business* (April 1984): 110.

102. Michael Closson, "A Disarming Solution," *Multinational Monitor* (February 1988): 18.
103. Speech given by Odessa Komer, Meeting of the International Metalworkers Federation, Milan, Italy, November 1990: 7.

Chapter 7: Cold War Communities

1. See Ann Markusen, Peter Hall, Sabina Deitrick, and Scott Campbell, *The Rise of the Gunbelt* (New York: Oxford University Press, 1991), ch. 7, for an analysis of the growth and interrelationship between government and private sector—oriented military work in Colorado Springs.
2. John Rae, *Climb to Greatness: The American Aircraft Industry, 1920–1960* (Cambridge, Mass.: MIT Press, 1968), pp. 9–10.
3. William Cunningham, *The Aircraft Industry: A Study in Industrial Location* (Los Angeles: Morrison, 1951), pp. 58–65.
4. Markusen, et al., *Rise of the Gunbelt,* ch. 2.
5. Jay Stein, "U.S. Defense Spending: Implications for Economic Development Planning" (working paper, City Planning Program, Georgia Institute of Technology, 1985), table 3.
6. Markusen, et al, *Rise of the Gunbelt,* p. 15 and Appendix, figure A.10.
7. Ibid., p. 15.
8. Jonathan Hicks, "The Long Shipyard Slump," *New York Times,* 15 November 1985, p. D1.
9. Charles Bright, *The Jet Makers: The Aerospace Industry from 1945 to 1972* (Lawrence: Regents Press of Kansas, 1978), p. 140.
10. For a fuller analysis of regional distributions, see Markusen, et al., *Rise of the Gunbelt,* ch. 2.
11. Ann Markusen, "The Military Industrial Divide," *Society and Space* 10, no. 1 (forthcoming in 1992).
12. Bureau of Labor Statistics data, as compiled in Philip Shapira, "Industry and Jobs in Transition: A Study of Industrial Restructuring and Worker Displacement in California" (Ph.D. dissertation, University of California at Berkeley, 1986, and updated).
13. Stephen Mehay and Loren Solnick, "Defense Spending and State Economic Growth," *Journal of Regional Science* 30, no. 4 (1990): 477–87. Their work updates the classic in the field, Roger Bolton, *Defense Purchases and Regional Growth* (Washington, D.C.: Brookings Institution, 1966). Other work suggests that the frequent fluctuations in defense spending diminish a region's growth potential; see William Weida and Frank Gertcher, *The Political Economy of National Defense* (Boulder, Colo.: Westview, 1987).
14. Markusen, et al., *Rise of the Gunbelt.*
15. Classic location theory is articulated in Walter Isard, *Location and Space Economy* (New York: John Wiley and Sons, 1956).
16. Extended analysis of the military-industrial locational question can be found in Ann Markusen, "Government as Market: Industrial Location in the U.S. Defense Industry," in Henry Herzog and Alan Schlottmann, eds., *Industry Location and*

Public Policy (Knoxville: University of Tennessee Press, 1991), pp. 137–68; and Ann Markusen, "Defense Spending and the Geography of High Tech Industries," in John Rees, ed., *Technology Regions and Policy* (New York: Praeger, 1986), pp. 94–119.

17. Geoffrey Rossano, "Suburbia Armed: Nassau County Development and the Rise of the Aerospace Industry, 1909–1960," in Roger Lotchin, ed., *The Martial Metropolis: U.S. Cities in War and Peace* (New York: Praeger, 1984), pp. 67–72.

18. David Johnson, "The Failed Experiment: Military Aviation and Urban Development in San Antonio, 1910–1940," in Lotchin, *Martial Metropolis,* p. 94.

19. See the case study of Harris Corporation in Amy Glasmeier, *The Structure, Location, and Role of High Technology Industries in United States Regional Development* (Ph.D. dissertation, University of California at Berkeley, 1986), ch. 8.

20. Edward Malecki, "Government-Funded R&D: Some Regional Economic Implications," *Professional Geographer* 33, no. 1 (1981): 72–82.

21. Scott Campbell, "From Dust Bowl to Defense Buildup: Labor Migration and Regional Development During the Second World War," *Annals of Regional Science* (forthcoming in 1992).

22. Ibid.

23. Ibid.

24. Ernest Schwiebert, *A History of the U.S. Air Force Ballistic Missiles* (New York: Praeger, 1965), pp. 58, 92, 117; Herbert York, *Race to Oblivion: A Participant's View of the Arms Race* (New York: Simon and Schuster, 1970), p. 93; Michael Armacost, *The Politics of Weapons Innovation: The Thor-Jupiter Controversy* (New York: Columbia University Press, 1969), p. 245.

25. Walter Dornberger, "The German V-2," in Eugene Emme, ed., *The History of Rocket Technology: Essays on Research, Development, and Utility* (Detroit: Wayne State University Press, 1964), pp. 29–37; Armacost, *Politics of Weapons Innovation,* pp. 159–60, 223.

26. Armacost, *Politics of Weapons Innovation,* p. 155.

27. Adam Yarmolinsky, *The Military Establishment: Its Impacts on American Society* (New York: Harper and Row, 1971), pp. 56–57.

28. John Mollenkopf, *The Contested City* (Princeton: Princeton University Press, 1983).

29. See Ann Markusen, *The Economics and Politics of Regions* (Totowa, N.J.: Rowman and Littlefield, 1987), pp. 117–20, for a summary of the studies on New England in the 1950s.

30. See Ann Markusen, *Profit Cycles, Oligopoly and Regional Development* (Cambridge, Mass.: MIT Press, 1985), ch. 3, 4, for an analysis of the impact of oligopoly on location.

31. Richard A. Barff and Prentice L. Knight III, "The Role of Federal Military Spending in the Timing of the New England Employment Turnaround," *Papers of the Regional Science Association* 65, no. 2 (1988): 151–66. For a discussion of New England's defense industries, see Bennett Harrison and Jean Kluver, "Re-assessing the 'Massachusetts Miracle': The Sources and Patterns of Employment and

Economic Growth in the Revitalization of a 'Mature' Region," in Lloyd Rodwin and Hidehiko Sazanami, eds., *Deindustrialization in the United States: Lessons for Japan* (Boston: Unwin Hyman, 1989), pp. 104–131.

32. See the summary of this literature in Barry Rundquist, "Politics' Benefits and Public Policy: Interpretation of Recent U.S. Studies," *Environment and Planning C: Government and Policy* 1, no. 3 (1983): 401–12.

33. Interview, December 1986.

34. Gordon Adams, *The Iron Triangle: The Politics of Defense Contracting* (New York: Council on Economic Priorities), pp. 185–95.

35. Roger Lotchin, "The City and the Sword in Metropolitan California, 1919–1941," *Urbanism Past and Present* 14 (Summer-Fall 1982): 1–16.

36. Markusen, *Economics and Politics of Regions,* p. 136.

37. See Norman Glickman and Amy Glasmeier, "The International Economy and the American South," in Rodwin and Sazanami, *Deindustrialization in the U.S.,* pp. 60–80, for an exposition of how unevenly Sunbelt growth has visited the South. Harrison and Kluver, "Re-assessing the 'Massachusetts Miracle'," shows that the Boston area accounts for almost all of Massachusetts's income gains in the last decade.

38. See, for instance, AnnaLee Saxenian, "The Genesis of Silicon Valley," in Peter Hall and Ann Markusen, eds., *Silicon Landscapes* (Boston: Allen and Unwin, 1985), pp. 20–34; Allen Scott, "High Technology Industry and Territorial Development: The Rise of the Orange County Complex, 1955–1984," *Urban Geography* 7, no. 1 (1986): 3–45; and David R. Lampe, ed., *The Massachusetts Miracle: High Technology and Economic Revitalization* (Cambridge, Mass.: MIT Press, 1988).

39. Ann Markusen and Virginia Carlson, "Deindustrialization in the American Midwest: Causes and Responses," in Rodwin and Sazanami, *Deindustrialization in the U.S.,* table 1.

40. See Ann Markusen, "Federal Budget Simplification: Preventive Programs Versus Palliatives for Local Governments with Booming, Stable, and Declining Economies," *National Tax Journal* 30, no. 3 (1977): 249–57, for a fuller exposition of this argument.

41. Kitty Gillman, "Technology and Economic Conversion" (draft outline) (Washington, D.C.: Office of Technology Assessment, August 1990) p. 3.

42. Charles Tiebout, "The Regional Impact of Defense Expenditure: Its Measurement and Problems of Adjustment," in Roger Bolton, ed., *Defense and Disarmament* (Englewood Cliffs, N.J.: Prentice-Hall, 1966), pp. 125–39.

43. See Markusen et al., *Rise of the Gunbelt,* ch. 7, for a fuller analysis of the relationship between military spending and the Seattle economy.

44. Brad Williams, "Quarterly General Fund Forecast," (Sacramento, Calif.: Commission on State Finance, March 1990), p. 3.

45. Michael Klare, "Behind Desert Storm: The New Military Paradigm," *Technology Review* 94, no. 4 (May-June 1991): 28–39.

46. Barton Gellman, "A Coming Revolution in Fighter Aircraft," *Washington Post,* 29 April–5 May 1991, national weekly edition, p. 10.

47. Clyde H. Farnsworth, "White House Seeks to Revive Credits for Arms Exports," *New York Times,* 18 March 1991, p. A1.
48. Steven Pearlstein, "Other Bidders Settle for Smaller Bites of the Aerospace Pie," *Washington Post,* 29 April–5 May 1991, national weekly edition, p. 11.
49. Gwen Ifill, "Powell Urges U.S. To Be 'Vicious' in Closing Wasteful Military Bases," *New York Times,* 27 April 1991, p. 1.
50. Quoted in Eric Schine, "Defenseless against Cutbacks," *Business Week,* 14 January 1991, p. 69.
51. Ifill, "Powell Urges U.S. To Be 'Vicious' in Closing Wasteful Military Bases."
52. Catherine Hill, "State and Local Legislation on Conversion of a Military to a Civilian Economy" (PRIE working paper no. 21, Center for Urban Policy Research, Rutgers University, November 1990).

Chapter 8: Scaling the Wall of Separation

1. Jacques Gansler, *The Defense Industry* (Cambridge, Mass.: MIT Press, 1980), pp. 48–50.
2. John Stodden, "Earnings Outlook Prompts Wall Street to Discount Aerospace/ Defense Stocks," *Aviation Week & Space Technology,* 30 May 1988, pp. 40–45; Rick Wartzman, "Defense Contractors Gird for Warming of the Cold War," *Wall Street Journal,* 11 November 1989, p. A8.
3. Michael Klare, "Behind Desert Storm: The New Military Paradigm," *Technology Review* 94, no. 4 (May-June 1991): 28–39.
4. Robert Hershey, Jr., "Marietta Optimistic as Boom Ends," *New York Times,* 28 November 1988, pp. B1, 24.
5. Quoted in Leslie Wayne, "Arms Makers Gird for Peace," *New York Times,* 17 December 1989, p. F8; see also Thomas Hayes, "FSX: Icing on the Cake for General Dynamics," *New York Times,* 2 May 1989, pp. 1, 34.
6. Gansler, *Defense Industry,* pp. 26, 171; Wartzman, "Defense Contractors Gird for Warming of the Cold War."
7. Charles Lane, et al., "Arms for Sale," *Newsweek,* 18 April 1991, pp. 22–27.
8. Stodden, "Earnings Outlook Prompts Wall Street to Discount Aerospace/Defense Stocks."
9. Eric Schine, "GM and Hughes: Is the Marriage Fizzling?" *Business Week,* 12 February 1990, pp. 54–55.
10. Quoted in ibid.
11. Eric Weiner, "Grumman Girds for Arms Cuts," *New York Times,* 12 December 1989, pp. D1, 8; Wartzman, "Defense Contractors Gird for Warming of the Cold War."
12. Joel Yudken, "Obstacles to Conversion," *Plowshare Press* 10, no. 1 (Winter 1984): 405; Robert DeGrasse, Jr., "Corporate Diversification and Conversion Experience," in John Lynch, ed., *Economic Adjustment and Conversion of Defense Industries* (Boulder, Colo.: Westview, 1987), pp. 95–97.
13. Murray Weidenbaum, "The Transferability of Defense Industry Resources to Civilian Uses," in James Clayton, ed., *The Economic Impact of the Cold War* (New York: Harcourt, Brace & World, 1970), p. 100.

14. DeGrasse, "Corporate Diversification and Conversion Experience," p. 111.
15. Cited in ibid., p. 92. See also John Gilmore and Dean Coddington, "Diversification Guides for Defense Firms," *Harvard Business Review* (May-June 1966): 146, for a review of Vietnam War–era efforts.
16. Weiner, "Grumman Girds for Arms Cuts."
17. John Rae, *Climb to Greatness: The American Aircraft Industry, 1920–1960* (Cambridge, Mass.: MIT Press, 1968), pp. 6, 12; Ronald Fernandez, *Excess Profits: The Rise of United Technologies* (Reading, Mass.: Addison-Wesley, 1983), p. 165; and J. L. Atwood, *North American Rockwell: Storehouse of High Technology* (New York: Newcomen Society, 1970), p. 15.
18. Quoted in Wartzman, "Defense Contractors Gird for Warming of the Cold War."
19. Quoted in William Baldwin, *The Structure of the Defense Market, 1955–1964* (Durham, N.C.: Duke University Press, 1967), p. 12.
20. M. Louise McNeilly, "Braving the New World," *Plowshare Press* 15, no. 1 (Winter 1990): 1, 6.
21. Quoted in Bruce Nissen, "Corporate Divestiture of a Calumet Region Foundry," in Charles Craypo and Bruce Nissen, eds., *Grand Designs: The Impact of Corporate Strategies on Workers, Unions, and Communities"* (forthcoming in 1992), ch. 3.
22. Robert Ady, "Normal Industrial Plant Redevelopment Process," in Lynch, *Economic Adjustment and Conversion of Defense Industries,* p. 138.
23. George Tibbits, "Boeing Defense Work Melts in 'Thaw'," *Chicago Tribune,* 2 January 1990, p. 15.
24. DeGrasse, "Corporate Diversification and Conversion Experience," pp. 97, 105, 108.
25. McNeilly, "Braving the New World."
26. Quoted in Michael Clossón, "A Disarming Solution," *Multinational Monitor* (February 1988): 18.
27. Walter Reuther, "Are War Plants Expendable? A Program for the Conversion of Government-Owned War Plants to the Mass Production of Modern Railroad Equipment and Low-Cost Housing" (pamphlet by Willow Run Local 50, UAW-CIO [Ypsilanti, Mich.], 4 July 1945); Walter Reuther, "Our Fear of Abundance," *New York Times Magazine,* 16 September 1945, pp. 8, 32–33, 35; Walter Reuther, "Let's Use the War Plants," *Antioch Review* (Fall 1945): 351–59.
28. William Winpisinger, "Technological Tyranny—Economic Conversion," in Betty Lall, ed., *Economic Dislocation and Job Loss* (New York: Cornell University, Extension and Public Service Division, 1985), p. 28.
29. Louis Jacobsen, National Commission on Economic Conversion and Disarmament, unpublished interview with Dick Greenwood, former special assistant to the president, International Association of Machinists, Washington, D.C., August, 1990.
30. Marion Anderson, *Converting the Work Force: Where the Jobs Would Be* (Lansing, Mich.: Employment Research Associates, 1983). See also Marion Anderson, *The Impact of Military Spending on the Machinists' Union* (Lansing, Mich.: Employment Research Associates, 1979).

31. Gearold Dargitz, District Secretary-Treasurer of the IAM, Boeing Lodge 751, quoted in Anderson, *Converting the Work Force,* p. 9; Bill Baker, quoted in Anderson, *Converting the Work Force,* p. 9.

32. Winpisinger, "Technological Tyranny—Economic Conversion," pp. 28, 29.

33. Lance Compa, "Conversion and the Labor Movement," *Labor Research Review* no. 7 (Fall 1985): 47.

34. Carol Taylor West, "A Survey of U.S. Unemployment Policies" (unpublished working paper, Bureau of Economic and Business Research, University of Florida, May 1990); Jane Kulik and Charles Fairchild, "Worker Assistance and Placement Experience," in Lynch, *Economic Adjustment and Conversion of Defense Industries,* pp. 191, 216. See also the description of the worker adjustment programs employed after the B-1B bomber program ended in 1988, in Fred Trueblood, Phillip Wyman, Vern Lawson, Jr., and Pete Eskis, "Organizing Industry Manpower Programs: Lancaster and Palmdale, California," in John Lynch, ed., *Plant Closures and Community Recovery* (Washington, D.C.: National Council for Urban Economic Development, January 1990), pp. 33–35.

35. Kulik and Fairchild, "Worker Assistance and Placement Experience," p. 204.

36. Department of Defense, Office of the Assistant Secretary of Defense, *Summary of Completed Military Base Economic Adjustment Projects, 1961–1977* (Washington, D.C.: U.S. Government Printing Office, February 1977), p. 1, and DOD's updated version, *Twenty-five Years of Civilian Reuse, 1961–1986: Summary of Completed Military Base Economic Adjustment Projects* (Washington, D.C.: U.S. Government Printing Office, May 1986). See also Robert Rauner and John Lynch, "Defense Economic Adjustment Program," in Lynch, *Plant Closures and Community Recovery,* pp. 98–100.

37. Alan Gregerman and R. Leo Penne, "Community Economic Adjustment to Defense Industrial Cutbacks," in Lynch, *Economic Adjustment and Conversion of Defense Industries,* pp. 64–66. The authors offer case studies of three other local economic development responses to military plant closures: Huntsville, Alabama, Taunton, Massachusetts, and Hagerstown, Maryland.

38. Seymour Melman, an economist, longtime scholar of the military-industrial complex, staunch advocate of conversion, and early advocate of alternative use planning, has most recently published *The Demilitarized Society: Disarmament and Conversion* (Montreal: Harvest House, 1988), which contains a blueprint for facility-based conversion planning. See also Seymour Melman, "An Economic Alternative to the Arms Race: Conversion from Military to Civilian Economy," (mimeograph, 18 November 1986); and Jonathan Feldman, Robert Krinsky, and Seymour Melman, "Criteria for Economic Conversion Legislation" (briefing paper no. 4, National Commission for Economic Conversion and Disarmament, December 1988).

39. How to judge the success of conversion efforts has been much discussed in the literature. See, for instance, the differences between Suzanne Gordon and Dave McFadden, "Introduction," in Suzanne Gordon and Dave McFadden, eds., *Economic Conversion: Revitalizing America's Economy* (Cambridge, Mass.: Ballin-

ger, 1984), p. xv, and John E. Lynch, "Introduction," and "Adjustment and Conversion Policy Issues," in Lynch, *Economic Adjustment and Conversion of Defense Industries,* pp. 5, 29–50. Other views on facility conversion are offered by the contributors to Lloyd Dumas and Marek Thee, eds., *Making Peace Possible: The Promise of Economic Conversion* (Oxford: Pergamon Press, 1989), especially Lisa Peattie, "Economic Conversion as a Set of Organizing Ideas," pp. 23–36, and Michael Renner, "Conversion to a Peaceful Economy: Criteria, Objectives, and Constituencies," pp. 37–54.

40. In a separate research project, the authors investigated six cases of community-union–initiated efforts at private-sector facility conversion. To find them, all groups in the United States that have been active in or interested in conversion—from peace groups to groups in the plant-closing, and labor movements—were canvassed. The sites chosen were by and large the best-known conversion efforts and constitute a set of "best practice" cases. For more on the methodology, see Catherine Hill, Sabina Deitrick, and Ann Markusen, "Converting the Military Industrial Economy," *Journal of Planning Education and Research* (forthcoming in 1992).

41. Quoted in Elizabeth McGannon and Steve Meacham, "Conversion: New Hope for Shipbuilding?" (testimony before Massachusetts congressional delegation, 16 April 1983, Weymouth, Mass.).

42. Ibid.

43. See the article written by Gary Guines, Vice-President of General Dynamics and head of the Quincy Shipbuilding Division, "Staying on the Course for the Future of Shipbuilding," *Quincy Patriot Ledger,* 28 September 1983.

44. This section is based on interviews with Joel S. Yudken in Menlo Park, California, and Kate Squire in Berkeley, California, in 1990. See also Joel S. Yudken, "Conversion in the Aerospace Industry: The McDonnell-Douglas Project," in Gordon and McFadden, *Economic Conversion,* pp. 130–143.

45. This section draws from Calumet Project on Industrial Jobs, "Preventing Plant Closings in Northwest Indiana: A Public Policy Program for Action" (November 1989); David Moberg, "Hooked on Tanks," *Progressive* (September 1986): 30–32; and Nissen, "Corporate Divestiture of a Calumet Region Foundry."

46. Greg LeRoy and Lynn Feekin, "Converting Tanks in Indiana," *Labor Research Review* no. 7, (Fall 1985): 59–68.

47. Nissen, "Corporate Divestiture of a Calumet Region Foundry."

48. Calumet Project on Industrial Jobs, "Preventing Plant Closings in Northwest Indiana."

49. The Unisys case is described in Jamie Markham and Associates, with the Alternative Product Development Committee, St. Paul, Minnesota, *The Unisys Alternative Use Project,* parts 1 and 2 (September 1989), and Mel Duncan, "Local Planning in Minnesota," *Nuclear Times* (Summer 1990): 14.

50. University of Minnesota professor Wilbur Maki researched the extent of Minnesota defense-dependency and conducted an analysis of job creation under an alternative social spending scenario. See Wilbur Maki, David Bogenschultz,

Christine Evans, and Michael Senese, *Military Production and the Minnesota Economy: A Report for the Minnesota Task Force on Economic Conversion* (St. Paul: Department of Jobs and Training, May 1989).

51. See Catherine Hill, "State and Local Legislation on Conversion of a Military to a Civilian Economy," *PRIE Working Paper No. 21,* Center for Urban Policy Research, Rutgers University, November, 1990); and Roger Kerson and Greg LeRoy, *State and Local Initiatives on Development Subsidies and Plant Closings* (Chicago: Federation for Industrial Retention and Renewal, September 1989), p. 6.

52. James Lawson, "Civilian Market Opportunities for Defense Industry," in Lynch, *Economic Adjustment and Conversion of Defense Industries,* pp. 172–173. See also John Ullmann, "Can Business Become a Participant?" in Gordon and McFadden, *Economic Conversion,* pp. 164–74.

Chapter 9: Dismantling the Cold War Economy

1. Dick Cheney, "A New Defense Strategy for Changing Times," *Defense* (21 February 1991): 12–17; Defense Budget Project, *Responding to Changing Threats: A Report of the Defense Budget Project's Task Force on the FY 1992–FY 1997 Defense Plan* (Washington, D.C.: Defense Budget Project, 1991); William Kaufman, *Glasnost, Perestroika and U. S. Defense Spending* (Washington, D.C.: The Brookings Institution, 1990); Lawrence R. Klein, "The Peace Dividend: Will There Be One and How Large Could it Be?" paper presented at the Conference on Economic Issues of Disarmament, Notre Dame University, November 30, 1990; Office of Technology Assessment, *Adjusting to a New Security Environment: The Defense Technology and Industrial Base Challenge* (Washington, D.C.: U.S. Government Printing Office, 1991).

2. Henry F. Howe, Stephen P. Hubbell, and David E. Blockstein, "Rationale for the National Institutes for the Environment," *Environmental Professional* 12 (1990): 360–63; Henry F. Howe and Stephen P. Hubbell, "Report, Towards the National Institutes for the Environment," *Global Environmental Change* (December 1990): 71–74.

3. For a more complete discussion of what a national needs–driven R&D policy might entail, see Joel S. Yudken and Michael Black, "Targeting National Needs: A New Direction for Science and Technology Policy," *World Policy Journal* vol. 7, no. 2 (Spring 1990): 251–88.

4. Kaufman, *Glasnost, Perestroika and U.S. Defense Spending.*

5. Quoted in Daniel Charles, "Reformers Seek Broader Military Role in Economy," *Science* 241 (12 August 1988): 779–81.

6. For discussion of technological innovation, developmental paths, and demand, see John Zysman, "Power, Wealth, and Technology: Industrial Decline and American National Security" (BRIE working paper no. 38, Berkeley, Calif.: Roundtable on the International Economy, January 1990), p. 21; Nathan Rosenberg, *Inside the Black Box: Technology and Economics* (Cambridge: Cambridge University Press, 1982), pp. 55–80.

7. Bennett Harrison, "Polishing the Rustbelt," *Technology Review* 93, no. 7 (October 1990), p. 74.

8. Lenny Siegel, Ted Smith, and Rand Wilson, "Sematech, Toxics, and U.S. Industrial Policy: Why We Are Concerned" (position paper, Campaign for Responsible Technology. See also "From Day Care to DARPA," "Bargaining for a New Industrial Policy," a 12-page report on CRT's meeting with SEMATECH, 17 May 1991. (Both are available from Campaign for Responsible Technology, 408 Highland Ave., Somerville, MA 02144.)

Index

■

Abrams, Richard, 116
ACE complex. *See* Aerospace-communi-
  cations-electronics (ACE) complex
Adams, Gordon, 53, 55, 88, 156, 167
Adams, James, 88, 92, 94
Adams, Walter, 88, 92, 94
Advanced Manufacturing Technology
  Act, 127
Advanced Research Projects Agency. *See*
  Defense Advanced Research Projects
  Agency
AEC. *See* Atomic Energy Commission
Aerospace-communications-electronics
  (ACE) complex: cold war and, 5, 8–9,
  13, 43–44, 55–56, 86–87; commercial
  conversion in, 215; company bailouts
  in, 53–54; company closings in, 212–
  13; costs and, 94–97; development of,
  34–39, 43–47, 80–82; economic issues
  and, 5, 55–68, 83–93, 96–97, 134,
  139–40, 210, 212; governmental support of, 33–34, 52–53, 56–58, 85–86,
  88–90, 96–97; industrial policies and,
  54–55; locations of, 171–72, 178; military and, 18, 31–32, 43; performance
  of, 97–99; research and development
  by, 116–19; technology of, 47–51;
  wall of separation in, xv, 5, 11, 69, 80,
  90–93, 99–100, 116, 133, 157, 210,

216, 219, 243; war and, 88–89. *See
  also* Contractors, defense; Military-in-
  dustrial complex; *individual corporations by name*
Aerospace industry, 34, 39–47, 49, 52,
  66–68, 79, 81, 82, 85, 93, 136, 174,
  186, 189, 191, 200, 205, 211, 216, 226.
  *See also individual corporations by
  name*
Aerospace Industry Association, 55, 97
Affirmative action, 164
AFL-CIO. *See* American Federation of
  Labor and Congress of Industrial Orga-
  nizations
Agriculture, Department of, 102, 107
Airbus, 56, 66, 74
Aircraft, 15–19, 27–28, 44–47, 57, 66,
  78–79, 86, 89, 177, 213; Aquila battle-
  field plane, 73; A-10 trainer, 89; B-1
  bomber, 66, 89, 97, 194, 197, 217;
  B-1B bomber, 95; B-2 bomber, 85;
  B-52, 89; Boeing 707, 57, 70; Boeing
  747, 71; Boeing KC-135, 57; C-5, 89,
  119; C-5A, 71–73; C-5B transport, 72;
  C-17, 89, 118–19, 215, 231, 233, 254;
  E-3A AWACS, 78, 89; E-4 AWACS, 89;
  F-15, 17, 22, 217; F-16, 78, 79; F-18,
  78, 89, 217; F-22, 73, 206; F-111, 89;
  Ford Trimotor, 28, 44, 45; KC-10, 89;

Aircraft *(continued)*
  KC-135, 89; L-1011, 69, 72; L-1011 Tri-Star, 71; Liberator bombers, 28, 44; Maiden Detroit, 45; Model 10 Electra, 70; P-40, 13; space shuttle, 73; Stealth fighter/bomber, 30, 31, 72, 73, 85, 94–95; Supersonic transport (SST), 71, 89; World Cruiser, 174
Aircraft industry. *See* Aerospace industry
Air Defense Command, 85
Air force. *See* Military services, air force
Air Force Association, 55
Air Force Scientific Advisory Board, 113
Air Mail Act (1925), 41
Air Policy (Finletter) Commission, 81
Alabama, 187, 190–91, 196, 198
Albrecht, Ulrich, 120
Allied-Signal, 76–77, 79, 147
Alternative-use planning, 228–29, 230, 236–37, 238, 251, 253. *See also* Conversion, economic; Dual-use policies
Alternative Use Project, 235–36
Ambrose, James, 218
American Aviation Mission to Europe (1919), 40
American Defense Preparedness Association, 55
American Federation of Labor and Congress of Industrial Organizations (AFL-CIO), 221, 222
American Telephone and Telegraph (AT&T), 50–51
AMRAAM. *See* Missiles, Advanced Medium Range Air-to-Air
Anders, William, 90
Anderson, Marion, 168
Anderson, Roy, 71, 74, 168
Applied Physics Laboratory, 113, 177
Army Arsenal Act (1853), 268*n*51
Army Mathematics Research Center, 113
Army Research Office, 106
Army Science Board, 113
Aspin, Les, 204
AT&T. *See* American Telephone and Telegraph

Atomic bomb, 19, 25, 102
Atomic Energy Commission (AEC), 52, 106, 107
Atwood, Lee, 215
Augustine, Norman, 19–20
Automation, 159–60
Automobile industry, 40, 44–47, 60, 61–62, 174, 212, 221
Avco, 82, 140
Avtex, 122

Babcock and Wilcox, 162
Bailouts, company, 53–54, 64
Ball Aerospace, 187
B&P Program. *See* Defense, Department of, Bids and Proposals Program
Bath Iron Works, 204
Bell, Alexander, 103
Bell, Daniel, 138
Bell Labs, 48, 81, 87
Bell System, 137
Bendix, 48, 90
Bennett, Marcus, 211
BENS. *See* Business Executives for National Security
Bingaman, Jeff, 126, 127
Blackwell, James, 216
Blaw-Knox Foundry, 218–19, 233–35, 238
Boeing: commercial business of, 43, 56, 69–70, 97, 156, 213–15, 219–20; employment practices of, 156, 166, 205, 227; government advisory committees and, 53; industry position of, 82; military contracts of, 41–42, 55, 75, 76, 79, 80, 87, 89, 189, 206; research and development awards to, 117, 177; U.S. industrial policy and, 54
Boeing-Vertol, 214
Bombing, 16, 19, 104
Boston (Mass.), 172
Bowen Machine Products, 217
Bradford, Bill, 152–53

Bradley, Omar, 23
Brandow, Jon, 231
Branscomb, Lewis, 118, 127, 129
Braun, Ernest, 57–58
Breaking Ranks, 149
Bright, Charles, 46
British Aerospace, 56
Broad, Williams, 149
Bromley, Alan, 126
Brown, George, 126, 196
Buffenbarger, Robert, 208
Burroughs, 82, 235. *See also* Unisys Defense Computer Systems
Bush, George: defense industry and, 4, 206; dual-use industrial policies and, 125–26; loan guarantees, overseas, 67; MX missiles and, 12–13; "new world order" of, 14, 27; nuclear weapons and, 97
Bush, Vannevar, 104, 106
Business community, 259
Business Executives for National Security (BENS), 259
Bussolini, Jake, 220
Buy-outs, 212, 238–39

C³I (command, control, communications, and intelligence systems), 22, 46, 47, 205
California, 174, 176–77, 178, 179, 190, 198, 203, 205, 231–33
Calumet Project on Industrial Jobs, 234
Campaign for Responsible Technology (CRT), 259
Carter, Jimmy, 12, 106, 203, 249
Celeste, Richard, 208, 209
Center for Defense Information, 259
Center for Economic Conversion, 153, 169, 232, 259
Center for Strategic and International Studies, 87
Chance-Vought, 80, 81. *See also* LTV

Chandler, Harry, 174
Charles Draper Laboratory, 113
Chaudet, Steve, 74
Cheney, Richard, 98, 167
China, 211
Chrysler, 45–46, 64, 212
Clark, Karen, 236
Clayton, James, 54
Closson, Michael, 169
Coalition for Science and Technology in a New Era, 258
Cohn, Carol, 149
Cold war: aerospace-communications-electronics complex and, 5, 8–9, 13, 43–44, 55, 81–82, 86–87, 93, 104; deterrence and, 5, 43; employment during, 135–36, 137; end of, 7, 168–69, 240, 260; foreign military sales during, 79; military contracting during, 174–75, 176, 179–80, 185; origins of, 25–26; technologies, development of, during, 101; weaponry of, 23–31
Colleges. *See* Employment, college education and; Universities
Colorado, 170–71, 177, 187, 188, 190, 191–92, 198, 203
Commerce, Department of, 92–93
Commercial industries/technologies. *See* Private sector
Commission on Industrial Competitiveness (MIT), 130
Communications equipment industry, 49. *See also* Aerospace-communications-electronics complex
Communication Workers of America, 258
Communities, military-industrial: Colorado Springs, Colo., 170–71, 187, 188, 190, 191–92, 198, 203; conversion and, 226–40, 251; Huntsville, Ala., 187, 190–91, 196, 198; locations of, 171–72, 197–99; Los Angeles, Calif., 172, 173–74, 179, 186–87, 190, 198, 204; problems of, 200–202; 204–5, 206, 243, 248; San Diego, Calif., 198;

Communities *(continued)*
Southern, 198, 200. *See also* Gunbelt
Compa, Lance, 224
Competitiveness: aerospace, 67, 85; "Buy America" policies, 35–36, 183; costs and, 94; economic factors of, 84, 245–46, 251, 256–57; high-technology, 126; industrial, 125; international, 4, 9, 11, 34, 60, 124–25; manufacturing, 124; military, 13–14, 18, 31–32, 49, 84, 105, 172, 190–91, 263n32; secrecy and, 93; targeted industry policies and, 51, 53–54, 64; United States and, 125, 250
Computer Professionals for Social Responsibility (CPSR), 258
Computers. *See* Technologies, computer
Computer Science Corporation (CSC), 51
Congress: defense contractors and, 36, 92, 194–99, 209; defense spending and, 8, 85, 124, 194–99; dual-use industrial policies and, 126; geographical constituency building and, 196–97; Gunbelt and, 172–73, 195, 203–4; military affairs committees in, 197; military installations and, 194–95; pork-barreling by, 194–97. *See also* Government, federal
Connecticut, 204
Consolidated, 28, 80, 81
Contractors, defense: bidding by, 98–99; cold war and, 14–15, 24, 25, 86–87, 94; commercial conversion of, 40–42, 43, 69–74, 76, 82, 85, 90–93, 99–100, 118–19, 162, 209–10, 211–16, 217–19, 220, 221–40, 243–44; commercial projects of, 152; corruption and, 71–72, 78, 94, 95, 235; costs of, 94–97, 118, 161, 185, 202; employment by, 66, 138–39, 145–65; establishment/expansion of, 80, 86–87, 103, 104, 105–6, 121–22; government and, 84–86, 87–88, 91; layoffs by, 165–69, 217, 219–20, 222–23, 227; locations of, 174–99; military services and, 80–81; military/space dependency of, 76–78, 79, 80–82, 140–45; procurement and, 31, 80, 85–86, 88, 95–96, 99, 177, 178–79, 196; production by, 27–31, 35, 47, 186; profits of, 96–97, 118; ranking of, 74–76; research and development by, 25, 26, 35, 48–49, 50–51, 52–53, 86, 91, 116–19; sole-source, 85–86; strategies of, 210–13; subcontractors and, 79–80, 87, 90, 95, 216–19, 272n29; takeovers of, 89–90; universities as, 110–16. *See also* Aerospace-communications-electronics complex; Defense industry; Military-industrial complex; Research and development; *individual corporations by name*
Convair, 43, 190. *See also* General Dynamics
Conversion, economic, xvi, 6–11, 69–74, 76, 162, 168–69, 200–201, 208–9, 211–16, 221–40, 243–44, 251, 252–55. *See also* Contractors, defense
Coproduction agreements, 183
Cost maximization, 95. *See also* Spending
Costs. *See* Spending
Council of Engineers and Scientists Organizations, 155
CPSR. *See* Computer Professionals for Social Responsibility
Critical Technologies Institute, 124
CRT. *See* Campaign for Responsible Technology
CSC. *See* Computer Science Corporation
Curtiss, 80, 81, 87
Curtiss-Wright, 28, 39, 42
Cybernetics, 22

DARPA. *See* Defense Advanced Research Projects Agency
Data sources, 250

Defense Advanced Research Projects Agency (DARPA), 9, 84, 107, 113, 120, 123, 124, 126–27, 129, 130, 259

Defense Authorization Act (1992), 127

Defense, Department of (DOD): aerospace-communications-electronics complex and, 50, 52, 53, 57; Bids and Proposals Program (B&P), 118; buying power of, 84; dual-use technology policies and, 121–27, 128–30; geographical constituency building and, 196–97; Independent Research and Development Program (IR&D), 118; manufacturing industries and, 33, 36; military services and, 191; physical capital of, 61; science and technology (S&T) programs of, 108–14, 127, 130

Defense industry: 1980s defense buildup and, 38–39, 66, 87, 96–97, 214, 217; cold war weaponry and, 5; cutbacks and, 209–20; domestic economy and, 7–8; economic aspects of, 83–90; employment in, 138–43; government support of, 1–2, 32–34, 51–55; role of, 2, 5–6; workers, redeployment of, 165–69; World War II and, 42–43, 174. *See also* Aerospace-communications-electronics complex; Contractors, defense; Economy, defense; Military-industrial complex; *individual corporations by name*

Defense Logistics Agency, 84

Defense Science Board, 113

Defense spending. *See* Spending, defense

Defense University Instrumentation Program, 111

Deficit, budget, 7, 242, 243

DeLauer, Richard, D., 111

Dellums, Ron, 196–97

Department of Defense–University Forum, 111

Dependency, defense: communities, of, xvi, 204–5, 244; defense-related industries and, xvi, 36–39, 76–78, 80–82,

87, 211–13; employment and, 139–46; politics and, xvi–xvii, 203; research and development and, 9–10; small companies, of, 216–19; United States, of, xvi, 4–8; universities, of, 110, 111. *See also* Contractors, defense

Deterrence: aerospace-communications-electronics complex and, 5; cold war, during the, 23

Detroit (Mich.), 46–47

Dickson, David, 105, 110

Digital Equipment, 51

DOD. *See* Defense, Department of

DOE. *See* Energy, Department of

Douglas Aircraft Company, 41, 42, 53–54, 80, 81, 96, 189, 215, 231–33. *See also* McDonnell-Douglas

Douglas, Donald, 174

Douglas, James, 189

DRAM. *See* Technologies, dynamic random access memory device

Draper Lab, 177

Dual-use policies, 121–31, 206–7, 242, 245, 259. *See also* Alternative-use planning; Conversion, economic

Dubinin, Yuri, 208–9

DuBois, Tom, 234

Dumas, Lloyd, 61

Eckert, J. Presper, 49

Economic development, 227–28

Economists against the Arms Race, 258

Economy, defense: 1980s military buildup and, 216; buyers and sellers in, 84–86; cold war and, 5, 14, 25–27, 34; diversification in, 211–16; dual-use technology policies and, 121–31; employment in, 132–46, 219–20; fixed-force structure, 30–31; government support and, 1–2, 9, 32–34, 52–53; Gulf War and, 4; market influences in, 183–84; postwar, 38, 40, 43, 70, 80, 81, 87–88, 90, 96–97; role of, 1–3, 4,

Economy *(continued)*
35–39, 82, 120–21, 242; technology development and, 47–51, 86, 200, 242; trade balance and, 59; vertical integration in, 93, 275*n*72; weaponry and, 14, 25–27; wall of separation in, xv, 5, 11, 69, 80, 90–93, 99–100, 116, 133, 157, 210, 216, 219, 243. *See also* Contractors, defense; Defense industry; Gunbelt

Economy, domestic: 1980s military buildup and, 133–34; capital, raising of, 52; computer sector and, 57; conversion of, 226–28, 252–55; defense economy and, 6–11, 35, 38, 50, 199–200, 242; defense industry and, 172, 242–43; deficit, budget, 7, 242, 243; development strategy for, 246–60; dual-use technology policies and, 130–31; Gunbelt and, 199–200, 204–5; peace dividend and, 251–55; targeted industry policies and, 58–65; technology development and, 9–10, 34; trade balance and, 58–60; war preparedness and, 1–3, 5, 6; world economy and, 125, 245

Economy, industrial: alternative-use planning and, 207; defense industry and, 2, 5, 33–39, 86, 120–21, 134, 172, 177, 200–202, 204–6, 243; dual-use technology policies and, 121–31, 206–7; manufacturing systems and, 27; New England, of, 192–94; postwar, 38, 40, 43, 70, 80, 81, 87–88, 96–97, 181; regional shifts in, 189–90; targeted industry policies, 51–65; vertical disintegration in, 93; warfare and, 13

Economy, regional, 200–201, 289*n*13. *See also individual regions by name*

EcoTech, 258

Edison, Thomas, 103

Eisenhower, Dwight D., 104

Electronics. *See* Technologies, electronics

Electronics industry, 47–49, 59–60, 63, 67–68, 86, 87, 93, 96. *See also* Aerospace-communications-electronics complex

Emerson, 49

Employees: blue-collar, 135, 138–39, 142, 157–63, 168–69, 221–24; conversion efforts for, 219–20, 222, 225–26, 254; defense workers, redeployment of, 165–69; engineers, 151–56, 166–67, 285*n*44; involvement of, in technology design, 257–58; military-industrial managers, 154, 155, 155–57, 160–61, 237–38, 254; pink-collar, 141–42; research scientists, 147–51; white-collar, 135–36, 138, 139, 141; women/minorities, 163–65. *See also* Engineering

Employment: 1980s military buildup and, 133–34, 137, 140, 222; aerospace industry and, 67; college education and, 136–37; commercial conversion and, 219–20, 221, 222–26, 228–39; costs of, 161, 234; defense dependency and, 139–46, 158–59, 201, 206; defense–nondefense shifts, 152–53, 206; defense technology and, 2–3, 13, 135–36; economic conversion and, 7–8; electronic industry and, 68; job blackmail, 221–22; layoffs in, 161–62, 165–69, 201, 204–5, 217, 222–23, 227; manufacturing, 132–33; nondefense, 145–46, 153; military-industrial complex, in, 136–37, 139–65; plant/base closings, 168, 226–27, 228–39; population shifts and, 202; salaries, 145, 154, 156, 160, 204; strikes/work stoppages, 160–61; trade balance and, 59–60; unemployment, 155, 165

Energy, Department of (DOE), 33, 84, 106, 116

Energy Research and Development Agency (ERDA), 106

Engineering: commercial needs for, 61; defense needs for, 137; economic con-

version and, 8; employment and, 139–41, 143–46, 151–55, 165–67; prestige of, 60, 136, 146; role of, 5, 14; unions of, 154–55
Engineers and Scientists Guild, 155
Environment, 248, 252, 258, 259
ERDA. *See* Energy Research and Development Agency
Etchell, Howard, 216, 217
Europe, 128–20
European Community, 63
Evangelista, Matthew, 18, 26
Everett, Melissa, 149, 150, 162
Export-Import Bank (U.S.), 54
Exports: aerospace, 56, 78–79; automobile, 61–62; military, 66–67, 78, 85, 206, 211, 242
Exxon, 82

Fairchild, 87, 89
Fallows, James, 23, 30, 31, 99
FCCSET. *See* Federal Coordinating Committee on Science, Engineering and Technology
Federal Coordinating Committee on Science, Engineering and Technology (FCCSET), 126
Federation for Industrial Renewal and Retention (FIRR), 257
Fermi, Enrico, 102
Fields, Craig, 127
Fighterplanes. *See* Aircraft
Fine, Stanley, 208
Firestone, 87
FIRR. *See* Federation for Industrial Renewal and Retention
Flamm, Kenneth, 49–50, 129
Florida, 187, 190
FMC, 82
Franks, Ray, 216, 217
Frisby Airborne Systems, 218, 220
Frisby, Greg, 218
Fokker, 56

Follow-on imperative, 89–90, 92
Fong, Glenn R., 122
Ford Aerospace, 46–47, 138–39, 140, 157
Ford, Gerald, 172, 203
Ford, Henry, 27–28, 45
Ford, Henry, II, 46, 221
Ford Motor Company, 28, 43, 44–45, 46, 47, 157, 212
Foreign policy (U.S.): military spending and, 204; military technology and, 14, 23, 26–27. *See also* Military policy
Foreign sales. *See* Exports
Forman, Paul, 115

Gansler, Jacques, 76, 79, 86, 87–88, 95–96, 122, 125
GE. *See* General Electric
General Dynamics, xv, 49, 54, 74, 76, 79, 81, 82, 87, 89, 90, 96, 160, 162, 177, 206, 210, 211, 215–16, 229–31
General Electric (GE), 74, 76, 79, 82, 87, 91, 161, 190
General Motors (GM), 43, 75, 77, 79, 82, 137, 157, 212
General Telephone & Electronics (GTE), 82, 88
General Tire and Rubber, 82
Georgia, 203
Gephardt, Richard A., 126
Germany, 6, 34, 60, 64
Glenn, John, 125
GM. *See* General Motors
GOCOs. *See* Government-owned, contractor-operated facilities
GOGOs. *See* Government-owned, government-operated facilities
Gold-plating, 99
Gorbachev, Mikhail, 208
Gordon, Harvey, 208
Government-owned, contractor-operated facilities (GOCOs), 90, 96, 161, 184, 188, 189, 201

Government-owned, government-operated facilities (GOGOs), 184

Government, federal: advisory committees of, 40, 53, 103, 113, 118; aerospace industry, support of, 40–41, 56–57, 64, 88–90; computer industry, support of, 49–50, 57–58; contractor locations and, 182–85, 187–88; conversion and, 239, 240; defense industry, support of, 1–2, 9, 32–34, 194–196; defense spending by, 35–39, 84–85; economic influences of, 84, 182; electronic industry, support of, 48–49, 57–58; plant ownership by, 90, 96, 161, 184, 188, 189, 201; targeted industry policies, 51–58. *See also* Congress

Gray, Harry, 156–57

Greenberg, Daniel S., 125

Greenwood, Dick, 222

Grissom, Tom, 150

Grumman, 49, 76, 80, 81, 82, 90, 117, 212, 213, 214, 220

GTE. *See* General Telephone & Electronics

Gulf War (1991), 3–4, 18–19, 23, 26, 31, 67, 68, 209

Gunbelt: 1980s military buildup and, 38, 243; air force and, 179–80; benefits/drawbacks of, 199–202; costs of, 173, 185; development of, 6, 181–82, 185–92; location of, 172–81, 182–99; politics of, 173, 182, 191, 192, 194–97, 203–4; post–cold war, 204–7; strategic concerns of, 184, 188–90. *See also* Communities, military-industrial

Guns, 99

Harris, 187

Harrison, Bennett, 257

Havemann, Ernest, 136

Health issues, 160, 248

Heinz, John, 126

Henry, David, 36

Hercules Powder, 177

Herres, John, 195

Herring, Richard, 187

Hicks, Donald, 167

High Tech Castings, 217

Hill, Bruce, 167

Hiroshima (Japan), 16, 19

Holley, Irving, Jr., 15, 17

Honeywell, 49, 50, 76, 82

Hoover, Herbert, 92–93

Houston space center, 196

Hughes, xv, 43, 48, 76, 77–78, 82, 98, 132, 140, 157, 177, 185, 187, 210, 212, 213

Huntsville Redstone Arsenal. *See* Alabama

IAM. *See* International Association of Machinists and Aerospace Workers

IBEW. *See* International Brotherhood of Electrical Workers

IBM. *See* International Business Machines

ICBM. *See* Missiles, intercontinental ballistic

Illinois Institute of Technology, 147

Imports, 58–60, 62, 183, 205

Incomes, 199–200. *See also* Employment, salaries

Indiana, 174, 178

Industrial policies: Germany, 34, 60, 64; Japan, 34, 60, 62, 63, 64, 67, 128–29, 130; United States, xvi, 33, 51–65, 119–21, 125, 242–43

Industrial Union of Marine and Shipbuilding Workers of America (IUM-SWA), 229–30

Industries. *See* Economy, industrial; Military-industrial complex; *individual industries by name*

Inflation, 8

Information Sciences Institute, 113

Institute of Electrical and Electronics Engineers, 167
Instrumentation Laboratory, 113
Intellectual property agreements, 148
Intercontinental ballistic missile (ICBM). *See* Missiles, intercontinental ballistic
Interest rates, 3
International Association of Machinists and Aerospace Workers (IAM), 158, 221
International Brotherhood of Electrical Workers (IBEW), 235, 237
International Business Machines (IBM), 50–51, 76, 79, 82
"Iron triangle," 88. *See also* Aerospace-communications-electronics complex
Invention and Development, Department of, 103
IR&D. *See* Defense, Department of, Independent Research and Development Program
IUMSWA. *See* Industrial Union of Marine and Shipbuilding Workers of America

Japan: automobile industry of, 62; competitiveness and, 245; economy of, 6; exports of, 60, 63; industrial policies of, 34, 60, 62, 63, 64, 67, 128–29, 130; Ministry for International Trade and Industry (MITI), 124
Jobs. *See* Employment
Job Training Partnership Act (JTPA), 230
Jobs with Peace, 236
Johns Hopkins University, 113, 177
Johnson, Lyndon, 196
Joyner, Russ, 160
JTPA. *See* Job Training Partnership Act

Kaldor, Mary, 120
Kaman, 147, 185, 188, 213, 220

Kaysen-Turner criterion, 76
Kennedy, John F., 107, 249
Kennedy, Joseph, 196
Keyworth, George, 63
Kilgore, Harley, 106
Kindelberger, Dutch, 28, 215
Klaw, Spencer, 114
Klein, Morton, 147, 241, 242
Komer, Odessa, 169
Korea, North, 211
Korean War, 189
Kramer, Ken, 197
Kurth, James, 32, 89

Laboratories, industrial, 109
Labor, Department of, 225
Labor unions. *See* Unions
LACAPS. *See* Los Angeles Coalition Against Plant Shutdowns
Lawrence Livermore National Laboratory, 97, 188, 206
Leapfrog Technology Program, 63
Leary, Frederick, 72
Legislation, conversion, 239, 253
Lerner, Joshua, 152, 166
Levine, Mel, 126
Licklider, J. C. R., 115–16
Litton, 82, 88
Location theory, 182. *See also* Gunbelt
Lockheed: bailout of, 54; commercial business of, 56, 96, 153, 210, 212, 213; electronics division of, 49; employment with, 159–60, 161; exports of, 78–79; government advisory committees and, 53; history of, 69–74; military contracts of, xv, 43, 66, 75, 76, 82, 89, 177, 206, 215–16; research and development contracts of, 117; takeover of, 90
Lockheed Missiles & Space Company, 140, 153
Lockheed Syndrome, 154
Los Alamos, 188, 190, 206

Los Angeles (Calif.), 172, 173–74, 179, 186–87, 190, 198, 204
Los Angeles Coalition Against Plant Shutdowns (LACAPS), 232
Lotchin, Roger, 198
Loughead, Allan, 70
Loughead, Malcolm, 70
LTV, 76, 81, 88, 90. *See also* Chance-Vought
Lugar, Richard, 235

MacDonald, Stuart, 57–58
Machine tool industry, 63–64, 129–30
Machinists' Union, 258
Maine, 204
Manhattan Project, 25, 30, 102, 103, 104, 136
Manno, Jack, 22
Mantech Program. *See* Manufacturing Technology Program
Manufacturers Aircraft Association, 40, 157
Manufacturing: 1980s military buildup and, 134; flexible, 27–28, 29; high-technology, 132; growth of, 33, 180–81; locations of, 180, 193–94; military, 29, 35, 91, 174; trade balance and, 58–60. *See also* Gunbelt
Manufacturing Technology Program (Mantech), 123
Market influences, 183
Market niche strategies, 210–11
Marketing, 91–92, 217
Markham, Jamie, 236
Marshall, Eliot, 127
Martin Company, 46, 49, 80, 87, 191, 215
Martin-Marietta, 75, 76, 89, 90, 117, 177, 187, 189, 210
Maryland, 177
Massachusetts, 174, 177, 179, 198, 203, 229–31, 291n37. *See also* New England

Massachusetts Center for Applied Technology, 257–58
Massachusetts Institute of Technology (MIT), 113, 177
Mass transit, 214, 223, 254, 257
Mauchly, John, 49
Mazzocchi, Tony, 162–63, 225
McClure, Gordon, 150
McDonnell Aircraft of St. Louis, 49, 231
McDonnell-Douglas: commercial business of, 56, 69–70, 74, 185, 213, 239, 254; government advisory committees and, 53, 55; history of, 231–33; location of, 189; military contracts of, xv, 76, 79, 81, 82, 89, 90, 118–19, 177, 187, 206, 215–16; research and development awards to, 117. *See also* Douglas Aircraft Company
McDonnell, Sanford, 157
McNamara, Robert, 85, 185
McNaugher, Thomas, 129
Melman, Seymour, 88, 95, 254
Mergers, 211–12
Michigan, 174, 178
Middle Atlantic region, 178
Mid-Peninsula Conversion Project (MPCP), 232
Midwest (region), 174, 178, 179–80, 193–94, 198–200, 201
Military affairs committees, 198–99
Military-industrial complex: 1980s defense buildup and, 38–39, 66, 87, 99, 105, 108, 133–34; cold war and, 15, 23, 24–25; concentration in, 87, 88, 90; conversion and, 241–42, 243–44; cost-plus contracts and, 95, 98–99, 118, 182, 183, 202; employment in, 138–46; industries involved, 36–39, 82; locations of, 170–81, 189; restructuring of, 205–7; technical evolution and, 68, 88–89; wall of separation and, xv, 5, 11, 69, 80, 90–93, 99–100, 116, 133, 157, 210, 216, 219, 243; weaponry and, 26, 27–31. *See also* Aero-

space-communications-electronics complex

Military installations, 185–88, 195

Military policy, 15, 17, 24, 26. *See also* Foreign policy

Military research. *See* Research and development, military

Military services: air force, 14, 17–18, 20–21, 57, 105, 114, 138, 172, 179, 185, 186, 190, 191, 217, 268n51; army, 185, 190, 191, 268n51; competition between, 18, 84, 105, 172, 190–91, 273n42; conflict between, 84–85; defense contractors and, 80–81, 184–85, 217; employment in, 137; minorities in, 165; navy, 178, 180, 191, 235; technology and, 120; weaponry and, 23, 24, 30–31, 45–46

Military spending. *See* Spending

MIMIC. *See* Technologies, microwave/millimeter wave monolithic integrated circuit

Mineta, Norman Y., 126

Mingos, Howard, 40, 41, 42

Minnesota, 239

Minnesota Task Force on Economic Conversion, 162

Minorities, 164–65

Missiles, 37, 49, 177–78, 180, 190, 211; Advanced Medium Range Air-to-Air (AMRAAM), 95, 98; Atlas, 43; cruise, 187; Dragon, 187; intercontinental ballistic (ICBM), 12, 19, 43, 46; Jupiter, 191; Maverick, 19–20; Minuteman, 48, 89; MX, 12–13, 89; Patriot, 26–27; Pershing, 191; Phoenix, 30; Polaris, 70; Poseidon, 70; radar-guided, 99; Sidewinder, 30; Sparrow, 30; submarine, 191; Tacit Rainbow antiradiation, 98; Titan, 189; Trident, 70, 73, 140, 264n49; tube-launched, optically traced, wire-guided (TOW), 99

Missouri, 177

MIT. *See* Massachusetts Institute of Technology

MITI. *See* Japan, Ministry for International Trade and Industry.

Mollenkopf, John, 192

Moorehead, William, 72

Mountain states, 177

MPCP. *See* Mid-Peninsula Conversion Project

Munson, Claudette, 240

NASA. *See* National Aeronautics and Space Administration

National Advisory Committee for Aeronautics, 40, 103

National Aeronautics and Space Administration (NASA): contractors, 76, 77; government advisory committees and, 53; space activities of, 84; spending by, 33, 52, 57, 76, 116

National Aerospace Place Technology Program, 57

National Bureau of Standards. *See* National Institute for Standards and Technology

National Cash Register (NCR), 50

National Commission for Economic Conversion and Disarmament, 259

National Critical Technologies Act, 127

National Defense Research Committee, 104

National Institute for Standards and Technology (NIST), 125

National Institutes of Health (NIH), 106–7, 110

National Science Foundation (NSF), 105, 106, 107, 110, 111

Naval Research Advisory Committee, 113

NCR. *See* National Cash Register

NESCO, 234

New England, 176, 177–78, 180, 192–94, 199, 201. *See also* Massachusetts

New Jersey, 174

Newport News Shipbuilding, 82

New York, 174

Nieburg, H. L., 102

NIH. *See* National Institutes of Health

1980s military buildup, 38–39, 66, 87, 96–97, 99, 105, 108, 133–34, 137, 140, 214, 216, 217, 222, 243

NIST. *See* National Institute for Standards and Technology

Nixon, Richard, 249

North American Aviation, 28, 42–43, 49, 80, 81, 174, 190, 215. *See also* Rockwell

Northeast region, 179–80

Northrup, xv, 53, 76, 85, 89, 90, 98, 206, 213

Noyce, Robert, 150–51

NSF. *See* National Science Foundation

Nuclear weapons: cold war and, 23; strategic, 17; submarines, 25, 30; tactical, 29

OCAW. *See* Oil, Chemical, and Atomic Workers International Union

Occupational Safety and Health Administration (OSHA), 160

OEA. *See* Office of Economic Adjustment

Office of Economic Adjustment (OEA), 54, 226–27, 228

Office of Naval Research (ONR), 105–6, 107

Office of Science and Technology Policy (OSTP), 124, 126

Office of Scientific Research, Air Force, 106

Office of Scientific Research and Development, 104, 105

Office of Technology Assessment (OTA), 64

Ohio, 174, 178, 208–9

Oil, Chemical, and Atomic Workers International Union (OCAW), 160, 162, 225

ONR. *See* Office of Naval Research

Orr, Verne, 161

OSHA. *See* Occupational Safety and Health Administration

OSTP. *See* Office of Science and Technology Policy

OTA. *See* Office of Technology Assessment

Pace, Stanley, 211, 215, 241

Pacific region, 174, 176, 177, 178, 179–80, 201

Packard, 28

Packard, David, 72

Parties, political, 203

Peace dividend, 251–55

Peacekeeper missile. *See* Missiles, MX

Peck, Merton, 83, 87, 94, 98

Perpich, Rude, 236

Philco, 46

Phillips, Almarin, 57

Pittsburgh (Pa.), 11

Plants/bases: closing of, 168, 226–27, 253, 254; conversion of, 228–39

Plant Site Board, 188, 189

Potter, Donald, 195

Powaski, Ronald, 30

Pratt & Whitney, 41, 160–61, 195

President's Commission on Industrial Competitiveness, 125

Press, Frank, 255–56

Private sector: defense workers of, 133; dual-use policies and, 121–23, 124–25; research capabilities of, 129

Production workers. *See* Employees, blue-collar

Proxmire, William, 204

Quayle, Dan, 235

Quincy Shipyards, 229–31, 238

Radar. *See* Technologies, radar
Radiation Corporation, 187
Ramo-Wooldridge, 190. *See also* TRW
R&D. *See* Research and development
Raymond, Louis, 162
Raytheon, 48, 75, 76, 82, 90, 98, 178, 220
RCA, 87
Reagan, Ronald: 1980s military buildup and, 38–39, 66, 87, 96–97, 99, 105, 108, 133–34, 137, 140, 214, 216, 217, 222, 243; defense industry and, 4, 38; employment and, 6; MX missiles and, 12; science and technology programs of, 108
Recession, 201, 226, 242, 259–60
RedZone, 257
Regulation, economic development and, 10, 250, 252, 256
Republic, 49, 82
Research and development (R&D): advanced technology development, 109; applied, 109; basic, 109; civilian industry and, 62, 63, 65, 120–21, 130; defense, 130, 150–51; dual-use technologies and, 121–31, 206; economic development and, 9–10, 107, 250–51; laboratories of, 147–51; layoffs in, 167–68; locations of, 176–77; military, 108–19; modern system, creation of, 105–8; private industry and, 116–19; spending for, 52–53, 107, 108–9, 110–11; universities and, 109, 110–16. *See also* Contractors, defense; Aerospace-communications-electronic complex
Recession, 10–11. *See also* Economy, domestic
Reppy, Judith, 120
Reuther, Walter, 168, 221
Rickover, Hyman, 25
Rivers, Mendel, 194
Rockwell International, xv, 43, 66, 75, 76, 79, 81, 82, 89, 177, 194, 197, 212, 213. *See also* North American Aviation

Rockwell Standard, 66
Rohr, 74, 213–14
Roosevelt, Franklin D., 27–28, 42
Ryan Aeronautical, 215

SAC. *See* Strategic Air Command
St. Clair, Dan, 162
San Antonio (Tex.), 186
Sanders Electronics, 73
Sandia Labs, 150, 188, 206
San Diego, 198
S&T programs. *See* Defense, Department of, science and technology programs of
Satellites, 34, 70, 140
Scheibel, Jim, 236
Scherer, Frederick, 83, 87, 94, 98
Science, 123
Science: The Endless Frontier, 106
Scientists, 147–51. *See also* Employment
SDI. *See* Strategic Defense Initiative
Seattle, 204–5. *See also* Boeing; Washington, State of
Seattle Professional Engineering Employees Association, 154
Secrecy, governmental, 30, 92–93
Sematech Program, 9, 58, 123, 126, 129, 259
Semiconductor Manufacturing Technology Program, 123
Sherry, Michael, 16
Shipbuilding, 178
Sibley, Gail, 162
Simmons, Harold, 90
Singer, 76, 82
Smith, Nathaniel, 219
Southern California Professional Engineering Association, 155
South (region), 180, 199, 201
South Shore Conversion Committee, 229–30
Soviet Union, 208–9, 253

Space Command, 191–92

Space industry, 73. *See also* Aerospace-communications-electronics (ACE) complex

Spending: aerospace-communications-electronics complex and, 94, 97–98; defense, 10–11, 17, 19, 23, 35–39, 54, 108, 110–11, 112*t*, 115, 116, 124, 127, 130, 158, 199, 203–7, 221, 241; cuts in, xvi, 204–5, 253, 261*n*5; manufacturing, 158; private industry and, 116, 123, 127; research and development, 52–53, 105, 108, 109, 110–11, 114, 115, 116, 123, 130, 140; universities and, 110–11, 112*t*, 114, 115, 116

Sperry, 82, 235. *See also* Unisys Defense Computer Systems

Sperry-Rand, 49

SSE. *See* Survey of Scientists and Engineers

SST. *See* Aircraft, supersonic transport

Standard Oil of California, 82

Stanford Research Institute, 113

Star Wars. *See* Strategic Defense Initiative

Steel industry, 62–63

Steel Valley Authority, 235, 257

Stekler, Herman, 34, 49, 83, 94

Stennis, John, 196

Stone, Pat, 147, 148

Stout, William, 45

Stowsky, Jay, 121

Strategic Air Command (SAC), 85, 191–92

Strategic Computing Program, 58, 113, 123

Strategic Defense Initiative (SDI), 24, 63, 107, 109, 111, 113–14, 117–18, 138, 149, 191–92, 205–6

Sundstrand Corporation, 135–36, 153, 189

Survey of Scientists and Engineers (SSE), 143–45, 152, 163, 164

Sweetser, Arthur, 19

Tanks: M-1, 96, 162, 218, 222, 233; M-60, 96, 218, 233, 234

Teaming, 93

Technologies, 2, 8–10, 14, 21–22, 24, 100, 119–20, 121–31, 200, 244–45, 255–56, 262*n*16, 276–77*n*6; aircraft, 16–17, 19–20, 263*n*31; computer, 21–22, 38, 49–51, 111, 112–13, 115, 120, 123, 124; dynamic random access memory (DRAM) device, 60; electronic, 20–23, 31, 48–49; integrated circuit, 122–23; laser, 31, 97; microwave/millimeter wave monolithic integrated circuit (MIMIC), 123; radar, 21, 31, 48, 49; robotic, 63–64, 257; semiconductor, 2, 9, 48, 123; transistor, 48; very high speed integrated circuit (VHSICs), 113, 121, 122–23; weaponry and, 14, 20; x-ray lithography, 124, 126. *See also* Research and development

Technology Mobilization and Reemployment Program (TMRP), 225–26

Technology transfer, 244–45

'Teeth to tail" ratio, 20

Teller, Edward, 97

Tellup, Daniel, 148

Tenneco, 74, 76, 82

Tennessee Valley Authority, 249

Texas, 203

Texas Instruments, 82

Textron, 82, 88, 140

Textron-Lycoming, 222–23

Thiokol, 177

Third World, 66, 205, 211

Thomas, Bill, 119

TMRP. *See* Technology Mobilization and Reemployment Program

TOW missiles. *See* Missiles, tube-launched, optically tracked, wire-guided

TRA. *See* Trade Readjustment Assistance Program

Trade: balance of, 59–60, 62, 67; policies of, 251. *See also* Exports; Imports

Trade Adjustment Assistance Act, 230
Trade Readjustment Assistance Program (TRA), 225
Training, conversion and, 225
Transportation, development of, 11. *See also* Mass transit
Trident submarine, 17
Tri-State Conference on Steel, 257
Truman, Harry S., 105, 106
TRW, 76, 140, 186, 210. *See also* Ramo-Wooldridge
21st Century Project, 258

UAW. *See* United Auto Workers
UE. *See* United Electrical, Radio, and Machine Workers of America
Ullmann, John, 120, 208
Unemployment. *See* Employment
Unions: commercial conversion and, 8, 220–24, 237; engineering, 154–55; production workers and, 160, 220–24, 258; work stoppages and, 161. *See also* Quincy Shipyards; Douglas Aircraft; Blaw-Knox Foundry; Unisys Defense Computer Systems
Unisys Defense Computer Systems, 76, 82, 177, 235–37, 238, 239
United Auto Workers (UAW), 160, 221, 232, 238, 258
United Community Organization, 234
United Electrical, Radio, and Machine Workers of America (UE), 224
United Nuclear Corporations, 162
United States: cold war and, xv; defense-dependency of, 4–8; economic development strategy for, 246–52; foreign policy of, 14; industrial policies of, xvi, 33, 51–65, 119–21, 125, 242–43; military exports of, 66–67; military policy of, 15; priorities of, 249, 250; public works investment in, 61; role of, 4, 242; science and technology policies of, 119–21, 125; standard of living of, 4, 11; war planning of, 14. *See also* Economy
United Steel Workers of America, 234, 238
United Technologies, 75, 76, 79, 82, 156–57, 195
Universities: defense and, 6, 112–16; priorities of, 115; research and development at, 109, 110–16, 146, 177
University of Southern California, 113
University Research Initiative, 111
Urban Mass Transit Program, 214
U.S. Steel. *See* USX
USX, 62
Utah, 177

Van Creveld, Martin, 16, 24, 33
Ver-Val Enterprises, 219
VHSICs. *See* Technologies, very high speed integrated circuits
Vietnam War, 38, 66, 107–8, 110
Vinson-Trammel Act (1934), 42
von Braun, Werner, 190

Warfare: airborne, 14, 15–20, 21, 22, 40; electronic, 20–23, 31–32, 33; guerrilla, 16; modern, 13, 18; postmodern, 13, 14, 15, 18, 19, 20, 99, 102; scientific, 102–4. *See also* Weaponry
War in the Air, 16
Washington (D.C.), 172, 183, 187
Washington, State of, 177, 179. *See also* Boeing; Seattle
Weaponry: atomic, 30, 102; automated, 19–23, 29; cold war, 23–32; conventional, 3–4; costs of, 30–31, 43–44, 94–95, 98–99, 105; Department of Defense and, 61; development of, 102–3; modern, 3–4, 7, 8, 103; postmodern, 12–15, 102–3, 205, 210–11; produc-

Weaponry *(continued)*
  tion of, 27–31, 91; Third World and, 3.
  See also Aircraft; Guns; Missiles; Nuclear weapons; Tanks
Weidenbaum, Murray, 81, 213
Weinberger, Caspar, 161
Weiss, Ted, 228–29, 239
Wells, H. G., 16
West, Patricia Salter, 136
West (region), 180, 199, 201. *See also* California
Western Electric, 48
Westinghouse, 76, 82
Wheaton, David J., 206
White Consolidated, 233, 234
Wichita Engineering Association, 154–55
Wichita (Kan.), 227

Wilson, David, 115
Winpisinger, William, 221–22, 223
Women, defense workers, as, 163
Workers. *See* Employees
Working Group on Economic Dislocation, 235–36
World Wars I and II, 13, 18, 19, 29, 39–40, 42, 70, 80, 86, 103–4, 157–58, 174, 189, 201, 249

Young, John, 125

Zikaris, Joseph, 223

DEC 1 2 1995

DEC 0 6 1996

BRODART

Cat. No. 23-221